BULLETIN OF THE OHIO BIOLOGICAL SURVEY

New Series

Volume 9	Number 1
THE OHIO LEPIDOPTERISTS	RESEARCH REPORT NO. 3

BUTTERFLIES AND SKIPPERS OF OHIO

David C. Iftner
John A. Shuey
John V. Calhoun

PUBLISHED BY

COLLEGE OF BIOLOGICAL SCIENCES
THE OHIO STATE UNIVERSITY

In Cooperation With

OHIO DEPARTMENT OF NATURAL RESOURCES,
DIVISION OF WILDLIFE
and
THE OHIO LEPIDOPTERISTS

COLUMBUS, OHIO 43210   1992

OHIO BIOLOGICAL SURVEY

BULLETIN NEW SERIES: ISSN 0078-3994
BULLETIN NEW SERIES VOLUME 9 NUMBER 1: ISBN 0-86727-107-8
LIBRARY OF CONGRESS NUMBER: 88-060896

EDITOR

Veda M. Cafazzo

EDITORIAL COMMITTEE

CITATION

Iftner, David C., John A. Shuey, and John V. Calhoun. 1992. Butterflies and Skippers of Ohio. Ohio Biol. Surv. Bull. New Series Vol. 9 No. 1 xii + 212 p. (includes 40 Pls.).

COVER ART—Marsh-inhabiting Baltimore, *Euphydryas phaeton phaeton* (Drury, 1773) taking nectar from black-eyed Susan, *Rudbeckia hirta* L., 1753. Cover painting and design by John V. Calhoun.

COLLEGE OF BIOLOGICAL SCIENCES
THE OHIO STATE UNIVERSITY
COLUMBUS, OHIO 43210
1992

7-92—1.8M

ABSTRACT

A dedication, foreword (by Paul A. Opler), and preface are followed by an overview of previous research on the State's butterflies and skippers, a section on education and conservation, and an overview of the ecological and historical factors which influence the distribution of species in Ohio. A methods section details the sources and handling of data presented, and describes the format used in the species accounts. A checklist of species reported from Ohio completes the introductory materials.

The bulk of the book consists of the individual species accounts. The 144 species treated are arranged by family. Each species account includes discussions describing resident status and distribution within the state and in adjacent areas. County distribution maps of Ohio are included for each species. Habitat associations, hostplants, and adult energy resources are discussed with emphasis upon the ecology of each species in Ohio. The adult flight period is detailed, and, where adequate data exist, is presented as a histogram. The similar species section discusses diagnostic characters which will separate those species which look very much alike. A section devoted to general comments synthesizes the previous sections, and includes observations on behavior, phenotypic variability, and aberrations. Each species account ends with a listing of unverified county records.

The text concludes with a discussion of species erroneously reported from the state, and those which, although not yet recorded from Ohio, might eventually be discovered. There is a glossary of unfamiliar terms, a bibliography with an excess of 300 entries, an appendix which lists regional lepidopterological societies, and an appendix which lists the abbreviation codes for Ohio counties as used in the plate captions. There is an index to reported Ohio hostplants, an index to common names of butterflies and skippers, and an index to taxa of butterflies and skippers.

There are 40 pages of color plates, some of which illustrate ecological features and a variety of habitats occupied by butterflies and skippers in the state. The bulk of the plates is devoted to illustrating the butterflies and skippers of the state, including those species not yet recorded from Ohio. For most species both ventral and dorsal figures of both sexes are illustrated. Over 600 specimens are figured.

DEDICATION

This book is dedicated to the many lepidopterists of Ohio, past and present, whose unquenchable curiosity has contributed to a more thorough understanding and heightened sense of awareness of the invertebrate fauna of North America.

ACKNOWLEDGEMENTS

This volume required the assistance and indulgence of many others during the course of its development. We are grateful to all. For their helpful suggestions and corrections on this manuscript during its various stages of development, we would like to thank Charles V. Covell, Jr., J. Richard Heitzman, Mogens C. "Mo" Nielsen, David K. Parshall, and especially John W. Peacock for their complete manuscript reviews. Additional reviews within their areas of expertise were provided by Jane L. Forsythe (Chapter 4), David J. Horn (Chapter 3 and Glossary), Robert C. Lederhouse (Chapter 8, Papilionidae), Paul A. Opler (Chapters 1-8 through the Pieridae), and Arthur M. Shapiro (Chapters 3-5).

Warm thanks are extended to all the curators of public and private collections listed in Chapter 6. In every case, our hosts displayed hospitality above and beyond the call of duty, and their graciousness enabled us to endure gathering the mass of data presented here. Several individuals lent specimens for the plates including John M. Burns, Loran D. Gibson, Harry Godwin, David K. Parshall, and John W. Peacock. Ronald L. Huber, Roy O. Kendall, Roy W. Rings, and Edward G. Voss provided biographical information used in Chapter 2. A special thanks to all the 4-H club members who let us peruse their State Fair collections. Battelle Memorial Institute provided access to the facilities used to generate Figure 8.2. Of course, the many members of The Ohio Lepidopterists supported this effort in many ways including the personal communications reported throughout Chapter 8. Those members not already mentioned who deserve special note include Leland L. Martin, Eric H. Metzler, Joseph E. Riddlebarger, and Reed A. Watkins.

Determinations of problem species were provided by John M. Burns *(Erynnis)*, Charles G. Oliver *(Phyciodes)*, and Paul A. Opler *(Phyciodes)*. Timothy P. Friedlander, Paul A. Opler, Austin P. Platt, Warren H. Wagner, and David M. Wright shared data with us and helped us to interpret ours. Blenn D. Bales, Ray W. Bracher, J. Donald Eff, Joseph W. Enke, Robert C. Hollister, Mrs. Louis A. Hoying, Ronald L. Huber, Roy O. Kendall, Jeanette Layman, Mogens C. Nielsen, Dorothy Parker, Homer F. Price, Roy W. Rings, Sonja E. Teraguchi, Edward G. Voss, and Albert E. Wyss provided historical information and/or photographs. Jim Iftner, Kaye Iftner, and Judith Cox-Shuey helped record specimen records. Nicki Miller prepared the flight period histograms. We are thankful for these services.

We thank Tommy G. Maloy, Photographer, The Ohio State University Department of Photography and Cinema, for devising the system necessary for creation of Plates 8 through 40, and for taking the photographs themselves.

Several people collected distribution and adult resource records specifically for this project; Valeriu Albu, James W. Becker, Larry E. Becker, Tomas W. Carr, Hoe H. Chuah, James H. Conover, Robert Dirig, Loran D. Gibson, J. Michael Gilligan, Todd Gilligan, Jeffrey D. Hooper, David J. Horn, Irving G. Loewit, Alma Long, Leland L. Martin, Joseph L. McMahon, Douglas Overracker, David K. Parshall, John W. Peacock, Maria W. Plonczynski, Roy W. Rings, Ronald F. Rockwell, Joseph E. Riddlebarger, Henri C. Seibert, Ann K. Stafford, Reed A. Watkins, Donald J. Wright, and Roger A. Zebold. The addition of their data adds immensely to the thoroughness of our coverage, and we are deeply indebted to all.

Most importantly, we thank our spouses, Kaye Iftner, Judith Cox-Shuey, and Julia Calhoun for their indulgence in our strange and time consuming pursuits. They endured many crises with uncanny patience and perspective during this project.

We thank the Ohio Department of Natural Resources, Division of Wildlife (especially Denis S. Case) and Division of Natural Areas and Preserves for their financial support during the data gathering phase of this project through grants to The Ohio Lepidopterists for The Ohio Survey of Lepidoptera and for work with endangered species. An additional contract with the Division of Wildlife contributed toward the costs of publication. These funds came from contributions checked off on the state income tax return form to the Nongame and Endangered Wildlife Special Account and the Natural Areas and Preserves Special Account. We thank the Reverand John E. Berger for his financial assistance, as well.

Finally, the Ohio Biological Survey supported this project from initial concept to completion. For their editorial and biological contributions, we are indebted to Charles C. King and Veda M. Cafazzo. This volume is a direct testament to their skills and perseverance, and to the mission of the Ohio Biological Survey.

CONTENTS

LIST OF FIGURES

Chapter 8 is comprised of the SPECIES ACCOUNTS and, as such, represents the bulk of the
text. Each account includes a distribution "dot" map, listed below as *Genus species —
Map*. Most accounts feature a histogram depicting the species' temporal distribution in
Ohio based upon adult capture records. These are titled *Genus species-Temporal
distribution*.

LIST OF FIGURES (cont'd)

TABLE

LIST OF PLATES

PHOTO CREDITS

Plates 8 through 40 were photographed by Tommy G. Maloy, Photographer, The Ohio State University Department of Photography and Cinema.

John V. Calhoun—Plate 3, Row 2 (No. 2); Plate 3, Row 3; Plate 6, Row 1 (No. 2); Plate 6, Row 2 (No. 1); Plate 6, Row 3; Plate 7, Row 1 (No. 3); Plate 7, Row 2 (No. 1).

Robert B. Gordon—Plate 1.

Charles C. King—Plate 4, Row 3 (No. 2).

Ohio Department of Natural Resources, Division of Geological Survey—Plate 2.

David K. Parshall—Plate 4, Row 3 (No. 1).

John A. Shuey—Plate 3, Row 1; Plate 3, Row 2 (No. 1); Plate 4, Row 1; Plate 4, Row 2; Plate 5; Plate 6, Row 1 (No. 1); Plate 6, Row 2 (No. 2); Plate 7, Row 1 (Nos. 1 and 2); Plate 7, Row 2 (Nos. 2 and 3); Plate 7, Row 3; Plate 7, Row 4.

FOREWORD

Of late, there has been a crescendo of publications that treat the butterfly faunas of many of the United States and Canadian provinces, and there are many more in the works.

Butterflies and Skippers of Ohio by David C. Iftner, John A. Shuey, and John V. Calhoun is the most thorough and complete treatment of a regional butterfly fauna yet published. The exhaustiveness of this study is the result of more than a decade of cooperation involving the authors, the Ohio Lepidopterists, the Ohio Biological Survey, and the Ohio Department of Natural Resources, Division of Wildlife.

The authors were the leaders of an effort to create a complete survey of the butterflies of every Ohio county, and to determine those species in need of conservation. Additionally, the authors were extremely conscientious and thorough in their combing of all available literature on Ohio Lepidoptera and their scouring of museum and private collections for historical records.

The treatment for each species carefully documents that butterfly's status through time. Moreover, there are included detailed distribution maps and charts of the seasonal flight periods for each species. Such seasonal charts have not previously been published in a general work.

This book will be an extremely valuable resource not only to lepidopterists, but also to natural historians, photographers, conservationists, wildlife managers, general biologists, and resource planners for many years to come. Butterflies are no longer just insects to be collected and placed on pins in an arranged assemblage like postage stamps, but have become important nongame wildlife to be appreciated through observation, photography, and study. New field guides emphasize features and behaviors that may be seen while stalking living animals in their natural environments.

The availability of these new field guides is most likely due to the increasing desire to appreciate nature in a world of growing urbanization. Perhaps butterfly-watching will take off for the stars in the 1990's as did bird-watching in the 1940's and 1950's!

I commend the authors for providing the reader with an accurately documented book on the status, occurrence, and biology of Ohio butterflies. It should prove to be a classic for many years to come.

Paul A. Opler
United States Department
of the Interior
Fish and Wildlife Service
Fort Collins, Colorado
13 September 1991

PREFACE

When we were children growing up in Illinois, Ohio, and Indiana, we often pedaled our bicycles past weedy meadows where white, yellow, and orange butterflies piqued our curiosity. With boyhood friends we soon captured and identified the largest and most showy, gathering them into small collections. Our authorities were *Butterflies and Moths* by Robert T. Mitchell and Herbert S. Zim (1962) and *A Field Guide to the Butterflies* by Alexander B. Klots (1951), two books that would eventually form the cornerstones of our modest libraries.

As we matured, our friends abandoned such devotion, and we were left to explore the fields alone. Even though our own interests in butterflies may have wavered over the years, they never totally disappeared. This passion transcended both peer pressure and puberty. How could we know that years later our mutual involvement with butterflies would bring us together in Ohio as friends and colleagues.

Together, we have spent more than 30 years studying butterflies and skippers in Ohio. In search of new discoveries, we travelled tens of thousands of miles, climbed steep forested ridges, plodded through mosquito-infested swamps, and (carefully) stepped through moss covered bogs. The more habitats we explored, the more familiar we became with the butterflies and skippers living there. Because we have always enjoyed sharing our knowledge with others, we wished to provide more information than was possible through lecturing, leading field trips, or identifying specimens. For that reason, we initiated the work that eventually led to this book.

Since that time in 1983, when we began, we have spent numerous hours in many museums, libraries, and homes of fellow lepidopterists. We left few stones unturned in our quest for available information. The end result, we feel, is a publication that will be equally useful to both the amateur and professional.

Finally, although we have tried to make this publication as complete as possible, we hope that it will be used primarily as a foundation or starting point for the continuing study of Ohio's butterflies and skippers. Much information remains to be gathered about our fauna. Whether you collect, photograph, or merely observe, you can take an active part in contributing to the knowledge of these fascinating animals.

May you have many enjoyable hours in the field.

15 June 1989

David C. Iftner
8 Alpine Trail
Sparta, NJ 07871

John A. Shuey
Battelle Great Lakes
   Environmental Center
739 Hastings Street
Traverse City, MI 49684

John V. Calhoun
1731 San Mateo Drive
Dunedin, FL 34698

1. INTRODUCTION

Prior to the early 1980's, the general consensus of most Ohio lepidopterists was that the overall status of the State's butterfly and skipper fauna was relatively unknown. Although various State (Hine, 1898a; b), regional (Price, 1970), and county checklists (Bales, 1909; Claypole, 1897; Porter, 1965; to name a few) had documented many of the species for Ohio, these lists as a whole provided little information about the animals themselves. In many cases, these lists contained dubious records and misdeterminations, and often omitted species that should have been present. The few Ohio papers that did pertain to biology, behavior, and occurrence were most often found in obscure and hard to obtain journals that were not generally available to the average lepidopterist.

Albrecht (1982), in his doctoral studies, partially filled this void. His work included an updated checklist, the first distribution maps for individual species, and the period of adult activity based upon capture records. However, this work remained unpublished.

In 1983, we jointly resolved to gather the available data on Ohio butterflies and skippers and to make it generally accessible. Since then, we have conducted thorough searches of the literature for information pertaining to Ohio, and have examined virtually all known collections containing Ohio specimens. Although we have relied heavily upon our own knowledge and experiences, resident collectors, as well as those who have spent time collecting in Ohio, were also consulted for their expertise. During this process, we were guided by four primary objectives. First and most importantly, we wanted to authenticate which butterfly and skipper species had been recorded from the State, and to provide accurate information on each species' biology and distribution. Secondly, we wished to highlight gaps in our current knowledge of these species, so that future studies might be developed. Thirdly, we hoped to provide the framework for the conservation of the State's terrestrial insect fauna. Finally, we wanted to present this information in such a way as to give as large an audience as possible the ability to utilize it. The end result is a publication that we feel achieves these goals.

This book is divided into a number of chapters, each representing an important part of the whole. Neither this work nor Ohio's fauna exists in a vacuum, and we have attempted to place both in perspective. Specific introductory chapters are devoted to historical overviews of butterfly studies in Ohio, geological history, plant ecology, and post-glacial biogeography. The bulk of this volume is devoted to the species accounts, which allow easy access to specific information. All of the species recorded from Ohio are figured in color. We have also provided brief accounts and color figures of those species which may eventually be discovered in Ohio, and we discuss species which have been erroneously reported from the State. Although we as authors contributed equally to most of the text, several chapters were conceived and written by a primary author. These are as follows; Chapters 2 and 10, John V. Calhoun; Chapter 3, John A. Shuey and John V. Calhoun; and Chapters 4 and 5, John A. Shuey.

Finally, although we have tried to keep errors and omissions to a minimum, some have undoubtedly escaped our attention. We would appreciate notification of any such problems.

2. THE HISTORY OF BUTTERFLY STUDY IN OHIO

The study of Ohio butterflies and skippers is not a recent endeavor. In fact, specimens collected in Ohio during the early 19th century still exist in the British Museum (Natural History) in London, England. Our present knowledge of these insects is enriched by more than a century of work by numerous individuals from many walks of life. Very few of these early naturalists were trained entomologists. Rather, the study of butterflies was, for most, an amateur interest, pursued strictly during times of leisure. Possessing careers as diverse as school teacher, florist, and clergyman, they shared a common interest and provided an invaluable legacy.

THE PIONEERS

During the 19th century, when an interest in the natural sciences was termed "natural philosophy," a few dedicated individuals explored the largely unknown wilderness of Ohio. Many were medical doctors who studied natural history only when their practices permitted a spare moment. Birds, rocks, wildflowers, shells, and insects were collected with great enthusiasm and curiosity. Because travel was difficult, either by horse or on foot, and often treacherous, collecting excursions rarely took place far from their homes. It is the early work of these natural philosophers that served as a foundation upon which future research on Ohio butterflies and skippers was based.

Two of the first individuals known to have collected in Ohio were the distinguished English entomologist **Edward Doubleday** (1810-1859) and his companion **Robert Foster.** In the autumn of 1837, Doubleday visited several Ohio cities including Portsmouth, Cincinnati, Huron, and Cleveland. Foster temporarily travelled separately and collected near Mt. Pleasant in eastern Ohio (Doubleday, 1838). Several species of Ohio butterflies collected during their Ohio visit were ultimately donated to the British Museum (Natural History) (Gray and Doubleday, 1844).

Jared P. Kirtland (1793-1877) (Figure 2.1) was the first individual to study the butterflies of Ohio seriously. Kirtland, a physician, was an eminent pioneer naturalist and was well acquainted with many facets of natural history (Mayfield, 1965). He published some of his initial observations of butterflies in 1851 (Kirtland, 1851a). To lepidopterists, Kirtland is best remembered for describing the snout butterfly (several times) from a specimen he collected in 1836 at Poland, Mahoning County, Ohio (Kirtland, 1851b; 1852a; 1874a). He also published the first list of butterflies known from Ohio, which included 53 species (Kirtland, 1854a; 1874b). Three additional publications contained remarks on Ohio butterflies (Kirtland, 1852b; 1854b; 1874c). His collection was donated to the former Cleveland Academy of Natural Science, but was later destroyed (Bubna, 1897).

In 1864, a colleague of Kirtland and a naturalist in his own right, **John Kirkpatrick** (1819-1869), a machinist by trade, published a list of butterflies found around Cleveland. This list contained 45 species, some of which were based on Kirtland's earlier list (Kirtland, 1854a). Kirkpatrick's collection was donated to the former Kirtland Society of Natural Science (Whittlesey, 1874) but was apparently destroyed.

In 1878, **Charles Dury** (1847-1931) (Figure 2.2), then curator of Ornithology and Entomology at the Cincinnati Society of Natural History, published an exhaustive list of Lepidoptera, including 58 species of butterflies, observed in the vicinity of Cincinnati. Over the years he continued to publish his remarks on butterflies new to Cincinnati and to Ohio (1898; 1900; 1910). His collection is deposited at the Cincinnati Museum of Natural History.

Although a brass machinist by trade, **George R. Pilate** (1856-1934) avidly studied insects, and in 1879 published a list of 52 species of butterflies he collected at Dayton. In 1882 he revised the list to include 61 butterflies and a large number of moths. Pilate also published two short notes about butterflies in 1880 and 1906. His father, **Eugene Pilate** (1804-1890), a physician, also collected Lepidoptera and was a regular correspondent of the renowned lepidopterist Ferdinand H. H. Strecker (Brown, 1967). Many of George's specimens are deposited in the Dayton Museum of Natural History and the Museum of Comparative Zoology, Harvard University.

In 1897, **Edward W. Claypole** (1835-1901) (Figure 2.3) published a list of the butterflies of Summit County which contained 48 species. Claypole was a geologist born and trained in England, who had broad natural history interests (Osborn, 1937). He also published two short entomological notes (Claypole, 1880; 1882) which included remarks on several species of Ohio butterflies. Efforts to locate his collection have been unsuccessful and it is assumed to have been destroyed.

William N. Tallant (1856-1905) lived in Columbus, where he worked as a clerk for the Pennsylvania Railway Company. During this time, he collected Lepidoptera in central Ohio until 1900 when he moved to Richmond, Indiana. Among his collecting companions was George R. Pilate. Tallant published a brief note in 1881 on his butterfly observations. His large worldwide collection was donated to The Ohio State University where it remains today. While he was a Columbus resident, Tallant lived in what is now the former home of literary humorist, James Thurber.

In 1898, the first comprehensive listings of Ohio butterflies were published by **James S. Hine** (1866-1930) (Figure 2.4). These lists of 92 and 93 species, respectively, were primarily based upon previously published lists and the collection of The Ohio State University, where he was an entomologist (Kennedy, 1931). In 1899, he updated his earlier publications and added seven species new to Ohio.

Several other individuals also contributed to our early knowledge of Ohio's butterflies, but less so than those discussed previously. **William V. Andrews,** a New York businessman, published a list (1875) of species he collected in Ohio and other eastern states. **John A. Bolton,** a Portsmouth schoolteacher, collected the the type specimen of *Hesperia nemoris* (W. H. Edwards, 1864), a synonym of *Amblyscrites hegon* (Scudder, 1864). **John F. Isom** (misspelled in literature as J. T. Ison), a Cleveland physician, made various observations of butterflies (Saunders et al, 1875; 1876). **Francis M. Webster** (Figure 2.5), Entomologist to The Ohio Agriculture Experiment Station in Wooster, published several papers (1892; 1893; 1900a; 1900b; 1912). Most of these dealt with economic entomology but included some information on butterflies. **Mathias Bubna,** a tailor, listed 42 species that he collected during 1896 in the vicinity of Cleveland (Bubna, 1897). **Rev. Albert I. Good** collected in the vicinity of Wooster and published a short note (1901) on his observations.

Ohio was also briefly visited by **Sherman F. Denton** (1857-1937) of Massachusetts. Denton was a taxidermist who authored *Moths and Butterflies of the United States ...* (1900), a publication which is now very rare. This exhaustive work is especially interesting because the plates depicting the species were partially constructed using the wing scales of actual butterflies and moths. Some of the specimens used for this purpose were collected in Ohio, especially in the vicinity of Fort Ancient, Warren County.

Two internationally-renowned entomologists temporarily resided in Ohio during the nineteenth century. **William J. Holland** (1848-1932) (Figure 2.6), the author of *The Butterfly Book* (1898), lived as a child in Dover and Tuscarawas. Here, Holland learned to appreciate the natural world through his father's teachings. Although it is not known if he actively collected in Ohio, the seed of his interest in Lepidoptera was undoubtedly planted during this time (Mallis, 1971). **Clarence M. Weed** (1864-1947) (Figure 2.7) was Entomologist to The Ohio Agriculture Experiment Station prior to Francis M. Webster. Although Weed's experience with Ohio butterflies was limited, he is remembered for his book *Butterflies Worth Knowing* (Weed, 1917).

NOTABLE SUCCESSORS

From the turn of the century through the 1960's, there were many individuals who contributed to our understanding of Ohio butterflies and skippers. Many of their specimens are still extant and much of what we know about Ohio's butterfly fauna is a direct result of their work.

Blenn R. Bales (1876-1946) (Figure 2.8), a Circleville physician who was interested in many aspects of natural history, published a list of the Lepidoptera of Pickaway County in 1909. This list included 50 species of butterflies he collected during 1907 and 1908. He also published a short note concerning butterflies in 1907. His collection was given to a young local collector during the 1920's and is presumed to have been destroyed (Blenn D. Bales, pers comm, 1988).

One of the most exhaustive local lists of Ohio Lepidoptera was published in 1910 by **Rev. Walter F. Henninger** (1873-1929) (Figure 2.9) of New Bremen. Although he was interested primarily in birds, Henninger accumulated much information on the Lepidoptera of Seneca County. His list, which included 82 species of butterflies, was based primarily upon material collected by **Lewis Ullrich** (?-1906). Ullrich, a druggist and florist who lived in Tiffin, exchanged specimens with William Tallant and provided invaluable information to William H. Edwards for his description of the life history of the northern pearly eye (Edwards, 1882b). A portion of Henninger's collection, which included many of Ullrich's specimens, was donated to the Ohio State Museum, but was almost completely without data and was badly damaged by dermestid beetles. The few specimens that still remain are in the Ohio Historical Society collection.

Henry Wormsbacher (?-1934), a Lakewood music teacher, amassed a large worldwide collection of Lepidoptera which included many specimens from northeastern Ohio. He was once the president (and apparently the founder) of the Cleveland Butterfly Association, an obscure organization of approximately 25 members. A rare form of the bronze copper was named in honor of Wormsbacher who had collected the type specimen, probably near Cleveland (Gunder, 1927). In 1918 he published a short paper about Lepidoptera. Many of his specimens remain in the Cleveland Museum of Natural History.

John C. Pallister (1891-1980) was an entomologist at the Cleveland Museum of Natural History. He collected Lepidoptera in northeastern Ohio from 1924-1931 (Sonja E. Teraguchi, pers comm, 1987). His greatest contribution to Ohio lepidopterology was the discovery of the rare Mitchell's satyr in Portage County (Pallister, 1927). Most of his specimens are deposited in the Cleveland Museum of Natural History.

One of the most influential collectors during this period was **Clement W. Baker** (1886-1958) (Figure 2.10). Baker, an accountant, studied the natural history of northeastern Ohio, especially in the vicinity of Waynesburg, where he resided. For several years he wrote a nature column for the Waynesburg newspaper. From 1924 until his death, he collected and reared Lepidoptera extensively, amassing a worldwide collection of about 60,000 specimens. He and several other local lepidopterists, including **Ray W. Bracher** (1908-1989), founded the Northeastern Ohio Lepidopterists Society. Although this short-lived organization had a small membership, it later evolved into the Neo-Naturalists Society with several hundred members. Baker wrote several unpublished manuscripts concerning Lepidoptera, and distributed them among the members of these societies (Ray W. Bracher, pers comm, 1985). An aberration of the aphrodite fritillary was named in honor of Baker who had collected the type specimen in Waynesburg (Clark, 1932). The bulk of Baker's collection was donated to his alma mater, Mt. Union College, Alliance, Ohio, where it remains today, stored in an attic above the Dean's office.

Two of the most important collectors of this period, and the first individuals to collect throughout the State, were **John S. Thomas** (1910-1988) (Figure 2.11) and his brother,

Edward S. Thomas (1891-1982) (Figure 2.12) of Columbus. John, a former staff member of the Ohio Historical Society, specialized in butterflies and was the more active lepidopterist of the two. His interest in butterflies waned when he left the Ohio Historical Society in the late 1930's. Edward was educated as a lawyer, but because of his incomparable knowledge of Ohio natural history, became the Curator of Natural History for the Ohio Archaeological and Historical Society in 1931 (Thomas, 1981). The Thomases and several student companions including **Joseph W. Enke** (1915-   ), travelled widely in Ohio and amassed a large collection of insects, mainly Lepidoptera and Orthoptera, for the Ohio State Museum. The Thomases published several observations on Ohio butterflies (Thomas, 1952; Potter and Thomas, 1970; Rawson and Thomas, 1939). Most of their specimens are now in the Ohio Historical Society collection.

Annette F. Braun (1884-1978) (Figure 2.13), a well known microlepidopterist and sister of plant ecologist E. Lucy Braun, collected many butterflies around Cincinnati. Her many specimens are currently deposited in various institutional collections including the Cincinnati Museum of Natural History, The Ohio Historical Society, and the Academy of Natural Sciences, Philadelphia.

Also collecting in the vicinity of Cincinnati were **Albert E. Wyss** (1909-   ) and his brother **Herbert E. Wyss** (1910-1985). While attending medical school at the University of Cincinnati, they authored several publications about the butterflies of the area (A. Wyss, 1930a; 1930b; 1931; 1932; and H. Wyss, 1930; 1931). Both served as curators of the Junior Society of Natural Sciences which was affiliated with the Cincinnati Museum of Natural History. Many of the Wyss' specimens are in the Cincinnati Museum of Natural History.

For nearly 40 years, **Hazel T. Chase** (1895-1977) (Figure 2.14) collected and reared the Lepidoptera of north-central Ohio. She was a naturalist of many interests, and wrote a nature column for the local Galion newspaper. Among her field companions were Clement W. Baker and Edward S. Thomas. She and **John S. Gill** (1929-   ), a young local collector, amassed a large collection which is now deposited in the Cleveland Museum of Natural History.

The Lepidoptera of the Oak Openings of Lucas County first received serious attention during the 1930's. Three individuals were especially active in the area at this time. **George W. Rawson** (1890-1986) was an English-born chemist who collected in northwestern Ohio while he resided in Detroit, Michigan (Rawson and Thomas, 1939). **J. Donald Eff** (1914-   ) (Figure 2.15), a postal employee, and **Robert C. Hollister** (1915-   ), a teacher, explored Lucas County while they lived in Sylvania, Ohio. Rawson's Ohio specimens are deposited in various institutional collections, including the Ohio Historical Society and the Carnegie Museum of Natural History. Most of Eff's specimens are deposited in the University of Colorado collection. A portion of Hollister's collection remains in his possession.

Best known for his research on the Hesperioidea, **Arthur W. Lindsey** (1894-1963) (Figure 2.16) collected in the vicinity of Granville, Ohio, where he taught at Denison University. One of his major contributions to the study of Hesperiidae was published while he was at the University (Lindsey, Bell, and Williams, 1931). His specimens were deposited in the collections of Denison University, The Ohio Historical Society, and the Carnegie Museum of Natural History.

From 1940 to 1965, **Homer F. Price** (1895-1987) (Figure 2.17) amassed in northwestern Ohio one of the most important collections of butterflies in the State. In 1970, Price, a farmer from Paulding County, published the results of his field work. A true naturalist, he collected many objects of natural history including bird eggs, land snails, and many types of insects. Among his correspondents and companions in the field were Clement W. Baker and Edward S. Thomas. His collection of 15,000 insects was sold to The Ohio State University where it remains today.

An authority on the natural history of Lorain and Huron Counties was **Leland L. Martin** (1912-1988) (Figure 2.18). A foundry administrator, he studied the butterflies and skippers of north-central Ohio for nearly 30 years. Although he was active until his death, a large portion of his collection was amassed during the 1960's. He generously shared his knowledge with others and published a short note about the American copper (Martin, 1962). Martin discovered a large population of Duke's skipper, *Euphyes dukesi*, at Findley State Park (Lorain County), prompting the Ohio Department of Natural Resources to create the first butterfly preserve in Ohio. His collection is deposited at the Cleveland Museum of Natural History.

Five other individuals who were active during this period published county and regional lists. **William Kayser,** a Wapakoneta businessman, compiled a list of insects of Auglaize County which included 50 species of butterflies (Williamson, 1905). **James W. Porter,** then a student, listed 61 species (1965) from Seneca County. **Orville N. Studebaker,** a printer, and his student son, **Dennis J. Studebaker** listed 49 species (1967) that they collected and reared in Miami County. **Louis A. Hoying,** a metallurgist, listed 56 species (1975) that he found from 1964-1973 in portions of Auglaize and Shelby Counties.

There are a number of additional collectors who built butterfly collections of local interest during this period. Many of their specimens still survive in institutional collections. Some of the more prominent collectors and the counties in which they primarily worked are **James W. Amrine, Jr.** (Franklin), **David F. Berringer** (Seneca), **Theodore Bock** (Hamilton), **Frank W. Case** (Hamilton), **Otto E. Ehrhart** (Paulding), **John F. Flenniken** (Jefferson), **Frank Hepp** (Seneca), **Josef N. Knull** (Franklin), **Gary Meszaros** (Cuyahoga), **Harry F. Murphy** (Seneca), **Charles E. Rhodes** (Seneca), **Raymond F. Romine** (Marion), **Stephen B. Smalley** (Hamilton), **William C. Stehr** (Athens), **William Thrasher** (Portage), **Edward G. Voss** (Lucas), and **Edward (Eduardo) C. Welling** (Cuyahoga).

CONTEMPORARY TRENDS

Since the 1960's, our understanding of Ohio's butterfly fauna has continued to increase at a dramatic pace. For example, Albrecht (1982) provided the first updated State list since Hine (1899) and included the first detailed data on the flight periods and distribution of Ohio's species. Much of our own work was initiated in response to obvious gaps in knowledge highlighted by Albrecht (eg Shuey, 1983; Calhoun, 1985[86]; Shuey, Iftner, and Calhoun, 1986). In addition, research on endangered and threatened butterflies and skippers has contributed to a heightened sense of awareness of Ohio's invertebrate fauna and its conservation (Shuey et al, 1987; Shuey, Calhoun, and Iftner, 1987).

Butterfly research in Ohio enjoys a rich history. Many individuals from Ohio and elsewhere are continuing to reveal much about Ohio's species. Nevertheless, there is still much to learn. No collection is too small nor is any observation unimportant. Both amateurs and professionals alike can continue to contribute to the work that was begun over 150 years ago.

Fig. 2.1 Jared P. Kirtland
(1793-1877)

Fig. 2.2 Charles Dury
(1847-1931)

Fig. 2.3 Edward W. Claypole
(1835-1901)

Fig. 2.4 James S. Hine
(1866-1930)

Fig. 2.5 Francis M. Webster
(?-1916)

Fig. 2.6 William J. Holland
(1848-1932)

Fig. 2.7 Clarence M. Weed
(1864-1947)

Fig. 2.8 Blenn R. Bales
(1876-1946)

Fig. 2.9 Walter F. Henninger
(1873-1929)

Fig. 2.10   Clement W. Baker
(1886-1958)

Fig. 2.11   John S. Thomas
(1910-1988)

Fig. 2.12   Edward S. Thomas
(1891-1982)

Fig. 2.13   Annette F. Braun
(1884-1978)

Fig. 2.14   Hazel T. Chase
(1895-1977)

Fig. 2.15   J. Donald Eff
(1914-   )

Fig. 2.16   Arthur W. Lindsey
(1894-1963)

Fig. 2.17 Homer F. Price (1895-1987) and his wife, Gladys, at home in 1963.

Fig. 2.18 A "collection" of Ohio Lepidopterists, 1985. From left to right: Joseph E. Riddlebarger, Leland L. Martin, John A. Shuey, John V. Calhoun, John W. Peacock, David C. Iftner, Vincent P. Lucas, Reed A. Watkins.

3. EDUCATION AND CONSERVATION

In order to encourage the study of Lepidoptera in Ohio, The Ohio Lepidopterists was founded in 1979. The purpose of this non-profit organization is to promote interest in, to provide information about, and to increase the knowledge of the butterflies, skippers, and moths of Ohio and neighboring states. This organization, in conjunction with the Ohio Department of Natural Resources, Division of Wildlife, initiated the Ohio Survey of Lepidoptera in 1986. The objectives of the Survey are to document the species of Lepidoptera present in Ohio, to record their distributions within the State, to identify species which are endangered and threatened in Ohio, and to provide access to the data for future research. Much of this publication is based upon data accumulated during the Survey.

For those who share our interests in Lepidoptera and would like to learn more, perhaps the best way to start is to join a regional organization such as the Ohio Lepidopterists, or one of the several other regional organizations devoted to the study of butterflies and moths. Consideration should be given also to the international professional organizations, all of which have a large amateur following. These organizations publish newsletters and journals, and sponsor meetings and field trips where beginners can learn from other amateur and

plete data with each specimen collected. The acceptable minimum data include the precise collection locality (state, county, nearest town, and township and section number if possible), date of capture, and the collector's name. Other information which is often helpful includes the habitat type, behavior of the butterfly when captured, and, if the specimen was reared, when the adult emerged and on what hostplant the larva fed. Additional information about collection techniques, preparation of data labels, and the preservation of specimens can be found in any of the general butterfly books available (eg Klots, 1951; Mitchell and Zim, 1987; Howe, 1975; Scott, 1986). We encourage all collectors to consider donating their collection to a natural history museum or a research university when its upkeep becomes a burden. Once passed into the public domain, a collection becomes a functional part of the resources available to other lepidopterists.

Understandably, some people are concerned about the effects of collecting upon butterfly populations. Fortunately, most butterfly populations are large enough that typical collecting activities do not threaten their long-term survival. However, many species occur as localized populations which may contain just a few breeding adults each generation. In these cases, we urge collectors to consider carefully the

Fig. 3.1 Butterfly early stages. a–egg (ovum); b-caterpillar (larva); c-chrysalis (pupa).

professional lepidopterists (see Appendix I. for names and addresses of these organizations).

Those wishing to observe living butterflies will find that many species can commonly be found in almost any habitat (Pyle, 1984). Butterflies are ideal subjects for photography, being abundantly available as models. Often, however, it requires patience and skill to approach them closely. Moreover, several species are restricted to unique habitats such as swamps, fens, and prairies, which adds to the adventure of capturing them on film.

The early stages of butterflies can also be observed closely and photographed. Butterflies are ideal house guests, and nothing is more amazing than the transformation of a caterpillar into an adult butterfly. Female butterflies will usually lay eggs when confined in bright light over suitable hostplants. Once the eggs have hatched, larvae can be reared by continuously supplying fresh hostplant cuttings. Cuttings can be kept fresh in refrigerated plastic bags. Larvae can also be found by searching hostplants in the field, but those found in this way are often parasitized by wasps and flies, and may not survive to adulthood. The butterfly lifecycle (Figure 3.1) is one of the best introductions available to the wonders of the natural world.

Those who would like to collect butterflies are urged to do so in an enlightened manner. Butterflies are more than postage stamps, and deserve better fates than becoming simple curios encased under glass. Butterfly collecting, intelligently done, can make real contributions to science by adding to our knowledge of geographic and temporal distributions. Furthermore, there are still taxonomic problems with several Ohio species which will only be resolved after more information about habitats, hostplants, geographic ranges, and flight periods is revealed. To insure that specimens are scientifically valuable, collectors are urged to include com-

number of specimens they intend to collect and to limit the number of individuals removed per generation. For particularly small populations, only one or two males should be collected and females should remain unharmed to lay eggs for the next generation. Of course, we strongly discourage the collection of endangered species, especially from known population sites where additional specimens add little to our understanding of the species and could have a negative impact on the viability of those populations. However, collectors should actively search for new population sites which may be important for the long-term survival of an endangered species in Ohio.

The greatest threats to most butterfly populations are habitat destruction and environmental degradation. Since European settlement, the natural landscape of Ohio has been radically altered, and many specialized habitats have become increasingly scarce. Presettlement Ohio was mostly forested, so species that require open habitats must have been restricted to the infrequent prairies, wetlands, beaver meadows, fire scars, and blowdowns scattered through the forest. By the late 1800's, most of the original forest had been cleared for agricultural purposes or to fuel iron furnaces. This clearing created potential habitats for many of the butterflies which are now ubiquitous, while perhaps leading to the extirpation of some forest-inhabiting species such as the diana fritillary, *Speyeria diana*. As a result of increased and improved forest management, woodland habitat has now returned to large portions of the State, especially the southern counties.

In a similar manner, most of western Ohio's prairies and many wetlands were destroyed as land was prepared for agricultural use. The extirpation of Mitchell's satyr, *Neonympha mitchellii*, probably resulted from the draining of the only known habitat for this species in the State (Shuey et al, 1987).

Recently, the Ohio Department of Natural Resources, Divisions of Natural Areas and Preserves, Parks and Recreation, and Wildlife, and some private conservation organizations such as The Nature Conservancy, have attempted to preserve endangered plant communities and their associated butterflies. Notable successes have been the preservation of many wetlands throughout the State, the establishment of a diverse series of preserves covering the Bluegrass Section of Adams County (Edge of Appalachia Preserve System), and the protection of the Oak Openings of Lucas County. Unfortunately, simply preserving representative plant communities does not guarantee that our endangered or threatened butterflies will be protected from extirpation; the past management of the Oak Openings serves as an excellent example. Until recently, the preservation of the Oak Openings depended solely upon keeping choice parcels of land from development. This policy included the suppression of many types of natural habitat maintenance, including fire. However, before the turn of the century, fire played an important role in the ecology of this area. Fires were frequent, and acted to maintain the openness of communities such as oak savannas, mesic prairies, and dune communities. Since the advent of fire suppression, many of these habitats have become overgrown with woody vegetation and are slowly converting to oak forests. Three currently endangered butterflies, the persius dusky wing *(Erynnis persius)*, the Karner blue *(Lycaeides melissa samuelis)*, and the frosted elfin *(Incisalia irus)* rely solely on these open communities, and their continued survival in Ohio depends upon maintenance of these habitats (Shuey, Calhoun, and Iftner, 1987; Metzler and Shuey, 1989). Unfortunately, populations of these butterflies have decreased to the point that direct burning of their population sites could be detrimental, and management plans must somehow improve the few available habitats without having a negative effect on the butterflies themselves. An aggressive initiative implemented in 1986 to restore many of the open communities on State and Toledo Metroparks land may eventually allow the natural expansion of populations of these endangered butterflies to the point that they would no longer be considered as endangered.

A new threat to Ohio's butterfly diversity is the gypsy moth *(Lymantria dispar* [L.]). This forest defoliator can reach extremely high larval densities, and is capable of defoliating large tracts of forest. However, it is the human response to gypsy moth defoliation that may cause the most ecological damage. In the past, most infestation sites have been sprayed with insecticides, which not only reduced the numbers of surviving gypsy moths, but also killed large numbers of nontarget arthropods as well. If major portions of the forests of southern Ohio are sprayed to protect them from gypsy moth defoliation, there may be major extirpations of arthropods from the region. Butterflies with limited distributions and early spring larvae (the likeliest period for spraying) are most susceptible (Shuey, Calhoun, and Iftner, 1987; Metzler and Lucas, 1990), but even common species will be affected. Given the failure of other states in the eastern United States to control the gypsy moth, any attempt to eradicate this pest from Ohio would seem futile. The gypsy moth is here to stay, and it is economically infeasible to spray for this species in perpetuity. Severe ecological damage could be inflicted while trying to prevent short term economic damage from this moth, resulting in the extirpation of untold numbers of arthropods from Ohio.

All biological communities are dynamic, and localized extinction of populations is a natural phenomenon. Thus, the loss of one population of a rare butterfly is not necessarily detrimental to the survival of the species **if new populations are founded at the same rate as others become extinct.** Unfortunately, human activities have increased the rate of localized extinction for many butterflies, while limiting the possibilities of new populations becoming established. If butterfly diversity (and all biological diversity) is to remain at its present level throughout Ohio and the eastern United States, a conscious effort must be directed towards preserving a significant percentage of the countryside in natural ecosystems.

4. THE ECOLOGICAL SETTING OF OHIO'S BUTTERFLIES

Many interacting factors influence the distribution of butterflies. The most obvious governing factor in Ohio is climate. More specifically, climate affects the ability or inability of butterflies to survive Ohio's cold winters or unpredictable springs. However, regardless of climate, butterflies cannot exist in a given area if suitable larval hosts and adult resources are absent. Although climate also affects the distribution of hostplants, Ohio's plant communities are greatly influenced by a combination of other factors as well, such as soil type, exposure to the sun, availability of moisture, and a multitude of other microclimatic features. In other words, specific plant communities generally develop under a given set of conditions. Therefore, if we recognize which factors exert the most control over the development of these plant communities, we can predict both the plants and thereby the butterflies which are likely to occur in an area. The following sections describe the geological factors which influence the distribution of Ohio's plants and butterflies, the botanical communities of the state, and finally the climatic factors that shape both sets of communities.

THE GEOLOGICAL SETTING OF OHIO

For the purposes of understanding the distribution of Lepidoptera, Ohio's bedrock can be lumped into two broad categories, alkaline and acidic. However, most of the bedrock in Ohio is buried beneath glacial deposits and has little direct influence over soil types or drainage. In unglaciated Ohio, the dominant bedrocks are the acidic sandstones and shales of the Mississippian, Pennsylvanian, and Permian periods, and the alkaline limestones and dolomites of the Silurian period (Plate 2). In these unglaciated regions, most of the soils are derived from the weathering of this bedrock; hence the bedrock types directly influence botanical and butterfly communities.

The soils that form from the weathering of the sandstones and shales in much of southern and eastern Ohio are often thin and usually acidic. These soils support a variety of cover types, the most important of which are mixed oak forests and mixed mesophytic forests. Many ridgetops and slopes in this region are very well drained and generally support mixed-oak vegetation, but localized stands of native pines and other species typical of xeric conditions are also present. Mixed-mesophytic forests are most common in deep moist ravines.

The limestones and dolomites in unglaciated Ohio weather forming nutrient-poor alkaline soils, which characterize a small but ecologically interesting portion of Ohio, the Bluegrass Section. The most notable communities occurring here are cedar glades and barrens and xeric prairies, all of which are important Lepidoptera habitats.

THE GLACIAL INFLUENCE

Before the first glacial advance, the drainage patterns in Ohio were radically different from those visible today. The major river in the region, the Teays River, flowed northwest through Ohio from the Appalachian Mountains. Most of the

8

feeder streams of the Teays River flowed northward in southwestern Ohio and westward in southeastern Ohio (Figure 4.1). When the first glacier moved in from the north over a million years ago, it effectively dammed these rivers and streams forming a huge lake, named Lake Tight, which flooded much of southern Ohio and adjacent Kentucky and West Virginia. Eventually, the water of Lake Tight reached such a level that it overflowed to the west, eroding deep ravines and reversing the direction of flow of most of the major channels in southern Ohio. For example, before the first glacial event, part of what we now call the Ohio River flowed northward from Monroe County into Pennsylvania. Once that stream was impounded, it overflowed and eroded through the highlands of its headwaters, and began to flow southward. Today part of this channel serves as the Ohio River channel. Likewise, several other channels in the southern part of the State were reversed, creating spectacular gorges and cliffs such as those east of Chillicothe.

Fig. 4.1 Teays River drainage pattern. This map was originally published as an insert *in* Stout, Wilbur E., Karl Ver Steeg, and G. F. Lamb. 1943. (Reprinted without revision in 1968). Geology of water in Ohio. Ohio Geol. Bull. 44. Ohio Department of Natural Resources, Division of Geological Survey. Columbus, Ohio. 694p.

9

The formation of Lake Tight over southern Ohio had a second far reaching effect. During its succesive stages, it flooded all but the highest ground until new drainage patterns were established. The lake deposited sediments which, upon exposure, weathered to form poorly drained soils in certain bottomlands. Today, the majority of wetlands in unglaciated Ohio occur over these lake sediments. Thus, although we refer to glaciated versus unglaciated Ohio throughout this text, glacial events have had an impact upon virtually the entire Ohio landscape.

Several separate glacial events have deposited recognizable debris in Ohio. The older deposits have been leached of their alkaline limestones near the surface, and the soils now formed over them are some of the most acidic in the State. Although some unique communities, such as sweet gum (*Liquidambar styraciflua* L.) swamps and oak-maple *(Quercus-Acer)* swamps, occur on these deposits, few entomologists have investigated them.

Deposits from the late Wisconsinan Stage (approximately 25,000-15,000 years ago) dominate Ohio's landscape today (Figure 4.2). This glacial drift is locally hundreds of feet thick, but generally ranges from 30 to 100 feet over the original bedrock in most of Ohio. Most of these deposits contain limestone fragments and are alkaline in reaction. The soils derived from these deposits are among the most agriculturally fertile in the world.

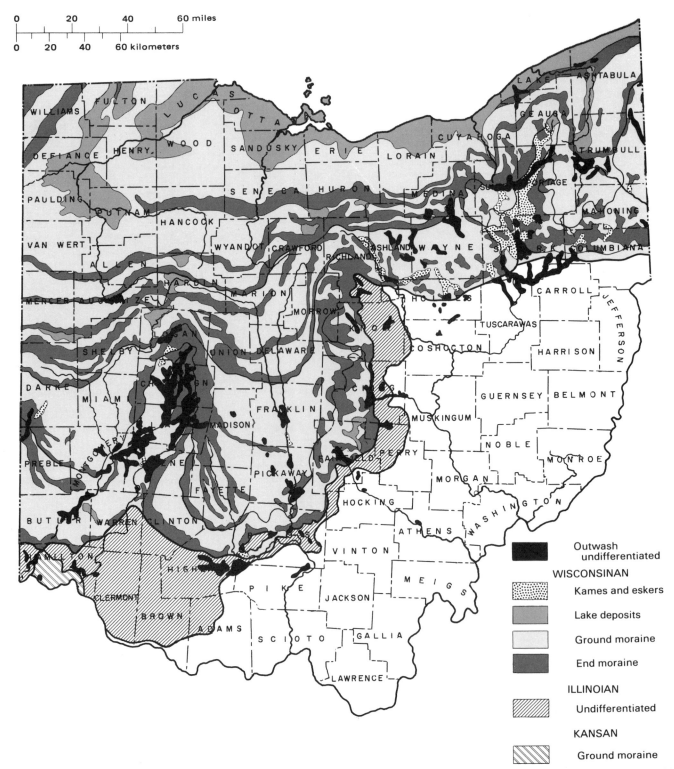

Fig. 4.2 Glacial deposits in Ohio. Modified from a map by the Ohio Department of Natural Resources, Division of Geological Survey. Columbus, Ohio.

Deposition of till into various patterns as the glacier retreated during the Wisconsinan Stage also has botanical implications. Where glaciers covered parts of the Allegheny Plateau, the till blocked the drainage patterns of the underlying topography, creating localized areas with abundant wetlands (eg the Portage County wetlands). Blocks of ice which were buried by glacial drift eventually melted forming depressions called glacial kettles which today form lakes, marshes, and bogs. Glacial deposits over pre-glacial river valleys often contain numerous springs, over which fens and marshes occur (Andreas, 1985). In areas where the surface of the till was deposited very evenly, poorly drained plains were formed which support swamps, marshes, and mesic prairies (eg west-central Ohio).

To understand the distribution of butterflies in Ohio today, it is helpful to follow the events that shaped our natural communities as the Wisconsinan Stage ended. This order is based upon pollen sequence-analyses of lake sediments and peat deposits (eg Knapp and Gooding, 1964; Ogden, 1966; 1967; Williams, 1962). Because both sediments and peat deposits are laid down chronologically, it is possible to look at the pollen preserved in the sequence of layers, and identify the sequence of plants that grew in the vicinity. Most lakes and peat deposits were formed as the glacier retreated, and the oldest are approximately 17,000 years old. The following generalized sequence is drawn primarily from King (1981).

It seems likely that as the glacier initially receded, a band of open ground and tundra with spruce and fir followed (Ogden, 1966; Shane, 1976). By about 14,000 years ago, the glacier had completely receded from Ohio. Pollen records indicate that spruce and fir forests (typical of much of Canada today) were well established, so the climate must have been cool and moist. As the glacier continued to recede to the north of Ohio, water was impounded between the ice margin and the drainage to the south creating glacial Lake Maumee, an earlier, higher, and ice-dammed predecessor of Lake Erie. Lake Maumee drained westward through Indiana, because the glacier still blocked all eastward drainage at Buffalo, New York. A later stage of this lake, Lake Warren, deposited sand beaches west of Toledo, which now underlay the soils of the Oak Openings.

By approximately 10,000 years ago, pollen profiles indicate that Ohio became dominated by pines as the climate became warmer and drier. Later, scattered oaks and elms became established as spruce and fir completely disappeared. However, wetland communities and deep valleys in eastern Ohio still supported many of the plants associated with northern habitats.

The Xerothermic Period began about 8,000 years ago and continued for 4000 years (Wright, 1968; Benninghoff, 1964). This period was marked by an increase in temperature and possibly decreased precipitation. The Xerothermic Period was too dry for forests to survive in many areas, and prairie dominated much of the landscape, especially to the west of Ohio (Transeau, 1935) (Figure 4.3). Groves of oaks and hickories probably occurred in moist, sheltered areas. Many marginal wetlands probably dried during this period, and

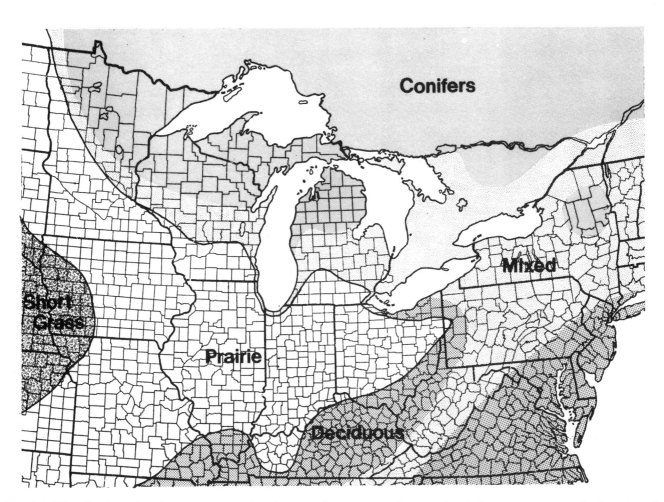

Fig. 4.3 Distribution of major ecotones during the Xerothermic Period. Note that habitat types currently distributed far to the west of Ohio were major features of the Ohio landscape during the height of this period. This rendering is from an original unpublished map prepared by E. N. Transeau and redrawn by Laurie Fletcher for Stuckey, Ronald L. and Karen J. Reese, eds. 1981. The Prairie Peninsula—in the "shadow" of Transeau: Proceedings of the Sixth North American Prairie Conference. Ohio Biological Survey Biological Notes Number 15. Columbus, Ohio. 278p. The original map is a glass lantern slide in the possession of R. L. Stuckey.

plants typical of prairies became established in the fens of central Ohio.

Since the Xerothermic Period (5,000 years ago to the present), the climate has cooled and become moister. Mesic deciduous forests became dominant over most of the State, although remnants of botanical communities derived from many of the other periods continued to survive within areas of unique microclimates.

THE PHYSIOGRAPHIC SECTIONS OF OHIO

The distribution of geological materials determines the boundaries of the physiographic sections (Figure 4.4). Although the boundary between sections is seldom conspicuous, there are differences in the botanical communities which are found within each section. This, in turn, limits some butterfly distributions. The following descriptions follow Anderson (1983). After the discussion of each section, we include a short list of the more uncommon habitat restricted butterflies which are found in the section. These lists are not meant to be inclusive, but rather to highlight these more uncommon (and therefore potentially more interesting) species.

The **Great Lake Section** occurs in Ohio just south and southwest of Lake Erie, largely within the former limits of glacial Lake Maumee. This area is characterized by flat terrain, broken only by scattered sand beach ridges. The soils are derived from till and lake deposits, and are generally fertile but poorly drained. The primary plant community which originally covered the western half of this section was

LEGEND

I Great Lake Section
II Till Plains Section
III Glaciated Allegheny Plateau
IV Unglaciated Allegheny Plateau
V Bluegrass Section

Fig. 4.4 The physiographic sections of Ohio (Anderson, 1983).

swamp, known to early European settlers as the Black Swamp. In Lucas, Henry, and Fulton Counties, a series of beach ridges support a complex of communities known collectively as the Oak Openings. Conditions in these communities range from extremely xeric to permanently flooded. Along the shore of Lake Erie, extensive marshes and strands of sand beach communities occur. The Lake Erie islands in Ohio consist mostly of dry, thin-soiled habitats perched on outcrops of limestone and dolomite. These islands support deciduous forest communities, gravel beaches, and small marshes. Habitat restricted butterflies which occur in the Great Lakes Section include *Erynnis persius, Poanes massasoit, Euphyes dion, E. dukesi, Atrytonopsis hianna, Satyrium acadica, S. edwardsii, Incisalia irus, Lycaeides melissa samuelis, Boloria selene, Satyrodes eurydice,* and *S. appalachia.*

The **Till Plains Section** occupies most of western Ohio and is characterized by the flat-to-rolling Wisconsinan glacial till found as flat ground maraine and low rolling end moraines over most of this section. The pre-settlement plant communities found here were various types of mesic deciduous forests, but naturally occurring treeless areas were common, as well. Most of Ohio's mesic prairies are found in this section, as well as scattered fens and marshes. Swamps and marshes are found in association with many glacial kettle lakes. Habitat restricted butterflies which occur in this section include *Polites mystic, Poanes massasoit, Euphyes dion, E. dukesi, Satyrium acadica, Fixsenia ontario, Calephelis muticum, Satyrodes eurydice,* and *S. appalachia.*

The **Glaciated Allegheny Plateau** is similar to the Till Plains Section in that it is characterized by a cover of glacial drift. However, in the Glaciated Allegheny Plateau, the deposits overlie a hilly topography produced by preglacial erosion, resulting in a much more varied terrain. Most of the plant communities prior to European settlement were mesic forests in valleys with oak forests on drier sites. Wetlands still dominate the landscape in many areas. Marshes, fens, swamps, bogs, and kettle lakes are more common in this section than in the remainder of the state. Habitat restricted butterflies which are typically encountered in this section include *Hesperia sassacus, Polites mystic, Poanes viator, Euphyes dion, E. conspicua, Pieris virginiensis, Satyrium acadica, Chlosyne harrisii,* and *Satyrodes eurydice.*

The **Unglaciated Allegheny Plateau** occupies the broad east and southeastern quarter of the State. This section is characterized by acidic soils derived from sandstone, siltstone, shale, and coal. The terrain is hilly, and relative relief may reach 100 meters. The vegetation before the coming of Europeans ranged from swamps in bottomland sites to mixed pine-deciduous forests on dry ridgetops. Natural treeless areas, including marshes, xeric prairies, and mesic prairies, were infrequent. Butterflies which typically inhabit this area include *Autochton cellus, Erynnis martialis, Pyrgus centaureae wyandot, Hesperia metea, Atrytonopsis hianna, Amblyscirtes hegon, Euchloe olympia, Anthocharis midea, Calycopis cecrops, Incisalia augustus, I. henrici, I. niphon, Celastrina neglecta-major, C. ebenina, Glaucopsyche lygdamus, Cyllopsis gemma,* and *Hermeuptychia sosybius.*

The **Bluegrass Section** is a small triangular portion of south-central Ohio characterized by Silurian limestone and dolomite substrates. The soils derived from these substrates are alkaline and nutrient poor. The terrain is rugged because of the deep dissection following the diversion of the Teays River westward by the first glacier, and relative relief may reach 100 meters. Several unusual botanical communities become common in this section of the state, especially xeric prairies and red cedar glades. The forests of this section range from mesic deciduous forests in the bottomlands to oak forests on xeric ridgetops. Habitat restricted butterflies occuring in this section include *Anthocharis midea, Satyrium edwardsii, Calycopis cecrops, Mitoura gryneus, Incisalia henrici, Calephelis borealis,* and *Hermeuptychia sosybius.*

THE BOTANICAL COMMUNITIES OF OHIO

Ohio lies at the edge of, and is influenced by, several ecological and physiographical regions: the prairies to the west, the Appalachian Mountains to the east and south, and the huge expanse of northern (boreal) forests and wetlands to the north. As such, the state is a mosaic of habitat types. Although forests may dominate the natural landscape to the extent that not much else is visible, there are usually small scattered habitats of other types within these areas which are important to Lepidoptera.

All attempts to classify botanical communities are, by definition, somewhat artificial. Very few communities fit perfectly into a specific community 'type', and intermediates between these 'types' are common. The "Natural Vegetation of Ohio" map (Gordon, 1966) (Plate 1) reflects those vegetational patterns present before European settlement, and is not necessarily indicative of the communities that exist today. It is presented as an aid to those who wish to maximize the diversity of habitats they investigate. Present-day communities reflect to a certain degree the original vegetation, or the unique conditions which originally supported unusual communities.

FOREST TYPES

The following brief descriptions of forests are primarily derived from Gordon (1966; 1969).

Beech Forests. These forests are characterized by large numbers of mesic species including beech (*Fagus grandifolia* Ehrh.), sugar maple (*Acer saccharum* Marsh.), red oak (*Quercus borealis* Michx.), white ash (*Fraxinus americana* L.), and white oak (*Quercus alba* L.) , with scattered individuals of basswood (*Tilia americana* L.), shagbark hickory (*Carya ovata* [Mill.] K. Koch), black cherry (*Prunus serotina* Ehrh.), and, more rarely, cucumber magnolia (*Magnolia acuminata* L.). The most familiar forest types are beech-sugar maple, and "wet beech" on poorly drained flatlands. In deep valleys in the dissected Allegheny Plateau, where mixed mesophytic forests occur, tulip tree (*Liriodendron tulipifera* L.), red maple (*Acer rubrum* L.), and/or sugar maple are associated with beech, forming the beech-maple-tuliptree subtype. Butterflies commonly encountered in beech-maple forests include *Papilio glaucus, Pieris virginiensis, Celastrina ladon, Polygonia interrogationis, P. comma, Nymphalis antiopa,* and *Enodia anthedon.*

Mixed Oak Forests (Plate 3). These forests include a wide variety of primary forest types, of which the most widespread are the white oak-black oak-hickory (*Quercus alba* L.-*Q. velutina* Lam.-*Carya* sp.) and the white oak types. The white oak-black oak-chestnut (*Castanea dentata* [Marsh.] Borkh.) type occurs in the low-lime glaciated plateau, chiefly on hilltops, and extends down south-facing slopes. Chestnut disappeared from Ohio woodlands during the 1920's and 1930's because of chestnut blight and is represented in older forests as snags or stump sprouts. Covering ridge tops of the Unglaciated Allegheny Plateau are forests of white oak-black oak and chestnut oak-chestnut, with sourgum (*Nyssa sylvatica* Marsh), flowering dogwood (*Cornus florida* L.), sassafras (*Sassafras albidum* [Nutt.] Nees), Virginia pine (*Pinus virginiana* Mill.), pitch pine (*Pinus rigida* Mill.), and/or shortleaf yellow pine (*Pinus echinata* Mill.) occurring locally. Butterflies which commonly occur in these forests include several *Erynnis* species, *Anthocharis midea, Satyrium calanus, Incisalia* species, *Celastrina ebenina, Cyllopsis gemma,* and *Hermeuptychia sosybius.*

Oak-Sugar Maple Forests. These forests include xeromesophytic forests in which white oak, red oak, black walnut (*Juglans nigra* L.), black maple (*Acer nigrum* Michx.), as well as sugar maple, white ash, elm (*Ulmus* sp.), basswood (*Tilia americana* L.), and bitternut (*Carya cordiformis* [Wang.] K. Koch) and shagbark hickories are among the dominant species. Local components often include black cherry, Kentucky coffee tree (*Gymnocladus dioica* [L.] K. Koch), chinquapin oak (*Quercus muehlenbergii* Engelm.), redbud (*Cercis canadensis* L.), and eastern red-cedar (*Juniperus virginiana* L.). Butterflies which are found in these areas include several *Erynnis* species, *Polygonia comma*, *P. interrogationis*, *Asterocampa celtis*, and *A. clyton*.

Elm-Ash Swamp Forests. These forests occur in flat, poorly drained areas (especially in the Black Swamp area of northwest Ohio) and are dominated by white elm (*Ulmus americana* L.), black ash (*Fraxinus nigra* Marsh.), and/or white ash (*Fraxinus americana* L.), silver maple (*Acer saccharinum* Marsh.), and/or red maple. Extremely wet areas contain cottonwood (*Populus deltoides* Marsh.) and/or sycamore (*Platanus occidentalis* L.). These "swamp oak-hickory" communities are enriched locally with swamp white oak (*Quercus bicolor* Willd.), pin oak (*Quercus palustris* Meunchh.), white oak, black walnut, and tulip tree. Contiguous areas are covered with "wet beech" forests, wet prairies, sedge swamps, and fens. Butterflies which are found in these habitats include *Euphyes dukesi*, *Polygonia progne*, *Fixsenia ontario*, and *Satyrodes appalachia*.

Mixed Mesophytic Forests. Mixed mesophytic forests are usually dominated by broad-leaved deciduous species, with no single species comprising a very large percentage of the dominants. Segregates of the mixed mesophytic association in Ohio include oak-chestnut-tulip tree, oak-hickory-tulip tree, white oak-beech-maple, and hemlock-beech-chestnut-red oak. North-facing slopes of the Portage Escarpment in Lake and Ashtabula Counties were covered with the latter forest type. The mixed mesophytic forests of southwestern Ohio were generally different from those of eastern Ohio in that the former contained a large percentage of beech, white basswood, and tulip tree. Butterflies encountered in these forests are several *Erynnis* species, *Papilio glaucus*, *Eurytides marcellus*, *Parrhasius m-album*, and *Celastrina* spp.

Bottomland Hardwood Forests (Plate 3). These forests occupy older valleys and terraces of major streams as well as recent alluvium and included vegetation types of variable composition. Several types and variations are recognized including beech-white oak, beech-maple, beech-elm-ash-yellow buckeye (*Aesculus octandra* Marsh.), and elm-sycamore-river birch (*Betula nigra* L.)-red maple and sweet gum (*Liquidambar styraciflua* L.)-river birch. Butterflies of bottomland hardwood forests include *Eurytides marcellus*, *Polygonia interrogationis*, *P. comma*, *Asterocampa celtis*, *A. clyton*, and *Libytheana bachmanii*.

PRAIRIES

Prairies are naturally occurring grasslands. In Ohio, there are three easily recognized prairie types; mesic, xeric, and savanna. **Mesic prairies** (Plates 4 and 5) occur on flat, poorly drained sites such as clayey till plains (eg Darby Plains—see King, 1981) or old lake beds (eg Killdeer Plains—see Troutman, 1981; Forsyth, 1981). They tend to be flooded in spring and early summer, but often experience very dry conditions by late summer. In Ohio these prairies are often dominated by big bluestem (*Andropogon gerardi* Vitman), which in favorable years can grow to 2.5 meters tall, giving these areas a very distinct appearance. Other conspicuous indicator species include little bluestem (*Andropogon scoparius* Michx.), Sullivant's milkweed (*Asclepias sullivantii* Engelm.), New England aster (*Aster novae-angliae* L.), purple coneflower (*Echinacea purpurea* [L.] Moench), sunflowers (*Helianthus* spp.), blazing-stars (*Liatris* spp.), and prairie-dock (*Silphium terebinthinaceum* Jacq.).

In Ohio, mesic prairies were among the last areas developed for agriculture (Transeau, 1981) and at the time of the first European settlers, mesic prairies were a conspicuous element of the west-central Ohio landscape (Figure 4.5), possibly occupying upwards of 500,000 hectares. Once the technologies were developed to drain and plow the prairies,

settlers soon discovered that these soils were among the most fertile in the state, and virtually every prairie was soon converted to agricultural use. Today, less than 1 percent of Ohio's original mesic prairies survive, mostly as small, highly disturbed, isolated remnants. The prairies that did survive often underwent a severe reduction in size at one point in their history. For example, Bigelow State Nature Preserve is a tiny (0.2 ha) remnant of the Darby Plains prairies located in a small cemetery (King, 1981). However, in the recent past, this site was manicured, restricting the native prairie plants to within centimeters of each tombstone. Under such conditions, it seems unlikely that any prairie insects could have survived at this site or at any other prairie remnants with a similar history. Lepidopterists searching for prairie butterflies should concentrate their efforts not only on larger remnants, but also on those which are known to have avoided a severe reduction in size.

There are no butterflies in Ohio which are considered to be restricted to mesic prairies. Given the large expanses once occupied by mesic prairies, it is conceivable that some species now extirpated did once occur in Ohio, but the occurrence of such classic prairie rarities as *Hesperia ottoe*, or *Lycaena xanthoides dione* now seems unlikely. Butterflies often encountered in and around mesic prairies today include *Atrytone logan*, *Euphyes conspicua*, *Harkenclenus titus*, *Nymphalis milberti*, *Satyrodes eurydice*, *Cercyonis pegala nephele*, and *Speyeria idalia*.

Xeric prairies (Plate 5) occur primarily in the Bluegrass Section of Ohio. Most xeric prairies are small openings surrounded by red-cedar (*Juniperus virginiana* L.), various oaks, and redbud. The prairies themselves are dominated by many of the same species that are found in mesic prairies, but the growth is less luxuriant and there are many more drought-tolerant species present. The native grasses in this region are a conspicuous component of early successional habitats, and prairie communities are found in many artificially created openings. In fact, there may actually be more of these prairies present in southern Ohio than there were 50 years ago (Cusick, 1981). Butterflies which are often seen in and around xeric prairies include *Thorybes* species, *Hesperia leonardus*, *Satyrium edwardsii*, *Mitoura gryneus*, *Incisalia henrici*, and *Calephelis borealis*.

Oak savannas (Plate 5) are primarily limited to a small region in the northwest corner of the state known as the Oak Openings. This region is actually a complex of habitats ranging from the very wet to the driest in the state. The soils occur over sand beaches formed from glacial Lake Warren, which was considerably higher than its present day counterpart, Lake Erie. Where the sand is well drained, oak savanna and dune communities occur. Oak savannas are xeric prairies dominated by drought-resistant herbaceous species with widely spaced black oaks. The common grass is usually little bluestem. These pockets of xeric vegetation are often surrounded by areas of poor drainage supporting wetlands and mesic prairies.

Dune communities (Plate 5) often have extensive areas of open unvegetated sand, and usually occur in association with the savannas. Both habitats usually support lupine (*Lupinus perennis* L.). The butterflies of these communities are among the most localized in the State and include *Erynnis persius*, *E. lucilius*, *Incisalia irus*, and *Lycaeides melissa samuelis*. Other species that are found here, but which are generally rare elsewhere in Ohio, are *Atrytonopsis hianna*, *Satyrium edwardsii*, and *Boloria selene*. Many of the uncommon butterflies associated with areas of poor drainage (eg sedge meadows, fens, and swamps) are also conspicuous inhabitants of the Oak Openings.

WETLANDS

There are several easily recognized types of wetlands in the Lower Great Lakes area. They are generally characterized as pioneer, now often relict, communities that occur in isolated pockets of poor drainage and cool microclimate.

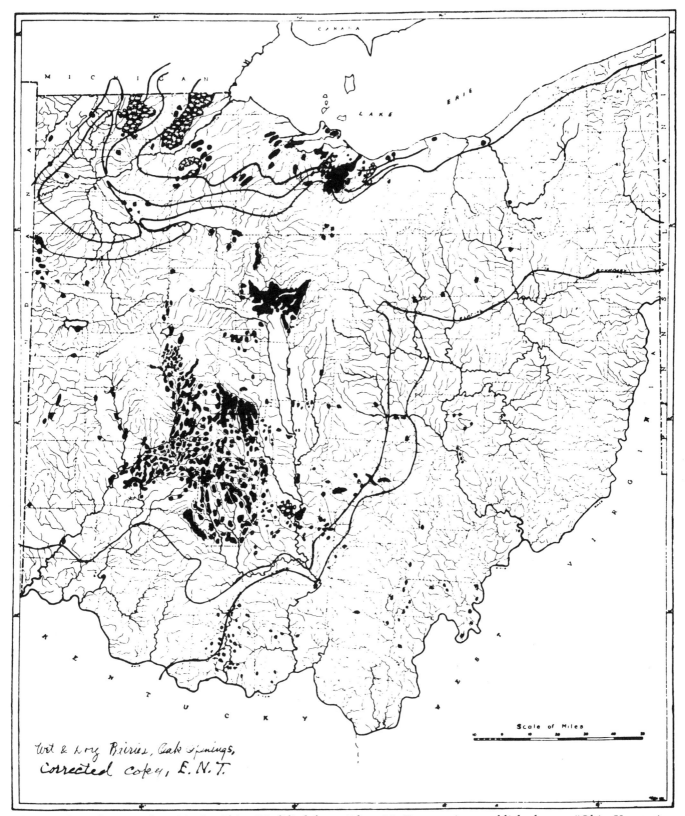

Wet & Dry Prairies, Oak openings,
corrected copy, E. N. T.

Fig. 4.5 Distribution of prairie in Ohio. Modified from Edgar N. Transeau's unpublished map "Ohio Vegetation: Prairies," first printed in 1950. The original is in the offices of the Ohio Biological Survey.

Open wetlands represent communities which may be directly derived from plant associations adjacent to the retreating glacier. Many of these wetlands have existed continuously since that era. Wooded wetlands may represent communities which replaced the pioneering communities as a result of natural habitat modifications. In addition to floristic differences, the wetland types differ in drainage patterns, soil types, and soil pH. The following descriptions are excerpted from Shuey (1985).

Marshes are the wettest of these habitats, with standing water present during most or all of the growing season. They often develop along streams and lake shores. The soils usually contain a high mineral content, even in areas where they superficially resemble organic muck. Typical plants are mostly herbaceous and include cattail (*Typha latifolia* L.), bulrush (*Scirpus validus* Vahl.), and occasionally blueflag (*Iris versicolor* L.). The only wetland butterflies that regularly occur in marshes are *Ancyloxypha numitor* and *Lycaena hyllus*.

15

Sedge meadows (Plate 4) are similar to marshes and occur in the same situations, but are only seasonally flooded. The soils are usually sedge peat or organic muck. These wetlands are open communities dominated by sedges (*Carex* spp.) with scattered horsetails (*Equisetum* spp.), blueflag, and cattails. Many butterflies occur in sedge meadows, including *Euphyes conspicua, E. dion, Poanes viator, P. massasoit, Lycaena helloides, L. hyllus, Satyrium acadica,* and *Satyrodes eurydice.*

Fens (Plate 4) occur in depressions with impeded drainage in areas of calcareous substrates, and are distributed almost exclusively in the glaciated portion of the State (Figure 4.6). They are generally found along streams or lake shores and are usually fed by springs. The soils are sedge peat and are neutral to highly alkaline. Two types of fens occur in Ohio, differing primarily in the relict plant species present (Stuckey and Denny, 1981). Bog fens (Plate 4) contain many plants of northern distribution such as pitcher-plant (*Sarracenia purpurea* L.), tamarack (*Larix laricina* [Du Roi] K. Koch), and poison sumac (*Rhus vernix* L.). **Prairie fens** (Plate 4) contain a significant number of prairie species, the most conspicuous of which is big bluestem. Both types of fens contain extensive stands of sedges and shrubby cinquefoil (*Potentilla fruticosa* L.), and often contain lady slippers (*C. ripedium* spp.). Both types of fens or parts thereof which are dominated by shrubs, such as red-osier dogwood (*Cornus stolonifera* Michx.) and willows (*Salix* spp.) are referred to as **carrs. Treed fens** are dominated by trees such as tamarack,

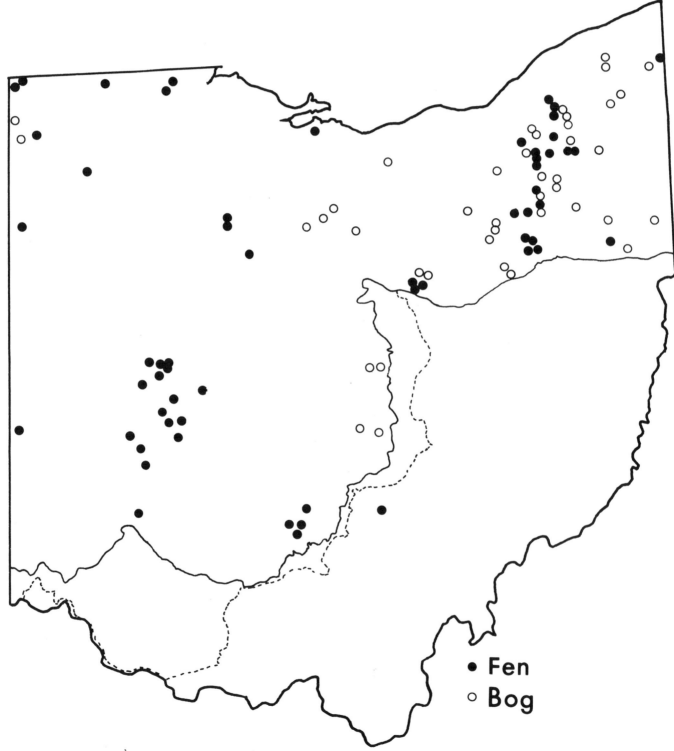

Fig. 4.6 Distribution of peatlands in Ohio. Modified from Andreas, 1985.

16

white cedar (*Thuja occidentalis* L.), or maples (*Acer* spp.). Because fens superficially resemble bogs, most named fens contain the term 'bog.' Butterflies which occur in fens are *Atrytone logan*, *Euphyes bimacula*, *E. dion*, *E. conspicua*, *Poanes viator*, *P. massasoit*, *Satyrium acadica*, *Lycaena dorcas*, *Calephelis muticum*, *Boloria selene*, *Euphydryas phaeton*, *Satyrodes eurydice*, *S. appalachia*, and *Neonympha mitchellii*.

Bogs (Plate 4) also occur in depressions, usually glacial kettle holes, and thus, in Ohio, are restricted to glaciated regions. Bogs have internal (inward) drainage and are fed by rain and ground water. There is often a remnant of open water in the center surrounded by a floating mat of sphagnum. The soil is sphagnum peat and is highly acidic. Bogs are dominated by *Sphagnum* mosses which form an almost complete ground cover that is usually obscured by taller plants. Ericaceous shrubs such as blueberries and cranberries (*Vaccinium* spp.) and leather-leaf (*Chamaedaphne calyculata* [L.] Moench) form a conspicuous element in these habitats. Other distinctive plants include pitcher-plant, cotton-sedges (*Eriophorum* spp.), sundews (*Drosera* spp.), and several orchids. **Wooded bogs** may be dominated by tamarack with red maple and scattered poison sumac. Butterflies are not common in bogs, but a few wetland species are usually present. In Ohio they include *Euphyes conspicua* and *Satyrodes eurydice*.

Swamps (Plate 4) occur along streams and rivers and in poorly drained plains, and are seasonally or permanently flooded. Swamp soils are high in organic matter but are not peaty. They are dominated by trees such as willows (*Salix* spp.), maples, elms (*Ulmus* spp.), white ash (*Fraxinus americana* L.) buttonbush (*Cephalanthus occidentalis* L.), and red-osier dogwood. Herbaceous plants include various sedges and skunk-cabbage (*Symplocarpus foetidus* [L.] Nutt). Three butterflies which are usually associated with swamps in Ohio are *Euphyes dukesi*, *Satyrodes appalachia*, and *Polygonia progne*.

MODIFIED HABITATS

Of course, human disturbance has had a dramatic impact upon the botanical communities of Ohio, and many such areas are important butterfly habitats (Plate 6). Some of these areas are similar to naturally occurring habitats and support many butterflies, whereas others are dominated by naturalized weeds and support few butterfly species.

Pastures (Plate 6) are maintained by grazing animals which very selectively eat plants that they find palatable. The surviving plants usually consist of grasses and 'tough' plants such as thistles (*Cirsium* spp.), and ironweed (*Vernonia* spp.). Butterflies which breed in pastures include several *Polites* species, *Wallengrenia egeremet*, *Vanessa virginiensis*, and *V. cardui*. **Orchards** generally support the same species as pastures, but the rotting fruit may also attract such species as *Polygonia comma*, *P. interrogationis*, and *Nymphalis antiopa*. **Hayfields** (Plate 6) often abound with species which visit nectar sources in open areas. This habitat does not actually support larval populations of many butterfly species, but adults from adjacent habitats avidly visit the abundant nectar sources in these fields, and 30 or more species may be observed in a single field. Species which often do breed in hayfields are *Ancyloxypha numitor*, *Colias eurytheme*, *C. philodice*, and *Everes comyntas*. Fields dominated by alfalfa and clover are especially productive. **Agricultural fields** planted in crop species generally do not support butterflies. However, many weeds associated with the edges of plowed fields may support a few butterflies, such as *Pholisora catullus*, *Pieris rapae*, and *Vanessa* spp.

Old fields form some of the most important butterfly habitats in Ohio. These are essentially abandoned agricultural fields which have been allowed through succession to develop into diverse assemblages of herbaceous plants. As succession proceeds, these habitats become increasingly dominated by woody plants until they eventually become young forests. Certain habitats, such as **railroad, powerline** (Plate 6), and **gasline rights-of-way** are essentially old fields that are maintained in a early successional stage by periodic disturbance. These habitats often develop a very diverse herbaceous flora which supports some of Ohio's rarest butterflies. Some of the more uncommon species that are found in these habitats are *Pyrgus centaureae wyandot*, *Hesperia metea*, *H. leonardus*, *Atrytonopsis hianna*, and *Calycopis cecrops*.

Landscaped urban/suburban habitats are generally well manicured and do not often support many butterfly species. Those butterflies that do breed in these settings often use trees as hostplants. For example, *Satyrium* species which feed on oaks and hickories, *Polygonia* species which feed on elms, and *Asterocampa* species which use hackberries. *Polites* species often use the various grasses present as hosts. *Pieris rapae* will exploit any weedy and cultivated mustard species present. If abundant nectar sources are available, many wide-ranging species may also be found. A recent trend in urban landscaping is the creation of **butterfly gardens,** which are consciously planned to include hostplants and nectar sources for butterfly species (see Rothschild and Farrell, 1983; Tekulsky, 1985; Tylka, 1987; Warren, 1988).

5. POSTGLACIAL BIOGEOGRAPHY

Because two-thirds of Ohio was completely denuded during the Wisconsinan Stage, plants and animals must have become re-established from populations located elsewhere. Much research has been undertaken to determine where these organisms originated (eg Peattie, 1922; Thompson, 1939; Benninghoff, 1964; Shapiro, 1970a). The most obvious answer is that vegetation simply spread northward as the climate warmed. For the majority of Ohio's flora and fauna, this seems to explain their present day distribution. However, some of the most localized and uncommon communities and their associated Lepidoptera entered the state by more indirect routes.

There is evidence that a few species of plants that were present before the first glacial event have survived to the present. These species occur in Ohio as disjunct populations of otherwise southern Appalachian species and may have migrated into southern Ohio via the Teays River before its direction of flow was reversed. These plants include mountain lover (*Paxistema canyi* Gray), bigleaf magnolia (*Magno-* *lia macrophylla* Michx.), and umbrella magnolia (*M. tripetala* L.) (Silberhorn, 1970; McCance and Burns, 1984). There are no known Ohio Lepidoptera which fit this distributional pattern.

Several species of plants occur on the shores of the Great Lakes that are otherwise restricted to the Atlantic Coastal Plain. Peattie (1922) suggested that these species followed habitats created in the St. Lawrence Valley or the Mohawk Valley of New York from the Coastal Plain to the Great Lakes area. Shapiro (1970) applied this model to wetland butterflies and suggested that several species reached the Great Lakes Region by dispersing from the Coastal Plain along the Mohawk Valley. Species which may have followed this route include *Euphyes bimacula*, *E. conspicua*, and *Neonympha mitchellii*. Shapiro further expanded the model to include species which may have followed the Mississippi Valley from the Gulf Coastal Plain into the Great Lakes Region, possibly following the Wabash River Valley (Figure 5.1). Species which may have followed this route include *Euphyes dukesi*

Fig. 5.1 Dispersal routes of wetland butterflies into Ohio (dotted line indicates the glacial maxima).

and *Calephelis muticum*. During the Xerothermic Period, many of the smaller wetlands along this route may have dried up, effectively isolating the Coastal Plain populations from the Great Lakes populations.

An additional route of wetland butterfly emigration into Ohio may have been from the west. For example, *Poanes massasoit* occurs only in western Ohio despite the abundance of seemingly suitable habitat available in northeastern Ohio (Shuey, 1985) (Figure 8.69). This may indicate that *P. massasoit* only relatively recently entered Ohio from Indiana or Michigan, but did not immigrate across central Ohio where wetlands are relatively scarce (Figure 4.6). The distribution of *Chlosyne harrisii* suggests a similar route (Figure 8.218). In northeastern Ohio, there are several very dark populations that are assignable to the subspecies *C. harrisii liggetti*. The limited material we have seen from northwestern Ohio is a lighter phenotype and seems referable to *C. h. harrisii*. This suggests that this species entered Ohio from two directions, the northeastern populations being genetical-

ly related to Pennsylvania populations, and the northwestern Ohio populations possibly derived from emigrants from southern Michigan.

The Xerothermic Period is most notable for the eastward expansion of prairie through Ohio and western Pennsylvania (Transeau, 1936) (Figure 4.3). Presumably these prairie communities included butterflies, but no known classic prairie species (eg *Hesperia ottoe*) have been reported from the State. Most of Ohio's prairies were destroyed for agricultural purposes long before they were entomologically surveyed.

Despite the absence of surviving prairie butterflies, the Xerothermic period probably did result in range expansions which brought *Lycaeides melissa samuelis* into the State (Shapiro, 1970), and possibly two other lupine-feeding species, *Incisalia irus* and *Erynnis persius*.

Of course, humans have had a tremendous impact upon the distribution of butterflies. To lepidopterists, the most obvious influence has been the introduction of two European species, *Pieris rapae* and *Thymelicus lineola*, both of which are very common in the State. Even more significant are the effects of European land use patterns which have eliminated many specialized habitats, reduced forest cover, and increased the amount of open disturbed habitats, resulting in the expansion or contraction of the ranges of several species in Ohio (see Chapter 3).

6. METHODS

The data summarized here are a subset of the Ohio Survey of Lepidoptera, sponsored by the Ohio Lepidopterists. We have collected information from virtually all available public and private collections with relevant data.

Public collections examined include:

COLLECTION	LOCATION	COLLECTION	LOCATION
American Museum of Natural History	New York, New York	Ohio Historical Society	Columbus, Ohio
Ashland College	Ashland, Ohio	Ohio Lepidopterists	Columbus, Ohio
Boardman Township Park	Boardman, Ohio	Ohio Northern University	Ada, Ohio
Bowling Green State University	Bowling Green, Ohio	The Ohio State University	Columbus, Ohio
Carnegie Museum of Natural History	Pittsburgh, Pennsylvania	Ohio University	Athens, Ohio
		Otterbein College	Westerville, Ohio
Cincinnati Museum of Natural History	Cincinnati, Ohio	Otto Ehrhart Museum	Antwerp, Ohio
Cleveland Museum of Natural History	Cleveland, Ohio	Academy of Natural Sciences of Philadelphia	Philadelphia, Pennsylvania
Dayton Museum of Natural History	Dayton, Ohio		
Denison University	Granville, Ohio	Rio Grande College	Rio Grande, Ohio
Field Museum of Natural History	Chicago, Illinois	Seneca County Museum	Tiffin, Ohio
Heidelberg College	Tiffin, Ohio	Stone Laboratory (The Ohio State University)	Bass Island, Ohio
Hiram College	Hiram, Ohio		
Marietta College	Marietta, Ohio	United States National Museum of Natural History	Washington, D.C.
Miami University	Oxford, Ohio		
Michigan State University	East Lansing, Michigan	University of Louisville	Louisville, Kentucky
		University of Michigan	Ann Arbor, Michigan
Mill Creek Park Ford Nature Center	Youngstown, Ohio	Upper Scioto Valley High School	McGuffey, Ohio
Mount Union College	Alliance, Ohio	Wilmington College	Wilmington, Ohio
Ohio Agricultural Research and Development Center	Wooster, Ohio	Wittenberg University	Springfield, Ohio
		Youngstown State University	Youngstown, Ohio

Private collections examined include:

INDIVIDUAL	LOCATION	INDIVIDUAL	LOCATION
Valeriu Albu	Charleston, West Virginia	Mitchell L. Magdich	Toledo, Ohio
		Mark E. Marshall	Springfield, Ohio
James W. Amrine	Westover, West Virginia	Leland L. Martin	Wakeman, Ohio
		Leroy Maybee	Toledo, Ohio
William F. Babcock	Akron, Ohio	John T. McBurney	Anaheim, California
Tim A. Bargar	Galena, Ohio	Joseph L. McMahon	Chillicothe , Ohio
James W. Becker	Hamilton, Ohio	Gary Meiter	Salem, Ohio
Larry E. Becker	Milford, Ohio	Steven J. and Richard G. Meyer	Napoleon, Ohio
Edward M. Binic	Akron, Ohio	Max E. Miller	Sugar Creek, Ohio
Roger S. Boone	Springfield, Ohio	Brian A. Nault	Wooster, Ohio
John V. Calhoun	Dunedin, Florida	Mogens C. Nielsen	Lansing, Michigan
Thomas W. Carr	Whitehouse, Ohio	Charles D. Overacker	Springfield, Ohio
Beatrice M. Chandler	Akron, Ohio	David K. Parshall	Columbus, Ohio
Hoe H. Chuah	Houston, Texas	John W. Peacock	Marion, Ohio
James H. Conover	Athens, Ohio	Maria W. Plonczynski	Jackson, Mississippi
Dennis A. Currutt	Chesterland, Ohio	James W. Porter	Athens, Georgia
Bastiaan M. and Carol F. Drees	Bryan, Texas	Diane A. Richards	Wellston, Ohio
Donald W. Dubois	Akron, Ohio	Joseph E. Riddlebarger	Logan, Ohio
Charles B. Fangboner	Fremont, Ohio	Ronald F. Rockwell	Galion, Ohio
John F. Flenniken	Bloomingdale, Ohio	Dale F. Roth	West Liberty, Ohio
Loran D. Gibson	Florence, Kentucky	Henri C. Seibert	Athens, Ohio
John S. Gill	Galion, Ohio	John A. Shuey	Williamsburg, Michigan
J. Michael and Todd Gilligan	Arcadia, Ohio		
Harry W. Godwin	Baltimore, Maryland	Ernest M. Shull	Fort Wayne, Indiana
Drew A. Hildebrant	Jackson, Mississippi	Ann K. Stafford	Springfield, Ohio
Jeffrey D. Hooper	Tallmadge, Ohio	Kenneth J. Stein	Blacksburg, Virginia
David J. Horn	Columbus, Ohio	Orville N. and Dennis J. Studebaker	Tipp City, Ohio
Louis A. Hoying	Minster, Ohio	James A. Toot	Cleveland, Ohio
John A. Hyatt	Kingsport, Tennessee	Edward G. Voss	Ann Arbor, Michigan
David C. Iftner	Sparta, New Jersey	William Ward	Girard, Ohio
Arno R. Kmentt	Youngstown, Ohio	Reed A. Watkins	Spring Valley, Ohio
Leroy C. Koehn	Coral Springs, Florida	Randall C. Wightman	Boardman, Ohio
Robert L. Langston	Kensington, California	Donald J. Wright	Cincinnati, Ohio
Irving G. Loewit	Bellbrook, Ohio	Steven R. Uecke	Newton Falls, Ohio
Alma M. Long	Ada, Ohio	Roger A. Zebold	Wilmington, Ohio
Vincent P. Lucas	Westlake, Ohio		

To date, over 25,000 **records** of Ohio butterflies have been compiled. The definition of a **record** is modified from Albrecht (1982), and is a documented collection of a single species from a specific locality on a specific date by a specific collector, regardless of how many specimens were actually collected. Thus, a series of 10 specimens taken at one time at one locality by a single individual or a group of individuals would constitute a single record. Two specimens taken under the same conditions but by two independent collectors would be considered as two records. The number of specimens examined during this study is at least twice the number of records recorded.

The data are stored electronically and have been deposited with the Ohio Lepidopterists and the Ohio Department of Natural Resources, Division of Wildlife. These data are presented graphically as geographic distribution maps and as histograms of adult capture (= record) dates.

Geographic Distribution-The distribution maps are based primarily upon material actually examined by the authors (solid circles). The maps indicate county records, and do not indicate precise collection localities. Literature records (open circles) are included only if they are not duplicated by actual specimen records. The source of each literature record is detailed under the discussion heading LITERATURE RECORDS. Although we have exercised some discretion in plotting dubious literature records and probable misdeterminations on the maps, these records are presented in the discussions. If there are no unsubstantiated literature records for a species, this section is omitted. The maps represent the distribution data accumulated up to 1 January 1989. County names refer to Figure 6.1.

Temporal Distribution-The histograms are based on capture records, and are estimations of the period of adult activity in Ohio and, to a degree, estimate the number of broods. They also allow relative comparisons of abundance between species. However, these histograms must be used

Fig. 6.1 Counties of Ohio.

with caution. They are based upon collection records accumulated over several decades, and are not direct measures of anything but the dates of capture on dead insects. However, if it is assumed that capture dates are a reflection of flight period, and that the probability of capture increases with actual abundance in the field, then these data illuminate the above parameters, often very well. We have exercised some discretion in plotting dubious extreme dates, most of which are based upon misleadingly labeled reared specimens. All extreme dates are presented in the discussion labeled FLIGHT PERIOD. Problems to be aware of when consulting the histograms include:

1. Flight period is generally over-estimated:
   a. Many species fly for only 2-3 weeks each year, but over a several year period generate histograms that indicate a 4-5 week flight period. This is the result of year-to-year differences in the timing of adult activity, which is dependent upon weather patterns. This problem is most noticeable in early spring species, where the year-to-year differences in the advent of warm weather have a major influence on the period of adult flight period;
   b. Although Ohio is a relatively small state, almost four degrees of latitude are covered from north to south. Because the histograms include data from throughout the State, there is some "smearing" of certain histograms due to the later adult emergence of most species in northern Ohio;
   c. Due to collectors' biases, the collection dates may overemphasize extreme dates (especially early dates when specimens are fresh) relative to the normal flight period.

2. The number of broods is often difficult to extract:
   a. The "smearing" effects of year to year and north to south differences in adult emergence often make it impossible to determine where one brood ends and the next begins. This is most pronounced in common wide-ranging species such as *Papilio glaucus* and *P. troilus*, for which an overabundance of data exists;
   b. Casual collectors often quit collecting for the season in late summer. Hence, late season broods are generally under-represented in the histograms.

3. Comparisons of relative abundance between species can be misleading:
   a. Some species are simply less often collected than others. Most collectors have favorite groups, and tend to collect those groups preferentially. Beginning collectors generally emphasize large showy species. The Hesperiidae are often ignored altogether. All collectors tend to ignore the more common species while rare species are collected at almost every opportunity. Thus, rare species are over-represented relative to common species (based on the actual numbers encountered in the field);
   b. Because the histograms are based upon collection records, and not the actual number of specimens collected, some species may seem rarer than they really are. Good examples are *Hermeuptychia sosybius* and *Satyrium edwardsii*, which are both intensely localized, but generally common when encountered. The number of preserved specimens of both these species is much larger than the number of records shown on the histograms.

4. The histograms cover only the months from March to November, which adequately covers the flight period of most of our species. However, some species have been recorded from the months of December, January, and February. This information can be found in the discusions labeled FLIGHT PERIOD.

With one exception, the histograms are based upon the data set collected up to December 1986 and are based on almost 16,000 records. We have included 1987 records for *Phoebis sennae* because the number of records collected during that summer quadrupled the number of records known for the State.

Under the heading, SIMILAR SPECIES, we have included brief descriptions which will separate potentially confusing species. These discussions emphasize reliable and easily seen differences, and are not meant to be exhaustive listings of species-level differences. The wing terminology used follows Figure 6.2. This section is omitted for those species which cannot be confused with any others within the State. Because we have figured every species recorded from Ohio, we have not included written descriptions of adults. Detailed descriptions of adults can be found in Klots (1951), Howe (1975), and Opler and Krizek (1984).

Resident species reside and breed every year in Ohio. **Stray species** are those that do not breed in Ohio, and only sporadically occur in the State. Strays generally do not reproduce in Ohio and do not survive the winters here. **Immigrants** are species that normally breed south of Ohio, but regularly or irregularly establish breeding populations in Ohio. These populations may occasionally survive mild winters, but are usually eliminated with the onset of cold weather, or in the case of *Danaus plexippus*, avoid winter conditions by migrating south in the autumn. **Naturalized residents** are those species which were not originally native to Ohio, but which now reside and breed every year.

Common denotes a species that is encountered in small to large numbers on almost every trip to the field while it is on the wing. **Uncommon** species are those that are not often encountered on the average collecting trip. These species are usually seen in small numbers when on the wing and are often restricted to specialized habitats. **Rare** species are those that are seldom encountered in the field. **Endangered** species are those that are known from five or fewer populations, and have very limited ranges in Ohio. These species occupy unique habitats, often ones that are vulnerable to disturbance or other factors which could render them unsuitable for the continued survival of the butterflies. **Threatened** species are those which have experienced a serious decline in range in Ohio. These species could become endangered if the factors precipitating the decline are not identified and alleviated. **Potentially threatened** species are those that occupy very limited ranges in Ohio, and for which specific threats are identifiable. **Extirpated** species are those which were once resident within the State, but for which there are no known viable populations.

All information in the discussions headed HABITAT, LARVAL HOSTPLANTS, and GENERAL COMMENTS is attributable to us unless otherwise noted. Most of the information in the ADULT ENERGY RESOURCES discussion is attributable to us, but we have included unattributed personal communications as well. These observations are based upon our collective field experience throughout the State. We have attempted to present the natural history of each species as it relates to Ohio, and the lists of hostplants are not comprehensive outside of the State. However, we have attempted to provide all relevant knowledge and citations that pertain to Ohio. We have purposely used precise language when referring to hostplants. For example, oviposition on a given hostplant does not imply that larvae successfully developed on that plant (unless it is so stated). Likewise, several species have been reared under artificial conditions on various plant species. We do not imply that these are the natural hostplants. We have included an index to reported Ohio hostplants on p. 166.

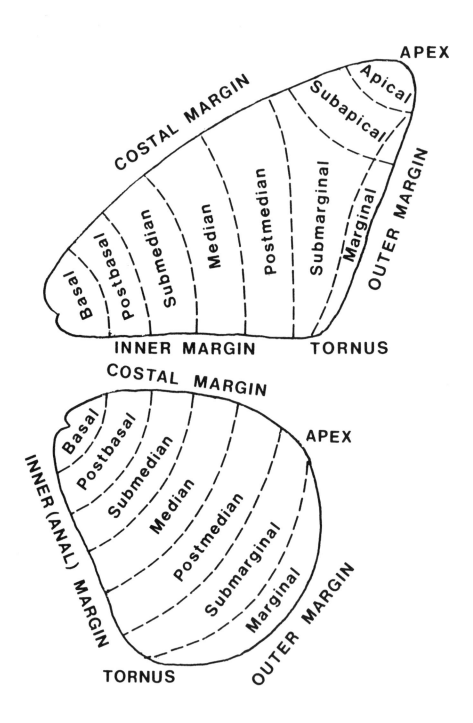

Fig. 6.2 Wing terminology.

7. CHECKLIST OF OHIO BUTTERFLIES AND SKIPPERS

With a few exceptions, the nomenclature used here conforms with Howe (1975) and Opler and Krizek (1984). For simplicity, the higher classification and the taxonomic order follow Miller and Brown (1981). Species' common names are in accordance with Opler and Krizek (1984). In theory, taxomomy should produce a stable nomenclature, but this has not been the trend for butterflies. Although it arrived too late for serious consideration, we include the "latest" nomenclatural amendments (Ferris, 1989) in brackets where they differ from our usage.

SUPERFAMILY Hesperioidea Latreille - Skippers

    FAMILY Hesperiidae Latreille - True Skippers

1. *Epargyreus clarus clarus* (Cramer, 1775). Silver-spotted Skipper
2. *Urbanus proteus proteus* (Linnaeus, 1758). Long-tailed Skipper
3. *Autochton cellus* (Boisduval & LeConte, 1837). Gold-banded Skipper
4. *Achalarus lyciades* (Geyer, 1832). Hoary Edge
5. *Thorybes bathyllus* (J.E. Smith, 1797). Southern Cloudy Wing
6. *Thorybes pylades* (Scudder, 1870). Northern Cloudy Wing
7. *Thorybes confusis* Bell, 1922. Confused Cloudy Wing
8. *Staphylus hayhurstii* (W.H. Edwards, 1870). Southern Sooty Wing
9. *Erynnis icelus* (Scudder & Burgess, 1870). Dreamy Dusky Wing
10. *Erynnis brizo brizo* (Boisduval & LeConte, 1834). Sleepy Dusky Wing
11. *Erynnis juvenalis juvenalis* (Fabricius, 1793). Juvenal's Dusky Wing
12. *Erynnis horatius* (Scudder & Burgess, 1870). Horace's Dusky Wing
13. *Erynnis martialis* (Scudder, 1869). Mottled Dusky Wing
14. *Erynnis lucilius* (Scudder & Burgess, 1870). Columbine Dusky Wing
15. *Erynnis baptisiae* (Forbes, 1936). Wild Indigo Dusky Wing
16. *Erynnis persius persius* (Scudder, 1863). Persius Dusky Wing
17. *Pyrgus centaureae wyandot* (W.H. Edwards, 1863). Grizzled Skipper
18. *Pyrgus communis* (Grote, 1872). Checkered Skipper
19. *Pholisora catullus* (Fabricius, 1793). Common Sooty Wing
20. *Nastra lherminier* (Latreille, 1824). Swarthy Skipper
21. *Ancyloxypha numitor* (Fabricius, 1793). Least Skipper
22. *Copaeodes minima* (W.H. Edwards, 1870). Southern Skipperling
23. *Thymelicus lineola* (Ochsenheimer, 1808). European Skipper
24. *Hylephila phyleus phyleus* (Drury, 1773). Fiery Skipper
25. *Hesperia leonardus leonardus* Harris, 1862. Leonard's Skipper
26. *Hesperia metea metea* Scudder, 1864. Cobweb Skipper
27. *Hesperia sassacus sassacus* Harris, 1862. Indian Skipper
28. *Polites coras* (Cramer, 1775). Peck's Skipper
29. *Polites themistocles* (Latreille, 1824). Tawny-edged Skipper
30. *Polites origenes origenes* (Fabricius, 1793). Cross Line Skipper
31. *Polites mystic mystic* (W.H. Edwards, 1863). Long Dash
32. *Wallengrenia egeremet* (Scudder, 1864). Northern Broken Dash
33. *Pompeius verna* (W.H. Edwards, 1862). Little Glassy Wing
34. *Atalopedes campestris huron* (W.H. Edwards, 1863). Sachem
35. *Atrytone logan logan* (W.H. Edwards, 1863). Delaware Skipper
36. *Poanes massasoit massasoit* (Scudder, 1864). Mulberry Wing
37. *Poanes hobomok hobomok* (Harris, 1862). Northern Golden Skipper
38. *Poanes zabulon* (Boisduval & LeConte, 1834). Southern Golden Skipper
39. *Poanes viator viator* (W.H. Edwards, 1865). Broad-winged Skipper
40. *Euphyes dion* (W.H. Edwards, 1879). Dion Skipper
41. *Euphyes dukesi* (Lindsey, 1923). Duke's Skipper
42. *Euphyes conspicua conspicua* (W.H. Edwards, 1863). [*Euphyes conspicuus*] Black Dash
43. *Euphyes bimacula bimacula* (Grote & Robinson, 1867). Two-spotted Skipper
44. *Euphyes vestris metacomet* (Harris, 1862). Dun Skipper
45. *Atrytonopsis hianna hianna* (Scudder, 1868). Dusted Skipper
46. *Amblyscirtes hegon* (Scudder, 1864). Pepper and Salt Skipper
47. *Amblyscirtes vialis* (W.H. Edwards, 1862). Roadside Skipper
48. *Amblyscirtes belli* H.A. Freeman, 1941. Bell's Roadside Skipper
49. *Lerodea eufala* (W.H. Edwards, 1869). Eufala Skipper
50. *Calpodes ethlius* (Stoll, 1782). Brazilian Skipper
51. *Panoquina ocola* (W.H. Edwards, 1863). Ocola Skipper

SUPERFAMILY Papilionoidea Latreille - True Butterflies

    FAMILY Papilionidae Latreille - Swallowtails

52. *Battus philenor philenor* (Linnaeus, 1771). Pipe Vine Swallowtail
53. *Eurytides marcellus marcellus* (Cramer, 1777). Zebra Swallowtail

54. *Papilio polyxenes asterius* Stoll, 1782. Black Swallowtail
55. *Papilio cresphontes* Cramer, 1777. [*Heraclides cresphontes*] Giant Swallowtail
56. *Papilio glaucus glaucus* Linnaeus, 1758. [*Pterourus glaucus*] Tiger Swallowtail
57. *Papilio troilus troilus* Linnaeus, 1758. [*Pterourus troilus*] Spicebush Swallowtail

FAMILY Pieridae Duponchel - Whites and Sulphurs

58. *Pontia protodice* (Boisduval & LeConte, 1829). Checkered White
59. *Pieris napi oleracea* Harris, 1829. Mustard White
60. *Pieris virginiensis* W.H. Edwards, 1870. West Virginia White
61. *Pieris rapae* (Linnaeus, 1758). European Cabbage White
62. *Euchloe olympia* (W.H. Edwards, 1871). Olympia Marble
63. *Anthocharis midea annickae* (dos Passos & Klots, 1969). [*Paramidea midea*] Falcate Orange-tip
64. *Colias philodice philodice* Godart, 1819. Clouded Sulphur/Common Sulphur
65. *Colias eurytheme* Boisduval, 1852. Alfalfa Butterfly/Orange Sulphur
66. *Colias cesonia cesonia* (Stoll, 1790). [*Zerene cesonia*] Dog Face
67. *Phoebis sennae eubule* (Linnaeus, 1767). Cloudless Sulphur
68. *Phoebis philea philea* (Johansson, 1763). Orange-barred Sulphur
69. *Eurema mexicana* (Boisduval, 1836). [*Eurema mexicanum*] Mexican Sulphur
70. *Eurema lisa lisa* (Boisduval & LeConte, 1829). Little Sulphur
71. *Eurema nicippe* (Cramer, 1779). Sleepy Orange
72. *Nathalis iole* Boisduval, 1836. Dainty Sulphur

FAMILY Lycaenidae Latreille - Gossamer Wings

73. *Feniseca tarquinius tarquinius* (Fabricius, 1793). Harvester
74. *Lycaena phlaeas americana* Harris, 1862. American Copper
75. *Lycaena hyllus* (Cramer, 1775). [*Hyllolycaena hyllus*] Bronze Copper
76. *Lycaena epixanthe epixanthe* (Boisduval & LeConte, 1833). [*Epidemia epixanthe*] Bog Copper
77. *Lycaena dorcas dorcas* (W. Kirby, 1837). [*Epidemia dorcas*] Dorcas Copper
78. *Lycaena helloides* (Boisduval, 1852). [*Epidemia helloides*] Purplish Copper
79. *Atlides halesus halesus* (Cramer, 1777). Great Purple Hairstreak
80a. *Harkenclenus titus titus* (Fabricius, 1793). Coral Hairstreak
    b. *H. titus mopsus* (Hübner, 1818).
81. *Satyrium acadica acadica* (W.H. Edwards, 1862). [*Satyrium acadicum*] Acadian Hairstreak
82. *Satyrium edwardsii* (Grote & Robinson, 1867). Edwards' Hairstreak
83. *Satyrium calanus falacer* (Godart, 1824). Banded Hairstreak
84. *Satyrium caryaevorum* (McDunnough, 1942). Hickory Hairstreak
85. *Satyrium liparops strigosum* (Harris, 1862). Striped Hairstreak
86. *Calycopis cecrops* (Fabricius, 1793). Red-banded Hairstreak
87. *Mitoura gryneus gryneus* (Hübner, 1819). [*Mitoura grynea*] Olive Hairstreak
88. *Incisalia augustus croesioides* Scudder, 1876. [*Incisalia augustinus*] Brown Elfin
89. *Incisalia irus irus* (Godart, 1824). Frosted Elfin
90. *Incisalia henrici henrici* (Grote & Robinson, 1867). Henry's Elfin
91. *Incisalia niphon niphon* (Hübner, 1823). Pine Elfin
92. *Fixsenia ontario ontario* (W.H. Edwards, 1868). Northern Hairstreak
93. *Parrhasius m-album m-album* (Boisduval & LeConte, 1833). White M Hairstreak
94. *Strymon melinus humuli* (Harris, 1841). Gray Hairstreak
95. *Erora laeta* (W.H. Edwards, 1862). Early Hairstreak
96. *Hemiargus isola alce* (W.H. Edwards, 1871). Reakirt's Blue
97. *Everes comyntas comyntas* (Godart, 1824). Eastern Tailed Blue
98. *Celastrina ladon ladon* (Cramer, 1780). [*Celastrina argiolus*] Spring Azure
99. *Celastrina neglecta-major* Tutt, 1908. Appalachian Blue
100. *Celastrina ebenina* Clench, 1972. Dusky Blue
101. *Glaucopsyche lygdamus lygdamus* (Doubleday, 1841). Silvery Blue
102. *Lycaeides melissa samuelis* Nabokov, 1944. Melissa Blue (Karner Blue)

FAMILY Riodinidae Grote - Metalmarks

103. *Calephelis borealis* (Grote & Robinson, 1866). Northern Metalmark
104. *Calephelis muticum* McAlpine, 1937. [*Calephelis mutica*] Swamp Metalmark

FAMILY Libytheidae Boisduval - Snouts

105. *Libytheana bachmanii bachmanii* (Kirtland, 1851). Eastern Snout Butterfly

FAMILY Heliconiidae Swainson - Heliconians

106. *Agraulis vanillae nigrior* Michener, 1942. Gulf Fritillary

FAMILY Nymphalidae Swainson - Brushfoots

107. *Euptoieta claudia* (Cramer, 1775). Variegated Fritillary
108. *Speyeria diana* (Cramer, 1775). Diana
109. *Speyeria cybele cybele* (Fabricius, 1775). Great Spangled Fritillary
110a. *Speyeria aphrodite aphrodite* (Fabricius, 1787). Aphrodite Fritillary
    b. *S. aphrodite alcestis* (W.H. Edwards, 1877).
111. *Speyeria idalia* (Drury, 1773). Regal Fritillary
112. *Speyeria atlantis atlantis* (W.H. Edwards, 1862). Mountain Silver-spot
113a. *Boloria selene myrina* (Cramer, 1777). [*Clossiana selene*] Silver-bordered Fritillary
    b. *B. selene nebraskensis* (Holland, 1928).
114. *Boloria bellona bellona* (Fabricius, 1775). [*Clossiana bellona*] Meadow Fritillary
115. *Chlosyne nycteis nycteis* (Doubleday & Hewitson, 1847). [*Charidryas nycteis*] Silvery Checkerspot
116a. *Chlosyne harrisii harrisii* (Scudder, 1864). [*Charidryas harrisii*] Harris' Checkerspot
    b. *C. harrisii liggetti* (Avinoff, 1930).
117. *Phyciodes tharos tharos* (Drury, 1773). Pearl Crescent
118. *Phyciodes pascoensis* Wright, 1905. Northern Pearl Crescent
119. *Euphydryas phaeton phaeton* (Drury, 1773). Baltimore
120. *Polygonia interrogationis* (Fabricius, 1798). Question Mark
121. *Polygonia comma* (Harris, 1842). Comma
122. *Polygonia progne progne* (Cramer, 1776). Gray Comma
123. *Nymphalis vau-album j-album* (Boisduval & LeConte, 1833). [*Nymphalis vaualbum*] Compton Tortoise Shell
124. *Nymphalis antiopa antiopa* (Linnaeus, 1758). Mourning Cloak
125. *Nymphalis milberti milberti* (Godart, 1819). [*Aglais milberti*] Milbert's Tortoise Shell
126. *Vanessa virginiensis* (Drury, 1773). American Painted Lady
127. *Vanessa cardui* (Linnaeus, 1758). Painted Lady
128. *Vanessa atalanta rubria* (Fruhstorfer, 1909). Red Admiral
129. *Junonia coenia* Hübner, 1822. Buckeye
130a. *Limenitis arthemis arthemis* (Dury, 1773). [*Basilarchia arthemis*] White Admiral
    b. *L. arthemis astyanax* (Fabricius, 1775). [*Basilarchia arthemis*] Red-spotted Purple
131. *Limenitis archippus archippus* (Cramer, 1776). [*Basilarchia archippus*] Viceroy

FAMILY Apaturidae Boisduval - Leaf Wing and Hackberry Butterflies

132. *Anaea andria* Scudder, 1875. Goatweed Butterfly
133. *Asterocampa celtis celtis* (Boisduval & LeConte, 1835). Hackberry Butterfly
134. *Asterocampa clyton clyton* (Boisduval & LeConte, 1835). Tawny Emperor

FAMILY Satyridae Boisduval - Satyrs and Wood Nymphs

135. *Enodia anthedon* A.H. Clark, 1936. Northern Pearly Eye
136. *Satyrodes eurydice eurydice* (Johansson, 1763). Northern Eyed Brown
137. *Satyrodes appalachia leeuwi* (Gatrelle & Arbogast, 1974). Appalachian Eyed Brown
138. *Cyllopsis gemma gemma* (Hübner, 1808). Gemmed Satyr
139. *Hermeuptychia sosybius* (Fabricius, 1793). Carolina Satyr
140. *Neonympha mitchellii mitchellii* French, 1889. Mitchell's Satyr
141. *Megisto cymela cymela* (Cramer, 1777). Little Wood Satyr
142a. *Cercyonis pegala alope* (Fabricius, 1793). Common Wood Nymph
    b. *C. pegala nephele* (W. Kirby, 1837).

FAMILY Danaidae Duponchel - Milkweed Butterflies

143. *Danaus plexippus plexippus* (Linnaeus, 1758). Monarch
144. *Danaus gilippus thersippus* (Bates, 1863) (= *strigosus* (Bates, 1864)). Queen

8. SPECIES ACCOUNTS

One hundred forty-four species of butterflies are known to occur in Ohio. Of these, 118 are residents, or likely residents. Five additional species have been extirpated. The remainder of the species are immigrants or strays.

More than 5,600 county records are presented, which equates to an average of 64 species from each of Ohio's 88 counties. The number of species known per county ranges from 35 for Allen County to 97 for Franklin County (Figure 8.1). In general, the counties with the highest totals have large cities or universities, and the number of species recorded from these counties is simply a reflection of the large sampling effort that these areas have received. The counties with the fewest reported species are generally highly agricultural and have simply been poorly collected. Nine species have been recorded from all of Ohio's 88 counties: *Papilio polyxenes, Pieris rapae, Colias philodice, Colias eurytheme, Everes comyntas, Celastrina ladon, Speyeria cybele, Phyciodes tharos,* and *Danaus plexippus.* Other species will undoubtedly be added to this list as collecting continues.

The number of resident species per county ranges from 33 for Allen County to 82 for Vinton and Lucas Counties (Figure 8.2) with approximately 57 breeding residents known

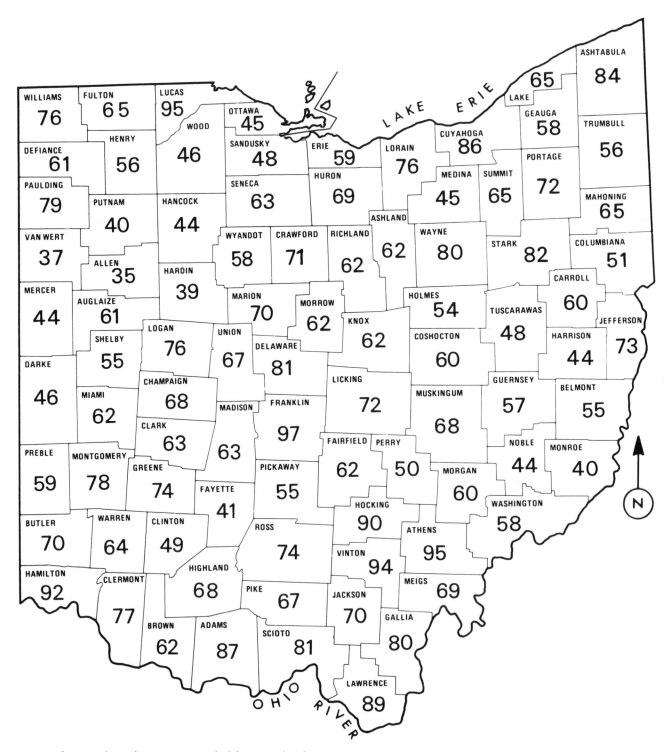

Fig. 8.1 The number of species recorded from each Ohio county.

26

per county. The true number of breeding residents should approach at least the high 60's for central and northern Ohio and the high 70's for the extreme southern counties.

Species richness, based on the number of breeding residents per county, is highest in the unglaciated counties of extreme southern Ohio and in the Oak Openings of Lucas County. This reflects the distributional trends of many species in Ohio. A large pool of species is primarily restricted to the unglaciated regions of the State, although several of these also occur in the Oak Openings. The wetland habitats of glaciated Ohio support another sizable community of restricted species. Thus, although the number of resident species per county is not that different between glaciated and unglaciated Ohio, there is often an abrupt shift in butterfly communities across the glacial maxima that involves approximately 30 species.

The nomenclature and common names used here generally follow those of Opler and Krizek (1984). Botanical nomenclature follows Weishaupt (1971).

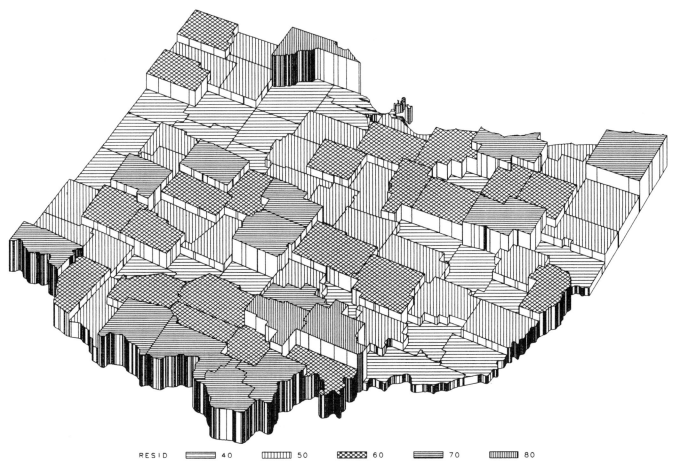

RESID ▭ 40　▥ 50　▨ 60　▭ 70　▥ 80

Fig. 8.2 Species richness based upon the number of resident species recorded from each county.

Family HESPERIIDAE-True Skippers

Eparygreus clarus clarus (Cramer, 1775). Silver-spotted Skipper. Plate 8.

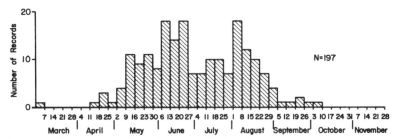

Fig. 8.4 *Eparygreus clarus*-Temporal distribution.

STATUS: Resident; common.

DISTRIBUTION/RANGE: Statewide (Figure 8.3).

HABITAT: This species is usually encountered along forest margins, areas containing young, brushy second growth, fence rows, powerline cuts through forest, and in virtually any other open area where the primary foodplants occur.

HOSTPLANT(S): In Ohio, this species has been found and reared on black locust (*Robinia pseudoacacia* L.), honey-locust (*Gleditsia triacanthos* L.), and hog-peanut *Amphicarpa bracteata* [L.] Fern.). Bales (1909) also reports wisteria (*Wisteria* sp.).

ADULT ENERGY RESOURCES: Red clover (*Trifolium pratense* L.), hop clover (*Trifolium agraium* L.), blue vervain (*Verbena hastata* L.), teasel (*Dipsacus sylvestris* Huds.), horseweed (*Conyza canadensis* [L.] Cronq.), alfalfa (*Medicago sativa* L.), multiflora rose (*Rosa multiflora* Thunb.), redbud (*Cercis canadensis* L.), tall ironweed (*Vernonia altissima* Nutt.), common milkweed (*Asclepias syriaca* L.), Canada thistle (*Cirsium arvense* [L.] Scop.), field thistle (*Cirsium discolor* [Muhl.] Spreng.), dame's rocket (*Hesperis matronalis* L.), black raspberry (*Rubus occidentalis* L.), tall bellflower (*Campanula americana* L.), self-heal (*Prunella vulgaris* L.), and many garden flowers. Adults also imbibe moisture from damp soil and mud.

FLIGHT PERIOD: Two to three broods, with peaks in May, June, and August (Figure 8.4). Extreme dates range from 4 March through 8 October.

SIMILAR SPECIES: *Achalarus lyciades* (Geyer) lacks the large silvery-white patch in the center of the ventral hindwing that characterizes *E. clarus*.

GENERAL COMMENTS: This is the largest and one of our most common resident skippers. Statewide in occurrence, this species is best sought in clover and alfalfa fields that border stands of the hostplant.

    Males perch on tree limbs and fly out to investigate almost any passing object. Because they often return to the same perch, they may be territorial. Females have a slow dipping flight when searching for oviposition sites in low underbrush. Both sexes often rest on the undersides of leaves. Because its flight is fast and powerful, it is almost impossible to observe on the wing. This species is best observed while it is visiting flowers or perching on leaves.

LITERATURE RECORDS: None.

Urbanus proteus proteus (Linnaeus, 1758). Long-tailed Skipper. Plate 8.

STATUS: Stray, rare. Only one Ohio specimen with complete data is known.

DISTRIBUTION/RANGE: *Urbanus proteus* is a resident of tropical and subtropical areas, and periodically migrates northward. Strays are also known from Kentucky (Covell, 1974) and Michigan (Moore, 1960). This species cannot survive freezing winters. In Ohio, it has only been collected in Franklin County (Figure 8.5).

HABITAT: In the southern United States, this species prefers brushy fields and woodland edges.

HOSTPLANT(S): Not known in Ohio. Where resident, *U. proteus* larvae feed on a variety of legumes, particularly beans (*Phaseolus* sp.) (Opler and Krizek, 1984). When present in large numbers, larvae can be a serious pest of cultivated beans (Klots, 1951). Strays may oviposit on these plants in Ohio.

ADULT ENERGY RESOURCES: None recorded for Ohio.

Fig. 8.5 *Urbanus proteus*.

FLIGHT PERIOD: The single Ohio record is dated 9 October 1945 and is deposited in The Ohio State Collection of Insects and Spiders. An additional specimen, also in The Ohio State Collection, was collected by William N. Tallant around the turn of the century and is labeled simply 'Columbus, Ohio.'

SIMILAR SPECIES: None.

GENERAL COMMENTS: This species probably occurs more frequently than our records indicate. It should be sought in late summer-early autumn. Jeffrey D. Hooper (pers comm, 1985) saw, but was unable to capture, a worn specimen of this species along a soybean field in Summit County. Because the larvae feed on this common crop, soybean fields may be a logical place to look for this stray.

The flight of this species is rapid. Adults readily visit nectar sources.

LITERATURE RECORDS: None.

Autochton cellus (Boisduval & LeConte, 1837). Gold-banded Skipper. Plate 8.

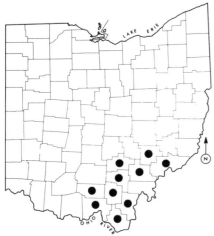

Fig. 8.6 *Autochton cellus*.

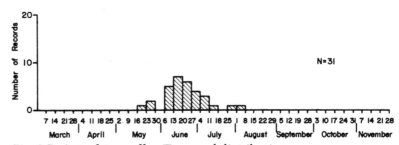

Fig. 8.7 *Autochton cellus*-Temporal distribution.

STATUS: Resident; uncommon to rare.

DISTRIBUTION/RANGE: The unglaciated counties of southeastern Ohio (Figure 8.6).

HABITAT: This skipper occurs in ridgetop clearings, wooded margins (especially oak forests), wooded ravines, and along roadsides which cut through bottomland forests.

HOSTPLANT(S): Not known in Ohio. The only reported foodplant is hog-peanut, *Amphicarpa bracteata* (L.) Fern., (Clark, 1936; Burns, 1984), a common plant in southern Ohio (Cusick and Silberhorn, 1977).

ADULT ENERGY RESOURCES: Red clover (*Trifolium pratense* L.), purple milkweed (*Asclepias purpurascens* L.), common milkweed (*Asclepias syriaca* L.), American ipecac (*Gillenia stipulata* [Muhl.] Trel.), New Jersey tea (*Ceanothus americanus* L.), wild bergamot (*Monarda fistulosa* L.), and fleabane (*Erigeron* sp.). Adults also imbibe moisture from damp soil and mud.

FLIGHT PERIOD: One brood, with an occasional second, flying from mid-May through early August (Figure 8.7). Extreme dates range from 19 May to 4 August.

SIMILAR SPECIES: None.

GENERAL COMMENTS: This species, generally considered rare throughout its range (Burns, 1984), is probably more continuously distributed through southern Ohio than our records indicate. Populations are very localized and adults are usually encountered singly or in low numbers. This skipper is possibly overlooked by casual collectors because of its general resemblance to *Epargyreus clarus*.

The flight of this species is the slowest of our large skippers but is usually highly erratic. Typically, both sexes fly low to the ground searching through vegetation. Males apparently patrol in search of potential mates and will chase after females and other similarly sized skippers. Adults bask on leaves with wings held outstretched.

Several individuals have been collected which have circular holes in their forewings. The cause of these deformities is unknown.

LITERATURE RECORDS: None.

A record from Lake County (Opler and Krizek, 1984) was unknowingly based on a specimen removed from a car radiator following a trip to Virginia (Leroy C. Koehn, pers comm, 1985). Because of this, we consider the record invalid.

Achalarus lyciades (Geyer, 1832). Hoary Edge. Plate 8.

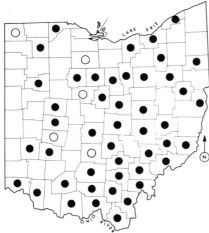

Fig. 8.8 *Achalarus lyciades.*

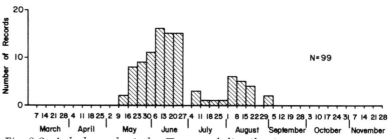

Fig. 8.9 *Achalarus lyciades*-Temporal distribution.

STATUS: Resident; uncommon. Although widely distributed, populations of this species tend to be localized.

DISTRIBUTION/RANGE: Statewide (Figure 8.8).

HABITAT: Typical habitats for this skipper include woodland borders, powerline cuts, along wooded roadsides, and open woodlands.

HOSTPLANT(S): Although no hostplant has been recorded for Ohio, this species is usually associated with tick-trefoil (*Desmodium* spp.). This is the primary foodplant throughout this butterfly's range (Opler and Krizek, 1984).

ADULT ENERGY RESOURCES: Red clover (*Trifolium pratense* L.), alfalfa (*Medicago sativa* L.), multiflora rose (*Rosa multiflora* Thunb.), blazing-star (*Liatris spicata* [L.] Willd.), common milkweed (*Asclepias syriaca* L.), Joe-Pye weed (*Eupatorium maculatum* L.), and vetch (*Vicia americana* Muhl.). Adults also visit damp soil and mud.

FLIGHT PERIOD: Two broods, the first peaking in late May through June, the second in early August (Figure 8.9). Extreme dates range from 11 May to 4 September.

SIMILAR SPECIES: See *Epargyreus clarus.*

GENERAL COMMENTS: This species resembles *Epargyreus clarus* enough that it may be overlooked by some collectors. However, the flight of this skipper is less powerful and usually closer to the ground than the flight of *E. clarus*. Males fly out to investigate similar sized skippers, possibly as part of their mate locating behavior.

This skipper is more common in southern Ohio than northern Ohio, although it is locally common in the Oak Openings, Lucas County. Price (1970) stated that *A. lyciades* was quite rare elsewhere in northwestern Ohio. Although this species is widely distributed in Ohio, the two areas where it is most common are disjunct (southern Ohio and the Oak Openings). This is a frequent distribution pattern in Ohio, which is better exemplified by species such as *Atrytonopsis hianna* and *Satyrium edwardsii.*

LITERATURE RECORDS: Seneca (Henninger, 1910), Williams, Clark, Pickaway (Albrecht, 1982), and Marion (Lepidopterists' Society, 1951) Counties.

Thorybes bathyllus (J.E. Smith, 1797). Southern Cloudy Wing. Plate 8.

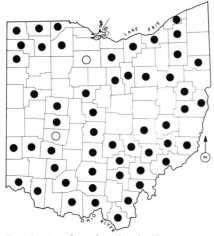

Fig. 8.10 *Thorybes bathyllus.*

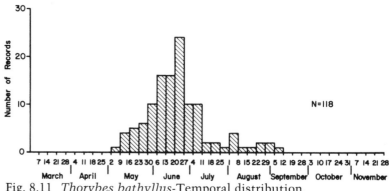

Fig. 8.11 *Thorybes bathyllus*-Temporal distribution.

STATUS: Resident; uncommon to common. This species is most common in southern Ohio, becoming much less frequent northward.

DISTRIBUTION/RANGE: Statewide (Figure 8.10).

HABITAT: This species occurs along forest margins (primarily oak forests), powerline cuts through woodlands, in dry upland fields, and in a variety of other open and brushy habitats.

HOSTPLANT (S): Not known in Ohio. Various legumes, including tick-trefoil (*Desmodium* spp.) and bush-clovers (*Lespedeza* spp.) are used in other parts of its range (Opler and Krizek, 1984). These plants are common in Ohio (Cusick and Silberhorn, 1977).

ADULT ENERGY RESOURCES: Red clover (*Trifolium pratense* L.), bull thistle (*Cirsium vulgare* [Savi] Tenore), common milkweed (*Asclepias syriaca* L.), and vetch (*Vicia americana* Muhl.).

FLIGHT PERIOD: Two broods, flying from May through early September. The first, which is more common, peaks in June (Figure 8.11). Extreme dates range from 4 May through 8 October (late). This skipper occurs slightly later in the season than *T. pylades*, which is single brooded.

SIMILAR SPECIES: *Thorybes pylades* and *T. confusis* are very similar. In *T. bathyllus* the hyaline forewing spots are usually broader and larger, and tend to be more aligned than in *T. pylades*. The palpi are light gray in *T. bathyllus* and are very dark in *T. pylades*. Males of *T. bathyllus* also lack the costal fold found on the forewings of *T. pylades*.
　　Thorybes bathyllus can be separated from *T. confusis* by the former's more pointed forewings, warmer brown ground color, and larger hyaline forewing spots. The hyaline forewing spots are greatly reduced in *T. confusis*.
　　Thorybes bathyllus flies later into the summer than does *T. pylades*, and most adults encountered in July and August will be *T. bathyllus*.

GENERAL COMMENTS: This species and the next are often confused with one another because they occupy the same habitats and have similar behavioral characteristics. Of the two species, *T. bathyllus* is the less common and is more southern in occurrence.
　　Thorybes bathyllus has a fast and erratic flight. Males like to perch on twigs and dried plant stalks. Males seem territorial and dart out to investigate other passing butterflies.

LITERATURE RECORDS: Seneca (Henninger, 1910) and Clark (Albrecht, 1982) Counties.

Thorybes pylades (Scudder, 1870). Northern Cloudy Wing. Plate 8.

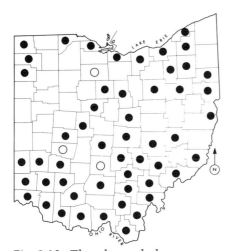

Fig. 8.12 *Thorybes pylades*.

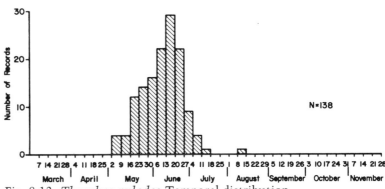

Fig. 8.13 *Thorybes pylades*-Temporal distribution.

STATUS: Resident; uncommon to common.

DISTRIBUTION/RANGE: Statewide (Figure 8.12).

HABITAT: This species occurs along forest margins (particularly oak forests), powerline cuts through wooded areas, in dry upland fields, along wooded roadsides, and in a variety of other open and brushy habitats.

HOSTPLANT(S): Not known in Ohio. In other areas it uses tick-trefoil (*Desmodium* sp.) and other legumes (Howe, 1975).

ADULT ENERGY RESOURCES: Red clover (*Trifolium pratense* L.), common milkweed (*Asclepias syriaca* L.), bull thistle (*Cirsium vulgare* [Savi] Tenore), and orange hawkweed (*Hieracium aurantiacum* L.). Adults also visit soil dampened with urine.

FLIGHT PERIOD: One brood flying primarily in late May and June (Figure 8.13). Extreme dates range from 2 May through 8 August (late).

SIMILAR SPECIES: See *Thorybes bathyllus*. *Thorybes pylades* is also similar to *T. confusis*, but can be distinguished from *T. confusis* by the former's non-aligned hyaline forewing spots. These hyaline spots tend to be more aligned in *T. confusis*. Male *T. pylades* have a costal fold on the forewing which is absent in *T. confusis*.

GENERAL COMMENTS: Of Ohio's two common *Thorybes* species, *T. pylades* is the more common and widespread. Both species occur in similar habitats and behave similarly.
　　The flight of *T. pylades* is fast and erratic. Males seem pugnacious because they fly out to investigate almost all passing objects from their perches of dead plant stalks and twigs. Males often rest with their wings held partially open.

LITERATURE RECORDS: Pickaway (Bales, 1909), Seneca (Henninger, 1910), and Clark (Albrecht, 1982) Counties.

Thorybes confusis Bell, 1922. Confused Cloudy Wing. Plate 8.

Fig. 8.14 *Thorybes confusis.*

STATUS: Uncertain, possibly a resident; rare. This species has only been collected once in Ohio.

DISTRIBUTION/RANGE: This species ranges from Florida north to Pennsylvania and westward to Texas and Kansas (Howe, 1975). The only Ohio record is from Adams County (Figure 8.14). Ohio represents a northern range limit for this species.

HABITAT: The single Ohio specimen was captured at Chapparal Prairie State Nature Preserve, a xeric prairie (David K. Parshall, pers comm, 1988). In Virginia *T. confusis* is found in open fields (Clark and Clark, 1951).

HOSTPLANT(S): Not known in Ohio. In other areas this species uses bush-clover (*Lespedeza* sp.) (Scott, 1986). Species of *Lespedeza* are widespread and common throughout southern Ohio (Cusick and Silberhorn, 1977).

ADULT ENERGY RESOURCES: None recorded for Ohio.

FLIGHT PERIOD: The single Ohio record is dated 29 May 1988. This species has two broods throughout most of its range, with the second brood being partial in many areas (Opler and Krizek, 1984). In Virginia, *T. confusis* flies from late May to late September (Clark and Clark, 1951).

SIMILAR SPECIES: See *Thorybes bathyllus* and *T. pylades.*

GENERAL COMMENTS: *Thorybes confusis* is a little-understood species that ranges widely in the south and will probably be found to occur over a greater geographic area as additional details of its ecology are revealed. This skipper, as its name implies, can easily be confused with other species of *Thorybes*, particularly *T. pylades*. This fact undoubtedly has caused it to be overlooked by collectors in many areas. Those hoping to find this skipper in Ohio should examine every *Thorybes* that they encounter, particularly those found in the more southern counties.

LITERATURE RECORDS: None.

Staphylus hayhurstii (W.H. Edwards, 1870). Southern Sooty Wing. Plate 9.

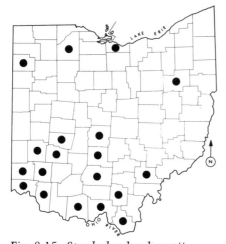

Fig. 8.15 *Staphylus hayhurstii.*

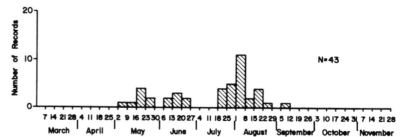

Fig. 8.16 *Staphylus hayhurstii*-Temporal distribution.

STATUS: Resident; rare to uncommon. This species is most often encountered in southern Ohio.

DISTRIBUTION/RANGE: Recorded primarily from the western and southern counties (Figure 8.15).

HABITAT: Forest margins, weedy gardens, sunlit stream banks, fallow pastures, disturbed areas, and moist woods. This skipper tends to favor shaded habitats.

HOSTPLANT(S): Although no hostplant has been reported for Ohio, *S. hayhurstii* is closely associated with common lamb's-quarters (*Chenopodium album* L.), a plant which is frequently encountered in highly disturbed situations. Native species of Amaranthaceae are probably used as well (Heitzman and Heitzman, 1987).

ADULT ENERGY RESOURCES: Purple loosestrife (*Lythrum salicaria* L.), yellow wood sorrel (*Oxalis europaea* Jord.), and white clover (*Trifolium repens* L.). This species also visits damp soil and mud.

FLIGHT PERIOD: Two broods, the first flying in mid-May and June, the second in late July and August (Figure 8.16). Extreme dates range from 6 May through 8 September.

SIMILAR SPECIES: *Pholisora catullus. Staphylus hayhurstii* has reduced forewing spotting and scalloped hindwing margins. The palpi are dark in *S. hayhurstii* and white in *P. catullus*. In flight these two species are almost indistinguishable .

GENERAL COMMENTS: This skipper is more common than our records indicate, and it appears to be increasing in numbers because it now feeds on the widespread naturalized weed, common lamb's-quarters. Colonies are very temporary, and are very succession sensitive. Typically, populations inhabit recently disturbed habitats such as fallow fields and other areas where bare soil has only recently been colonized by wild plants. As these areas undergo succession and are transformed into old field communities, *S. hayhurstii* populations decline to the point of localized extinction, even though the hostplant may still be relatively common.

Adults fly close to the ground and for only short distances. Unlike *P. catullus* which rests with its wings only partially open, adults often bask on low vegetation in sunlit clearings, wooded margins, and along wooded trails and roadsides with their wings outstretched. When disturbed, *S. hayhurstii* flies into shaded or wooded areas, whereas the similar *P. catullus* flies toward sunlit areas.

LITERATURE RECORDS: None.

Erynnis icelus (Scudder & Burgess, 1870). Dreamy Dusky Wing. Plate 9.

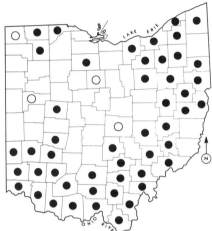

Fig. 8.17 *Erynnis icelus.*

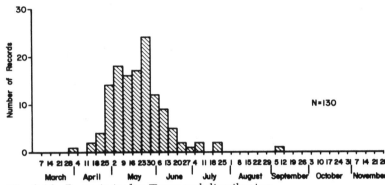

Fig. 8.18 *Erynnis icelus*-Temporal distribution.

STATUS: Resident; uncommon to common. This species is most common in southern Ohio, and becomes progressively less common northward, except in the Oak Openings of Lucas County where it is locally common.

DISTRIBUTION/RANGE: Statewide (Figure 8.17).

HABITAT: Associated with oak forests, this species is commonly found along wooded roadsides and trails, forest edge habitats, in woodland openings, and oak savannas.

HOSTPLANT(S): Not known in Ohio. Although Burns (1964) lists willows (*Salix* spp.) and poplars (*Populus* spp.) as the primary foodplants in the eastern United States, this species is usually associated with oaks in Ohio, which may serve as the hostplants.

ADULT ENERGY RESOURCES: Spring beauty (*Claytonia virginica* L.), winter cress (*Barbarea vulgaris* R. Br.), redbud (*Cercis canadensis* L.), wild strawberry (*Fragaria virginiana* Duchesne), multiflora rose (*Rosa multiflora* Thunb.), dandelion (*Taraxacum officinale* Weber), honeysuckle (*Lonicera* sp.), and birdsfoot violet (*Viola pedata* L.). This species also visits damp soil and mud.

FLIGHT PERIOD: One brood, peaking in May, with hints of an occasional partial second brood (Figure 8.18). The specimen from September is fresh, and probably represents a rare partial summer brood. Clark and Clark (1951) also report the possibility of a partial second brood in Virginia. Extreme dates range from 1 April through 5 September.

SIMILAR SPECIES: All *Erynnis* species, but particularly *E. brizo*. *Erynnis icelus* and *E. brizo* both lack subapical spots on the forewings, which allows these species to be easily separated from the remaining *Erynnis* species. *Erynnis icelus* is usually smaller than *E. brizo*, and *E. icelus* does not have as complete a postmedial, chain-like band across the forewing. The gray patch on the forewing is more prominent in *E. icelus*. The antennal club in *E. icelus* is pointed, whereas it is blunt in *E. brizo*. In addition, the palpi of *E. icelus* are longer than those of *E. brizo*.

GENERAL COMMENTS: An early spring species, *E. icelus* flies slightly after the peak flight of *E. brizo*. It is a more common and widespread species than *E. brizo*, although it does experience occasional population fluctuations and may seemingly disappear from an area for one or two years.

The flight of *E. icelus* is fast, erratic, and usually close to the ground. Adults often bask on sunlit leaves, exposed soil and gravel, with their wings held parallel to the ground. Males perch on twigs and plant stalks in a similar posture.

LITERATURE RECORDS: Auglaize (Williamson, 1905), Williams (Price, 1970), Crawford, and Licking (Albrecht, 1982) Counties.

Erynnis brizo brizo (**Boisduval & LeConte, 1834**). Sleepy Dusky Wing. Plate 9.

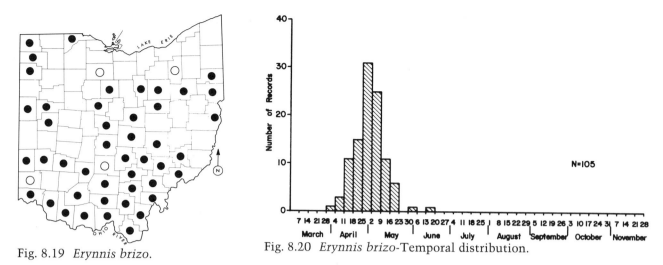

Fig. 8.19 *Erynnis brizo*.

Fig. 8.20 *Erynnis brizo*-Temporal distribution.

STATUS: Resident; uncommon to common. This species is very common in southern Ohio, but becomes rarer northward.

DISTRIBUTION/RANGE: Statewide (Figure 8.19).

HABITAT: Associated with oak forests, this species is commonly found along wooded roadsides and trails, forest margins (eg powerline cuts), and in woodland openings.

HOSTPLANT(S): In Ohio, this species has been observed ovipositing on young black oak leaves (*Quercus velutina* Lam.). Oaks are the principle reported hosts in the eastern United States (Burns, 1964).

ADULT ENERGY RESOURCES: Spring beauty (*Claytonia virginica* L.), redbud (*Cercis canadensis* L.), wood vetch (*Vicia caroliniana* Walt.), winter cress (*Barbarea vulgaris* R. Br.), ragwort (*Senecio* sp.), Greek valarian (*Polemonium reptans* L.), Russian olive (*Elaeagnus angustifolia* L.), pussy-toes (*Antennaria* sp.), dandelion (*Taraxacum officinale* Weber), buttercup (*Ranunculus hispidus* Michx.), birdsfoot violet (*Viola pedata* L.), and common blue phlox (*Phlox divaricata* L.). Bales (1909) reports *Phlox carolina* L. Adults also frequently feed at damp soil and animal dung, where they often congregate in large numbers.

FLIGHT PERIOD: One brood, flying from mid-April through mid-June (Figure 8.20). Extreme dates range from 1 April through 15 June.

SIMILAR SPECIES: See *E. icelus*.

GENERAL COMMENTS: This is one of the earliest spring species, and it usually flies before *E. icelus*. It tends to be less common than *E. icelus*, especially outside of southeastern Ohio. *Erynnis brizo* also experiences population fluctuations over several year periods.

In flight, *E. brizo* is fast and erratic, more so than *E. icelus*. Adults often bask on sunlit leaves, exposed soil and on gravel roads, with their wings outstretched. Males perch on dried plant stalks and twigs in a similar posture. At night, adults rest with their wings wrapped around twigs or grass stalks.

LITERATURE RECORDS: Pickaway (Bales, 1909), Summit (Claypole, 1897; Hine, 1898a), Seneca (Henninger, 1910), and Butler (Albrecht, 1982) Counties.

Erynnis juvenalis juvenalis (Fabricius, 1793). Juvenal's Dusky Wing. Plate 9.

Fig. 8.21 *Erynnis juvenalis.*

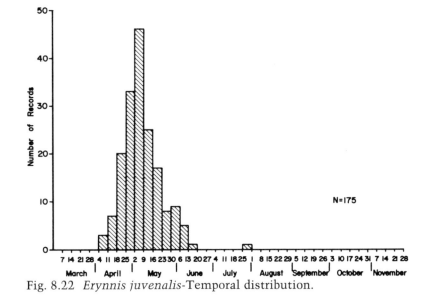

N=175

Fig. 8.22 *Erynnis juvenalis*-Temporal distribution.

STATUS: Resident; common.

DISTRIBUTION/RANGE: Statewide (Figure 8.21).

HABITAT: Associated with oak forests, this species is commonly found along wooded trails and roadsides, forest margins, and in woodland openings.

HOSTPLANT(S): In Ohio, this species has been observed ovipositing on leaves of young white oak (*Quercus alba* L.). A variety of oaks are used throughout this skipper's range (Opler and Krizek, 1984).

ADULT ENERGY RESOURCES: Redbud (*Cercis canadensis* L.), multiflora rose (*Rosa multiflora* Thunb.), Russian olive (*Elaeagnus angustifolia* L.), dandelion (*Taraxacum officinale* Weber), spring beauty (*Claytonia virginica* L.), garlic-mustard (*Alliaria officinalis* Andrz.) buttercup (*Ranunculus hispidus* Michx.), ragwort (*Senecio* sp.), fleabane (*Erigeron* sp.), violets (*Viola* sp.), cut-leaved toothwort (*Dentaria laciniata* Muhl.), narrow-leaved toothwort (*Dentaria multifida* Nutt.), and wood vetch (*Vicia caroliniana* Walt.). Hoying (1975) listed common cleavers (*Galium aparine* L.). Adults also utilize damp soil, mud, and animal dung, upon which they may congregate in large numbers.

FLIGHT PERIOD: One brood, flying in April and May (Figure 8.22). Extreme dates range from 4 April through 30 July (late).

SIMILAR SPECIES: All *Erynnis* species, but particularly *E. horatius*. *Erynnis juvenalis* can be separated from the majority of the other *Erynnis* species by its large size (17 mm-22 mm wing span) and the presence of two apical pale spots on the ventral hindwing. These spots are the easiest character with which to determine most specimens of *E. juvenalis*, but they are occasionally reduced or very rarely absent. When these spots are absent, *E. juvenalis* can usually be separated from *E. horatius* by the darker ground color present in *E. horatius*.

Because *E. juvenalis* is single-brooded, specimens collected in the summer are referable to *E. horatius*, which is double-brooded.

GENERAL COMMENTS: This is the most common of the early spring skippers. Its flight period overlaps those of the rarer *Erynnis* species, often making it difficult to pick out the rarer species from among the hoards of *E. juvenalis*.

The flight is usually fast and tends to be more direct and higher off the ground then other *Erynnis* species. Males repeatedly patrol fairly large areas. Adults bask on sunlit dead leaves, exposed soil and on gravel roads, with the wings held outstretched. Males perch on twigs several feet off the ground in a similar posture.

LITERATURE RECORD: Seneca County (Henninger, 1910).

Erynnis horatius (Scudder & Burgess, 1870). Horace's Dusky Wing. Plate 9.

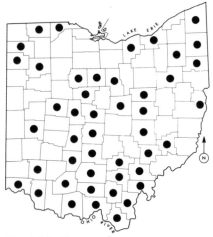

Fig. 8.23 _Erynnis horatius_.

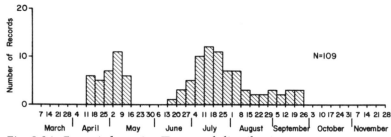

Fig. 8.24 _Erynnis horatius_-Temporal distribution.

STATUS: Resident; uncommon. This species is most frequently encountered in southern Ohio and in the Oak Openings of Lucas County.

DISTRIBUTION/RANGE: Statewide (Figure 8.23).

HABITAT: Associated with oak forests, this species is usually found along wooded trails and roadsides, forest margins, powerline cuts, and in woodland openings.

HOSTPLANT(S): In Ohio, this species is closely associated with oaks (_Quercus_ spp.) and has been observed ovipositing on young burr-oak (_Quercus macrocarpon_ Michx.) (David K. Parshall, pers comm, 1987). Burns (1964) lists a variety of oaks as known hostplants.

ADULT ENERGY RESOURCES: Redbud (_Cercis canadensis_ L.), common milkweed (_Asclepias syriaca_ L.), American ipecac (_Gillenia stipulata_ [Muhl.] Trel.), ironweed (_Vernonia_ sp.), rough blazing-star (_Liatris aspera_ Michx.), blazing-star (_Liatris spicata_ [L.] Willd.), red clover (_Trifolium pratense_ L.), fleabane (_Erigeron_ sp.), and purple vetch (_Vicia americana_ Muhl.). Adults also imbibe moisture from damp soil and mud.

FLIGHT PERIOD: Two broods, the first in late April-early May, the second from late June through September (Figure 8.24). Extreme dates range from 14 April through 23 September.

SIMILAR SPECIES: All _Erynnis_ species, but particularly _E. juvenalis_ and _E. baptisiae_. _Erynnis horatius_ usually does not have the two light apical spots on the ventral hindwing that characterize almost all specimens of _E. juvenalis_. Also, because _Erynnis juvenalis_ has only a spring brood, 'juvenalis'-like individuals from mid-summer and later are almost certainly variants of _E. horatius_.
　　Erynnis horatius is larger, and has larger apical spots on the forewing than does _E. baptisiae_. _Erynnis baptisiae_ is usually darker (almost black with a purplish sheen) and has a more mottled ventral hindwing than _E. horatius_.

GENERAL COMMENTS: Unlike _E. juvenalis_, this species is double-brooded. _Erynnis horatius_ is probably more widespread than our records indicate, and is overlooked in many areas.
　　The flight of this species is fast and often erratic. Adults bask in the sun on dried leaves and exposed soil with the wings held outstretched. Males perch on twigs in a similar posture.

LITERATURE RECORDS: None.

Erynnis martialis (Scudder, 1869). Mottled Dusky Wing. Plate 9.

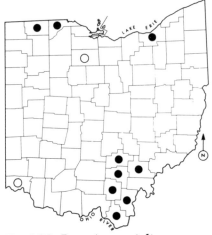

Fig. 8.25 _Erynnis martialis_.

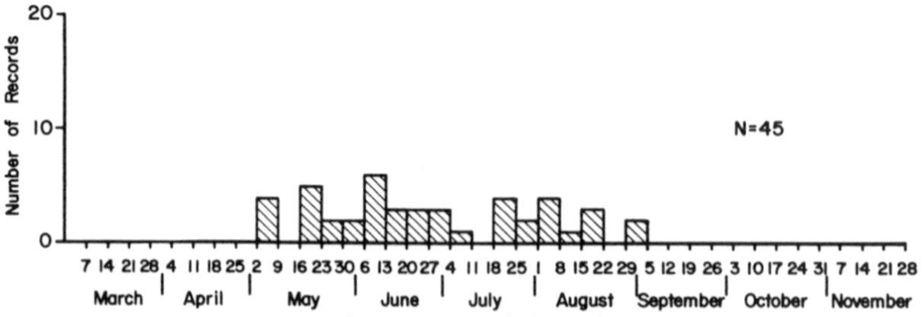

Fig. 8.26 _Erynnis martialis_-Temporal distribution.

STATUS: Resident; rare. Populations are usually localized. Price (1970) considered this species to be common in the Oak Openings (Lucas County), but absent elsewhere in northwestern Ohio. We have been unable to locate this species in the Oak Openings, which may indicate a decline in abundance since Price collected in the area.

DISTRIBUTION/RANGE: Currently known from only extreme northern Ohio (Fulton, Lucas, and Cuyahoga Counties) and from several counties in southern Ohio where it may be limited to the hill country (Figure 8.25).

HABITAT: This skipper occurs along wooded margins, ridgetop clearings, and in prairie openings where New Jersey tea, *Ceanothus americanus* L., occurs.

HOSTPLANT(S): In Ohio, larvae have been found and reared on New Jersey tea (*Ceanothus americanus* L.). This is the primary hostplant in eastern North America (Opler and Krizek, 1984).

ADULT ENERGY RESOURCES: Blazing-star (*Liatris* sp.). Adults also imbibe moisture from damp soil and gravel.

FLIGHT PERIOD: Two broods, the first flying in May and June, the second in late July and August (Figure 8.26). Extreme dates range from 4 May through 4 September.

SIMILAR SPECIES: None, although superficially, all *Erynnis* could be confused with this species. The highly mottled wings and small size (wing span 15 mm-16 mm) are distinctive. Female *E. juvenalis* and *E. horatius* often have the same highly mottled appearance, but are much larger. *E. juvenalis* almost always has two pale apical spots on the ventral hindwing which are absent in *E. martialis*.

GENERAL COMMENTS: Although this species is relatively rare in Ohio, it can be locally common when a population is found. It is puzzling why the distribution of *E. martialis* is so limited when the hostplant ranges widely and commonly throughout the State. It is probably overlooked in many areas.

Adults fly close to the ground and often perch on small twigs and small stones. They often bask in sunlight with the wings outstretched.

There are two seasonal phenotypes. Spring brood individuals are smaller and paler than summer brood individuals.

LITERATURE RECORDS: Seneca (Henninger, 1910; Porter, 1965) and Hamilton (Wyss, 1930b, 1932) Counties.

Erynnis lucilius (Scudder & Burgess, 1870). Columbine Dusky Wing. Plate 9.

Fig. 8.27 *Erynnis lucilius*.

STATUS: Possible resident; rare. There are only two probable records of this species from Ohio.

DISTRIBUTION/RANGE: Both known specimens were collected in the Oak Openings of Lucas County (Figure 8.27).

HABITAT: Unknown, although the habitat is presumably one of the several communities unique to the Oak Openings in Ohio.

HOSTPLANT(S): Although no host has been reported from Ohio, the only known hostplant is wild columbine, *Aquilegia canadensis* L. (Burns, 1964).

ADULT ENERGY RESOURCES: None recorded for Ohio.

FLIGHT PERIOD: Two broods, the first flying in late April and May, the second in July. The two probable specimens from Ohio are dated 27 April and 20 July.

SIMILAR SPECIES: Although all *Erynnis* species are similar, *E. persius* and *E. baptisiae* are most easily confused with this species. *Erynnis lucilius* lacks the white hair-like scales that cover the dorsal forewings of *E. persius*. *Erynnis lucilius* tends to be smaller (wing span=14-16 mm) than *E. baptisiae* (wing span=15-18 mm), but otherwise these two species are almost impossible to separate. Although not reliable throughout their ranges, the subapical white spots of *E. persius* tend to be close together and aligned, whereas in *E. lucilius*, and especially *E. baptisiae*, these spots tend to zigzag. The subapical spots of *E. baptisiae* tend to be more separated than those of *E. lucilius* and *E. persius*. These characters seem fairly reliable in the Oak Openings where all three of these species have been recorded. The surest method of identification is to collect *E. lucilius* in association with its foodplant, wild columbine.

This species is very difficult to separate from smaller specimens of *E. baptisiae*. The specimens from Ohio have been "tentatively" determined as *E. lucilius* by John M. Burns.

GENERAL COMMENTS: Very little is known about this skipper in Ohio (Shuey, Calhoun, and Iftner, 1987). The two records are several years apart, which may indicate that it is a very rare resident in the Oak Openings. It may be overlooked because of its very similar appearance to the other *Erynnis* species. Collectors should look for this species around stands of columbine.

LITERATURE RECORDS: None.

Albrecht (1982) recorded this species from Cuyahoga County, but his record was based on a misdetermined specimen of *E. baptisiae*.

Erynnis baptisiae **(Forbes, 1936).** Wild Indigo Dusky Wing. Plate 9.

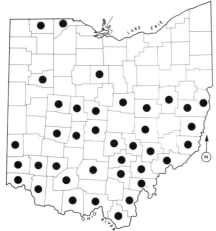

Fig. 8.28 *Erynnis baptisiae.*

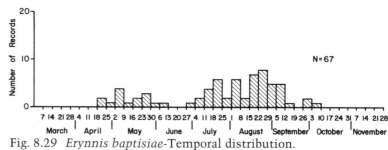

Fig. 8.29 *Erynnis baptisiae*-Temporal distribution.

STATUS: Resident; uncommon to common.

DISTRIBUTION/RANGE: Statewide (Figure 8.28).

HABITAT: This species is most often encountered in prairie openings where wild indigo occurs, and along roadsides where crown vetch has been planted. It is has also been collected in woodland openings and hayfields.

HOSTPLANT(S): In eastern and central Ohio, this species has been observed ovipositing on crown vetch (*Coronilla varia* L.), an alien species planted extensively along roads to stabilize soil. In the Oak Openings this species is associated with wild indigo, *Baptisia tinctoria* (L.) R.Br. (Price, 1970). In the 1930's, John S. Thomas (pers comm, 1985) found that populations near Columbus were associated with white indigo (*Baptisia leucantha* T.&G.). Today, most populations seem to be associated with crown vetch. *Erynnis baptisiae* has been reared on columbine (*Aquilegia*) from eggs laid on *Baptisia* (John S. Thomas, pers comm, 1985), but columbine is not a likely natural host in Ohio.

ADULT ENERGY RESOURCES: Red clover (*Trifolium pratense* L.), white clover (*Trifolium repens* L.), alsike clover (*Trifolium hybridum* L.), yellow sweet clover (*Melilotus officinalis* [L.] Lam.), white sweet clover (*Melilotus alba* Desr.), crown vetch (*Coronilla varia* L.), tickseed-sunflower (*Bidens aristosa* [Michx.] Britt.), ironweed (*Vernonia* sp.), birdsfoot trefoil (*Lotus corniculatus* L.), wild carrot (*Daucus carota* L.), blue vervain (*Verbena hastata* L.), heal-all (*Prunella vulgaris* L.), peppermint (*Mentha piperita* L.), horse-nettle (*Solanum carolinense* L.), teasel (*Dipsacus sylvestris* Huds.), black-eyed susan (*Rudbeckia hirta* L.), chicory (*Cichorium intybus* L.), horseweed (*Conyza canadensis* [L.] Cronq.), dandelion (*Taraxacum officinale* Weber), winter cress (*Barbarea vulgaris* R. Br.), garlic mustard (*Alliaria officinalis* Andrz.), Joe-Pye weed (*Eupatorium maculatum* L.), Canada thistle (*Cirsium arvense* [L.] Scop.), blazing-star (*Liatris* sp.), and *Aster* species.

FLIGHT PERIOD: At least three broods in most years, the first flying primarily in May, the second in July, and the third in late August (Figure 8.29). The late September-October records may represent a fourth brood. Extreme dates range from 19 April through 7 October.

SIMILAR SPECIES: All *Erynnis* species, but especially *E. persius* and *E. lucilius*. See the discussion under *E. lucilius* for characters which help separate these species. Spring brood individuals are sometimes small enough to be confused with *E. icelus* in the field.

GENERAL COMMENTS: This species was not as common in the past as it is today, and outside of the Oak Openings, most of our records are from the last few years. Prior to the widespread planting of crown vetch along roadsides to prevent erosion, *E. baptisiae* was local and uncommon. Although this skipper probably still uses *Baptisia* in certain prairie areas, it now appears to be using crown vetch as the primary foodplant throughout most of Ohio. It is becoming one of our most common skippers. Shapiro (1979) noted a similar situation in Pennsylvania.

   The flight of this species is rapid and close to the ground. Adults usually confine their activities to the near vicinity of the hostplants, but may wander to adjacent areas in search of nectar sources. Males patrol open areas, presumably in search of mates.

LITERATURE RECORDS: None.

***Erynnis persius persius* (Scudder, 1863).** Persius Dusky Wing. Plate 10.

Fig. 8.30 *Erynnis persius.*

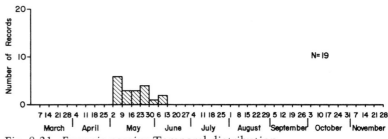

Fig. 8.31 *Erynnis persius*-Temporal distribution.

STATUS: Resident; rare (endangered). Populations of this species are extremely localized. Currently there are only two known populations in Ohio (Shuey, Calhoun, and Iftner, 1987).

DISTRIBUTION/RANGE: This species has never been reliably reported outside of the Oak Openings of Lucas County (Figure 8.30).

HABITAT: This species is limited to oak savannas and dune communities where lupine (*Lupinus perennis* L.) is common.

HOSTPLANT(S): In Ohio, this species has been observed ovipositing on lupine (*Lupinus perennis* L.). Various *Baptisia* species serve as alternate hosts in other eastern areas (Dale F. Schwietzer, pers comm, 1985).

ADULT ENERGY RESOURCES: Lupine (*Lupinus perennis* L.).

FLIGHT PERIOD: One brood, flying in May and early June (Figure 8.31). Extreme dates range from 5 May through 10 June.

SIMILAR SPECIES: All *Erynnis* species, but especially *E. lucilius* and *E. baptisiae*. *Erynnis persius* is easily recognized by the abundant white hair-like scales that cover the dorsal forewings. This species flies only in the spring, hence individuals from early summer and later are referable to other species. Although an unreliable character throughout much of their ranges, the forewing apical spots are aligned on most Ohio specimens of *E. persius* but tend to zigzag in *E. baptisiae* and *E. lucilius*. (See *E. lucilius* account, p. 37).

GENERAL COMMENTS: This skipper is one of the characteristic butterflies of the Oak Openings. Recently, it has experienced a decline in numbers, probably the result of uncontrolled succession in the Oak Openings. Originally, fire was a major force in maintaining the open habitats that this species requires. The recent advent of fire suppression has resulted in shrub encroachment into the oak savannas and dune communities. Although lupine often survives in the shade of these shrubs, *E. persius* apparently will not oviposit on shaded plants. If controlled burning or shrub removal is not implemented in the few remaining areas where this skipper survives, this species may become extirpated from Ohio.

This species is usually seen flying around and landing on lupine. When frightened this species flies rapidly and erratically into the underbrush. Adults rest on low vegetation with their wings held outstretched.

LITERATURE RECORDS: None.

Although reported from Pickaway (Bales, 1909), Seneca (Henninger, 1910), and Summit (Hine, 1898a) Counties, these records probably refer to other *Erynnis* species such as *E. baptisiae*, a more common and closely related species that was not yet described at the time these papers were published. During the period of these reports, identification of skippers was very difficult and most published records from this period must be viewed with suspicion. A specimen mentioned by Price (1970) was determined by John M. Burns as probably *E. lucilius*.

Pyrgus centaureae wyandot (W.H. Edwards, 1863). Grizzled Skipper. Plate 10.

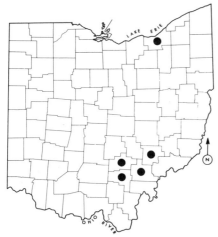

Fig. 8.32 *Pyrgus centaureae.*

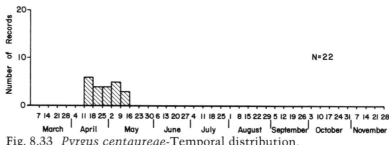

Fig. 8.33 *Pyrgus centaureae*-Temporal distribution.

STATUS: Resident; rare. Populations of this species are very localized and usually occur at low densities.

DISTRIBUTION/RANGE: Most of our records are from a limited region of unglaciated Ohio (Figure 8.32). There is also one record from Cuyahoga County.

HABITAT: In southern Ohio, this species is associated with openings in mature oak forests (eg open hillsides, disturbed ridgetops, powerline cuts, and roadsides) that support stands of dwarf cinquefoil (*Potentilla canadensis* L.). Most of these areas are highly disturbed, and are characterized by fair amounts of exposed soil and rock. We know nothing about the northern Ohio locality.

HOSTPLANT(S): Although no hostplant has been reported from Ohio, *P. centaureae wyandot* appears to be associated with dwarf cinquefoil, *Potentilla canadensis* L., the reported host in Virginia (Scott, 1986) and the associated host in West Virginia (Thomas J. Allen, pers comm, 1986). In Michigan, the hostplant is wild strawberry, *Fragaria virginiana* Dene. (Nielsen, 1985).

ADULT ENERGY RESOURCES: Dwarf cinquefoil (*Potentilla canadensis* L.), coltsfoot (*Tussilago farfara* L.), wood vetch (*Vicia caroliniana* Walt.), and spring beauty (*Claytonia virginica* L.).

FLIGHT PERIOD: One brood, flying in late April and early May (Figure 8.33). Extreme dates range from 16 April through 10 May.

SIMILAR SPECIES: *Pyrgus communis.* In Ohio, the flight periods of the two *Pyrgus* do not normally overlap. *Pyrgus c. wyandot* flies in early spring, but *P. communis* is rarely seen before mid-summer. If morphological characters are needed, the light spots on *P. c. wyandot* forewings are more square; these light spots are more rectangular in *P. communis. Pyrgus c. wyandot* also tends to be much darker and smaller.

GENERAL COMMENTS: This species is probably more widespread than our records indicate. The early flight period and the very local nature of the small populations probably account for this species' rarity in collections. Because this species is currently known from just a few localized populations, all of which occupy small clearings within oak forests, it could be very susceptible to gypsy moth control measures if they are implemented (Shuey, Calhoun, and Iftner, 1987).

   The flight of this species is fast, erratic, and close to the ground, which makes it quite difficult to follow visually in the field. The checkered pattern tends to blend in with the habitat background, allowing the skipper to seemingly disappear while on the wing. Males appear to patrol most of the day, occasionally stopping to perch and visit flowers. Adults rest on exposed soil and dead leaves.

LITERATURE RECORDS: None.

Pyrgus communis (Grote, 1872). Checkered Skipper. Plate 10.

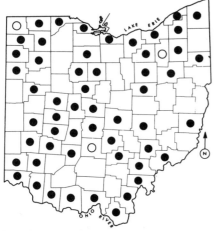

Fig. 8.34 *Pyrgus communis.*

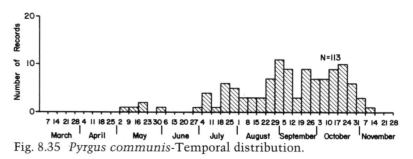

Fig. 8.35 *Pyrgus communis*-Temporal distribution.

STATUS: Regular immigrant; uncommon to rare. This species is occasionally locally common, especially in southern Ohio.

DISTRIBUTION/RANGE: This species is a resident of the southern U.S. (Tropical to Lower Austral Life Zones) which immigrates into Ohio yearly. Our records are scattered statewide (Figure 8.34).

HABITAT: Virtually any open area (eg yards, vacant lots, waste areas, roadsides, and farmyards) with low, weedy vegetation. These areas usually contain numerous nectar sources.

HOST PLANT(S): Although no host has been reported from Ohio, this skipper is closely associated with several species of mallows (Malvaceae) (Price, 1970). In southern Ohio, this species is usually associated with common mallow (*Malva neglecta* Wallr.). Mallows are the primary hosts for this skipper (Opler and Krizek, 1984).

ADULT ENERGY RESOURCES: Alfalfa (*Medicago sativa* L.), red clover (*Trifolium pratense* L.), and white *Aster* species. Adults also imbibe moisture from damp soil and mud.

FLIGHT PERIOD: Although our histogram shows no discrete broods (Figure 8.35), this species is capable of producing one or more generations in Ohio. Extreme dates range from 3 May through 13 November.

SIMILAR SPECIES: See *Pyrgus centaureae wyandot*.

GENERAL COMMENTS: Although this skipper is primarily a resident of the southern U.S., it does wander into Ohio yearly, where it establishes temporary populations. From the literature, it appears that this species was more regularly collected in the past. Hine (1898a), Bales (1909), Henninger (1910), Price (1970), and Hoying (1975) all considered this species to be common. Today, with the exception of the Ohio River Valley, this skipper is seldom seen. There are relatively few collection records between 1965 and 1988. The cause of this reduction is unknown, but the use of herbicides to control weeds in urban and agricultural areas may have reduced populations of this skipper's weedy hostplants. In 1988, this skipper was unusually widespread in Ohio, and several temporary populations were discovered.

Under typical conditions, *P. communis* does not appear to survive Ohio's winters; hence most Ohio records are the result of yearly immigrations. Because populations are not stable from year to year, one seldom finds this species in the same locality in successive years.

Males patrol most of the day for females, and often seem pugnacious, darting after other passing insects. The flight is very fast and erratic. Males seem to disperse away from hostplant-containing areas in early afternoon to imbibe nectar and are most often seen in alfalfa fields, red clover fields, and in closely grazed pastures with an abundance of low-growing asters.

LITERATURE RECORDS: Williams (Price, 1970), Pickaway (Bales, 1909), and Summit (Claypole, 1897) Counties.

Pholisora catullus (Fabricius, 1793). Common Sooty Wing. Plate 10.

Fig. 8.36 *Pholisora catullus*.

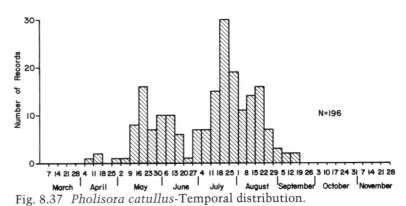

Fig. 8.37 *Pholisora catullus*-Temporal distribution.

STATUS: Resident; common.

DISTRIBUTION/RANGE: Statewide (Figure 8.36).

HABITAT: This species is associated with pastures, farmyards, waste areas, and almost any other open area where the hostplant occurs.

HOSTPLANT(S): In Ohio this species has been found and reared on amaranth (*Amaranthus* sp.) (Leland L. Martin, pers comm, 1988) and common lamb's-quarters, (*Chenopodium album* L.), a naturalized weed of disturbed areas. This skipper appears to be much more efficient at locating and using stands of the foodplant than does the very similar (ecologically and morphologically) *Staphylus hayhurstii*.

ADULT ENERGY RESOURCES: White clover (*Trifolium repens* L.), red clover (*T. pratense* L.), alfalfa (*Medicago sativa* L.), fleabane (*Erigeron* sp.), dogbane (*Apocynum* sp.), crown vetch (*Coronilla varia* L.), stiff-haired sunflower (*Helianthus hirsutus* Raf.), birdsfoot trefoil (*Lotus corniculatus* L.), chicory (*Cichorium intybus* L.), Canada thistle (*Cirsium arvense* [L.] Scop.), and common dandelion (*Taraxacum officinale* Weber). Adults also utilize damp soil and mud.

FLIGHT PERIOD: At least two broods, the first flying in May and June, the second in July through early September (Figure 8.37). There may be a partial third brood in some years. Extreme dates range from 8 April through 16 September.

SIMILAR SPECIES: *Staphylus hayhurstii* and possibly *Amblyscirtes vialis. Pholisora catullus* has rounded hind wings and white palpi whereas *S. hayhurstii* has scalloped hindwings and dark palpi. The black ground color of *P. catullus* will differentiate it from *A. vialis.* In addition, *A. vialis* has gray palpi.

The number and size of the spots on the dorsal forewing in *P. catullus* are highly variable.

GENERAL COMMENTS: This is one of our most abundant and widespread skippers. Unlike the very similar *S. hayhurstii,* which prefers more shaded areas, *P. catullus* flies in the sun.

The flight of this skipper is fast, erratic, and usually close to the ground. When disturbed it continues to fly in open areas. When resting, the wings are held partially open, whereas in *S. hayhurstii,* they are held outstretched. Males often chase other similar butterflies.

LITERATURE RECORDS: None.

Nastra lherminier (Latreille, 1824). Swarthy Skipper. Plate 10

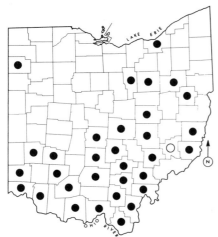

Fig. 8.38 *Nastra lherminier.*

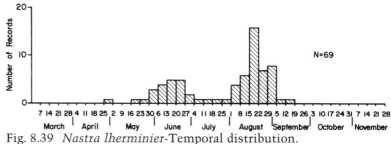

Fig. 8.39 *Nastra lherminier*-Temporal distribution.

STATUS: Resident; uncommon to rare. This species is most frequently encountered in southern Ohio, but rarely encountered in northern counties. Opler and Krizek (1984) consider this species to be an immigrant in Ohio, but our records indicate that it is probably a resident in southern Ohio (see GENERAL COMMENTS).

DISTRIBUTION/RANGE: Probably statewide, although most of our records fall south of a line running from the southwestern to northeastern corners of the State (Figure 8.38).

HABITAT: This species is most often found in disturbed xeric fields, reclaimed strip mined areas, powerline cuts, dry hillsides, in forest clearings, and along roadsides where *Andropogon scoparius* Michx. is common.

HOSTPLANT(S): In Ohio, *N. lherminier* has been observed mating, ovipositing, and feeding on little bluestem, *Andropogon scoparius* Michx. (David K. Parshall, pers comm, 1987). This is the only reported foodplant (Opler and Krizek, 1984).

ADULT ENERGY RESOURCES: Blazing-star (*Liatris spicata* [L.] Willd.), self-heal (*Prunella vulgaris* L.), and ironweed (*Vernonia* sp.). Adults also imbibe moisture from damp soil and mud.

FLIGHT PERIOD: Two broods, the first flying primarily in June, the second in August (Figure 8.39). Extreme dates range from 26 April through 16 September.

SIMILAR SPECIES: *Lerodea eufala* is similar, but has several white spots on the forewing that are absent in *N. lherminier.* Although *N. lherminier* occasionally has some faint obscure forewing markings, it generally lacks any discernible pattern. As Klots (1951) stated, "If you have a specimen that looks as neutral, dull, drab and undistinguished as possible, think of *lherminier.*"

GENERAL COMMENTS: This is possibly the most overlooked skipper in Ohio, and is much more frequent and widespread than our records suggest. In the field, this species is almost impossible to see. When at rest, the dull brown color of this species blends in perfectly with the exposed soil and dried grasses that characterize many of its haunts. Even in flight, this species stays close to the ground and more often than not, simply disappears into the background. As a result, very few Ohio collections contain this skipper.

In southern Ohio, this species is found yearly in a number of localities in both late spring and summer. This persistence and several early capture dates leads us to believe that *N. lherminier* is a resident in at least southern Ohio. Records from northern Ohio are more sporadic and are more likely to represent immigrants or strays from southern Ohio. The lack of records from northwestern Ohio may be a reflection of the lack of suitable habitats for colonization there. This is one of the most intensively farmed regions in Ohio, and, with the exception of the Oak Openings, few fields remain idle long enough to develop stands of *Andropogon scoparius.*

LITERATURE RECORD: Noble County (Lepidopterists' Society, 1984).

Ancyloxypha numitor (Fabricius, 1793). Least Skipper. Plate 10.

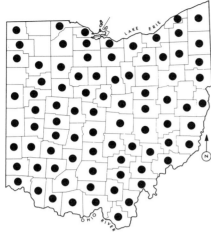

Fig. 8.40 *Ancyloxypha numitor.*

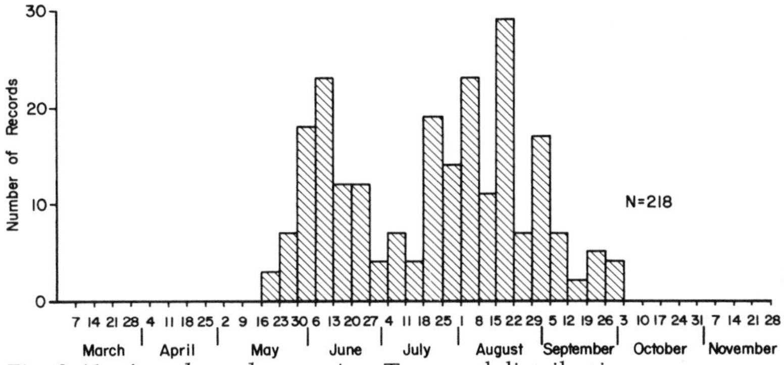

Fig. 8.41 *Ancyloxypha numitor*-Temporal distribution.

STATUS: Resident; common.

DISTRIBUTION/RANGE: Statewide (Figure 8.40).

HABITAT: This species is associated with moist, open habitats, particularly wet meadows, sedge meadows, fens, and seeps. It is also commonly found in tall grasses bordering ditches, stream banks, and pond edges. If suitable grasses are present, the summer broods will also spread into old fields and pastures.

HOSTPLANT(S): Not known in Ohio. A variety of grasses are used throughout this species' range (Opler and Krizek, 1984).

ADULT ENERGY RESOURCES: Red clover (*Trifolium pratense* L.), oxeye daisy (*Chrysanthemum leucanthemum* L.), alfalfa (*Medicago sativa* L.), Canada thistle (*Cirsium arvense* [L.] Scop.), bull thistle (*C. vulgare* [Savi] Tenore), blue vervain (*Verbena hastata* L.), and peppermint (*Mentha piperita* L.). Adults also utilize damp soil and mud.

FLIGHT PERIOD: Probably three broods, the first flying in late May and June, the second in late July and August, and the third in September (Figure 8.41). Extreme dates range from 17 May through 30 September.

GENERAL COMMENTS: This diminutive skipper is relatively common and widespread throughout Ohio. Populations are generally larger during wetter years.

The flight of this species is weak, slow, and usually low within the tall grasses it inhabits. This low, bobbing flight often makes this skipper difficult to observe. Males patrol through grasses at a height of approximately one meter or less. Adults perch with their wings slightly open. Females are darker and larger than males and are encountered less frequently in the field.

LITERATURE RECORDS: None.

Copaeodes minima (W.H. Edwards, 1870). Southern Skipperling. Plate 10.

Fig. 8.42 *Copaeodes minima.*

STATUS: Uncertain, either a stray or a transported individual; rare. Only one Ohio specimen is known.

DISTRIBUTION/RANGE: The sole Ohio record is from Hancock County, 2 miles south of Findley (Figure 8.42). This species is a resident of Tropical and Lower Austral Zone habitats. Other than the Ohio record, it is not known from north of Arkansas and central North Carolina (Opler and Krizek, 1984).

HABITAT: In the south, *C. minima* is found in open grassy areas. The Ohio specimen was taken while the animal was collecting nectar along the banks of a creek.

HOSTPLANT(S): Not known in Ohio. Bermuda grass (*Cynodon dactylon* [L.] Pers.) is the hostplant elsewhere (Opler and Krizek, 1984). It is doubtful if this skipper ever reproduces in Ohio.

ADULT ENERGY RESOURCES: None recorded for Ohio.

FLIGHT PERIOD: The single specimen was collected on 10 September 1928 by George W. Rawson.

SIMILAR SPECIES: *Thymelicus lineola* is larger and lacks the pale stripe on the ventral hindwing that characterizes *C. minima.*

GENERAL COMMENTS: How this individual got to Ohio will always remain an enigma. Is it a legitimate stray or was it transported? It is obvious that Rawson realized the uniqueness of this record by the very complete label data he recorded (date, exact locality, habitat, and what it was doing when captured). Unless additional evidence refutes his, Rawson's reputation as an extremely competent lepidopterist leaves us no choice but to accept the validity of this record. The specimen is deposited in The Ohio State Collection of Insects and Spiders.

LITERATURE RECORDS: None.

Thymelicus lineola (Ochsenheimer, 1808). European Skipper. Plate 10.

Fig. 8.43 *Thymelicus lineola.*

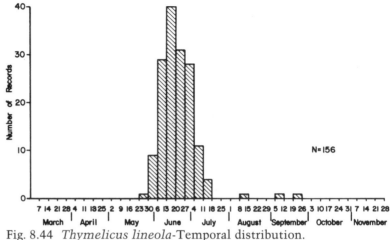

Fig. 8.44 *Thymelicus lineola*-Temporal distribution.

STATUS: Naturalized resident; common. Local, but generally common throughout the northern two-thirds of the State. Uncommon to rare in the lower third.

DISTRIBUTION/RANGE: Statewide (Figure 8.43).

HABITAT: This species can be found in almost any open, moist grassy area, such as prairies, clover and alfalfa fields, grassy roadsides, wetlands, and along streams and ponds.

HOSTPLANT(S): Not known in Ohio. The preferred larval foodplant throughout its range is timothy (*Phleum pratense* L.) (Opler and Krizek, 1984). This species has the potential to become a minor pest in timothy pastures.

ADULT ENERGY RESOURCES: Alfalfa (*Medicago sativa* L.), red clover (*Trifolium pratense* L.), alsike clover (*Trifolium hybridum* L.), crown vetch (*Coronilla varia* L.), purple vetch (*Vicia americana* Muhl.), Canada anemone (*Anemone canadensis* L.), upright cinquefoil (*Potentilla recta* L.), cinquefoil (*Potentilla* sp.), wild carrot (*Daucus carota* L.), Indian hemp (*Apocynum cannabinum* L.), dogbane (*Apocynum* sp.), and Canada thistle (*Cirsium arvense* [L.] Scop.).

FLIGHT PERIOD: One brood, flying in June and early July, with a possible partial second brood in August and September (Figure 8.44). Extreme dates range from 28 May through 20 September.

SIMILAR SPECIES: *Atrytone logan* males are similar, but *T. lineola* is smaller, duller orange, and lacks most of the dark forewing markings found in *A. logan*.

GENERAL COMMENTS: The European skipper was first discovered on the North American continent near London, Ontario in 1910 (Saunders, 1916). Since that time it has spread southward into Kentucky and Virginia (Opler and Krizek, 1984). It was first collected in northern Ohio by Rawson (1931) in 1927. Thomas (1952) reported the first captures from central Ohio. Today it probably occurs throughout Ohio, although it has not yet been reported from some of the southern counties. It is known from northern Kentucky (Charles V. Covell Jr., pers comm, 1985). Several authors (Ehle, 1958; Pengelly, 1961; Burns, 1966a) have suggested that the spread of *T. lineola* may be linked primarily to the transportation of hay containing eggs. Populations fluctuate in numbers from year to year.

Males patrol grassy areas in search of potential mates (Pivnick and McNeil, 1985) with a slightly faster flight than *Ancyloxypha numitor*. Both sexes perch frequently on low vegetation and bask in sunlight to thermoregulate (Pivnick and McNeil, 1987). Adults are easily approached while they are taking nectar.

The pale or light form, 'pallida' Tutt, 1875, has been collected in Franklin, Lucas, and Lorain Counties.

LITERATURE RECORDS: None.

Hylephila phyleus phyleus (**Drury, 1773**). Fiery Skipper. Plate 10.

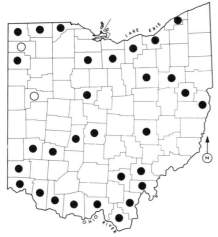

Fig. 8.45 *Hylephila phyleus*.

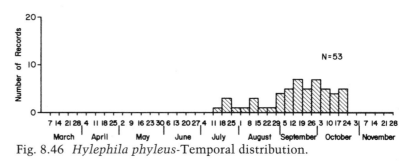

Fig. 8.46 *Hylephila phyleus*-Temporal distribution.

STATUS: Regular immigrant; uncommon to rare. This species is occasionally locally common, especially in the extreme southern portion of the State.

DISTRIBUTION/RANGE: Primarily a resident of the southern U.S. and southward, this skipper regularly appears as far north as Wisconsin, Michigan, and New York (Scott, 1986). Although Ohio records are scattered statewide (Figure 8.45), *H. phyleus* is most often encountered in the Ohio River Valley in southern Ohio. Price (1970) reported it as occasionally common in northwestern Ohio.

HABITAT: Typical habitats include open and disturbed areas, particularly weedy vacant lots, fields with brushy growth, roadsides, lawns, and alfalfa and clover fields.

HOSTPLANT(S) : Not known in Ohio. Various grasses are utilized throughout its range (Opler and Krizek, 1984).

ADULT ENERGY RESOURCES: Red clover (*Trifolium pratense* L.), alfalfa (*Medicago sativa* L.), white aster (*Aster* sp.), and various garden flowers.

FLIGHT PERIOD: Although there are no discrete broods in Ohio (Figure 8.46), this skipper is capable of at least one generation a year in Ohio. Extreme dates range from 17 July through 22 October.

SIMILAR SPECIES: Male *H. phyleus* can be confused with male *Polites vibex*, a species which is known from areas close to Ohio and which eventually could be recorded here (see Chapter 9). The length of the antennae will distinguish these two species. In *H. phyleus* the antennae are short, less than one-half the length of the forewing, whereas in *P. vibex* the antennae are longer than one-half the length of the forewings. The yellow rays on the dorsal hindwing of *H. phyleus* will also separate it from *P. vibex*, which lacks them.

Females of *H. phyleus* can be confused with females of *Atalopedes campestris*, but the distinctive hyaline discal spots on the forewing of *A. campestris* will separate these species. These spots are absent in *H. phyleus*.

GENERAL COMMENTS: This species probably does not overwinter in Ohio and it is usually most common following mild winters. Year-to-year abundance seems to be dependant upon this species' ability to establish itself early in the year, which allows population numbers to build up for a longer period. After mild winters, this skipper can become locally common by mid-summer. After typical winters, *H. phyleus* is not seen until late summer or early autumn.

The flight of this skipper is rapid and difficult to follow visually, especially if it is startled. However, *H. phyleus* is easily observed while it is visiting nectar sources. Males are more frequently collected than females.

LITERATURE RECORDS: Auglaize (Hoying, 1975) and Defiance (Price, 1970) Counties.

Hesperia leonardus leonardus **Harris, 1862.** Leonard's Skipper. Plate 10.

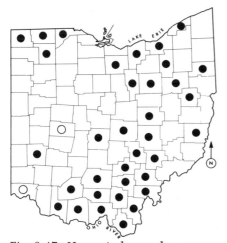

Fig. 8.47 *Hesperia leonardus*.

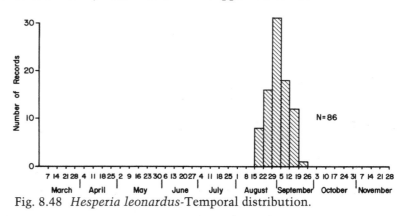

Fig. 8.48 *Hesperia leonardus*-Temporal distribution.

STATUS: Resident; uncommon to rare. This species is sometimes locally common, especially in southern Ohio and the Oak Openings of Lucas County.

DISTRIBUTION/RANGE: Statewide (Figure 8.47).

HABITAT: This species is associated with prairie openings, dry grassy hillsides, xeric ridgetops, and moist meadows where purple nectar sources occur. It is sometimes found in localities that contain *Atrytonopsis hianna* earlier in the season.

HOSTPLANT(S): Although no hostplant has been reported from Ohio, *H. leonardus* is usually associated with areas containing stands of *Andropogon* species. This skipper uses a number of grass species throughout its range (Opler and Krizek, 1984).

ADULT ENERGY RESOURCES: Blazing-stars (*Liatris aspera* Michx. and *L. squarrosa* [L.] Michx.), wild bergamot (*Monarda fistulosa* L.), poke-weed (*Phytolacca americana* L.), ironweed (*Vernonia* spp.), and thistles (*Cirsium vulgare* (Savi) Tenore, and others). Price (1970) records teasel (*Dipsacus sylvestris* Huds.) and purple boneset (*Eupatorium perfoliatum* L.). This species seems strongly attracted to purple flowers. Adults are also attracted to damp soil and mud.

FLIGHT PERIOD: One brood from late August through September (Figure 8.48). This species appears first in northern Ohio, and then gradually emerges southward. This is opposite of the general trend, where most species occur earlier in southern Ohio, then gradually later northward. Extreme dates range from 15 August through 23 September.

SIMILAR SPECIES: None.

GENERAL COMMENTS: This is the latest of our native skippers to appear on the wing each season. It is probably more common and widespread than our records indicate, because it flies after most lepidopterists have stopped collecting for the year.

The flight of this species is powerful and extremely rapid. Individuals seem to disappear instantly once they take flight. However, this species is easily observed at flowers.

The median band of spots on the ventral hindwing ranges in color from white to yellow (ochrous), with yellow being the most common phenotype. Individuals with white spots are more frequent in northern Ohio. The male holotype and female allotype of the form 'stallingsi' Freeman (1943) (the yellow spotted form) were collected in Franklin and Jackson Counties, respectively.

LITERATURE RECORDS: Hamilton (Wyss, 1930b; 1932) and Champaign (Albrecht, 1982) Counties.

Hesperia metea metea Scudder, 1864. Cobweb Skipper. Plate 11.

Fig. 8.49 *Hesperia metea.*

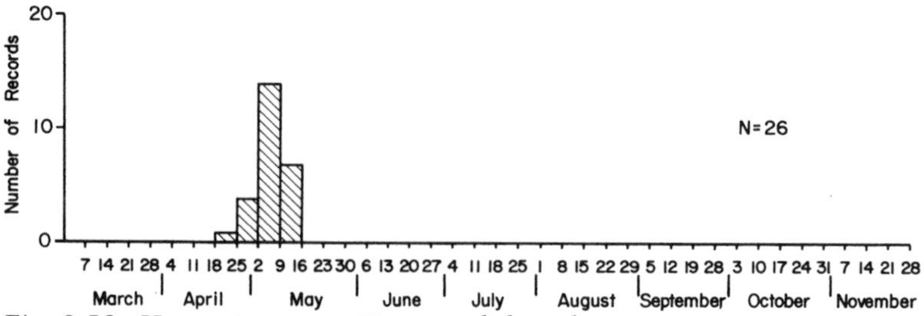

Fig. 8.50 *Hesperia metea*-Temporal distribution.

STATUS: Resident; uncommon to rare.

DISTRIBUTION/RANGE: This skipper is disjunctly distributed in Ohio, occurring in the hill country of southern Ohio, and also in the Oak Openings, Lucas County (one record) (Figure 8.49).

HABITAT: This species is associated with xeric open habitats and prairie-like openings (eg powerline cuts, ridgetop openings, old pastures, and rocky hillsides) that contain stands of *Andropogon scoparius*. Most of the known populations have been found along powerline cuts.

HOSTPLANT(S): In Ohio, eggs of this species have been placed on and larvae reared to adulthood on little bluestem (*Andropogon scoparius* Michx.) (David K. Parshall, pers comm, 1987). Big bluestem (*A. gerardi* Vitman) and broom-sedge (*A. virginicus* L.), two widespread grasses in Ohio (Braun, 1967) may also be used (Opler and Krizek, 1984; Scott, 1986).

ADULT ENERGY RESOURCES: Dwarf cinquefoil (*Potentilla canadensis* L.), wild strawberry (*Fragaria virginiana* Dene.), dwarf larkspur (*Delphinium tricorne* Michx.), and blackberry and other *Rubus* species. Adults also visit damp soil and mud.

FLIGHT PERIOD: One brood flying in late April through early May (Figure 8.50). Extreme dates range from 21 April through 25 July (this unusually late date may be the result of a labeling error).

SIMILAR SPECIES: None.

GENERAL COMMENTS: Although only recently reported from the State (Iftner, 1983a), this species may have always been present but overlooked. Prior to human intervention, this skipper was probably restricted to ridgetop openings, recently burned areas, blowdowns, and xeric prairies. As the original forest cover was removed and, more recently, as cultivated areas have been abandoned, areas conducive to the primary foodplant, *Andropogon scoparius*, have become common. However, this foodplant is an early successional species, and unless some artificial disturbance maintains these habitats, it is quickly shaded out. In Pennsylvania, *H. metea* colonizes such areas and flourishes for a few years at each site (Shapiro, 1965). Shapiro noted that females disperse readily from suitable habitats, and suggested that this was an adaptation toward the ephemeral nature of its early successional habitats. In Ohio, this skipper is usually found in areas that are artificially maintained in early succession (eg powerline cuts). Shapiro noted that *H. metea* and *Atrytonopsis hianna* generally occupy the same habitats, but in Ohio, these two species have so far been found together in only Lucas, Vinton, and Hocking Counties. *Hesperia metea* is usually gone or badly worn by the time *A. hianna* appears on the wing.

The original xeric prairies that probably supported this species in the past have all but been destroyed through human activities. The few xeric prairies that do survive occur primarily in the Bluegrass Section (Adams County), where *H. metea* has not yet been collected, and in the Oak Openings (Lucas County) where there is a single old record (25 July 1937, collected by George W. Rawson). Although abundant (seemingly suitable) habitat still exists in the Oak Openings, *H. metea* has not been reported despite the recent intensive collecting in the area, suggesting that it is very rare or perhaps extirpated from this portion of the State.

Several factors may contribute to this skipper being overlooked. Few collectors are in the field during the early spring flight period, and those who are generally ignore the lifeless looking habitats that support this skipper. In spring, habitats dominated by *Andropogon scoparius* appear "dead" and unproductive. In this grass, new growth is concealed by the dried remnants of last year's leaves, and this gives a sterile appearance to the habitat.

Hesperia metea is well camouflaged when resting on the foodplant. Even in flight, this species stays close to the ground, and is almost invisible. Its very rapid flight coupled with its wariness, make it very difficult to collect. Males are most easily observed when perching on the dried leaves of the foodplant or on exposed soil. Females tend to fly short distances when disturbed and usually land on the ground.

This skipper should be found in many more counties, once collectors become more familiar with the habitat. *Andropogon scoparious* is known from at least 69 of Ohio's 88 counties (Braun, 1967).

LITERATURE RECORDS: None.

Hesperia sassacus sassacus Harris, 1862. Indian Skipper. Plate 11.

Fig. 8.51 *Hesperia sassacus*.

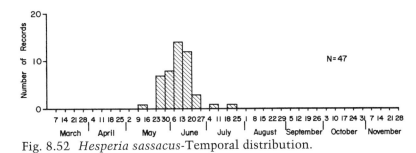

Fig. 8.52 *Hesperia sassacus*-Temporal distribution.

STATUS: Resident; uncommon. This skipper is most common in the northeastern corner of the State, where it occasionally reaches high densities.

DISTRIBUTION/RANGE: Eastern Ohio (Figure 8.51).

HABITAT: In northeastern Ohio, this species has been found in dry grassy fields, on open hillsides, and in forest openings. In southeastern Ohio, it has only been taken from xeric powerline cuts through wooded areas.

HOSTPLANT(S) : In Ohio, this species has been observed ovipositing on red fescue (*Festuca rubra* L,) (Dennis A. Currutt, pers comm, 1988). Several populations are closely associated with stands of broom-sedge (*Andropogon virginicus* L.) (David K. Parshall, pers comm, 1987) and little bluestem (*Andropogon scoparius* Michx.), and these may be important foodplants as well. Various grasses are used throughout this skipper's range (Opler and Krizek, 1984).

ADULT ENERGY RESOURCES: Orange hawkweed (*Hieracium aurantiacum* L.) and brambles (*Rubus* sp.).

FLIGHT PERIOD: One brood flying in late May and June (Figure 8.52). Extreme dates range from 15 May through 19 July.

SIMILAR SPECIES: *Hesperia sassacus* can be confused with *Polites mystic*, which usually has much less orange on the wings, and a less angled band of spots on the ventral hindwings. The stigma of male *P. mystic* is more robust, and lacks the silver gray center found in *H. sassacus*. The stigma of *P. mystic* often connects with the dark apical patch, creating a long black dash that transverses the entire forewing (hence the common name, long dash). In *H. sassacus* the stigma rarely connects with this pattern element.

GENERAL COMMENTS: This species is probably frequently overlooked in southern Ohio, because it occurs in the same 'dead' appearing habitats as *H. metea* and *A. hianna*. In northern Ohio, the habitat usually appears to be more productive (ie 'green-looking') and as a result, more collectors find this species there. In northern Ohio, *H. sassacus* habitats often border wetter habitats supporting *P. mystic*, sometimes making it difficult to distinguish the two species in the field, particularly around nectar sources. Generally, the rarer *H. sassacus* is found up-slope from the often abundant *P. mystic*. *Hesperia sassacus* also appears on the wing slightly earlier than *P. mystic*.

The flight of this species is rapid and close to the ground. Because of their coloration, adults blend in with the ground cover and are difficult to follow visually while in flight. Both sexes rest on dead grasses, and males chase after other passing butterflies.

LITERATURE RECORDS: Franklin (Hine, 1898a) and Seneca (Henninger, 1910) Counties.

Polites coras (Cramer, 1775). Peck's Skipper. Plate 11.

Fig. 8.53 *Polites coras*.

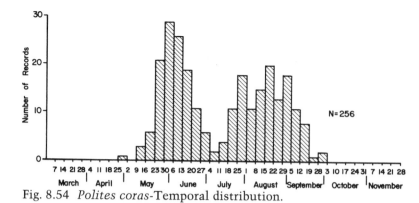

Fig. 8.54 *Polites coras*-Temporal distribution.

STATUS: Resident; common.

DISTRIBUTION/RANGE: Statewide (Figure 8.53).

HABITAT: This skipper can be found in almost any open grassy habitat, such as old pastures, moist meadows, powerline cuts, roadsides, drainage ditches, grassy areas along streams, and lawns. *Polites coras* is often seen in large numbers obtaining nectar in alfalfa and clover fields.

HOSTPLANT(S): Not known in Ohio. In New York, Shapiro (1974) found rice cutgrass (*Leersia oryzoides* [L.] Swartz) to be the foodplant. This grass is widespread in Ohio (Braun, 1967). Other grasses are also probably used.

ADULT ENERGY RESOURCES: Red clover (*Trifolium pratense* L.), white clover (*T. repens* L.), alfalfa (*Medicago sativa* L.), winter cress (*Barbarea vulgaris* R.), teasel (*Dipsacus sylvestris* Huds.), Canada thistle (*Cirsium arvense* [L.] Scop.), field thistle (*Cirsium discolor* [Muhl.] Spreng.), swamp thistle (*Cirsium muticum* Michx.), purple coneflower (*Echinacea purpurea* [L.] Moench), ironweed (*Vernonia* sp.), blazing star (*Liatris spicata* [L.] Willd.), and many garden flowers. Adults also imbibe moisture from moist soil and mud.

FLIGHT PERIOD: Two broods, the first flying in late May and June, the second in late July through early September (Figure 8.54). Extreme dates range from 26 April through 27 September.

GENERAL COMMENTS: This species is very common throughout the State, and it is probably our most common skipper. When it is nectaring in alfalfa fields, this species can be so numerous that it is difficult to spot less common skippers.

    The flight of this species is usually rapid and close to the ground. Adults perch on blades of grass and occasionally on exposed soil. Males fly out from their perches to chase other passing skippers, probably as part of their mate locating behavior.

LITERATURE RECORDS: None.

Polites themistocles (Latreille, 1824). Tawny-edged Skipper. Plate 11.

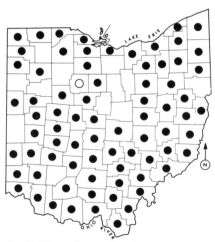

Fig. 8.55 *Polites themistocles*.

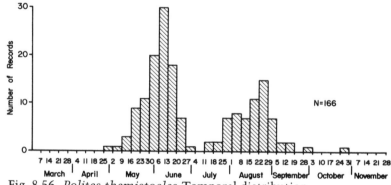

Fig. 8.56 *Polites themistocles*-Temporal distribution.

STATUS: Resident; common.

DISTRIBUTION/RANGE: Statewide (Figure 8.55).

HABITAT: This species is found in almost any open grassy area such as roadsides, pastures, moist meadows, prairie remnants, powerline cuts, and old fields. *Polites themistocles* is also very fond of alfalfa and clover fields.

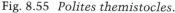

48

HOSTPLANT(S): Not known in Ohio. Opler and Krizek (1984) list panic grasses (*Panicum* spp.). These grasses are widespread and common in Ohio (Braun, 1967).

ADULT ENERGY RESOURCES: Alfalfa (*Medicago sativa* L.), red clover (*Trifolium pratense* L.), two-flowered cynthia (*Krigia biflora* [Walt.] Blake), common milkweed (*Asclepias syriaca* L.), and blazing-star (*Liatris spicata* [L.] Willd.). Bales (1909) listed jewel-weed (*Impatiens* sp.). Adults also visit damp soil and mud.

FLIGHT PERIOD: Two broods, the first flying in late May and June, the second in late July and August (Figure 8.56). Extreme dates range from 26 April through 24 October.

SIMILAR SPECIES: *Polites origenes* males are larger and have a relatively narrower and less S-shaped stigma than *P. themistocles*. The tawny costal area of the dorsal forewing is more brassy in *P. origenes* than *P. themistocles*. *Polites origenes* females usually lack the orange forewing costal area (ventral and dorsal) that is present in *P. themistocles*. See Table (p. 49) for a key to the easily confused female skippers.

GENERAL COMMENTS: This is one of our most common skippers, rivaling *P. coras* in numbers. *Polites themistocles* and *P. coras* generally occur in the same habitats, and both seem to be very fond of clover and alfalfa fields. *Polites themistocles* is more widespread and more frequently encountered than *P. origenes*.

The flight of this species is rapid and close to the ground. Males perch on grass blades and other vegetation. Males dart out at other passing skippers, probably to search for potential mates.

LITERATURE RECORD: Wyandot County (Albrecht, 1982).

Table. A key to easily confused females of five skipper species.

This simplified key uses easily discernable morphological characters to separate a group of small dark female skippers. Often referred to as the "black witches", this group of female skippers is characterized by their uniformly drab coloration. Although the males of these species are more easily identified, these females can confuse even the most seasoned taxonomists. This key should be used in conjunction with the plates. Occasional specimens may need to be determined by an authority on the Hesperiidae.

1. Tibiae of middle pair of legs without spines ....*Euphyes vestris*.

   Tibiae of middle pair of legs with spines 2

2. Forewings dark, with orange coloring confined to areas near the costal margin ....*Polites themistocles*.

   Forewings dark, without orange near the costal margin, or with orange coloring near the dorsal wing bases 3

3. Ventral hindwings with a curved light patch made up of indistinct spots ....*Wallengrenia egeremet*.

   Ventral hindwing unmarked, or with a row of small round spots 4

4. Forewings with fairly large light spots which are slightly transparent ....*Pompeius verna*.

   Forewings with small light spots which are not transparent ....*Polites origenes*.

***Polites origenes origenes* (Fabricius, 1793).** Cross Line Skipper. Plate 11.

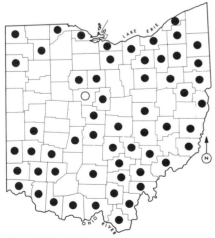

Fig. 8.57 *Polites origenes*.

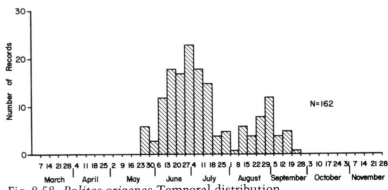

Fig. 8.58 *Polites origenes*-Temporal distribution.

STATUS: Resident; uncommon.

DISTRIBUTION/RANGE: Statewide (Figure 8.57).

HABITAT: This species can be found in a variety of open grassy areas. Examples include powerline cuts, prairie remnants, brushy fields, and pastures. The habitat of *P. origenes* tends to be drier than that of *P. themistocles*, although both species often fly together.

HOSTPLANT(S): Not known in Ohio. Scott (1986) lists purple-top (*Triodia flava* [L.] Smyth) and little bluestem (*Andropogon scoparius* Michx.). Both of these grasses are common and widespread in Ohio (Braun, 1967).

ADULT ENERGY RESOURCES: Alfalfa (*Medicago sativa* L.), red clover (*Trifolium pratense* L.), common milkweed (*Asclepias syriaca* L.), thistles (*Cirsium arvense* [L.] Scop., and others), and dogbane (*Apocynum* sp.).

FLIGHT PERIOD: Two broods, the first flying from late May through mid July, the second from mid-August through mid-September (Figure 8.58). Extreme dates range from 23 May through 19 September.

SIMILAR SPECIES: See *P. themistocles*. See Table (p. 49) for a breakdown of the many similar females.

GENERAL COMMENTS: The cross line skipper is more local and less common than the tawny-edged skipper. Although they often occur together, *P. origenes* tends to inhabit drier sites, and often occurs in the very xeric habitats that support *Hesperia metea* and *Atrytonopsis hianna* earlier in the season.
  The flight of this species is more rapid than that of the other *Polites* species. Males perch on grass blades and other vegetation. Both sexes are wary and can be difficult to approach. However, this species is easily observed while it feeds at flowers.
  A bilateral gynandromorph of this skipper was collected in Adams County by David K. Parshall.

LITERATURE RECORD: Marion County (Albrecht, 1982).

Polites mystic mystic (W.H. Edwards, 1863). Long Dash. Plate 11.

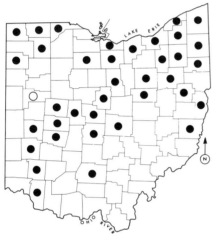

Fig. 8.59 *Polites mystic.*

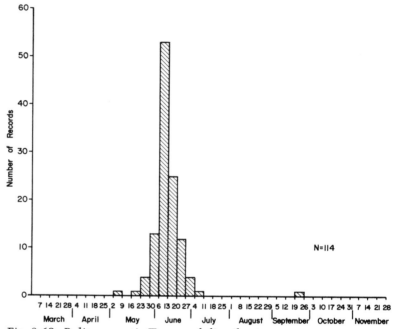

Fig. 8.60 *Polites mystic*-Temporal distribution.

STATUS: Resident; uncommon. In northwestern Ohio, Price (1970) considered this species to be locally common in Lucas, Fulton, and Williams Counties, but absent in the remaining counties that he studied. Although populations of this species are localized, they often reach fairly high densities and adults are often common in northeastern Ohio wetlands.

DISTRIBUTION/RANGE: Glaciated Ohio (Figure 8.59).

HABITAT: This skipper inhabits open, wet, marshy areas (eg fens, sedge meadows, moist grassy clearings, and pipeline and powerline cuts through swamps).

HOSTPLANT(S): Although no host has been recorded in Ohio, *P. mystic* is usually associated with dense stands of sedges (*Carex* spp.). It is probable that these are the foodplants. Shapiro (1966) listed bluegrass (*Poa* sp.) as the foodplant in Pennsylvania.

ADULT ENERGY RESOURCES: Red clover, (*Trifolium pratense* L.), swamp milkweed (*Asclepias incarnata* L.), and Canada thistle (*Cirsium arvense* [L.] Scop.).

FLIGHT PERIOD: One brood flying primarily in June (Figure 8.60). Extreme dates range from 4 May through 1 September. The September date may indicate a partial second brood in some years.

SIMILAR SPECIES: See *Hesperia sassacus*.

GENERAL COMMENTS: This skipper can be easily confused with *H. sassacus*, a species that sometimes occurs in adjacent habitats in northeastern Ohio. *Polites mystic* generally flies in wetter areas than does *H. sassacus*, and the species sometimes occur together at nectar sources.

In flight, *P. mystic* stays low and flies just above the top of the ground cover. Both sexes perch on the upper leaves of sedges, and are generally easy to observe. Males dart out from their perches at passing objects, probably in an effort to locate potential mates.

The common name, long dash, refers to the long streak on the dorsal forewing, which is created by the connection of the stigma and the dark subapical patch.

LITERATURE RECORD: Auglaize County (Williamson, 1905).

Wallengrenia egeremet (Scudder, 1864). Northern Broken Dash. Plate 11.

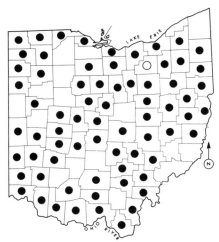

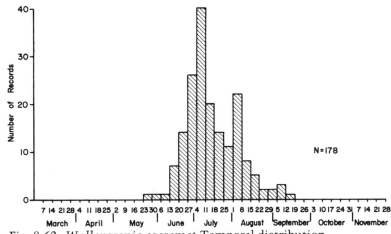

Fig. 8.61 *Wallengrenia egeremet*.

Fig. 8.62 *Wallengrenia egeremet*-Temporal distribution.

STATUS: Resident, uncommon to common.

DISTRIBUTION/RANGE: Statewide (Figure 8.61).

HABITAT: This species is found in old fields, areas with brushy second growth, grassy clearings, pastures, and along roadsides. These habitats usually tend to be near wooded areas.

HOSTPLANT(S): Not known in Ohio. Panic grasses (*Panicum*, particularly *P. dichotomum* L.) are used elsewhere (Shapiro, 1974). These grasses are widespread in Ohio (Braun, 1967).

ADULT ENERGY RESOURCES: Red clover (*Trifolium pratense* L.), alfalfa (*Medicago sativa* L.), white sweet clover (*Melilotus alba* Desr.), thistles (*Cirsium* spp.), teasel (*Dipsacus sylvestris* Huds.), swamp milkweed (*Asclepias incarnata* L.), and common yarrow (*Achillea millefolium* L.). Adults also visit damp soil and mud.

FLIGHT PERIOD: One brood, flying from mid-June through August (Figure 8.62). September captures may indicate a partial second brood. Extreme dates range from 26 May through 18 September.

SIMILAR SPECIES: Although males are distinctive, females of this species can be confused with *Polites origenes, Polites themistocles, Pompeius verna,* and *Euphyes vestris metacomet* (See Table, p. 49).

GENERAL COMMENTS: The common name, "broken dash", refers to the male stigma, which is separated into two parts. *Wallengrenia egeremet* is a close but distinct relative of the more southern *W. otho,* which should eventually be recorded from Ohio (Burns, 1985). See Chapter 9 for more information.

Although widespread, *W. egeremet* is seldom abundant. As with most skippers, the flight is rapid. Adults are intensely attracted to nectar sources.

LITERATURE RECORD: Medina County (Albrecht, 1982).

Pompeius verna (W.H. Edwards, 1862). Little Glassy Wing. Plate 11.

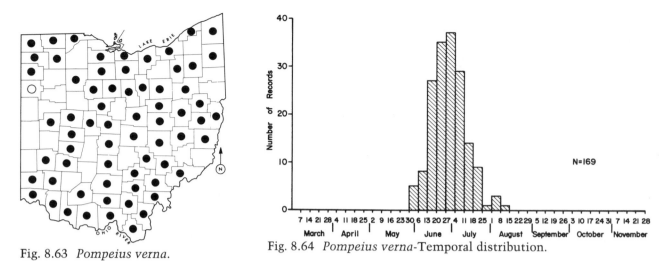

Fig. 8.63 *Pompeius verna.*

Fig. 8.64 *Pompeius verna*-Temporal distribution.

STATUS: Resident; uncommon. Populations in southern Ohio occasionally become locally common.

DISTRIBUTION/RANGE: Statewide (Figure 8.63).

HABITAT: This skipper is usually associated with brushy old fields, wooded margins, grassy clearings, and pastures.

HOSTPLANT(S): Not known in Ohio. Purple-top (*Triodia flava* [L.] Smyth), a common species throughout Ohio (Braun, 1967), is the only reported foodplant (Opler and Krizek, 1984).

ADULT ENERGY RESOURCES: Red clover (*Trifolium pratense* L.), common milkweed (*Asclepias syriaca* L.), swamp milkweed (*Asclepias incarnata* L.), Canada thistle (*Cirsium arvense* [L.] Scop.), and dogbane (*Apocynum* sp.). Adults also visit moist soil and mud.

FLIGHT PERIOD: One brood, flying in June and July (Figure 8.64). Extreme dates range from 30 May through 11 August.

SIMILAR SPECIES: Females of this species can be confused with the females of *Polites origenes, Polites themistocles, Wallengrenia egeremet,* and *Euphyes vestris* (See Table, p. 49). The square hyaline (clear) spots in the forewing cell will distinguish *P. verna* from these similar species.

GENERAL COMMENTS: This is an early summer species that is characteristic of open areas. It often flies with the four species with which it is easily confused.

The flight of this species is rapid and close to the ground. Both sexes are strongly attracted to nectar sources, and can be easily observed while feeding.

LITERATURE RECORD: Van Wert County (Price, 1970).

Atalopedes campestris huron (W.H. Edwards, 1863). Sachem. Plate 12.

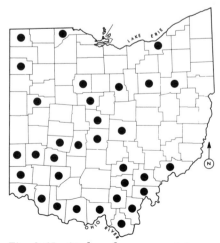

Fig. 8.65 *Atalopedes campestris.*

Fig. 8.66 *Atalopedes campestris*-Temporal distribution.

STATUS: Regular immigrant; rare to uncommon. Occasionally, this species establishes itself in southern Ohio, and can become locally abundant. Price (1970) collected only four males of this species in northwestern Ohio over a 25-year period. This species may have been more abundant in the past as Hine (1898a) considered it to be "very common all over the State."

DISTRIBUTION/RANGE: This skipper is a resident species in the southern half of the United States. It is an immigrant or stray as far north as Wisconsin and New York (Opler and Krizek, 1984). Although our records are scattered statewide, most are from southern Ohio (Figure 8.65).

HABITAT: Virtually any open area (eg pastures, vacant lots, old fields, alfalfa and clover fields, and roadsides). This species can even be found in open woodlands during years of high abundance.

HOSTPLANT(S): Not known in Ohio. Crabgrass (*Digitaria* sp.), goose grass (*Eleusine indica* [L.] Gaertn.), and Bermuda grass (*Cynodon dactylon* [L.] Pers.) are used in other portions of its range (Opler and Krizek, 1984). These grasses are common and widespread in Ohio (Braun, 1967).

ADULT ENERGY RESOURCES: Alfalfa (*Medicago sativa* L.), red clover (*Trifolium pratense* L.), wild bergamot (*Monarda fistulosa* L.), bur-marigold (*Bidens aristosa* [Michx.] Britt), ironweed (*Vernonia* sp.), zinnias (*Zinnia* spp.), marigolds (*Tagetes* spp.), and *Aster* species. This species also imbibes moisture from damp soil and mud.

FLIGHT PERIOD: Probably several broods in Ohio, with noticeable peaks in late July-early August, and September through October (Figure 8.66). Extreme dates range from 22 May through 26 October.

SIMILAR SPECIES: Females of *A. campestris* are superficially similar to females of *Hylephila phyleus*, *Hesperia leonardus*, *Polites mystic*, *Euphyes dion*, and *Euphyes conspicua*. However, the rectangular hyaline spot at the distal end of the forewing cell will distinguish *A. campestris* from all these species.

GENERAL COMMENTS: Although this skipper cannot survive the typically cold winters of Ohio, early capture dates suggest that it may survive particularly mild winters. Alternatively, adults are occasionally able to invade the State earlier than usual. During typical years, *A. campestris* is found only along the Ohio River flood plain, but when established, it can be found in scattered localities statewide. In 1983, this species was the most common butterfly seen in Lawrence County from July through October. During this period, hundreds of individuals were seen in fields where grew abundant nectar sources (Calhoun, 1985[86]).

The flight of this species is extremely rapid and close to the ground, and it can be difficult to follow with the eye. Males perch on blades of grass and other vegetation, and dart out at other passing skippers, presumably in search of potential mates. Both sexes are wary and can be difficult to approach. However, they are strongly attracted to nectar sources, and are easily observed while they are feeding.

LITERATURE RECORD: None.
Porter (1965) listed this species from Seneca County, but his record was based on a misdetermined female of *Hylephila phyleus*.

***Atrytone logan logan* (W.H. Edwards, 1863).** Delaware Skipper. Plate 12.

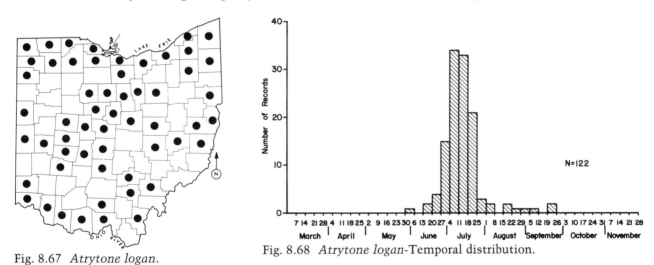

Fig. 8.67 *Atrytone logan*.

Fig. 8.68 *Atrytone logan*-Temporal distribution.

STATUS: Resident; uncommon. Populations are usually localized, and occasionally reach high enough densities to become locally common.

DISTRIBUTION/RANGE: Statewide (Figure 8.67).

HABITAT: *Atrytone logan* occurs in a variety of open, grassy habitats, and is frequently encountered in prairie remnants, fens, bogs, marshes, old fields, and alfalfa and clover fields.

HOSTPLANT(S): Not known in Ohio. Elsewhere, bluestems (*Andropogon* spp.), silver plume grass (*Erianthus alopecuroides* [L.] Ell.), and switchgrass (*Panicum virgatum* L.) are the reported foodplants (Sedman and Hess, 1985; Shapiro, 1966; 1974). This skipper is often found in sedge meadows, suggesting that some *Carex* species may also serve as hostplants.

ADULT ENERGY RESOURCES: Alfalfa (*Medicago sativa* L.), red clover (*Trifolium pratense* L.), common milkweed (*Asclepias syriaca* L.), and swamp milkweed (*Asclepias incarnata* L.).

FLIGHT PERIOD: One brood, flying primarily in July with stragglers or indicators of a possible partial second brood through September (Figure 8.68). Extreme dates range from 2 June through 21 September.

SIMILAR SPECIES: See *Thymelicus lineola*. Hoying (1975) confused this species with *Atrytone arogos*, a species which is not known from Ohio.

GENERAL COMMENTS: This species is more widespread than was once thought (Hine, 1898a; Hoying, 1975). Although generally uncommon, this skipper can be locally common in wetlands and prairie remnants.

    Atrytone logan has a rapid flight, and can be difficult to approach. It can be easily observed while it is nectaring or perching on grassy vegetation. Males fly out from their perches to investigate passing objects, probably in an attempt to locate females.

LITERATURE RECORDS: None.

Poanes massasoit massasoit (Scudder, 1864). Mulberry Wing. Plate 12.

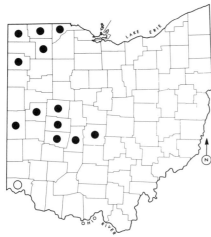

Fig. 8.69 *Poanes massasoit*.

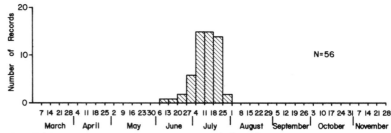

Fig. 8.70 *Poanes massasoit*-Temporal distribution.

STATUS: Resident; uncommon. Populations are intensely localized, although once found, this species can be locally common.

DISTRIBUTION/RANGE: This species is known from extreme northwestern Ohio and from a few scattered localities within the Teays River drainage in west-central Ohio (Figure 8.69). Although suitable habitats exist in northeastern Ohio, this species has not been found in this region (Shuey, 1985).

HABITAT: In west-central Ohio, this species inhabits sedge meadows and fens. In extreme northwestern Ohio, it also occurs along the edges of swamps and in sedge-lined ditches.

HOSTPLANT(S): In Ohio, larvae of this species have been found and reared through the third instar on the sedge, *Carex stricta* Lam., the only reported foodplant for the species (Shapiro, 1974). Adults are usually associated with *C. stricta* in the field.

ADULT ENERGY RESOURCES: Common milkweed, (*Asclepias syriaca* L.), swamp milkweed (*Asclepias incarnata* L.), wild bergamot (*Monarda fistulosa* L.), pickerel-weed (*Pontederia cordata* L.), and vetchling (*Lathyrus palustris* L.).

FLIGHT PERIOD: One brood, flying primarily in July (Figure 8.70). Extreme dates range from 10 June through 31 July.

SIMILAR SPECIES: None.

GENERAL COMMENTS: This wetland species is more widespread than once thought (see Albrecht, 1982). Populations are extremely localized and easily overlooked, but this skipper can be quite common when found. Adults occasionally stray out of their usual habitats, especially to adjacent areas with abundant nectar sources.

    The flight of this species is weak and low, and they are usually seen flying through, rather than over, the sedges that dominate their habitat. Because of this, they are often difficult to follow visually. Adults frequently rest on sedges and surrounding vegetation. Males exhibit a patrolling, mate seeking behavior.

LITERATURE RECORD: Hamilton County (Wyss, 1930b; 1932). Although today this record seems implausible because of the absence of suitable wetlands this far south, it is conceivable that wetlands existed in this area when Wyss was actively collecting.

    Shapiro (1970a) incorrectly included northeastern Ohio in this species' range.

Poanes hobomok hobomok (Harris, 1862). Northern Golden Skipper. Plate 12.

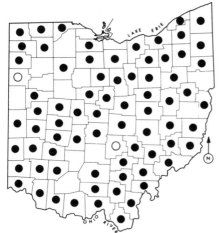

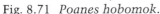

Fig. 8.71 *Poanes hobomok.*

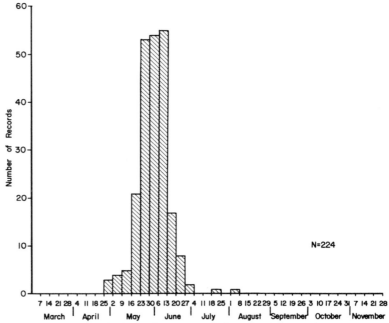

Fig. 8.72 *Poanes hobomok*-Temporal distribution.

STATUS: Resident; uncommon to common.

DISTRIBUTION/RANGE: Statewide (Figure 8.71).

HABITAT: This skipper occurs in a variety of open forest habitats (eg forest margins, sunlit openings within forests, powerline cuts through forests, and along woodland roads). Adults will move into more open habitats to obtain nectar.

HOSTPLANT(S): Not known in Ohio. Panic grasses (*Panicum* spp.) and meadow grasses (*Poa* spp.) are used in other portions of this skipper's range (Opler and Krizek, 1984). Both of these grass genera are common throughout Ohio (Braun, 1967).

ADULT ENERGY RESOURCES: Red clover (*Trifolium pratense* L.), wild cranesbill (*Geranium maculatum* L.), oxeye daisy (*Chrysanthemum leucanthemum* L.), and irus (*Irus versicolor* L.). Adults also imbibe moisture from damp soil and mud.

FLIGHT PERIOD: One brood, flying from mid-May through June (Figure 8.72). Fresh specimens from July and August may indicate that a partial second brood is occasionally produced. Extreme dates range from 26 April through 2 August.

SIMILAR SPECIES: Both forms of this species can be confused with *Poanes zabulon*. The tawny form of *P. hobomok* can be identified by the ventral hind wing pattern, which consists of a central yellow patch sharply outlined by dark brown. In males of *P. zabulon*, the yellow central patch is outlined by diffuse spots of dark brown, and the yellow patch itself usually contains three diffuse spots.

The females of *P. hobomok* are sometimes melanic (form 'pocahantas' [Scudder, 1864]), and can be confused with the females of *P. zabulon*, which are always melanic. In these females, the dorsal forewings of *P. hobomok* are marked by a series of blurry light spots, and often there is a hint of tawny coloration in the cell. In *P. zabulon*, the dorsal forewing is marked by sharply defined light spots, and there is no hint of tawny coloration in the cell. In females of both species, despite their dark patterns, it is usually possible to see hints of the normal ventral hindwing pattern found on males.

GENERAL COMMENTS: This species and *P. zabulon* are often confused. Not only are they very similar looking, but they usually fly together.

Females of *P. hobomok* are sexually dimorphic; the majority of the females are tawny and look very much like males. However, some females (less than 20%) are melanic and are very dissimilar looking. This dark brown form, 'pocahantas' (Scudder, 1864), is most frequently encountered in southern Ohio.

Males perch on sunlit leaves and twigs, and fly out rapidly to investigate passing objects, probably in search of potential mates. These males often return to the same perches, suggesting that they may be somewhat territorial. Females are more often found in shaded areas.

Pilate (1882), Bales (1909), Henninger (1910), and Wyss (1932) incorrectly associated the form name 'pocahantas' with *P. zabulon*. This may have been due to errors in the literature of the period (eg Holland, 1898).

LITERATURE RECORDS: Van Wert (Lepidopterists' Society, 1976) and Fairfield (Albrecht, 1982) Counties.

Poanes zabulon (Boisduval & LeConte, 1834). Southern Golden Skipper. Plate 12.

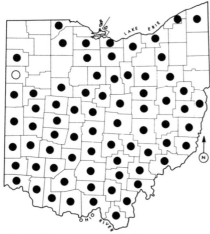

Fig. 8.73 *Poanes zabulon.*

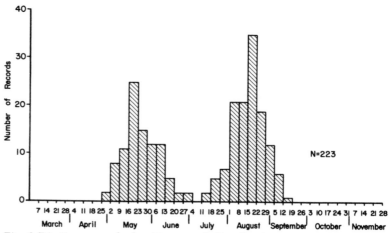

Fig. 8.74 *Poanes zabulon*-Temporal distribution.

STATUS: Resident; common to uncommon. Ohio is near the northern limit of this skipper's range, and it is most common in the central and southern counties.

DISTRIBUTION/RANGE: Statewide (Figure 8.73).

HABITAT: This species is found in a variety of open forest habitats such as forest margins, openings within forests, powerline cuts, and woodland roads. Adults are also found at nectar sources in open areas.

HOSTPLANT(S): Not known in Ohio. The larvae feed on a variety of grasses such as purple-top (*Triodia* sp.) and love grass (*Eragrostis* sp.) in other areas (Howe, 1975). These are widespread grasses in Ohio (Braun, 1967).

ADULT ENERGY RESOURCES: Red clover (*Trifolium pratense* L.), thin-leaved sunflower (*Helianthus decapetalus* L.), coneflower (*Rudbeckia laciniata* L.), common milkweed (*Asclepias syriaca* L.), swamp thistle (*Cirsium muticum* Michx.), field thistle (*Cirsium discolor* [Muhl.] Spreng), bull thistle (*Cirsium vulgare* [Savi] Tenore), dame's rocket (*Hesperis matronalis* L.), wild cranesbill (*Geranium maculatum* L.), sweet alyssum (*Lobularia maritima* [L.] Desv.), chicory (*Cichorium intybus* L.), purple coneflower (*Echinacea purpurea* [L.] Moench), *Phlox* species, and ironweed (*Vernonia* sp.). Bales (1909) listed blackberry (*Rubus* sp.) as a nectar source for this species. Adults also imbibe moisture from damp soil and mud.

FLIGHT PERIOD: Two broods, the first flying during May to mid-June, the second primarily in August (Figure 8.74). Extreme dates range from 26 April through 18 September.

SIMILAR SPECIES: See *P. hobomok.*

GENERAL COMMENTS: The males of this species are tawny, but the females are always melanic. Unlike *P. hobomok,* there are never tawny females. *Poanes zabulon* is very similar to *P. hobomok,* and in the spring these two species often fly together. *Poanes zabulon* is double-brooded, but *P. hobomok* flies primarily in the spring. Hence all specimens found in mid-summer and later are generally referable to *P. zabulon.*

    Males perch on sunlit leaves and twigs, from which they investigate and pursue passing objects. Males often return to the same perch, which suggests that they may be territorial. Females are generally found at nectar or in more shaded areas. The flight of *P. zabulon* appears to be slightly more rapid than that of *P. hobomok.*

    Pilate (1882), Bales (1909), Henninger (1910), and Wyss (1932) incorrectly associated the form name 'pocahantas' (= *P. hobomok* melanic females) with *P. zabulon.* This may have been due to errors in the literature of the period (eg Holland, 1898).

LITERATURE RECORD: Van Wert County (Lepidopterists' Society, 1984).

Poanes viator viator (W.H. Edwards, 1865). Broad-winged Skipper. Plate 12.

Fig. 8.75 *Poanes viator.*

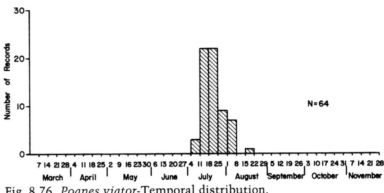

Fig. 8.76 *Poanes viator*-Temporal distribution.

STATUS: Resident; uncommon.

DISTRIBUTION/RANGE: Scattered localities throughout the northern half of the State (Figure 8.75).

HABITAT: This skipper inhabits a variety of wetland habitats such as sedge meadows, fens, swamps, and scrubby marshes.

HOSTPLANT(S): In Ohio this species has been reared on the sedge, *Carex lacustris* Willd., under greenhouse conditions. This and other species of broad-leaved sedges are also probably used in nature. *Carex rostrata* Stokes, a sedge known from scattered locations in Ohio (Braun, 1967), has been reported as a foodplant elsewhere (Scott, 1986). Adults are usually associated with broad-leaved sedges like *Carex lacustris* in the field (Shuey, 1985).

ADULT ENERGY RESOURCES: Common milkweed (*Asclepias syriaca* L.), swamp milkweed (*Asclepias incarnata* L.), alfalfa (*Medicago sativa* L.), wild bergamot (*Monarda fistulosa* L.), blazing star (*Liatris spicata* [L.] Willd.), and vetchling (*Lathyrus palustris* L.).

FLIGHT PERIOD: One brood, flying primarily in July (Figure 8.76). Extreme dates range from 7 July through 20 August.

GENERAL COMMENTS: Populations of this skipper are very localized, but scattered throughout the northern counties. Although this species is usually uncommon, it can be locally common, particularly in small, restricted areas of sedge. It tends to prefer sedges that are partially shaded, and is sometimes associated with *Euphyes dukesi*.

The flight of this skipper is weak, bobbing, and somewhat meandering, creating the illusion that it drops several centimeters between each wing beat. Like *P. massasoit*, *P. viator* flies through the sedges rather than over them, and can be difficult to follow visually. Alarmed individuals fly rapidly over the sedges. Both sexes perch on sedges, but males usually patrol through sedges, probably in search of mates.

This species is probably more widespread in northern Ohio than our records indicate, and continued efforts to search likely habitats should increase the number of counties from which this skipper is known.

LITERATURE RECORD: Ashtabula County (Lepidopterists' Society, 1984).

Euphyes dion (W.H. Edwards, 1879). Dion Skipper. Plate 12.

Fig. 8.77 *Euphyes dion.*

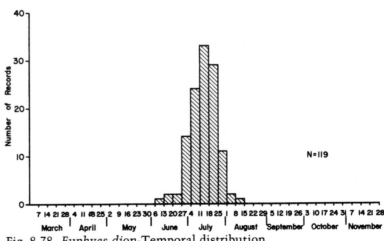

Fig. 8.78 *Euphyes dion*-Temporal distribution.

STATUS: Resident; uncommon to common.

DISTRIBUTION/RANGE: Northern Ohio (Figure 8.77).

57

HABITAT: This skipper occurs in a variety of open wetlands, including sedge meadows, fens, bogs, marshes, and roadside ditches. Within glaciated Ohio, this species can be expected almost anywhere its hostplants occur.

HOSTPLANT(S): In Ohio, this species has been found and reared on the sedge, *Carex lacustris* Willd. It undoubtedly feeds on other species of sedges, as *C. lacustris* is absent from several *E. dion* localities. *Carex hyalinolepis* Steud., *Carex stricta* Lam., and wool grass, *Scirpus cyperinus* [L.] Kunth., are used in other parts of its range (Opler and Krizek, 1984). All of these sedges are widespread in Ohio (Braun, 1967), and could be used as foodplants.

ADULT ENERGY RESOURCES: Common milkweed (*Asclepias syriaca* L.), swamp milkweed (*Asclepias incarnata* L.), Sullivant's milkweed (*Asclepias sullivantii* Engelm.), Canada thistle (*Cirsium arvense* [L.] Scop.), bull thistle (*Cirsium vulgare* [Savi] Tenore), pickerelweed (*Pontederia cordata* L.), buttonbush (*Cephalanthus occidentalis* L.), teasel (*Dipsacus sylvestris* Huds.), and vetchling (*Lathyrus palustris* L.).

FLIGHT PERIOD: One brood, flying primarily in July (Figure 8.78). Extreme dates range from 10 June through 12 August.

SIMILAR SPECIES: See *E. dukesi*.

GENERAL COMMENTS: This species is the most common and widespread of the large sedge-feeding skippers in Ohio. It can be found almost anywhere within its range where sunny stands of sedges occur. It often occurs in sedge patches as small as six meters in diameter, or in sedge-filled ditches, one to two meters wide.
　　Adults are powerful and rapid fliers. Males perch on the tops of sedges and chase after nearby passing objects. Females usually settle lower in the sedges, and are more difficult to observe. Both sexes are wary and hard to approach unless visiting nectar sources. Generally, adults are not seen far from wetlands.

Euphyes dukesi (**Lindsey, 1923**). Duke's Skipper. Plate 12.

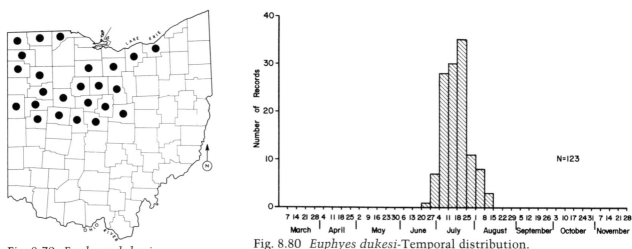

Fig. 8.79　*Euphyes dukesi*.

Fig. 8.80　*Euphyes dukesi*-Temporal distribution.

STATUS: Resident; uncommon. Although populations are localized, they can reach high densities.

DISTRIBUTION/RANGE: Primarily the black swamp area of northwestern Ohio (Figure 8.79).

HABITAT: This species is restricted to shaded swamps where *Carex lacustris* Willd. and other wide-leaved sedges occur. It is occasionally encountered in open areas at nectar.

HOSTPLANT(S): In Ohio, this species has been found and reared on *Carex lacustris* Willd.; and is usually associated with this sedge in the field. South of Ohio, it also uses *Carex hyalinolepis* Steud. (Opler and Krizek, 1984). This sedge is widespread in northwestern Ohio (Braun, 1967), and may also be used as a foodplant.

ADULT ENERGY RESOURCES: Alfalfa (*Medicago sativa* L.), red clover (*Trifolium pratense* L.), common milkweed (*Asclepias syriaca* L.), swamp milkweed (*Asclepias incarnata* L.), and buttonbush (*Cephalanthus occidentalis* L.).

FLIGHT PERIOD: One brood, flying primarily in July (Figure 8.80). A second brood is produced when larvae are reared under natural photoperiods in greenhouse conditions. Extreme dates range from 26 June through 10 August. A natural second brood is produced in September in western Kentucky (Charles V. Covell, Jr., pers comm, 1982).

SIMILAR SPECIES: Females of *E. dion* are similar, but the blunt forewing tips and darker ground color of *E. dukesi* females will separate these species.

GENERAL COMMENTS: This species is much more common and widespread in Ohio than was once generally believed. For years after its initial discovery, it was considered to be one of the rarest species in the country, and newly discovered populations were well documented (Pliske, 1957[58]; Mather, 1963). It was not reported from Ohio until 1940 (Mather, 1963). The mosquito-infested swamps it inhabits and the localized nature of its populations have definitely led to its being overlooked in the past.

In central Ohio, populations exist in patchwork form along neglected railroad rights-of-way through swampy woodlands, and in small natural clearings within woodlands. These populations generally occur in low densities. In northwestern Ohio, populations generally achieve higher densities.

This skipper has a slower flight than other *Euphyes* species. Males seem to patrol over, and perch on sedges when seeking potential mates. Females fly lower through the sedges. Both sexes are attracted to nectar, especially buttonbush (*Cephalanthus occidentalis* L.). Although the primary habitat is densely shaded, individuals will fly into adjacent sedge meadows or alfalfa fields to visit nectar sources.

Continued investigation of swamps in central Ohio should yield additional populations of this species. This skipper should be looked for in areas where *Carex lacustris* grows in shaded situations.

The discovery of this skipper in 1980 in Findley State Park by Leland L. Martin prompted the Ohio Department of Natural Resources to establish the Duke's Skipper Butterfly Sanctuary. This sanctuary is the first of its type in Ohio.

LITERATURE RECORDS: None.

Euphyes conspicua conspicua (Edwards, 1863). Black Dash. Plate 13.

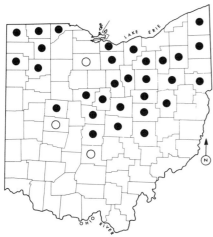

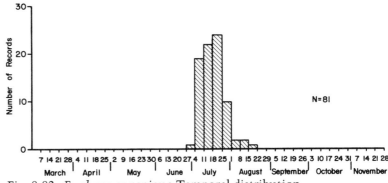

Fig. 8.82 *Euphyes conspicua*-Temporal distribution.

STATUS: Resident; uncommon. The localized populations of this species are most numerous in the northern portion of its Ohio range, where it is sometimes locally common.

Fig. 8.81 *Euphyes conspicua*.

DISTRIBUTION/RANGE: There are scattered records over the northern half of the State (Figure 8.81).

HABITAT: This skipper can be found in bogs, fens, sedge meadows, and wet prairies.

HOSTPLANT(S): Although no hostplant has been recorded in Ohio, this species is associated with the sedge *Carex stricta* Lam., and other narrow-leaved sedges. Although *C. stricta* is the only reported foodplant for this skipper, attempts to rear *E. conspicua* on this sedge in Ohio have been unsuccessful.

ADULT ENERGY RESOURCES: Common milkweed (*Asclepias syriaca* L.), swamp milkweed (*Asclepias incarnata* L.), wild bergamot (*Monarda fistulosa* L.), pickerel-weed (*Pontederia cordata* L.), and vetchling (*Lathyrus palustris* L.).

FLIGHT PERIOD: One brood, peaking in July (Figure 8.82). Extreme dates range from 2 July through 20 August.

SIMILAR SPECIES: Although several species are superficially similar (*Euphyes dion, Polites mystic,* and female *Atalopedes campestris*), the large pale patch on the ventral hindwing of *E. conspicua* will reliably separate this species from the others.

GENERAL COMMENTS: In the areas of northeastern and northwestern Ohio, where sedge meadows and fens are more common, this skipper occurs in almost every seemingly suitable habitat. At the southern edge of its range in Ohio, populations are widely scattered and difficult to find.

Adults are less wary than the other *Euphyes* species, and are more easily observed. The flight of this species is rapid and usually within one meter of the ground. Males perch on sedge tops and dart out at passing objects, whereas females rest lower in the sedges or fly weakly through them.

LITERATURE RECORDS: Pickaway (Bales, 1909), Seneca (Henninger, 1910), and Champaign (Albrecht, 1982) Counties.

Pilate (1882) recorded this species from Montgomery County, but his record was based on a misdetermined series of *Polites mystic*.

Euphyes bimacula bimacula (Grote & Robinson, 1867). Two-spotted Skipper. Plate 13.

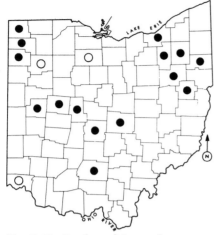

Fig. 8.83 *Euphyes bimacula.*

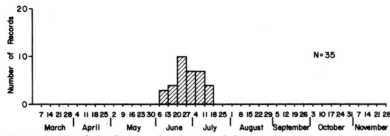

Fig. 8.84 *Euphyes bimacula*-Temporal distribution.

STATUS: Resident; rare. The few known populations are extremely localized and occur at low densities.

DISTRIBUTION/RANGE: Widely scattered localities throughout glaciated Ohio (Figure 8.83).

HABITAT: This species is restricted to sedge meadows and fens.

HOSTPLANT(S): Although no hostplant has been recorded in Ohio, *E. bimacula* is always associated with dense stands of sedges, particularly *Carex stricta* Lam. In New York, this skipper feeds on *Carex trichocarpa* Muhl. (Shapiro, 1974). Although this sedge occurs in scattered localities throughout the State (Braun, 1967), it has not been reported from all the counties where *E. bimacula* has been recorded. It is likely that this skipper feeds on several species of sedge in Ohio.

ADULT ENERGY RESOURCES: Common milkweed (*Asclepias syriaca* L.), swamp milkweed (*Asclepias incarnata* L.), and Indian hemp (*Apocynum cannabinum* L.). In Michigan, blue flag (*Irus versicolor* L.) is commonly visited (John W. Peacock, pers comm, 1989).

FLIGHT PERIOD: One brood flying from mid-June through mid-July (Figure 8.84). Extreme dates range from 9 June through 17 July.

SIMILAR SPECIES: *Polites origenes* is superficially similar, but the white fringed hindwings and the light veins on the ventral hindwing of *E. bimacula* are distinctive.

GENERAL COMMENTS: This species is the rarest of our wetland skippers and very little is known about its hostplants or habitat associations (Shuey, 1985). From the few specimens collected in the past 25 years (fewer than 20), it is apparent that this skipper has declined from years past. Claypole (1897), Baker (unpublished notes, ca 1950), and Price (1970) all found this species to be common at times, and Price and Baker both included large series of *E. bimacula* with their collections. Although the early flight period of this species relative to other wetland butterflies may limit the number of collectors that encounter it, the most likely reason for its rarity may be the lack of suitable habitats. This species occupies a limited number of wetlands relative to other sedge-feeding skippers, indicating that its needs are more limited. Massive draining and filling of wetlands have occurred in the past 35 years, and it is likely that *E. bimacula* has suffered to a greater extent than most wetland butterflies from this habitat loss. The recently renewed interest of many lepidopterists in wetland butterflies may increase the number of known populations as more wetlands are investigated.

This skipper seems to be most active in the late morning, and tends to avoid flying during the heat of the day. It flies less frequently than other wetland skippers, and is more likely to be flushed out of the sedges than observed flying about. Males perch on sedge tops and investigate passing objects, but generally do not fly far before they settle back into the sedges. Adults will fly into adjacent fields to search for nectar sources.

LITERATURE RECORDS: Hamilton (Hine, 1898a), Putnam (Price, 1970), and Seneca (Henninger, 1910) Counties.

Euphyes vestris metacomet (Harris, 1862). Dun Skipper. Plate 13.

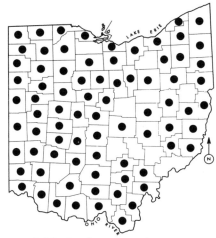

Fig. 8.85 *Euphyes vestris.*

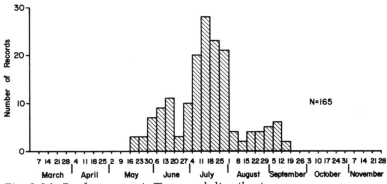

Fig. 8.86 *Euphyes vestris*-Temporal distribution.

STATUS: Resident; common.

DISTRIBUTION/RANGE: Statewide (Figure 8.85).

HABITAT: This skipper is associated with open areas. Typical habitats include meadows, prairie remnants, alfalfa and clover fields, old fields, powerline cuts, roadsides, woodland edges and clearings, sedge meadows, and fens.

HOSTPLANT(S): In Ohio, a larva of this species has been found and reared on *Carex stricta* Lam., a common sedge in fens. It undoubtedly feeds on other upland sedges as well. Sedges may be the only hosts (Opler and Krizek, 1984; Heitzman, 1964).

ADULT ENERGY RESOURCES: Red clover (*Trifolium pratense* L.), white clover (*Trifolium repens* L.), common milkweed (*Asclepias syriaca* L.), swamp milkweed (*Asclepias incarnata* L.), fleabane (*Erigeron* sp.), thistles (*Cirsium* spp.), dogbane (*Apocynum* sp.), and teasel (*Dipsacus* sp.). Edward S. Thomas (unpublished notes) lists Indian hemp (*Apocynum cannabinum* L.) as a nectar source. Adults also visit damp soil and mud.

FLIGHT PERIOD: Probably two broods, with an occasional partial third brood. The first brood flies in mid-May to mid-June, the second in July, and the third in August and September (Figure 8.86). Extreme dates range from 17 May through 13 September.

SIMILAR SPECIES: Females of *Pompeius verna*, *Wallengrenia egeremet*, *Polites origenes*, and *Polites themistocles* can all be confused with females of *E. vestris* (See Table, p. 49). However, all of these species have spines on their middle tibiae (visible with a hand lens), whereas the middle tibiae of *E. vestris* are smooth.

GENERAL COMMENTS: This is the most common and widespread *Euphyes* in Ohio. Pilate (1882) considered this species to be rare, but today this species is well adapted to many human-modified habitats, and may have increased in abundance since Pilate collected. This species, along with those listed as similar species, is one of the truly ubiquitous skippers in Ohio.

The flight of this species is rapid and usually close to the ground. Males perch on blades of grass in open habitats and on sunlit twigs and leaves in forest openings. Males fly out at passing objects, presumably in search of potential mates. Both sexes are strongly attracted to nectar sources.

LITERATURE RECORDS: None.

Atrytonopsis hianna hianna (Scudder, 1868). Dusted Skipper. Plate 13.

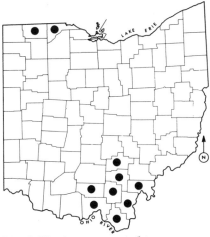

Fig. 8.87 *Atrytonopsis hianna.*

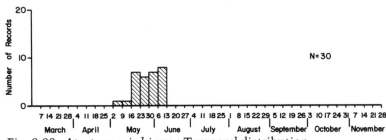

Fig. 8.88 *Atrytonopsis hianna*-Temporal distribution.

STATUS: Resident; uncommon. In the Oak Openings (Lucas and Fulton Counties) this species is locally common. This skipper was only recently discovered in southern Ohio, and is much more uncommon there.

DISTRIBUTION/RANGE: This species is disjunctly distributed in Ohio, and is found in the hill country of southern Ohio and in the Oak Openings of northwestern Ohio. (Figure 8.87).

HABITAT: In the Oak Openings, this species is associated with prairies and savannas where *Andropogon* grasses are common. In southern Ohio, this species is associated with xeric openings where *Andropogon scoparius* Michx. is common. Typical habitats include dry hillsides, powerline cuts, and ridgetop clearings.

HOSTPLANT(S): In Lucas County, this species has been observed ovipositing on little bluestem (*Andropogon scoparius* Michx.). This grass and big bluestem (*Andropogon gerardi* Vitman) are the only reported foodplants (Shapiro, 1965; Heitzman and Heitzman, 1974). Both of these grasses are widespread in Ohio (Braun, 1967).

ADULT ENERGY RESOURCES: Red clover (*Trifolium pratense* L.), dwarf dandelion (*Krigia biflora* [Walt.] Blake), goat's-beard (*Tragopogon* sp.), brambles (*Rubus* sp.), Russian olive (*Elaeagnus angustifolia* L.), cinquefoil (*Potentilla* sp.), and purple vetch (*Vicia americana* Muhl.).

FLIGHT PERIOD: One brood, flying from mid-May through early June (Figure 8.88). Extreme dates range from 4 May through 12 June.

SIMILAR SPECIES: Female *Euphyes vestris* are superficially similar, but the more pointed forewing apex and spined middle tibiae (visible with a hand lens) of *A. hianna* will separate these two species.

GENERAL COMMENTS: This is another of the spring skippers that is overlooked because of the seemingly unproductive habitat in which it occurs. The bluestems (*Andropogon* spp.) that dominate these habitats look dead until early summer because dead blades from the previous season obscure new growth until then. Most lepidopterists avoid these fields in favor of the more productive woodlands and other areas in early spring, thus overlooking this species (and *Hesperia metea*).

This skipper was only recently discovered in southern Ohio (Calhoun, 1985[86]), where it is very local and usually uncommon. As more collectors search for this species, it will probably be found to occur in additional southern counties. Although Price (1970) considered this skipper to be rare in the Oak Openings, we have found it to be locally common in xeric fields dominated by prairie grasses.

Shapiro (1966) noted that *Atrytonopsis hianna* usually occurs in the same habitats as *Hesperia metea*. So far these species have been found together only in Lucas, Vinton, and Hocking Counties, although they probably co-exist throughout most of their Ohio ranges. Where occurring together, these species' flight periods overlap only briefly. *Hesperia metea* appears first and is usually gone or very worn by the time *A. hianna* appears on the wing (Figures 8.50 and 8.88).

This species has probably always been present in southern Ohio, but overlooked until recently. The recent practice of maintaining powerline cuts through forested areas has created abundant habitats for this skipper. Conversely, Shapiro (1966) noted that this species is very vagrant, and often disperses from suitable habitats. He speculated that this could be an adaptation for locating new habitats as current habitats become unsuitable through natural succession. Thus it is also conceivable that the species may have only recently colonized southern Ohio from adjacent areas.

The flight of this skipper is fast and erratic. Both sexes perch on exposed soil and dead blades of grass. Males dart out to investigate passing objects, but do not usually return to their original perch. When flushed from these perches, males tend to fly rapidly off into the distance whereas females usually settle just a few meters from their original perch.

LITERATURE RECORDS: None.

Hoying (1975) listed this species from Shelby County (near Egypt), but his record was based on a misdetermined female *Euphyes vestris*.

Amblyscirtes hegon (Scudder, 1864). Pepper and Salt Skipper. Plate 13.

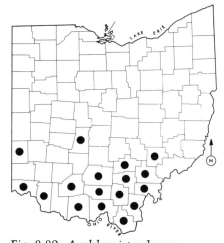

Fig. 8.89 *Amblyscirtes hegon*.

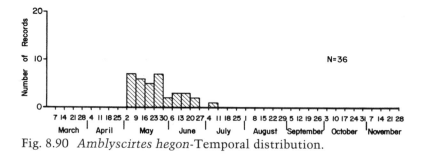

Fig. 8.90 *Amblyscirtes hegon*-Temporal distribution.

STATUS : Resident; uncommon to rare.

DISTRIBUTION/RANGE: This species is found only in southern Ohio (Figure 8.89). Opler and Krizek (1984) indicated that its overall range closely approaches the northeastern and northwestern corners of Ohio, and it is conceivable that this species may eventually be found in these portions of the State.

HABITAT: This species is usually found in openings within forests, along wood land roads, and in fields adjacent to forests.

HOSTPLANT(S): Not known in Ohio. Various grasses, including Kentucky bluegrass (*Poa pratensis* L.), Indian grass (*Sorghastrum nutans* [L.] Nash), and broadleaf uniola (*Uniola latifolia* Michx.) are used in other portions of its range (Opler and Krizek, 1984). All of these grasses occur in Ohio (Braun, 1967).

ADULT ENERGY RESOURCES: Blackberry and other brambles (*Rubus* spp.). Adults also visit damp soil and mud.

FLIGHT PERIOD: One brood, flying in May and June (Figure 8.90). Extreme dates range from 4 May through 4 July.

SIMILAR SPECIES: Both *Amblyscirtes vialis* and *A. belli* can be confused with this skipper. *Amblyscirtes hegon* can be identified by its more extensive pattern above and below, especially the ventral hindwing postmedial spots, which are well developed and form a thin linear band. In *A. belli*, the ventral hindwing postmedial band is curved and broken into faint spots. The ventral hindwing postmedial band is absent in *A vialis*.

GENERAL COMMENTS: This species is probably more widespread in Ohio than present records indicate, especially in the Unglaciated Plateau. Clement W. Baker (unpublished notes) listed this species from Stark and Carroll Counties, over 100 km northeast of our nearest records. Unfortunately a review of his collection failed to locate these specimens.

Adults are usually seen flying beneath the forest understory and males often perch on sunlit leaves, especially in small sunlit openings within the forest itself. The flight of this species is rapid and difficult to follow visually. However, males usually return to the vicinity of their original perch. *Amblyscirtes hegon* is easily overlooked because of its small size, its low erratic flight, and its spring flight period.

The type locality of *Hesperia nemoris* W.H. Edwards, 1864, a synonym of *A. hegon*, was originally Portsmouth, Ohio (Scioto County). Miller and Brown (1981) amended the type locality to 3 miles (approximately 5k) east of Zaleski, Vinton County, Ohio.

LITERATURE RECORDS: None.

Amblyscirtes vialis (W.H. Edwards, 1862). Roadside Skipper. Plate 13.

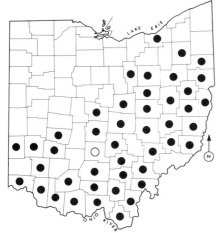

Fig. 8.91 *Amblyscirtes vialis*.

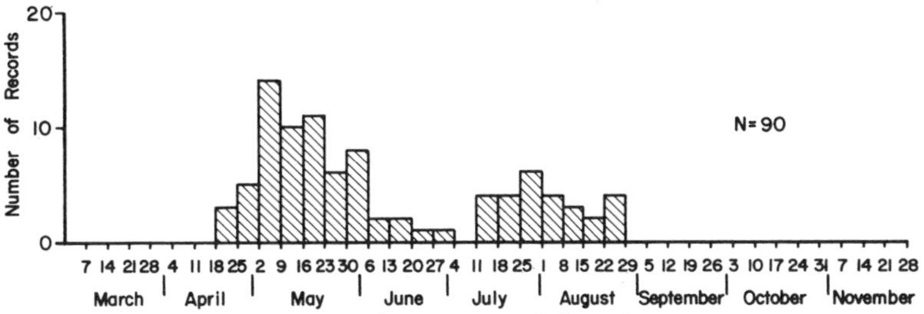

Fig. 8.92 *Amblyscirtes vialis*-Temporal distribution.

STATUS: Resident; common to uncommon. Most of our records are from southeastern Ohio, where this species can be locally common. In northeastern Ohio, this species is decidedly uncommon.

DISTRIBUTION/RANGE: The southern and eastern portions of the State (Figure 8.91).

HABITAT: This species is usually found in open deciduous woodlands, along woodland roads, and along woodland margins. It is occasionally found in shrubby old fields.

HOSTPLANT(S): Not known in Ohio. The larvae feed on a variety of grasses throughout its range. Bluegrasses (*Poa* spp.) and bent grasses (*Agrostis* spp.) are used in Pennsylvania (Shapiro, 1966). Both of these grass genera are widespread in Ohio (Braun, 1967).

ADULT ENERGY RESOURCES: White clover (*Trifolium repens* L.) and blackberries (*Rubus* spp.). This species also visits damp soil and mud.

FLIGHT PERIOD: Two broods, the first flying from late April through early June, the second from mid-July through August (Figure 8.92). Extreme dates range from 19 April through 27 August.

SIMILAR SPECIES: *Amblyscirtes hegon* and *A. belli* (see *A. hegon*). In flight this species strongly resembles *Pholisora catullus*, but once either of these insects are in hand, they are easily separated.

GENERAL COMMENTS: Although usually encountered in low numbers, this skipper can be locally common, especially in southern Ohio. Its small size, drab color, and the localized nature of its populations have probably resulted in this skipper being overlooked by many lepidopterists. Most of the early collectors (eg Dury, 1878; Pilate, 1882; Bales, 1909) may have considered it to be rare for these reasons.

This skipper flies rapidly, erratically, and close to the ground, making it difficult to follow visually. Adults perch on dried leaves, low vegetation, exposed soil, and small rocks along woodland trails. They are very wary and difficult to approach. When at rest, the wings are held at an angle or together above the body.

Although this species is apparently absent from northwestern Ohio and adjacent areas of Indiana and Michigan (Opler and Krizek, 1984), it may occur there in very low numbers.

LITERATURE RECORD: Pickaway County (Bales, 1909).

Hoying (1975) listed this species from west-central Ohio, but his record was based on a misdetermined female *Pholisora catullus*.

Amblyscirtes belli H.A. Freeman, 1941. Bell's Roadside Skipper. Plate 13.

Fig. 8.93 *Amblyscirtes belli.*

STATUS: Uncertain, possibly a resident; rare. Only one specimen from Ohio is known.

DISTRIBUTION/RANGE: In the eastern United States, this is a skipper of the mid-south that occurs northward at least to Louisville, Kentucky along the Ohio River (Opler and Krizek, 1984). The Ohio record is from Elk Lick, Clermont County (Figure 8.93).

HABITAT: In Kentucky, this species is found in forest clearings and in fields near forests (Charles V. Covell, Jr., pers comm, 1985). In Missouri it is found in moist ravines where the foodplant grows (Heitzman, 1965a).

HOSTPLANT(S): Not known in Ohio. Broadleaf uniola, *Uniola latifolia* Michx., is the foodplant in Missouri (Heitzman, 1965a), and it may serve as the host in Ohio as well. This grass is common along the Ohio River and its feeder streams in the southern part of the State (Braun, 1967), and is most often encountered in moist woodlands and along shaded river and stream banks.

ADULT ENERGY RESOURCES: None recorded for Ohio.

FLIGHT PERIOD: The single Ohio specimen, dated April 1938, was collected by Frank W. Case (deposited in the Cincinnati Museum of Natural History). In Missouri there are several broods which fly from mid-April to mid-September (Heitzman and Heitzman, 1987).

SIMILAR SPECIES: *Amblyscirtes vialis* and *A. hegon* (see *A. hegon*).

GENERAL COMMENTS: The single Ohio record represents the farthest northeast that this species has been found. Although this record could represent a stray, the early season capture date and the specimen's good wing condition suggest that it emerged locally. The reported foodplant is locally common in the county where it was captured, increasing the probability that the specimen originated there.

The small size of *A. belli* and its general resemblance to other *Amblyscirtes* could lead collectors to overlook it. If it is a resident in Ohio, it is probably limited to the extreme southwestern portion, an area where few lepidopterists have ventured in recent years. Collectors should search in moist forests and along wooded stream banks where the foodplant occurs.

Some authors consider *A. belli* to be a subspecies of *Amblyscirtes celia* (Skinner, 1895).

LITERATURE RECORDS: None.

Lerodea eufala (W.H. Edwards, 1869). Eufala Skipper. Plate 13.

Fig. 8.94 *Lerodea eufala.*

STATUS: Stray; rare. Only one Ohio specimen is known.

DISTRIBUTION/RANGE: In the eastern United States, *L. eufala* is resident from coastal South Carolina, south through Florida and west to Texas. Although this species emigrates northward each summer, its seasonal expansion does not include Ohio (Opler and Krizek, 1984). Strays have been reported from as far north as Minnesota (Opler and Krizek, 1984), Michigan (Mogens C. Nielsen, pers comm, 1985), and Indiana (Shull, 1987). The single Ohio specimen is from Wooster, Wayne County (Figure 8.94).

HABITAT: Within its normal range this skipper is usually associated with open disturbed habitats, such as grassy fields, vacant lots, and residential areas. Presumably, it would occur in similar situations in Ohio.

HOSTPLANT(S): Not known in Ohio. In other portions of its range, this skipper feeds on Johnson grass (*Sorghum halepense* [L.] Pers.) and sorghum (*Sorghum vulgare* Pers.) (Opler and Krizek, 1984). Both of these agriculturally associated plants occur in Ohio (Braun, 1967).

ADULT ENERGY RESOURCES: None recorded for Ohio.

FLIGHT PERIOD: The single specimen was captured on 17 June 1976.

SIMILAR SPECIES: *Nastra lherminier* is similar, but the white forewing spots will identify *L. eufala*.

GENERAL COMMENTS: Although this species had been reported from Ohio (Hoying, 1975), its occurrence was not verified until recently when a specimen was discovered in the United States National Museum collection. Our lone record probably represents a stray, because it is far removed from any area into which it emigrates.

In Ohio, it should be searched for in late summer and autumn in areas where nectar sources are abundant, such as clover and alfalfa fields. Its small size, dull coloration, and low erratic flight make it easy to overlook. It is doubtful that this species overwinters or reproduces in Ohio.

LITERATURE RECORDS: None.

Hoying (1975) reported this species from Auglaize County, but his record was based upon a misidentified female *Euphyes vestris metacomet*.

Calpodes ethlius (Stoll, 1782). Brazilian Skipper. Plate 13.

Fig. 8.95 *Calpodes ethlius*.

STATUS: Uncertain, either a transported introduction or a stray; rare. There is only one known capture of this species from Ohio.

DISTRIBUTION/RANGE: In eastern North America, *C. ethlius* is a permanent resident in only southern Florida and southern Texas. It periodically colonizes the Atlantic and Gulf Coasts and the Mississippi Valley (Opler and Krizek, 1984), but these populations presumably perish during severe winters. Strays are known as far north as Chicago, Illinois (Irwin and Downey, 1973) and New York (Shapiro, 1974). The single Ohio record is from Vinton County (Figure 8.95).

HABITAT: Where resident, this species is usually found in open areas where cannas (*Canna* spp.) grow. The single Ohio record was collected near a stand of cultivated canna (David K. Parshall, pers comm, 1985)

HOSTPLANT(S): Not known in Ohio. Cannas (*Canna* spp.) are the primary hosts in areas where this skipper is resident (Opler and Krizek, 1984).

ADULT ENERGY RESOURCES: Rough blazing star (*Liatris aspera* Michx.).

FLIGHT PERIOD: The single known specimen was collected on 31 July 1981 by David K. Parshall.

GENERAL COMMENTS: The only Ohio individual was taken near an ornamental planting of canna. Because canna is not usually hardy north of Georgia and must be replanted each year, it is possible that the specimen was imported as a larva on growing plants. Conversely, canna is also planted as a bulb, suggesting that the specimen may have arrived under its own power. Adults are extremely strong fliers and are certainly capable of reaching Ohio on their own. However it arrived, *C. ethlius* is not capable of surviving our winters. Large outdoor plantings of canna, especially in southern Ohio, should be examined during late summer and early autumn for the presence of *C. ethlius* larvae.

LITERATURE RECORDS: None.

Panoquina ocola (W.H. Edwards, 1863). Ocola Skipper. Plate 13.

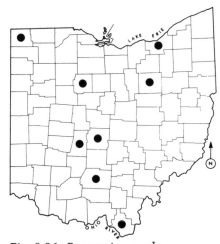

Fig. 8.96 *Panoquina ocola*.

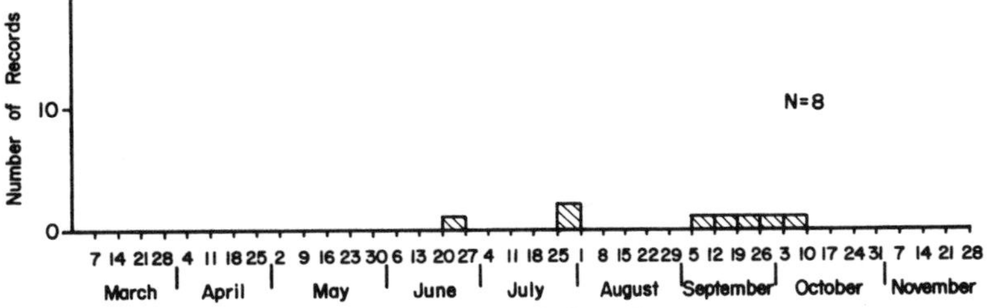

Fig. 8.97 *Panoquina ocola*-Temporal distribution.

STATUS: Irregular immigrant or stray; rare.

DISTRIBUTION/RANGE: Although this species is primarily a resident of tropical and subtropical habitats, it periodically strays as far north as Indiana, Pennsylvania, and Ohio (Opler and Krizek, 1984). Our few records are scattered statewide (Figure 8.96).

HABITAT: In Ohio, this skipper has been found in a variety of open habitats, including disturbed old fields, pastures, and prairies. Price (1970) collected his only specimen in a slough of the St. Joseph River.

HOSTPLANT(S): Not known for Ohio. Of the several recorded foodplants (Howe, 1975), only rice (*Oryza sativa* L.) is known from Ohio (Braun, 1967).

ADULT ENERGY RESOURCES: White *Aster* species.

FLIGHT PERIOD: Although there are no recognizable broods in Ohio (Figure 8.97), this species may be capable of producing at least one generation if immigrating females arrive early enough in the summer. Extreme dates range from 26 June through 7 October.

GENERAL COMMENTS: This species is probably more frequent in Ohio than our records suggest. Because of its dull color and small size, it can be easily overlooked.

It should be looked for in late summer and early autumn in open areas with an abundance of nectar sources (eg alfalfa and clover fields and open fields containing asters). Although the flight of this skipper is very fast and erratic, adults are easily observed at flowers. When resting, this skipper holds its wings slightly open or close together over its thorax, with the forewings pulled down inside the hindwings. This is another skipper that does not survive Ohio's cold winters. Although most of the known captures represent strays, the good wing condition of several specimens may indicate that they developed from eggs deposited in Ohio.

LITERATURE RECORDS: None.

Family PAPILIONIDAE-Swallowtails

Battus philenor philenor (Linnaeus, 1771). Pipevine Swallowtail. Plate 14.

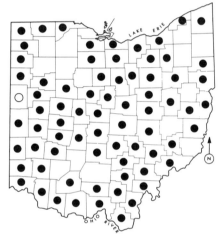

Fig. 8.98 *Battus philenor*.

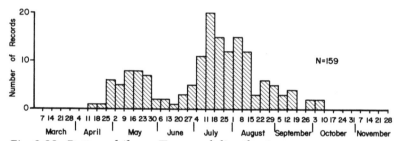

Fig. 8.99 *Battus philenor*-Temporal distribution.

STATUS: Resident; uncommon to common. This species is most frequently encountered in southern Ohio, becoming less common northward.

DISTRIBUTION/RANGE: Statewide (Figure 8.98).

HABITAT: This species is found in open woodlands, along roadsides through wooded areas, open fields, and occasionally in gardens. It is most commonly encountered in forested areas.

HOSTPLANT(S): This swallowtail uses various species of pipevines (Aristolochiaceae). In Ohio, it has been reported feeding on ornamental Dutchman's pipe (*Aristolochia durior* Hill) (Kirtland, 1854a), Virginia snakeroot (*Aristolochia serpentaria* L.) (Kirtland, 1851; Pilate, 1882), and wild ginger (*Asarum canadense* L.) (Hoying, 1975).

ADULT ENERGY RESOURCES: Alfalfa (*Medicago sativa* L.), red clover (*Trifolium pratense* L.), common milkweed (*Asclepias syriaca* L.), swamp milkweed (*Asclepias incarnata* L.), butterfly-weed (*Asclepias tuberosa* L.), Joe-Pye weed (*Eupatorium fistulosum* Barrett), teasel (*Dipsacus sylvestris* Huds.), bull thistle (*Cirsium vulgare* [Savi] Tenore), thistle (*Cirsium discolor* [Muhl.] Spreng), ironweed (*Vernonia* sp.), common blue phlox (*Phlox divaricata* L.), brambles (*Rubus* spp.), wild cranesbill (*Geranium maculatum* L.), and hawthorn (*Crataegus* sp.). Adults also imbibe moisture from moist soil and urine deposits. Males are often seen congregated at mud puddles in the early spring and during the summer.

FLIGHT PERIOD: Two, possibly three broods, with peaks in May and July (Figure 8.99). Extreme dates range from 16 April to 5 October.

SIMILAR SPECIES: *Papilio troilus* females are superficially similar, but use of the color plates will easily distinguish these species.

GENERAL COMMENTS: The pipevine swallowtail is unpalatable (distasteful) to potential predators, and serves as a Batesian model for five supposedly palatable species in Ohio (*Papilio troilus*, dark form female *P. glaucus*, *P. polyxenes*, *Limenitis arthemis astynax*, and female *Speyeria diana*). These species are probably attacked less often than most butterflies because predators mistake them for the unpalatable model.

The rarity of *B. philenor* in northern Ohio is probably a reflection of hostplant availability. In the past, this species was locally common throughout the State around home sites where Dutchman's pipe was planted. Kirtland (1854a) discovered that this previously rare butterfly became quite common around his home in Cleveland after he planted the hostplant. Bracher (1976) made the same observation in northeastern Ohio. The decline of this species in northern Ohio is thus probably the result of discontinued cultivation of Dutchman's pipe as an ornamental vine.

66

The flight of this species is usually low (1-1.5 m) and fairly rapid. In flight, adults are wary and often difficult to observe but the species visits flowers readily. Adults may roost communally.

This species is often referred to as the blue swallowtail because of the bright blue metallic sheen on the dorsal hindwings.

LITERATURE RECORD: Mercer County (Price, 1970).

Eurytides marcellus marcellus (Cramer, 1777). Zebra Swallowtail. Plate 14.

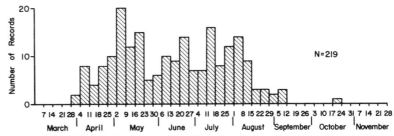

Fig. 8.101 *Eurytides marcellus*-Temporal distribution.

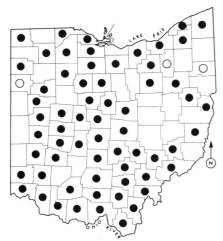

Fig. 8.100 *Eurytides marcellus*.

STATUS: Resident; uncommon to common. This species is most frequently seen in southern Ohio, becoming less common and more localized northward. There are very few known populations in the northern third of the State.

DISTRIBUTION/RANGE: Statewide (Figure 8.100).

HABITAT: This species is found in open deciduous forest, along woodland roads and trails, and in wet woodlands where its hostplant, pawpaw (*Asimina triloba* [L.] Dunal) occurs. Adults will fly to open areas in search of nectar sources.

HOSTPLANT(S): In Ohio, this species has been found and reared on pawpaw (*Asimina triloba* [L.] Dunal). Species of pawpaws are the only known host. Pawpaw is an understory tree in rich deciduous forests, usually occurring along streams or in other wet areas. Although females usually deposit their eggs on the leaves of pawpaw, Leland L. Martin (pers comm, 1987) saw a female deposit an egg on a blade of grass near the base of a pawpaw tree.

ADULT ENERGY RESOURCES: Red clover (*Trifolium pratense* L.), loosestrife (*Lythrum salicaria* L.), butterfly-weed (*Asclepias tuberosa* L.), American ipecac (*Gillenia stipulata* [Muhl.] Trel.), brambles (*Rubus* spp.), *Phlox* sp., redbud (*Cercis canadensis* L.), and cut-leaved toothwort (*Dentaria laciniata* Muhl.). Adults take moisture from damp soil, sand, gravel, and urine deposits, presumably to obtain salts and amino acids. Males are often seen congregating at puddles in early spring.

FLIGHT PERIOD: Two to three broods, possibly with an occasional partial fourth brood in southern Ohio, with peaks in April-May, June-July, and August (Figure 8.101). Extreme dates range from 2 April to 23 October (late).

GENERAL COMMENTS: This species is closely associated with its hostplant, pawpaw, and its rarity in northern Ohio is a reflection of the decreasing abundance of this shrub throughout this region. Many populations of *E. marcellus* in central and northern Ohio inhabit small second growth woodlots. These populations are sensitive to human disturbance, and generally become extinct in the wake of housing developments. It seems likely that this species rarely finds and repopulates the suitable second growth habitats that occur in highly urbanized and agricultural areas.

This species has three distinctive seasonal phenotypes. The early spring brood, form 'marcellus', is the smallest and lightest of the forms. It has shorter tails, the least extensive black markings, and the most extensive red spots of the phenotypes. Individuals from late spring, form 'telamonides' (C. & R. Felder, 1864) are larger, have more extensive black markings, smaller red spots, and more extensive white on the tail tips than does the early spring phenotype. Form 'lecontei' (Rothschild and Jordan, 1906), the summer form, is the largest and darkest of the phenotypes. The white bands and red spots on the wings are greatly restricted. The tails of this form are extremely long and have the most extensive white scaling of all the forms. This species seems to decrease in abundance as the season progresses, and form 'lecontei' is collected less frequently than the other two forms.

The flight of this species is fast and erratic. In the spring, most adults are seen hilltopping in forested areas, but in the summer they are most often encountered in fields adjacent to woodlands. Both sexes are easily observed at flowers.

LITERATURE RECORDS: Summit (Claypole, 1880; 1897; Kirtland, 1854a), Mahoning (Kirtland, 1854a), and Van Wert (Lepidopterists' Society, 1976) Counties.

67

Papilio polyxenes asterius Stoll, 1782. Black Swallowtail. Plate 14.

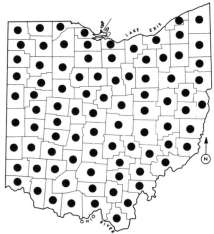

Fig. 8.102 *Papilio polyxenes*.

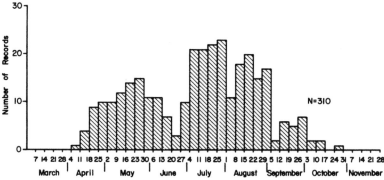

Fig. 8.103 *Papilio polyxenes*-Temporal distribution.

STATUS: Resident; common.

DISTRIBUTION/RANGE: Statewide (Figure 8.102). This species has been recorded from all 88 counties.

HABITAT: Virtually any open habitat. This species can be found in old fields, pastures, along roadsides, in meadows, and flower gardens.

HOSTPLANT(S): This species uses virtually any cultivated or wild member of the carrot family, Apiaceae. In Ohio, it has been found and reared on wild and cultivated carrot (*Daucus carota* L.), parsley (*Petroselinum crispum* [Mill.] Nym.), cultivated celery (*Apium graveolens* L.), and wild parsnip (*Pastinaca sativa* L.). Scriber and Finke (1978) considered *Daucus carota* L. to be the primary host in west-central Ohio. It has also been reported from dill (*Anethum graveolens* L.) (Price, 1970), fennel (*Foeniculum vulgare* Mill.) (Kirtland, 1854a), poison-hemlock (*Conium maculatum* L.) (Kirtland, 1854a), bulb-bearing water-hemlock (*Cicuta bulbifera* L.) (Scriber and Finke, 1978), angelica (*Angelica atropurpurea* L.) (Scriber and Finke, 1978), honewort (*Cryptotaenia canadensis* L.) (Scriber and Finke, 1978), and cultivated anise (*Pimpinella anisum* L.) (Studebaker and Studebaker, 1967). This butterfly can be a pest in gardens and truck farms which specialize in crops such as carrots, celery, dill, and parsley. The larva is sometimes referred to as the "parsley worm".

Webster (1900b) reported larvae on the composite, cosmos (*Cosmos* sp.). Larvae of closely related species of *Papilio* have been reported to eat Asteraceae (Scott, 1986), so this may represent a valid record.

ADULT ENERGY RESOURCES: Alfalfa (*Medicago sativa* L.), red clover (*Trifolium pratense* L.), common milkweed (*Asclepias syriaca* L.), swamp milkweed (*Asclepias incarnata* L.), thistle (*Cirsium discolor* [Muhl.] Spreng.), purple coneflower (*Echinacea purpurea* [L.] Moench), winter cress (*Barbarea vulgaris* R. Br.), teasel (*Dipsacus sylvestris* Huds.), and ironweed (*Vernonia* sp.). Adults also gather at damp soil and mud puddles to imbibe moisture.

FLIGHT PERIOD: Two broods, with an occasional partial third brood, with major peaks in May, July, and August (Figure 8.103). Extreme dates range from 4 April to 24 October.

SIMILAR SPECIES: None. The wing pattern will differentiate this butterfly from all other Ohio swallowtails. However, collectors should watch for *Papilio joanae*, a closely related and very similar species not yet reported for Ohio (see Chapter 9).

GENERAL COMMENTS: This is one of the species that has undoubtedly benefited from human disturbance of the original countryside. The most frequently used hostplants, wild and domestic carrots, are naturalized plants that owe their presence in Ohio to human intervention. Before the forests were cleared, this species was probably restricted to prairies, wetlands, and other openings in the forest.

The flight of this species is rapid, erratic, and close to the ground. It tends to be more wary than our other swallowtails and can be difficult to capture. Males are territorial (Lederhouse, 1982) and actively defend small territories in open fields, especially on hilltops. The males often perch on the tallest herbaceous vegetation present within their territories and fly out to investigate other passing butterflies. Both sexes are avid flower visitors, and are easily observed while they are feeding.

LITERATURE RECORDS: None.

Papilio cresphontes Cramer, 1777. Giant Swallowtail. Plate 15.

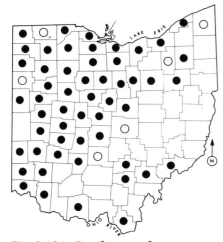

Fig. 8.104 *Papilio cresphontes*.

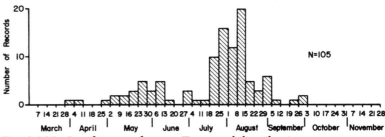

Fig. 8.105 *Papilio cresphontes*-Temporal distribution.

STATUS: Resident; uncommon. This species is most frequently seen in glaciated Ohio, and is rare in the unglaciated portion of the State. Populations are locally common in certain years.

DISTRIBUTION/RANGE: Statewide, but most of our records are from glaciated Ohio (Figure 8.104).

HABITAT: This species is found in open areas adjacent to woodlands and scrubby wetlands where the primary hostplant is common.

HOSTPLANT(S): This swallowtail uses various species of the rue family (Rutaceae). In Ohio, the primary host is prickly ash (*Xanthoxylum americanum* Mill.), but other reported hosts include hop tree (*Ptelea trifoliata* L.) (Hine, 1898b; John W. Peacock, pers comm, 1985), and Hercules club (*Aralia spinosa* L.) (Kirtland, 1854a). Clement W. Baker (unpublished notes) listed osage orange (*Maclura pomifera* [Raf.] Schneid.), a report that needs to be confirmed. Kirtland (1852b) also lists *Fraxinella* (= *Dictamnus albus* L.), gas plant, a cultivated member of the Rutaceae.

Females of the two broods apparently oviposit in different habitats (Mac Albin, pers comm, 1987). Spring brood females select plants in open areas, whereas summer brood females select plants in wooded areas. This may be a strategy to avoid placing larvae on plants which may be more likely to suffer water stress later in the season.

In Florida, larvae are sometimes a pest of citrus trees, and are called "orange dogs."

ADULT ENERGY RESOURCES: Alfalfa (*Medicago sativa* L.), red clover (*Trifolium pratense* L.), common milkweed (*Asclepias syriaca* L.), swamp milkweed (*Asclepias incarnata* L.), teasel (*Dipsacus sylvestris* Huds.), dame's rocket (*Hesperis matronalis* L.), appendaged waterleaf (*Hydrophyllum appendiculatum* Michx.), and ironweed (*Vernonia* sp.). Adults also visit damp soil, damp gravel, feces, and carrion.

FLIGHT PERIOD: Two broods in most years, with an occasional third brood (Figure 8.105). The second brood, which peaks in late July and early August, is more often encountered than the first. Extreme dates range from 2 April (early) to 30 September.

SIMILAR SPECIES: None.

GENERAL COMMENTS: This is our rarest swallowtail, especially in unglaciated Ohio. Populations are local, and usually only single individuals are found. However, populations fluctuate, and in good years, several adults may be observed especially around swamps where the primary hostplant can be locally common.

The flight of this species is strong and powerful, but seemingly effortless. When alarmed, this species is almost impossible to pursue. Males patrol regular flyways (along rivers, and woodland edges), flying back and forth 1.5 to 2.5 m above the ground. Both sexes are often encountered while sunning themselves in sunlit clearings or while they are visiting flowers.

LITERATURE RECORDS: Fulton (Hine, 1898b), Pickaway (Bales, 1909), Summit (Claypole, 1897), Van Wert (Lepidopterists' Society, 1975; 1976), Ashtabula (Robertson-Miller, 1912), and Licking (Albrecht, 1982) Counties.

Papilio glaucus glaucus Linnaeus, 1758. Tiger Swallowtail. Plates 15 and 16.

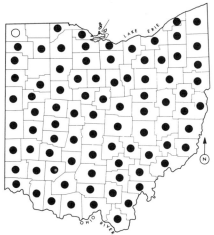

Fig. 8.106 *Papilio glaucus*.

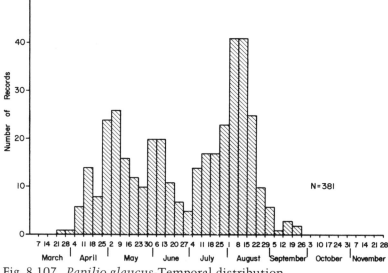

Fig. 8.107 *Papilio glaucus*-Temporal distribution.

STATUS: Resident; common.

DISTRIBUTION/RANGE: Statewide (Figure 8.106).

HABITAT: This butterfly is found almost anywhere that there is deciduous forest. Although it is most frequently encountered in wooded areas, it can be a common sight in old fields, clover and alfalfa fields, and in city yards and gardens.

HOSTPLANT(S): In Ohio, this species has been recorded feeding on ash (*Fraxinus* spp.) (John W. Peacock, pers comm, 1989), tulip tree (*Liriodendron tulipifera* L.), and sassafras (*Sassafras albidum* [Nutt.] Nees). It has also been reported from wild black cherry (*Prunus serotina* Ehrh.) (Ray W. Bracher, pers comm, 1987) and prickly ash (*Xanthoxylum americanum* Mill.) (Studebaker and Studebaker, 1967). This butterfly undoubtedly uses a number of other broad-leaved trees and shrubs in Ohio.

ADULT ENERGY RESOURCES: Alfalfa (*Medicago sativa* L.), red clover (*Trifolium pratense* L.), rue-anemone (*Anemonella thalictroides* [L.] Spach), dandelion (*Taraxacum officinale* Weber), common blue phlox (*Phlox divaricata* L.), common milkweed (*Asclepias syriaca* L.), butterfly-weed (*Asclepias tuberosa* L.), Joe-Pye weed (*Eupatorium purpureum* L.), spotted Joe-Pye weed (*Eupatorium maculatum* L.), redbud (*Cercis canadensis* L.), ironweed (*Vernonia* sp.), teasel (*Dipsacus sylvestris* Huds.), Canada thistle (*Cirsium arvense* [L.] Scop.), swamp thistle (*Cirsium muticum* Michx.), thistle (*Cirsium discolor* [Muhl.] Spreng.), dame's rocket (*Hesperis matronalis* L.), Indian hemp (*Apocynum cannabinum* L.), rosin-weed (*Silphium trifoliatum* L.), purple coneflower (*Echinacea purpurea* [L.] Moench.), ragwort (*Senecio* sp.), hawthorn (*Crataegus* sp.), lilac (*Syringa* sp.), and garden flowers such as impatiens (*Impatiens* spp.), violets (*Viola* spp.), periwinkle (*Vinca minor* L.), and garden phlox (*Phlox paniculata* L.). Adults also imbibe moisture from damp soil, mud and sand, feces, carrion, and urine deposits. Adults often congregate in large numbers at puddles along woodland roads, especially in the spring.

FLIGHT PERIOD: Two broods, with an occasional partial third in southern Ohio (Figure 8.107). Extreme dates range from 24 March to 24 September.

SIMILAR SPECIES: Dark females are superficially similar to female *Papilio troilus*, but referral to the plates will allow easy separation of these two species.

GENERAL COMMENTS: This is one of our most common and conspicuous species. The females are dimorphic, occurring as yellow or black phenotypes. The black phenotype is generally assumed to be a mimic of the unpalatable *Battus philenor*. By resembling this species, female *P. glaucus* may be avoided by predators, and hence protected from them to a certain degree. However, males may not recognize black females as potential mates as easily as they recognize yellow females (Burns, 1966b). Hence, neither form has a clearcut evolutionary advantage over the other, and they coexist in a balanced equilibrium (the black females partially protected from predators, and the yellow females better able to attract males with which to mate). In Ohio, dark females are most common in the southern counties, where they predominate. The yellow females become progressively more common northward, and in the extreme north seem to comprise more than half the population. Occasionally, intermediate females are found. Scriber and Evans (1986[87]) have studied the genetics of the black/yellow females extensively, and have discovered genetic abnormalities in one southern Ohio population.

There is pronounced seasonal variation in this species. Spring brood adults are generally smaller. Occasional individuals may be only half the size of typical adults. Late summer adults are often very large, sometimes with a deep orange-yellow ground color resembling individuals of *Papilio glaucus australis* Maynard, 1891, from the Gulf Coast, suggesting that this is a temperature-induced phenotype.

In forests, the tiger swallowtail is a true canopy (treetop) flyer, and can be seen sailing and gliding around treetops, often descending into small sunlit openings. In more open areas, this species flies closer to the ground with a fast direct flight that can make it very difficult to capture. However, both sexes avidly visit flowers and can be easily observed while they are taking nectar.

LITERATURE RECORD: Williams County (Price, 1970).

***Papilio troilus troilus* Linneaus, 1758.** Spicebush Swallowtail. Plate 16.

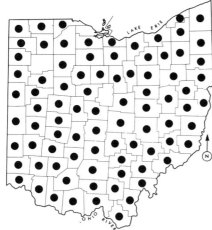

Fig. 8.108 *Papilio troilus.*

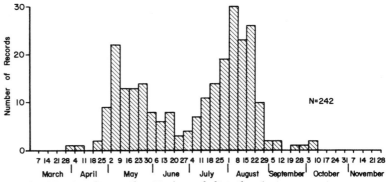

Fig. 8.109 *Papilio troilus*-Temporal distribution.

STATUS: Resident; uncommon to common.

DISTRIBUTION/RANGE: Statewide (Figure 8.108).

HABITAT: The spicebush swallowtail inhabits deciduous forests and adjacent open habitats such as old fields, woodland roads, and brushy areas. Adults are common in flower gardens and clover fields.

HOSTPLANT(S): Sassafras (*Sassafras albidum* [Nutt.] Nees) and spicebush (*Lindera benzoin* [L.] Blume) are the principal hosts in Ohio. These plants are the primary hostplants throughout this butterfly's range (Opler and Krizek, 1984).

ADULT ENERGY RESOURCES: Red clover (*Trifolium pratense* L.), winter cress (*Barbarea vulgaris* R. Br.), common milkweed (*Asclepias syriaca* L.), swamp milkweed (*Asclepias incarnata* L.), butterfly-weed (*Asclepias tuberosa* L.), Joe-Pye weed (*Eupatorium purpureum* L.), thistle (*Cirsium discolor* [Muhl.] Spreng.), swamp thistle (*Cirsium muticum* Michx.), honeysuckle (*Lonicera* sp.), teasel (*Dipsacus sylvestris* Huds.), monarda (*Monarda fistulosa* L.), dame's rocket (*Hesperis matronalis* L.), brambles (*Rubus* spp.), lilac (*Syringa vulgaris* L.), weigela (*Weigela* sp.), and common blue phlox (*Phlox divaricata* L.). Adults also take moisture from damp soil, mud, and urine deposits. Large gatherings of adults, especially males, at mud puddles are a common sight along woodland roads and stream mudflats, particularly in the spring.

FLIGHT PERIOD: Two broods in typical years, with peaks in May and August (Figure 8.109). Extreme dates range from 1 April to 4 October.

SIMILAR SPECIES: Use of the plates will allow easy determination of this species. Dark females of *P. glaucus* are superficially similar, but always have traces of dark bands on the ventral wing surfaces which are always absent in *P. troilus.*

GENERAL COMMENTS: This species is sometimes referred to as the green-clouded swallowtail, a reference to green scaling on the dorsal hindwings of the males (rarely, males have blue scaling on the dorsal hindwing). Although it occurs statewide, this species is especially abundant in the forests of southern Ohio, where adults are frequently encountered flying through the understory.

Both sexes of this swallowtail resemble *Battus philenor*, a species which is distasteful to predators. This mimicry may result in reduced predation of *P. troilus* because some predators may not be able to distinguish them from *B. philenor* and hence, are reluctant to eat them.

The flight of this species is fairly rapid and direct. When alarmed, the flight becomes extremely fast and very erratic. Both sexes visit flowers freely.

Family PIERIDAE-Whites and Sulphurs

***Pontia protodice* (Boisduval and LeConte, 1829).** Checkered White. Plate 17.

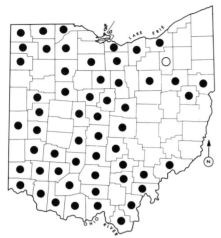

Fig. 8.110 *Pontia protodice.*

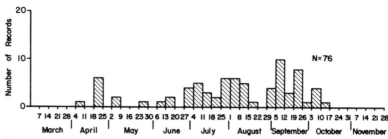

Fig. 8.111 *Pontia protodice*-Temporal distribution.

STATUS: Uncertain; probably a regular immigrant, although it may be a permanent resident along the Ohio River (Shuey, Calhoun, and Iftner, 1987). This butterfly can be locally common along the Ohio River, but is rare elsewhere in Ohio.

DISTRIBUTION/RANGE: Statewide (Figure 8.110). Most individuals are encountered in the southern quarter of the State.

HABITAT: This species is usually seen near stands of pepper-grass (*Lepidium virginicum* [L.] R. Br.) in disturbed, open habitats such as vacant lots, old fields, along railroad rights-of-way, pastures, and even in yards. In the spring it is also found along forest edges and in woodland clearings.

HOSTPLANT(S): Various species of mustards (Cruciferae). In Ohio, *P. protodice* has been found and reared on pepper-grass (*Lepidium virginicum* [L.] R. Br.). It has also been reported on pepper-grass (*Lepidium densiflorum* Schrad.) (Robert Dirig, pers comm, 1988), shepherd's purse (*Capsella bursa-pastoris* [L.] Medic.), cultivated cabbage (*Brassica oleracea* L.), and turnip (*Brassica rapa* L.) (Kirtland, 1854a). Additional species of mustards are also probably used.

ADULT ENERGY RESOURCES: Alfalfa (*Medicago sativa* L.), red clover (*Trifolium pratense* L.), ironweed (*Vernonia* sp.), dogbane (*Apocynum* sp.), Canada thistle (*Cirsium arvense* [L.] Scop.), and aster species.

FLIGHT PERIOD: This species produces continuous and overlapping broods throughout the summer (Figure 8.111). Although it is difficult to tell from the histogram, there are two to five generations a year. Extreme dates range from 4 April to 11 October.

SIMILAR SPECIES: None.

GENERAL COMMENTS: In Ohio, as in much of the northeastern United States, this species has suffered a dramatic decline. At least through the 1930's, this species was fairly common and widespread throughout Ohio, with most early collectors reporting its presence (Dury, 1878; Kirtland, 1854a; Pilate, 1882; Hine, 1898a; Bales, 1909; Henninger, 1910). Since Wyss (1930b) first noted a general reduction in *P. protodice* numbers, this butterfly has declined dramatically. We found only one individual collected from 1967 through 1981, and all but a few of the records since 1982 are from southern Ohio. In the drought year of 1988, however, this species was widespread and temporary populations were located.

In some past years this species was a resident, and there are many spring brood specimens in older collections to verify this yearly presence. However, the spring brood has been collected only once since 1953, and recent efforts to obtain spring brood material from sites where this butterfly was captured the previous summer have only yielded a single specimen. This may indicate that populations rarely survive Ohio's winters. However, the spring brood is generally considered to be rare relative to later broods, and it may be easily overlooked.

Several authors have speculated about the decline of this species. Klots (1951) felt that naturalized populations of *Pieris rapae* may have competed with *P. protodice*, or that parasites may have reproduced in the abundant *P. rapae* to such an extent that they depressed populations of native *Pieris* and closely related species. Pyle (1981) suggested that changing land use patterns may have reduced available habitats for the species, reducing its numbers. In Ohio, however, old fields and other disturbed open habitats have long been common. Perhaps the best explanation is that native whites cannot distinguish between native and naturalized mustards (Chew, 1977). Most naturalized mustards contain lethal quantities of mustard oils, and *P. protodice* larvae are unable to develop on them. Given the abundance of naturalized mustards in many disturbed habitats, ovipositing females may not lay sufficient numbers of eggs on suitable hosts to maintain populations in Ohio. The use of modern farm herbicides may also have eliminated hostplants from many of the agricultural habitats that once supported this butterfly.

Today, the best places to locate the checkered white are in disturbed habitats along the Ohio River, where it is often locally common in late summer and early autumn. Most other sites are also located in or near river valleys, suggesting that dispersing adults may follow valleys northward through the State. Females which immigrate early in the season should be able to establish temporary populations throughout the State.

Adults of this species are extremely variable in appearance. The spring form 'vernalis' (W. H. Edwards) is smaller, possesses darker ventral hindwings, and has more restricted dark markings above than do individuals from later broods. Some autumn individuals may resemble the spring form.

This species flies more rapidly than *Pieris rapae*, but is otherwise very difficult to separate in the field. *Pontia protodice* also tends to fly closer to the ground and in a more direct fashion. *Pieris rapae* is usually common in areas where *P. protodice* occurs, and collectors should examine every white butterfly if they hope to detect *P. protodice*. The current rarity of *P. protodice* in collections may partially be a reflection of the difficulty in separating these two species in the field.

William N. Tallant (unpublished notes) observed a natural interspecific pairing of a female *P. protodice* and a male *P. rapae* in September 1884, in Columbus.

LITERATURE RECORD: Summit County (Claypole, 1897).

Pieris napi oleracea Harris, 1929. Mustard White. Plate 17.

Fig. 8.112 *Pieris napi.*

STATUS: Resident; rare, probably extirpated. We only have literature records for this species.

DISTRIBUTION/RANGE: In the eastern United States, this species is primarily a resident of the transition and Canadian life zones. Northeastern Indiana and northwestern Ohio represent the southern limit of this species in the Midwest (Opler and Krizek, 1984). Literature records from Seneca and Lucas Counties (Figure 8.112) represent the extreme southern limit for this species.

HABITAT: In southern Michigan and Indiana, this butterfly inhabits moist deciduous forests and fens (Wagner and Hansen, 1980; Shull, 1987).

HOSTPLANT(S): Not known in Ohio. In northeastern Indiana, *P. napi* uses naturalized water cress (*Nasturtium officinale* R. Br.) (Shull, 1977), a species that is often common in many wetland habitats. This species uses a variety of mustards (Cruciferae) throughout its range (Chew, 1977).

ADULT ENERGY RESOURCES: None recorded for Ohio.

FLIGHT PERIOD: The only date available for Ohio is 6 July (Henninger, 1910). In Indiana there are three broods (Shull, 1987).

SIMILAR SPECIES: *Pieris rapae* and *Pieris virginiensis* are both easily confused with this species. The spring brood of *P. napi* is easily identified by the bold dark veins on the ventral hindwing. This pattern is completely absent in *P. rapae* and is very faint in *P. virginiensis*. Only the summer brood of *P. napi* can be confused with *P. rapae*, because *P. virginiensis* normally flies only in early spring (Figure 8.114). Summer individuals of *P. napi* are usually immaculate white on all wing surfaces, and are easily separated from the well marked summer broods of *P. rapae*. If any melanic pattern is evident at all in *P. napi*, it is very diffuse and faint.

GENERAL COMMENTS: This butterfly is known from Ohio only from literature records. Kirtland (1854a) observed this species in the vicinity of Toledo while he was travelling by train from Detroit to Cleveland (this sighting predates the invasion of *P. rapae* into Ohio). Scudder (1889) also reported this species from Toledo, but used Kirtland (1854a) as his source. Henninger (1910) captured a individual on 6 July 1905 in Seneca County. Although he reported this capture as *Pieris napi virginiensis*, the July date indicates that he was referring to *P. napi* (in addition, *P. virginiensis* has not been recorded from northwestern Ohio). The Cleveland Museum of Natural History contains a small series of this species with Ohio locality labels, but these specimens represent a western subspecies and must have been mislabeled.

This species may have occurred throughout much of the original Black Swamp of northwestern Ohio. This area, and the adjacent Oak Openings, was a complex mosaic of wetlands similar to areas in northeastern Indiana and southern Michigan which still support this species. Today, virtually all of the wetlands of northwestern Ohio have been drained, and the butterfly faunas of the few wetlands which remain (primarily in the Oak Openings) are well known. It is remotely possible that a population may survive in some small undocumented fen or wet woodland in the northwestern corner of the State.

Although many of the same arguments that have been applied to the decline of *P. protodice* have also been applied to the decline of *P. napi* (eg Klots, 1951; Chew, 1977; Pyle, 1981), the extirpation of this species from Ohio can be attributed directly to habitat destruction.

The flight of this species is usually weak and within one meter of the ground. Even when harassed by collectors, the flight remains relatively calm and direct. Although summer brood adults tend to wander somewhat, they generally remain in their cool, partially shaded habitats.

LITERATURE RECORDS: Lucas (Kirtland, 1854a; Scudder, 1889) and Seneca (Henninger, 1910) Counties.

Pieris virginiensis W. H. Edwards, 1870. West Virginia White. Plate 17.

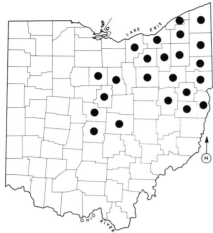

Fig. 8.113 *Pieris virginiensis.*

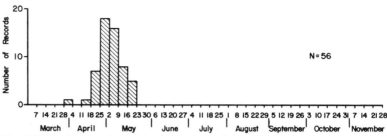

N = 56

Fig. 8.114 *Pieris virginiensis*-Temporal distribution.

STATUS: Resident; rare to common. *Pieris virginiensis* is most common in the extreme northeastern counties, becoming less common and more local southward.

DISTRIBUTION/RANGE: This species is found in the northeastern quarter of the State, and a few north-central counties (Figure 8.113).

HABITAT: This species is usually associated with deciduous woodlands and is only rarely found in open areas. In northeastern Ohio this species is usually associated with beech-maple forests, but in central Ohio it is most frequently encountered in wooded shale ravines.

HOSTPLANT(S): In Ohio, this species has been observed ovipositing on, and reared on, two-leaved toothwort (*Dentaria diphylla* Michx.), cut-leaved toothwort (*Dentaria laciniata* Muhl.), narrow-leaved toothwort (*Dentaria multifida* Muhl.), and rock cress (*Arabis laevigata* Muhl.) (Shuey and Peacock, 1988[89]; Calhoun and Iftner, 1988[89]). Throughout most of *P. virginiensis'* range, *D. diphylla* is the primary hostplant (Cappuccino and Kareiva, 1985) but in some central Ohio populations, *A. laevigata* is the primary host (Shuey and Peacock, 1989).

ADULT ENERGY RESOURCES: Trillium (*Trillium grandiflorum* [Michx.] Salisb.), two-leaved toothwort (*Dentaria diphylla* Michx.), and bluebell (*Mertensia virginica* [L.] Pers.). Adults also imbibe moisture from damp soil.

FLIGHT PERIOD: One brood, peaking in late April and early May (Figure 8.114). Extreme dates range from 3 April to 20 May. A rare partial second brood sometimes occurs in Kentucky (Charles V. Covell Jr., pers comm, 1987), and should be watched for in Ohio.

SIMILAR SPECIES: See *P. napi.*

GENERAL COMMENTS: For many years *P. virginiensis* was thought to be a race of *P. napi.* However, the discovery of sympatric populations of both species confirmed their distinctness. *Pieris virginiensis* tends to replace *P. napi* in the southern portion of their collective ranges. In Ohio, there is no overlap in the ranges of these two species.

Strictly a woodland species, *P. virginiensis* seldom strays from its forested habitat. Because of its reluctance to cross open habitats, very little recolonization of second growth forest takes place in areas of scattered woodlands (Cappucinno and Kreiva, 1985). Before most of the forests of Ohio were removed around the turn of the century, this species was probably more widespread in the State. It is still fairly common in northeastern Ohio where forest cover is fairly complete. Cappucinno and Kareiva (1985) speculate that viral diseases, unfavorable weather, and poor dispersal may play important roles in determining the present day distribution of this species.

Although this butterfly is known from only central and northeastern Ohio, it may occur in southern counties as well. Populations are known from nearby areas of West Virginia, Kentucky, and Indiana, and the foodplants are locally common throughout the southern portion of the State. If *P. virginiensis* is present, it must be localized and rare, given the large amount of attention collectors have devoted to southern Ohio. The early flight period and the presence of other spring flying whites (*Pieris rapae, Anthocharis midea,* and *Euchloe olympia*) in the area may result in casual collectors overlooking populations in this region.

Ohio populations are phenotypically intermediate between the well marked populations which occur in the northern Great Lakes Region and the pale populations of the Appalachian Region (Wagner, 1978). Within populations, individuals vary from those that possess fairly heavy scaling along the ventral hindwing veins to those which are almost devoid of any markings.

The normal flight of this butterfly is slow and relatively weak, and adults usually stay within one meter of the ground. Unlike *P. napi,* which remains fairly calm when pursued, *P. virginiensis* is capable of wildly erratic flight when disturbed, and sometimes flies upwards into the canopy.

LITERATURE RECORDS: None.

Pieris rapae (Linnaeus, 1758). European Cabbage White. Plate 17.

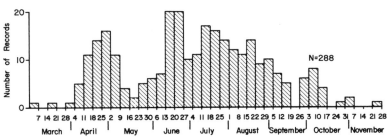

Fig. 8.116 *Pieris rapae*-Temporal distribution.

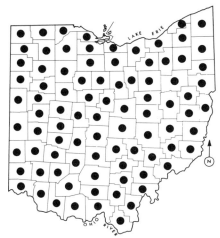

Fig. 8.115 *Pieris rapae*.

STATUS: Naturalized resident; common.

DISTRIBUTION/RANGE: Statewide (Figure 8.115). This was the first butterfly to be recorded from all 88 Ohio counties by the Ohio Survey of Lepidoptera.

HABITAT: This species inhabits virtually any open area, but particularly old fields, pastures, vacant lots, roadsides, and gardens. This species is also encountered within woodlands in early spring.

HOSTPLANT(S): Primarily species of cultivated and wild mustards (Cruciferae). In Ohio this species has been found and reared on garlic mustard (*Alliaria officinalis* Andrz.) and cut-leaved toothwort (*Dentaria laciniata* Muhl.), and has been reared on horseradish (*Armoracia rusticana* Gaertn., Mey., and Scherb.) (Studebaker and Studebaker, 1967), and a variety of cole crops (*Brassica oleracea* L., such as cabbage, kohlrabi, broccoli, cauliflower, Brussels sprouts, and collards). It has also been observed ovipositing on water cress (*Nasturtium officinale* R. Br.), and winter cress (*Barbarea vulgaris* R. Br.). This butterfly undoubtedly uses other mustards as well. Saunders et al (1875) reported this butterfly on mignonette (*Reseda odorata* L., Resedaceae), a host record that needs to be verified.

ADULT ENERGY RESOURCES: Alfalfa (*Medicago sativa* L.), red clover (*Trifolium pratense* L.), white clover (*Trifolium repens* L.), white sweet clover (*Melilotus alba* Desr.), yellow sweet clover (*Melilotus officinalis* [L.] Lam.), dame's rocket (*Hesperis matronalis* L.), black mustard (*Brassica nigra* [L.] Koch.), cauliflower, broccoli, and Brussels sprouts (*Brassica oleracea* L.), shrubby cinquefoil (*Potentilla fruticosa* L.), wood sorrel (*Oxalis stricta* L.), loosestrife (*Lythrum alatum* Pursh), Indian-hemp (*Apocynum cannabinum* L.), self-heal (*Prunella vulgaris* L.), catnip (*Nepeta cataria* L.), giant hyssop (*Agastache nepetoides* [L.] Ktze.), peppermint (*Mentha piperita* L.), swamp milkweed (*Asclepias incarnata* L.), blue vervain (*Verbena hastata* L.), whorled rosin-weed (*Silphium trifoliatum* L.), wing-stem (*Verbesina alternifolia* [L.] Britt.), sunflower (*Helianthus hirsutus* Raf.), dandelion (*Taraxacum officinale* Weber), bur-marigold (*Bidens aristosa* [Michx.] Britt.), chicory (*Cichorium intybus* L.), horseweed (*Erigeron canadensis* L.), Canada thistle (*Cirsium arvense* [L.] Scop.), *Aster* spp., ironweed (*Vernonia* sp.), Joe-Pye weed (*Eupatorium purpureum* L.), spotted Joe-Pye weed (*Eupatorium maculatum* L.), common boneset (*Eupatorium perfoliatum* L.), ground-ivy (*Glechoma hederacea* L.), red henbit (*Lamium purpureum* L.), sweet alyssum (*Lobularia maritima* [L.] Desv.), teasel (*Dipsacus sylvestris* Huds.), and loosestrife (*Lythrum salicaria* L.). Adults also take moisture from mud puddles and damp soil.

FLIGHT PERIOD: This species produces continuous and overlapping broods throughout the summer (Figure 8.116). Although it is difficult to tell from the histogram, there are three to five generations a year. We have records for this species from every month but December and February.

SIMILAR SPECIES: See *P. napi* and *P. virginiensis*.

GENERAL COMMENTS: Accidentally introduced into Quebec around 1860 (Scudder, 1887), this European species rapidly spread throughout North America. Its spread through Ohio is well documented. It was first reported in the vicinity of Cleveland in 1873 (Webster, 1893), where it was considered common by 1875. This butterfly reached western Ohio and the vicinity of Cincinnati by at least 1875 (Saunders et al, 1875; Dury, unpublished notes). By 1878 it was regarded as very abundant in southwestern Ohio (Dury, 1878). By 1882 this butterfly was already considered a serious economic pest (Anonymous, 1883). Today, *P. rapae* is our most common and widespread butterfly.

Although this species feeds on a wide variety of cruciferous plants, it is particularly fond of cole crops (cabbage, broccoli, cauliflower, etc), upon which it is a destructive pest. Virtually any gardener who plants these crops will encounter the larvae of this butterfly. The myriad of common names reflect the pest status of this species (cabbage white, European cabbage white, imported cabbageworm, cabbage moth, and cabbage butterfly) (Albrecht and Watkins, 1983).

This is one of the first butterflies to emerge in the spring and flies continuously until the first major frost. The flight of this species is relatively slow, although it can be quite rapid and erratic when disturbed.

In September, 1884, a male of this species was observed in copula with a female *Pontia protodice* near Columbus (William N. Tallant, unpublished notes).

LITERATURE RECORDS: None.

Euchloe olympia (**W. H. Edwards, 1871**). Olympia Marble. Plate 18.

Fig. 8.117 *Euchloe olympia*.

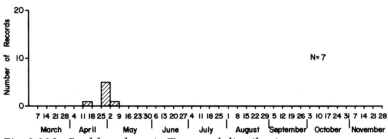

Fig. 8.118 *Euchloe olympia*-Temporal distribution.

STATUS: Resident; rare.

DISTRIBUTION/RANGE: This species is known only from the Lake Vesuvius area of Lawrence County (Riddlebarger, 1984; Calhoun, 1985[86]) and Monroe County (Figure 8.117).

HABITAT: This species has been captured only on dry ridgetops in and adjacent to open oak forests.

HOSTPLANT(S): Not known in Ohio. Rockcresses, *Arabis* spp., are the primary foodplants throughout its range (Clench and Opler, 1983). In southern Ohio, *Arabis laevigata* (Muhl.) Poir., may be the host (Riddlebarger, 1984).

ADULT ENERGY RESOURCES: None recorded for Ohio.

FLIGHT PERIOD: One brood, peaking in late April and early May (Figure 8.118). Extreme dates range from 13 April to 5 May.

SIMILAR SPECIES: Females of *Anthocharis midea* are superficially similar, but use of the plates will identify *E. olympia*.

GENERAL COMMENTS: This species was first collected in Ohio in 1984 (Riddlebarger, 1984) after years of speculation that it could occur in the southern part of the State or in the Oak Openings of Lucas County. It is certainly more widespread than our records indicate, and collectors should search for it in other southern counties. Where it occurs, *E. olympia* maintains very low population densities and seems to be very localized. Many hours of search time were expended locating the few known Ohio specimens.

Ohio populations belong in the Appalachian distribution isolate described by Opler and Clench (1983). There is a slight chance that the Great Lakes population isolate will be found in the Oak Openings of Lucas County. Populations in Michigan occupy habitats similar to the oak savannas found in the Oak Openings.

This species is one of the first butterflies of spring, and is found in areas that also support *Pieris rapae* and *Anthocharis midea*. In flight, *E. olympia* is difficult to separate from the other two species. The flight of *E. olympia* is usually more direct and rapid than the other two species, and leaves one with the impression that this species "knows where it is going," whereas the other species tend to wander. Because it is so difficult to separate from the others, searchers should examine every white butterfly they encounter. *Euchloe olympia* has only been encountered as single individuals in Ohio, and the majority have been males patrolling near hilltops. Individuals usually fly within one meter of the ground.

Individuals with rosy markings on the ventral hindwing are known as form 'rosa' (W. H. Edwards, 1882). These rosy markings fade and disappear on pinned specimens.

LITERATURE RECORDS: None.

Anthocharis midea annickae (dos Passos and Klots, 1969). Falcate Orange-Tip. Plate 18.

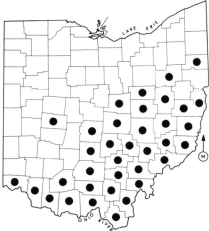

Fig. 8.119 *Anthocharis midea.*

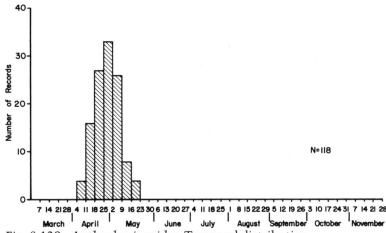

Fig. 8.120 *Anthocharis midea*-Temporal distribution.

STATUS: Resident; uncommon to common. This species is usually common throughout unglaciated Ohio, but is uncommon in the glaciated counties bordering this region. It is a rare find elsewhere. Dury (1878) and Wyss (1930b; 1932) considered it to be rare in the Cincinnati area, and our records support this.

DISTRIBUTION/RANGE: This species occurs primarily in the Unglaciated Allegheny Plateau and adjacent counties (Figure 8.119). The records from outside of this area are mostly based upon single individuals.

HABITAT: This butterfly is most often encountered in open oak-hickory forests and associated clearings. Along the Ohio River it also occurs in thinly wooded lowland areas. This species is occasionally encountered in open areas far from woodlands.

HOSTPLANT(S): In Ohio, this butterfly has been observed ovipositing on field pepper-grass (*Lepidium campestre* [L.] R. Br.). Ova have been found and reared on bitter cress (*Cardamine parviflora* L.), cut-leaved toothwort (*Dentaria laciniata* Muhl.), and field pepper-grass (*Lepidium campestre* [L.] R. Br.). Various species of mustards are the only known hosts (Opler and Krizek, 1984).

ADULT ENERGY RESOURCES: Early saxifrage (*Saxifraga virginiensis* Michx.), cut-leaved toothwort (*Dentaria laciniata* Muhl.), bluets (*Houstonia caerulea* L.), rock cress (*Arabis* sp.), and spring-beauty (*Claytonia virginica* L.).

FLIGHT PERIOD: One brood, peaking in late April and early May (Figure 8.120). Extreme dates range from 4 April to 22 May.

SIMILAR SPECIES: Females of this species can be confused with *Euchloe olympia,* but the hooked (falcate) forewing apex of *A. midea* will separate these two species.

GENERAL COMMENTS: This is one of the earliest spring species. It is usually common throughout the forested areas of southeastern Ohio, although populations fluctuate and in some seasons this species can be rare. To the north and west, populations become fewer and smaller, and there are very few records from northern Ohio. This species was probably more common and more widely distributed prior to the clearing of the State's virgin forests.

Males appear several days before females, and spend most of their lives patrolling roadsides, hilltops, and forest clearings in search of females. The flight of this species is low to the ground (less than one meter), slow, and quite erratic.

LITERATURE RECORD: Seneca County (Henninger, 1910).

Colias philodice philodice Godart, 1819. Clouded Sulphur/Common Sulphur. Plate 18.

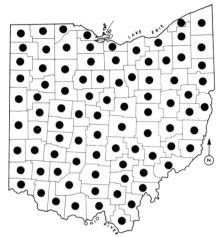

Fig. 8.121 *Colias philodice.*

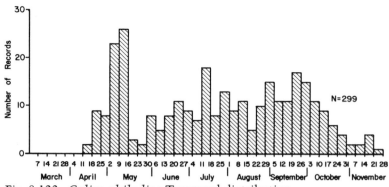

Fig. 8.122 *Colias philodice*-Temporal distribution.

STATUS: Resident; common.

DISTRIBUTION/RANGE: Statewide (Figure 8.121). This species has been recorded from all 88 counties.

HABITAT: This species can be found in virtually any open area. It is especially common in clover and alfalfa fields, pastures, old fields, and along roadsides,

HOSTPLANT(S): In Ohio, this species has been recorded on two introduced plants, red clover (*Trifolium pratense* L.) and white clover (*Trifolium repens* L.). Other legumes are also probably used.

ADULT ENERGY RESOURCES: Alfalfa (*Medicago sativa* L.), red clover (*Trifolium pratense* L.), white clover (*Trifolium repens* L.), dandelion (*Taraxacum officinale* Weber), winter cress (*Barbarea vulgaris* R. Br.), common milkweed (*Asclepias syriaca* L.), butterfly-weed (*Asclepias tuberosa* L.), peppermint (*Mentha piperita* L.), butter-and-eggs (*Linaria vulgaris* Hill), sunflower (*Helianthus hirsutus* Raf.), horseweed (*Erigeron canadensis* L.), and asters (*Aster* spp.). Adults also imbibe moisture from damp soil and mud.

FLIGHT PERIOD: Many overlapping broods throughout the summer (Figure 8.122). Although it is difficult to tell from the histogram, there are between three to five generations a year. Extreme dates range from 17 April to 2 December.

SIMILAR SPECIES: Both sexes of *C. eurytheme* can be confused with *C. philodice*. These two species hybridize frequently, and intermediates are common (Plate 18). For this study, only pure yellow specimens are considered to represent *C. philodice*. White females of these two species are not as easily separated. On average, white females of *C. philodice* have narrower black margins on the dorsal wings than do white females of *C. eurytheme*. Unfortunately, many females, especially hybrids, are essentially impossible to identify with any certainty.

GENERAL COMMENTS: This is one of Ohio's most common butterflies. This species is most abundant in late summer and reaches its highest densities in clover and alfalfa fields. Prior to the introduction of its agriculturally important foodplants, this species was probably less common than it is today.

This species is extremely variable both is size and color pattern. Spring brood individuals tend to be smaller, darker below, and a paler yellow than summer brood individuals. White females are common, particularly in late summer and may represent up to 40% of the females in some populations (Shapiro, 1966). Females range from white, to buff, to yellow. Aberrations and somewhat melanic individuals are fairly common.

In flight, this butterfly flies rapidly and erratically, usually within one meter of the ground. *Colias philodice* is usually less common than *C. eurytheme.*

LITERATURE RECORDS: None.

Colias eurytheme Boisduval, 1852. Alfalfa Butterfly/Orange Sulphur. Plate 18.

Fig. 8.123 *Colias eurytheme.*

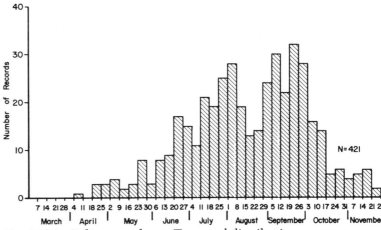

Fig. 8.124 *Colias eurytheme*-Temporal distribution.

STATUS: Naturalized resident; common.

DISTRIBUTION/RANGE: Statewide (Figure 8.123). This species has been recorded from all 88 counties.

HABITAT: Virtually any open area. This butterfly is especially common in open fields, vacant lots, pastures, and along roadsides. It is most frequent in alfalfa and clover fields.

HOSTPLANT(S): In Ohio, as its common name suggests, this species uses alfalfa (*Medicago sativa* L.) as its primary host. It has also been observed ovipositing on yellow hop clover (*Trifolium agrarium* L.) (Xerces Society, 1987). Other legumes are probably utilized as well.

ADULT ENERGY RESOURCES: Alfalfa (*Medicago sativa* L.), red clover (*Trifolium pratense* L.), alsike clover (*Trifolium hybridum* L.), common milkweed (*Asclepias syriaca* L.), swamp milkweed (*Asclepias incarnata* L.), self-heal (*Prunella vulgaris* L.), teasel (*Dipsacus sylvestris* Huds.), peppermint (*Mentha piperita* L.), horseweed (*Erigeron canadensis* L.), purple coneflower (*Echinacea purpurea* L.), sunflower (*Helianthus hirsutus* Raf.), wing-stem (*Verbesina alternifolia* [L.] Britt), chicory (*Cichorium intybus* L.), asters (*Aster* spp.), Canada thistle (*Cirsium arvense* [L.] Scop.), ironweed (*Vernonia altissima* Nutt.), common boneset (*Eupatorium perfoliatum* L.), great blue lobelia (*Lobelia siphilitica* L.), and goldenrods (*Solidago* spp.). Adults also imbibe moisture from damp soil and mud, and are often seen in large numbers around puddles in mid-summer.

FLIGHT PERIOD: Many overlapping broods throughout the summer, peaking in early autumn (Figure 8.124). Although it is difficult to distinguish from the histogram, there are between three to five generations a year. This is one of the last butterflies to disappear each autumn. Extreme dates range from 10 April to 2 December.

SIMILAR SPECIES: See *C. philodice. Eurema nicippe* is superficially similar, but the silver spot in the ventral hindwing cell of *C. eurytheme* will separate it from *E. nicippe*.

GENERAL COMMENTS: This species is probably our third most common butterfly after *Pieris rapae* and *Phyciodes tharos*. However, *C. eurytheme* usually becomes the most abundant species in late summer and early autumn. Statewide in occurrence, this species is most frequently encountered with its near relative, *C. philodice*, in alfalfa and clover fields. Often hundreds of adults can be seen flying about in these fields in the summer.

Originally a species of the far west, this species was not part of Ohio's native fauna. *Colias eurytheme* spread eastward during the 1870's following the widespread cultivation of alfalfa (Shapiro, 1966). The first report of this species in Ohio was in 1874 near Cincinnati (Dury, unpublished notes). It was considered rare in the State (Pilate, 1882; Claypole, 1897; Bales, 1909; Henninger, 1910) until about 1930 when Baker (unpublished notes) reported it as common in Stark County. This increase in numbers is similar to trends found in other eastern states (Shapiro, 1966). Prior to the widespread cultivation of alfalfa, this species used native legumes as its primary foodplants. Today this butterfly feeds almost exclusively on alfalfa in Ohio and can be a minor pest at times.

The recent range expansion of this species has resulted in contact with *C. philodice*, and subsequent hybridization between these two species. Despite the prevalence of hybrids throughout Ohio, both butterflies have retained their integrity and must be considered as distinct species (Silberglied and Taylor, 1973).

As is the case with *C. philodice*, *C. eurytheme* is also phenotypically variable. In early spring and autumn, adults are smaller and have the orange areas greatly reduced on the dorsal forewing. Summer individuals are larger and usually brighter orange. White females are common, particularly in late summer. In Pennsylvania, white females can represent up to 40% of the autumn population (Shapiro, 1966). Females range from white to buff to orange. Aberrations and somewhat melanic individuals are fairly common.

The flight of *C. eurytheme* is fairly rapid, slightly erratic, and usually within one meter of the ground. Males patrol back and forth over open fields and hillsides in search of recently emerged receptive females (Paul A. Opler, pers comm, 1989). *Colias eurytheme* is best observed while the adults are feeding at nectar sources.

LITERATURE RECORDS: None.

Colias cesonia cesonia (Stoll, 1790). Dog Face. Plate 19.

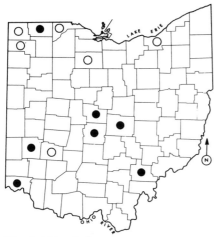

Fig. 8.125 *Colias cesonia.*

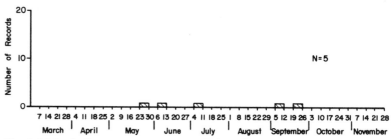

Fig. 8.126 *Colias cesonia*-Temporal distribution.

STATUS: Irregular immigrant; rare.

DISTRIBUTION/RANGE: In the eastern United States, this species is a resident only in the Gulf States. It regularly wanders northward, occasional reaching states as far north as Wisconsin, Michigan, and New Hampshire (Opler and Krizek, 1984). Our few records are scattered throughout the western two-thirds of the State (Figure 8.125). This species does not survive Ohio's winters.

HABITAT: *Colias cesonia* is usually found in open habitats such as fields, pastures, clover fields, and along roadsides and river levees and river banks.

HOSTPLANT(S): Not known in Ohio. In other areas this species uses false indigo (*Amorpha fruticosa* L.), alfalfa (*Medicago sativa* L.), clover (*Trifolium* spp.), and other legumes (Howe, 1975). West of Cincinnati, *C. cesonia* has been found flying in stands of false indigo (*Amorpha fruticosa* L.), a known host in Kentucky and Indiana (Reed A. Watkins, pers comm, 1987). This plant can be common along the Ohio River, especially near Cincinnati.

ADULT ENERGY RESOURCES: Goldenrod (*Solidago* sp.). It has also been collected in a clover (*Trifolium* sp.) field (Hine, 1898b).

FLIGHT PERIOD: Although our records do not indicate any trends (Figure 8.126), this species may occasionally produce one or two broods in Ohio. Extreme dates range from 28 May to 22 December.

SIMILAR SPECIES: This species is superficially similar to the other two Ohio *Colias*, but the hooked forewing apex and distinctive pattern will readily identify *C. cesonia*.

GENERAL COMMENTS: Although Kirtland (1854a) called this species locally "very numerous," it is in reality an infrequent and very rare immigrant into our area. Most records are based on single individuals, which were encountered in late summer and early autumn. Hine (1898b) noted that several specimens were captured in Columbus in the spring of 1895, in a field of clover (a potential hostplant). Thus, it is possible that this species occasionally establishes breeding colonies in the State, possibly even surviving mild winters. This species is known to establish temporary colonies well to the north of Ohio in Ontario and New York (Opler and Krizek, 1984). Collectors seeking this species in Ohio should watch stands of the hostplant, *Amorpha fruticosa* L., particularly along the Ohio River near Cincinnati where the host is abundant in late summer, especially after mild winters.

The flight of this species is swift and direct, usually within one and one-half meter of the ground. Males patrol all day, presumably searching for receptive females, and pause only to visit nectar sources or when clouds obscure the sun. Although difficult to observe on the wing, this species stops frequently at flowers.

LITERATURE RECORDS: Seneca (Henninger, 1910), Williams, Lucas, Defiance (Price, 1970), Greene (Kirtland, 1854a) and Cuyahoga (Bubna, 1897) Counties.

Phoebis sennae eubule (Linnaeus, 1767). Cloudless Sulphur. Plate 19.

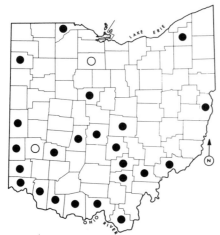

Fig. 8.127 *Phoebis sennae.*

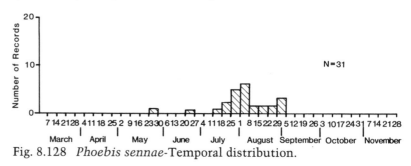

Fig. 8.128 *Phoebis sennae*-Temporal distribution.

STATUS: Irregular immigrant; rare.

DISTRIBUTION/RANGE: In the eastern United States, this species is a resident only in the lower Gulf States. Although this butterfly annually wanders northward, it rarely reaches Ohio. However, it is capable of occasionally establishing temporary populations. These populations cannot survive Ohio's winters. Ohio records are scattered statewide (Figure 8.127).

HABITAT: This species is most frequently encountered in open, disturbed habitats such as old fields, pastures, vacant lots, residential areas, parks, and along waterways and roadsides.

HOSTPLANT(S): In Ohio, this species has been found and reared on wild senna (*Cassia hebecarpa* Fern) and partridge-pea (*Cassia fasciculata* Michx.) (Calhoun, Allen, and Iftner, 1989[90]). It may also use other *Cassia* species as well. Populations of *Cassia* species are generally quite localized in Ohio.

ADULT ENERGY RESOURCES: Wild senna (*Cassia herbecarpa* Fern), cultivated geranium (*Pelargonium* sp.), thistle (*Cirsium* sp.), jewel-weed (*Impatiens capensis* Meerb.), and salvia (*Salvia* sp.).

FLIGHT PERIOD: Depending on how early temporary populations are established, this species has the potential to produce two or more broods per summer in Ohio. There are no discrete broods, and generations apparently overlap considerably (Figure 8.128). Extreme dates range from 23 May to 5 September. (This histogram includes data from 1987).

GENERAL COMMENTS: This species is a rare sight in Ohio, and because of its very rapid flight, is even less often collected. Both Dury (1898) and Price (1970) reported seeing only a handful of individuals each during their respective 25 plus years of collecting. Only twice (Kirtland, 1854a; Calhoun, Allen, and Iftner, 1989[90]) has this species been reported in numbers in Ohio. In 1987, individuals were sighted in numbers as early as May, and the first documented temporary populations were discovered. During this single season, the number of county records accumulated for this butterfly (in over 125 years of collecting) increased from eight to 24.

This 1987 invasion may have been the result of two successive mild winters, which could have allowed populations to survive the winter well to the north of *P. sennae's* normal range. Thus, wandering females had less distance to cover before reaching our borders, and were able to establish populations early in the season. Populations of *Cassia* species were also abnormally vigorous in 1987. This may have provided abundant and easily discoverable resources for wandering females to exploit relative to most years. Under more typical conditions (ie, after "normal" winters), the one or two adults which may be sighted over the entire State probably represent wandering individuals that did not originate from within the State. Adults may use waterways as dispersal routes, because most of the sightings in off years are along rivers.

The flight of this species is very rapid, direct, and usually several meters above the ground. Individuals are almost impossible to observe at close range unless they are visiting flowers. Even then, flower visits are brief, and the butterflies usually speed off after a few seconds. When populations are located, males can be easily collected by attracting them with "decoys." Males will investigate dead specimens of their species or even bright yellow paper, presumably as part of their search for females. Collectors can use this predictable behavior to lure males to within net range, but even then success is not guaranteed.

LITERATURE RECORDS: Montgomery (Kirtland, 1854a; Scudder, 1889; Pilate, 1906), and Seneca (Henninger, 1910) Counties.

Phoebis philea philea (Johansson, 1763). Orange-barred Sulphur. Plate 20.

Fig. 8.129 *Phoebis philea.*

STATUS: Stray; rare. This species is only known from one literature record.

DISTRIBUTION/RANGE: In the eastern United States, this butterfly is resident only in peninsular Florida. Strays have been reported from several states adjacent to Ohio (Opler and Krizek, 1984). The single Ohio record was collected in Franklin County (Hine, 1898a; 1898b) (Figure 8.129).

HABITAT: Where resident, this species occurs near forest edges and in open areas, and is frequently seen in residential areas, vacant lots, and along forest margins.

HOSTPLANT(S): Not known in Ohio. Sennas (*Cassia* spp.) are the primary hosts in areas where this butterfly is resident (Opler and Krizek, 1984).

ADULT ENERGY RESOURCES: None recorded for Ohio.

FLIGHT PERIOD: The single report of this species from Ohio is 16 September 1895.

SIMILAR SPECIES: None.

GENERAL COMMENTS: This species is known only from a literature record (Hine, 1898a; 1898b). The specimen was collected on the grounds of The Ohio State University, Franklin County, by Edward Orton. The whereabouts of this specimen is unknown, and we believe it to be lost. A single male of this species reportedly was observed 2 September 1990 at Gilmore Ponds, Hamilton County, but unfortunately escaped capture (James W. Becker, pers comm, 1990).

This species only rarely reaches Ohio. Its behavior is very similar to *P. sennae*, and any specimen seen in Ohio would likely remain uncaptured. One larva was found and reared in Indiana (Shull, 1987), indicating that this species could reproduce in Ohio if immigrating females arrive early in the season and can locate suitable stands of the hostplant. This species cannot survive Ohio's winters.

LITERATURE RECORD: Franklin County (Hine, 1898a; 1898b).

Eurema lisa lisa (Boisduval and Leconte, 1829). Little Sulphur. Plate 20.

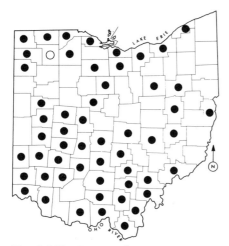

Fig. 8.130 *Eurema lisa.*

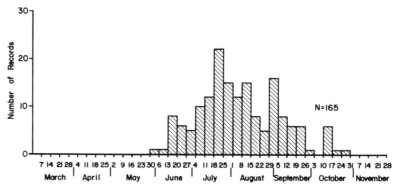

Fig. 8.131 *Eurema lisa*-Temporal distribution.

STATUS: Regular immigrant; rare to common. This species is most regularly encountered in southern Ohio and in the Oak Openings of Lucas County, where at times it is locally common. It becomes progressively less common northward. With the exception of the Oak Openings, it is rarely encountered in the northern counties.

DISTRIBUTION/RANGE: This species has been recorded throughout the State (Figure 8.130). In the eastern United States, this species is resident throughout the South. Each summer, *E. lisa* wanders northward and establishes temporary populations well north of its permanent range.

HABITAT: In Ohio, this species inhabits open areas such as prairie openings, old fields, forest clearings, clover fields, and along railroad rights-of-way and roadsides.

HOSTPLANT(S): Although no hostplant has been reported in Ohio, temporary populations of this species are usually found in association with partridge-pea (*Cassia fasciculata* Michx.). Various *Cassia* species are the primary foodplants throughout this butterfly's range (Opler and Krizek, 1984).

ADULT ENERGY RESOURCES: Self-heal (*Prunella vulgaris* L.), red clover (*Trifolium pratense* L.), and blazing-star (*Liatris* sp.). Adults also take moisture at damp soil and mud, especially if they have been wetted with urine.

FLIGHT PERIOD: Depending on how early wandering females reach Ohio, this species has the potential to produce up to three broods (Figure 8.131). Extreme dates range from 2 June to 25 October.

SIMILAR SPECIES: None.

GENERAL COMMENTS: This is our most common immigrant sulphur. Although it is usually uncommon and encountered as single individuals, it can be quite common once a temporary population is established. It is seen regularly only along the Ohio River, where populations are probably formed yearly. It is more sporadic northward where populations are more localized, except in the Oak Openings, where this butterfly is often common in late summer. Most adults are seen in late summer and early autumn. All of the temporary populations are eliminated each winter.

   The flight of this species is fairly rapid, very erratic, and usually within a few centimeters of the ground. When alarmed, this species can be very difficult to follow visually.

   Females are polymorphic, and can be white (form 'alba' [Strecker, 1878]), pale yellow, or yellow. Although Henninger (1910) found the white form to be very common in Seneca County, this form is quite uncommon in Ohio.

LITERATURE RECORD: Henry County (Hine, 1898a; 1898b).

Eurema mexicana (Boisduval, 1836). Mexican Sulphur. Plate 20.

Fig. 8.132 *Eurema mexicana.*

STATUS: Stray: rare. This species has only been reported once from Ohio.

DISTRIBUTION/RANGE: This species is resident from southern Texas, Arizona, and New Mexico, south to northern South America (Opler and Krizek, 1984). Although this species seldom wanders north and east of Nebraska and Missouri, strays have been recorded as far north as southern Michigan (Opler and Krizek, 1984), Minnesota (Macy and Shepard, 1941), and Point Pelee, Ontario (Wormington, 1982). The single Ohio specimen was captured in Sylvania, Lucas County (Figure 8.132) (Robert C. Hollister, pers comm, 1989).

HABITAT: This species prefers dry open habitats in the northern portion of its range (Opler and Krizek, 1984). The Ohio record was captured in a yard near open fields.

HOSTPLANT(S): Not known in Ohio. Various legumes, including *Cassia* species, are used in areas where this butterfly is a resident. There is no evidence to suggest that *E. mexicana* has ever reproduced within Ohio.

ADULT ENERGY RESOURCES: Although no specific adult energy resource has been reported, the single Ohio record was collected while it was feeding at a garden flower.

FLIGHT PERIOD: The single Ohio individual was collected during the summer of 1934 (Robert C. Hollister, pers comm, 1989).

SIMILAR SPECIES: None.

GENERAL COMMENTS: This species regularly wanders northward from its breeding range, but seldom occurs as far north as Ohio. However, during the drought years of the early 1930's, this species was collected in states far to the north of its usual range, including Michigan (Moore, 1960), Minnesota (Macy and Shepard, 1941), and Ohio. The prolonged drought of that period may have provided ideal conditions for the northward spread of this species. Because this butterfly wanders widely from the areas in which it is a resident, it should be watched for in Ohio, especially in open habitats during late summer and early autumn.

LITERATURE RECORDS: None.
The single Ohio record is based on a personal communication from Robert C. Hollister (1989). Unfortunately, the specimen upon which this record is based no longer exists.

Eurema nicippe (Cramer, 1779). Sleepy Orange. Plate 20.

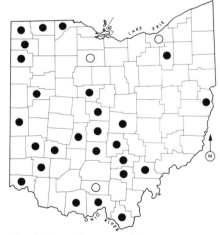

Fig. 8.133 *Eurema nicippe.*

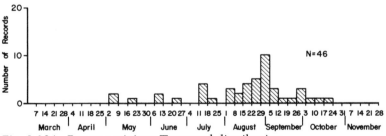

Fig. 8.134 *Eurema nicippe*-Temporal distribution.

STATUS: Regular immigrant; rare to uncommon. This species is encountered most frequently in southern Ohio.

DISTRIBUTION/RANGE: In the eastern United States, this species is resident in the southern Atlantic and Gulf States. It regularly wanders well north of Ohio (Opler and Krizek, 1984). Although this species has been recorded over most of the State, most of our records are from southern Ohio (Figure 8.133).

HABITAT: This butterfly usually inhabits open disturbed habitats such as old fields, pastures, vacant lots, wet meadows, disturbed fens, and roadsides.

HOSTPLANT(S): In Ohio this species has been found and reared on wild senna (*Cassia hebecarpa* Fern). Pilate (1882) also listed *Cassia marilandica* L., but may have been referring to the more common *C. hebecarpa*, which had not yet been described. *Cassia* species are the primary foodplants throughout the range of *E. nicippe* (Opler and Krizek, 1984).

ADULT ENERGY RESOURCES: Alfalfa (*Medicago sativa* L.), velvet-leaf (*Abutilon theophrasti* Medic.), asters (*Aster* spp.), ironweed (*Vernonia* sp.), and monkey flower (*Mimulus* sp.). Adults also imbibe moisture from damp soil and mud.

83

FLIGHT PERIOD: Depending on how early wandering females reach Ohio, this species has the potential to produce two or three overlapping broods (Figure 8.134). Extreme dates range from 4 May to 20 October.

SIMILAR SPECIES: See *Colias eurytheme.*

GENERAL COMMENTS: Although Price (1970) suggested that *E. nicippe* was resident (because it appeared to inhabit the same areas year after year), this butterfly forms only temporary populations in Ohio. However, Hine (1898b), Henninger (1910), and Tallant (unpublished notes) all report seeing or collecting adults as early as April, so it is possible that this species may survive an occasional mild winter. Most of the older literature (Dury, 1878; Hine, 1898a; Kirtland, 1854a; Pilate, 1882) lists this butterfly as common, which may indicate that it might have been a more regular immigrant than at present.

The flight of this species is rapid, low, and erratic, and is anything but "sleepy", as its common name might suggest. Contrary to popular belief, "sleepy" does not refer to sluggish behavior. Rather, it was coined by John H. Comstock (Comstock and Comstock, 1904) in reference to the small discal black lines on the dorsal forewings which resemble closed eyes. Alarmed individuals can be almost impossible to pursue. This species is most easily observed while it is visiting nectar sources.

Eurema nicippe is seasonally polyphenic. Summer brood individuals have a yellowish ventral hindwing whereas those of the autumn brood are reddish. A rare yellow form, 'flava' (Strecker, 1878), has not been reported from Ohio.

LITERATURE RECORDS: Cuyahoga (Bubna, 1897; Lepidopterists' Society, 1977), Seneca (Henninger, 1910), and Pike (Albrecht, 1982) Counties.

Nathalis iole Boisduval, 1836. Dainty Sulphur. Plate 20.

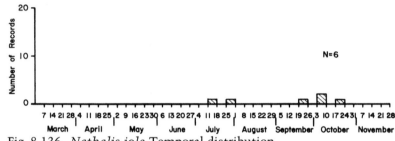

Fig. 8.136 *Nathalis iole*-Temporal distribution.

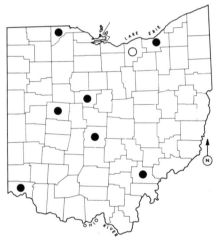

Fig. 8.135 *Nathalis iole.*

STATUS: Irregular immigrant or stray; rare.

DISTRIBUTION/RANGE: In the eastern United States, this species is a resident only in the deep south. Individuals from populations located west of the Mississippi River wander northward each season and may travel as far north as Minnesota, Ohio, and Pennsylvania (Clench, 1976; Douglas and Grula, 1988). Our few records are scattered statewide (Figure 8.135).

HABITAT: This butterfly prefers dry, open areas, particularly roadsides, railroad rights-of-way, and weedy fields.

HOSTPLANT(S): Not known in Ohio. Where this butterfly is resident, various species of composites (Asteraceae) including marigold (*Tagetes* spp.) and sneezeweeds (*Helenium* spp.) are used (Opler and Krizek, 1984). These plants are found throughout Ohio.

ADULT ENERGY RESOURCES: Red clover (*Trifolium pratense* L.).

FLIGHT PERIOD: Although our data are inconclusive, this species could produce at least one brood in Ohio, if females became established by early summer (Figure 8.136). Extreme dates range from 11 July to 20 October.

GENERAL COMMENTS: The dainty sulphur, the smallest of our pierids, is very rarely encountered in Ohio. Most of our records are based upon single individuals, although it has been noted (at least once) as being common. In a letter to Homer F. Price, Edward S. Thomas noted that there was a large flight of *N. iole* in 1931, and that he had collected this species at several localities in Ohio. Thus, it seems likely that temporary populations were established in 1931. Since that time, the few individuals that have been captured probably represent wandering individuals that have not originated from within the State. This butterfly cannot survive Ohio's winters.

Because of its small size, and the fact that it flies within a few centimeters of the ground in a rapid, erratic flight, this species can be easily overlooked. It should be looked for in open areas, particularly near potential dispersal corridors such as river valleys, railroads, and highways during late summer and early autumn.

LITERATURE RECORD: Lorain County (Lepidopterists' Society, 1967). This record is based upon a confirmed sighting and the individual was not captured (Leland L. Martin, pers comm, 1988).

Family LYCAENIDAE-Gossamer Wings

Feniseca tarquinius tarquinius (Fabricius, 1793). Harvester. Plate 21.

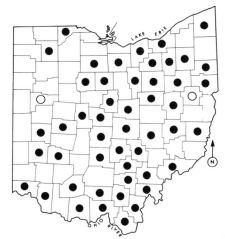

Fig. 8.137 *Feniseca tarquinius.*

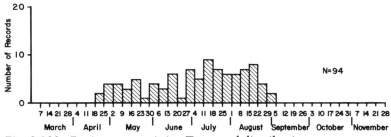

Fig. 8.138 *Feniseca tarquinius*-Temporal distribution.

STATUS: Resident; uncommon to rare. Populations are generally localized. Harvesters are usually encountered as solitary individuals.

DISTRIBUTION/RANGE: Statewide (Figure 8.137). *Feniseca tarquinius* is most often found in southern Ohio and in the Oak Openings.

HABITAT: This species is most often encountered in or near deciduous forests and along shrub-lined creeks. In the Oak Openings, it is often found near swamps and ditches.

HOSTPLANT(S) : This butterfly is predacious, with the larvae feeding on woolly aphids (Eriosomatidae). In Ohio, it has been reared on the aphid *Schizoneura tessellata* Fitch, which in turn were feeding on winterberry, (*Ilex verticillata* [L.] Gray) (Good, 1901). Larvae have also been found eating aphids on wild balsam-apple (*Echinocystis lobata* [Michx.] T. & G.) (Mogens C. Nielsen, pers comm, 1986). In addition, adults have been found in association with woolly aphids on common alder (*Alnus serrulata* [Ait.] Willd.) and hawthorns (*Crataegus* spp.).

ADULT ENERGY RESOURCES: Golden ragwort (*Senecio aureus* L.). Although this butterfly may occasionally visit flowers, most often it is found sipping honeydew secreted on leaves and twigs by woolly aphids. Adults also imbibe moisture from damp soil and wet rocks along creeks. Hine (1898a) reported this butterfly visiting carrion.

FLIGHT PERIOD: Three or more overlapping broods (Figure 8.138). Extreme dates range from 18 April to 2 September.

GENERAL COMMENTS: This is probably Ohio's most unusual butterfly. Whereas the larvae of all other butterflies in Ohio feed exclusively on plants, the harvester's larvae are carnivorous and eat woolly aphids.

    The flight of this species is rapid and erratic. Although not as fast, the darting flight is reminiscent of many hairstreaks. Males perch on sunlit leaves two to six meters above the ground and will fly out to investigate other males. Alarmed individuals fly only a short distance, often returning to their original perches. Adults are seldom encountered away from their larval hosts, and can often be found resting on leaves and twigs covered with aphid honeydew.

    Light individuals which lack or have reduced submarginal black spots on the dorsal hindwings may resemble the northeastern subspecies *F. t. novascotiae* McDunnough, 1935. Most of these individuals are seen in early spring, suggesting that this is a temperature-induced polyphenism.

LITERATURE RECORDS: Auglaize (Price, 1970) and Carroll (Albrecht, 1982) Counties.

Lycaena phlaeas americana Harris, 1862. American Copper. Plate 21.

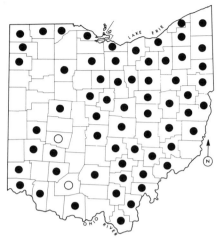

Fig. 8.139 _Lycaena phlaeas._

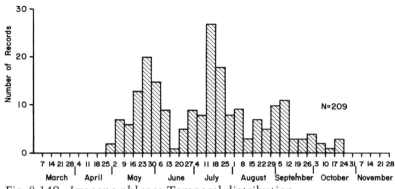

Fig. 8.140 _Lycaena phlaeas_-Temporal distribution.

STATUS: Resident, possibly naturalized; uncommon to common. This butterfly is more often encountered in the northern counties.

DISTRIBUTION/RANGE: Statewide (Figure 8.139).

HABITAT: This species is most often seen in open areas such as old fields, prairies, oak savannas, brushy areas, pastures, farmyards, alfalfa fields, and clover fields.

HOSTPLANT(S): Although no hostplant has been recorded for Ohio, this species is usually found in association with sheep sorrel (_Rumex acetosella_ L.), a common naturalized weed of disturbed areas. This is the primary hostplant throughout the eastern United States (Opler and Krizek, 1984).

ADULT ENERGY RESOURCES: Oxeye daisy (_Chrysanthemum leucanthemum_ L.), blazing star (_Liatris spicata_ [L.] Willd.), dwarf cinquefoil (_Potentilla canadensis_ L.), wild strawberry (_Frageria virginiana_ Dushesne), red clover (_Trifolium pratense_ L.), mountain mint (_Pycnanthemum virginianum_ L.), butterfly-weed (_Asclepias tuberosa_ L.), and alfalfa (_Medicago sativa_ L.).

FLIGHT PERIOD: Three, possibly four broods with peaks in May, July, and September (Figure 8.140). Extreme dates range from 23 May to 21 October.

SIMILAR SPECIES: None.

GENERAL COMMENTS: This is the most common copper in Ohio. Populations tend to be localized, but are numerous throughout the State. Males often seem quite aggressive, and will dart out to investigate almost any passing object, airplanes included! Adults often rest on bare soil with their wings held partially open. The flight of this species is rapid, erratic, and close to the ground.

   This species exhibits great individual variation. Aberrations with enlarged or suffused spots and small blue markings have been reported from the State, as well as the genetically based form 'fasciata' (Strecker, 1878). A rare white form of this species has been collected in Lorain County (Martin, 1962).

   Despite its common name, the American copper may be a naturalized resident from Europe (Opler and Krizek, 1984). This is supported by its choice of hostplants, which are all naturalized weeds from Europe, and its resemblance to certain European populations.

LITERATURE RECORDS: Clark and Highland Counties (Albrecht, 1982).

Lycaena hyllus (Cramer, 1775). Bronze Copper. Plate 21.

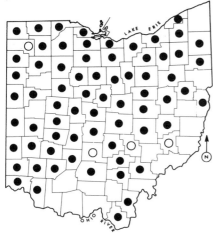

Fig. 8.141 *Lycaena hyllus*.

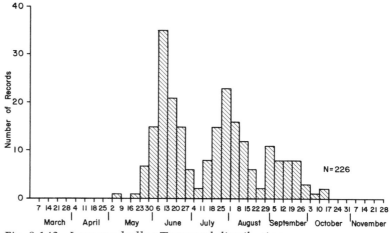

Fig. 8.142 *Lycaena hyllus*-Temporal distribution.

STATUS: Resident; uncommon. This species is most frequently encountered in the northern half of the State where it is occasionally locally common. In southern Ohio, this species is fairly rare.

DISTRIBUTION/RANGE: Statewide (Figure 8.141). This is one of the few butterflies reported from Kelleys Island, Erie County.

HABITAT: The bronze copper is restricted to moist habitats. In northern Ohio, suitable habitats include sedge meadows, fens, marshes, wet drainage ditches, pond edges, stream edges, and swamps. In unglaciated areas, it is associated with poorly drained bottomland swamps, and marshes, and occasionally is found in small hillside seeps. One population in Athens County persisted for at least three years in a 3 m² seep which supported fewer than ten stems of potential hostplant. This butterfly will move to drier habitats to visit nectar sources.

HOSTPLANT(S): In Ohio, this species has been found and reared on great water dock (*Rumex orbiculatus* Gray) (Jewett, 1880; Pilate, 1882). It is also associated with knotweeds (*Polygonum* spp.). Docks and knotweeds are the primary hostplants throughout its range (Opler and Krizek, 1984).

ADULT ENERGY RESOURCES: Alfalfa (*Medicago sativa* L.), red clover (*Trifolium pratense* L.), swamp milkweed (*Asclepias incarnata* L.), common milkweed (*Asclepias syriaca* L.), dogbanes (*Apocynum* spp.), thistles (*Cirsium* spp.), asters (*Aster* spp.), and knotweed (*Polygonum* sp.).

FLIGHT PERIOD: Three broods, peaking in June, July, and late August-early September (Figure 8.142). Extreme dates range from 8 May to 15 October.

SIMILAR SPECIES: None.

GENERAL COMMENTS: Although widely distributed, this butterfly is very localized, and usually encountered in low numbers. Adults are usually restricted to the vicinity of their presumed hostplants, even when visiting nectar sources.

   Although Opler and Krizek (1984) and Pyle (1981) both mention that this butterfly seldom visits flowers, we have found just the opposite. Adults take nectar at a variety of flower species, but are especially frequent on swamp milkweed, red clover, and Indian hemp. Adults perch on flower heads, grass blades, and other plants, often with their wings held partially open. The flight of this species is erratic and close to the ground cover. Males perch and fly out to investigate passing objects. An aberration of this species, "wormsbacheri" (Gunder, 1927), was probably described from a specimen collected in northeastern Ohio by Henry Wormsbacher.

LITERATURE RECORDS: Defiance (Price, 1970), Pickaway (Bales, 1909), Perry, and Noble (Albrecht, 1982) Counties.

Lycaena epixanthe epixanthe (Boisduval and LeConte, 1833). Bog Copper. Plate 21.

Fig. 8.143 *Lycaena epixanthe.*

STATUS: Resident; rare, probably extirpated. We have seen no authentic Ohio specimens.

DISTRIBUTION/RANGE: This butterfly has been reported from Cuyahoga County (Kirtland, 1854a; Kirkpatrick, 1864) (Figure 8.143). Northern Ohio represents the extreme southern limit of this species' range in the Great Lakes region.

HABITAT: This species is limited to acidic peat deposits (bogs) that support an abundant growth of cranberries.

HOSTPLANT(S): Although no hostplant has been recorded for Ohio, the only known hostplants for this butterfly are species of cranberries (*Vaccinium macrocarpon* L. and *V. oxycoccus* Ait.) (Wright, 1983). Although cranberries have been reported from at least 16 northern and central Ohio counties, very few populations are extant. Northeastern Ohio contains the only remaining bogs which might support this butterfly.

ADULT ENERGY RESOURCES: None recorded for Ohio.

FLIGHT PERIOD: Populations in southern Michigan have one brood, which flies from mid-June through mid-July.

SIMILAR SPECIES: Both sexes of *Lycaena dorcas* and *L. helloides* can be confused with this species. Males of both *L. dorcas* and *L. helloides* have six or more dark spots on the dorsal forewings, but male *L. epixanthe* have only three such spots. Females of *L. epixanthe* are duller brown dorsally, and lack the orange patches that are found on females of *L. dorcas* and *L. helloides*. Ventrally, both sexes of *L. epixanthe* are light gray with a hint of yellow while *L. dorcas* and *L. helloides* have more orange. Finally, *L. epixanthe* tends to be smaller than the other two species.

GENERAL COMMENTS: This butterfly may have once occurred throughout northern Ohio. Prior to human intervention, cranberry bogs were widespread throughout northern and central Ohio. Today, most of the documented bogs in Ohio have been destroyed, and only a handful of these unique habitats survive (Andreas, 1985). The majority of these wetlands was drained, but a few of the larger and more spectacular areas were flooded to provide reservoirs for Ohio's canal system. Notable examples include Buckeye Lake in Licking County and Pymatuning State Park in Ashtabula County, both of which originally supported large expanses of cranberry. Likewise, the large bog complex that once dominated parts of Morrow and Crawford Counties may have also supported *L. epixanthe* prior to the drainage of this area for agricultural purposes. Cranberries were also common in the wet depressions between sand dunes in the Oak Openings (Moseley, 1928). Unfortunately, these communities have also been eliminated through draining.

This species has not been reported from Ohio since the nineteenth century (Kirtland, 1854a; and Kirkpatrick, 1864). Searches of potential habitats in central and northeastern Ohio by John and Edward Thomas (Rawson, 1948), Albrecht (1982), Shuey (1985), David M. Wright (pers comm, 1987), and others have all failed to locate this species. A small series of this species was seen in a private collection in Pennsylvania, labelled simply "Ohio". However, there is conflicting information regarding the origin of these specimens and unless further evidence suggests otherwise, they should not be seriously considered. It is possible that this species is still resident in extreme northeastern Ohio in some unexplored peatland. If this species is rediscovered in the State, it and its habitat should be preserved as an example of a once widespread community type in northern Ohio. Populations of this butterfly still survive in areas that are close to Ohio in Michigan (Moore, 1960) and Pennsylvania (Prescott, 1984).

In southern Michigan this species occurs in small, very localized populations. Adults seldom stray far from their hostplants. The flight of *L. epixanthe* is slow, weak, and very close to the ground. Because of the two-toned color pattern of this species (dark dorsally, pale ventrally), the species seems to disappear between each wing beat. Adults perch on cranberry, sedges, and other low-growing plants. Although we have not seen authenic Ohio specimens, we have assigned the Ohio reports to *L. e. epixanthe*, rather than the weakly differentiated putative subspecies *L. e. michiganensis* (Rawson, 1948).

LITERATURE RECORD: Cuyahoga County (Kirtland, 1854a; Kirkpatrick, 1864).

Lycaena dorcas dorcas **(W. Kirby, 1837).** Dorcas Copper. Plate 21.

Fig. 8.144 *Lycaena dorcas.*

STATUS: Resident; rare, probably extirpated. This species is known from a single literature record (Price, 1970).

DISTRIBUTION/RANGE: The only Ohio record is from Mud Lake State Nature Preserve, Williams County (Price, 1970) (Figure 8.144).

HABITAT: The single known Ohio locality is a fen. This is the only reported habitat type throughout this region (Shull, 1987; Shuey, 1985). Although fens are widespread and fairly frequent throughout glaciated Ohio, in northwestern Ohio, where *L. dorcas* could most likely occur, fens are rare.

HOSTPLANT(S): The single individual reported from Ohio was a female which was collected while it appeared to be ovipositing on the leaves of shrubby cinquefoil (*Potentilla fruticosa* L.) (Price, 1970). This is the only reported hostplant in the eastern United States (Opler and Krizek, 1984). Shrubby cinquefoil generally is restricted to fens in the Great Lakes region (Stuckey and Denney, 1981).

ADULT ENERGY RESOURCES: None recorded for Ohio. In populations near Ohio, adults have been observed visiting shrubby cinquefoil (*Potentilla fruticosa* L.) and black-eyed Susans (*Rudbeckia hirta* L.).

FLIGHT PERIOD: The single report (Price, 1970) is dated 11 July 1948. In northeastern Indiana, the single brood of this species peaks in July.

SIMILAR SPECIES: See *L. epixanthe. Lycaena helloides* can also be confused with *L. dorcas.* Although these two species are indistinguishable in other parts of their ranges, in Ohio they are easily separated. Specimens of *L. dorcas*, especially females, are smaller and tend to have more pronounced spotting on the ventral wing surfaces than does *L. helloides*. Female *L. dorcas* also have less orange dorsally. Male *L. dorcas* are darker (bronze-brown) and have wider dark forewing margins than does the lighter (orange-brown) *L. helloides*.

GENERAL COMMENTS: This is another species that is known only from a literature report. Price's single specimen was not found with the rest of his collection (which is housed at The Ohio State Museum of Insects and Spiders), and we consider it to be lost or deposited in some other collection. We have also learned that although Price (1970) named Mogens C. Nielsen as the individual who identified the *L. dorcas* specimen, the specimen was actually determined by Edward S. Thomas.

Prior to human intervention, this species was probably established in northwestern Ohio. Unfortunately, the massive agricultural rearrangement of the landscape in this region eliminated almost all of the wetlands which might have supported this butterfly. Populations still survive in appropriate habitats in southern Michigan and northeastern Indiana, such as Marsh Lake, Stuben County, Indiana, which is less than 12 km from Ohio.

The flight of this species is slower and less erratic than the very similar *L. helloides*. Adult *L. dorcas* are usually seen flying just over the ground cover, and seldom stray from the fens they inhabit. Adults perch on shrubby cinquefoil, sedges, and other low plants within their habitats.

LITERATURE RECORD: Williams County (Price, 1970; Lepidopterists Society, 1949).

Studebaker and Studebaker (1967) recorded this species from Miami County, but based their record on a misdetermined series of *L. helloides*.

Lycaena helloides **(Boisduval, 1852).** Purplish Copper. Plate 21.

Fig. 8.145 *Lycaena helloides.*

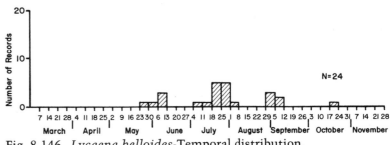

Fig. 8.146 *Lycaena helloides*-Temporal distribution.

STATUS: Resident; rare. Populations are extremely localized, and usually occur at low densities.

DISTRIBUTION/RANGE: Although our records are scattered throughout the western half of the State (Figure 8.145), this butterfly is most often encountered in northwestern Ohio. South of this region, *L. helloides* is very rare. The single record from Hamilton County was collected in 1917.

HABITAT: This species inhabits a variety of disturbed moist areas, such as fallow fields with poor drainage, sedge meadows, wet prairies, wet ditches, and low damp areas of cultivated fields.

HOSTPLANT(S): In Ohio this species has been found and reared on water smartweed (*Polygonum amphibium* L.) (David K. Parshall, pers comm, 1987). It has also been observed in association with sheep sorrel (*Rumex acetosella* L.). These, and other species within these genera are the primary hostplants throughout this butterfly's range (Opler and Krizek, 1984).

ADULT ENERGY RESOURCES: Arrow-head (*Sagittaria latifolia* Willd.), red clover (*Trifolium pratense* L.), and swamp milkweed (*Asclepias incarnata* L.). Price (1970) also lists this species at May-apple (*Podophyllum peltatum* L.) and at damp soil.

FLIGHT PERIOD: Three, possibly four broods peaking in June, July, and late August-early September (Figure 8.146). Extreme dates range from 23 May to 21 October.

SIMILAR SPECIES: See *L. epixanthe* and *L. dorcas*.

GENERAL COMMENTS: This species is probably more widespread in western Ohio than our records indicate. It occurs as localized populations and usually flies with *L. phlaeas*, which makes *L. helloides* very easy to overlook. Although populations of *L. helloides* are rare, population densities are occasionally high.

This butterfly has probably been negatively affected by agricultural activities. Wetland drainage and herbicide use have eliminated vast areas that once might have been suitable habitat for this species. Because the type of wetland that this species requires is often not botanically unique, few if any of its habitats have been protected by preservation groups. If the general trend of losing these wetlands continues, *L. helloides* could become endangered in Ohio.

The flight of this species is rapid, erratic, and usually close to the ground and wetland vegetation. Males chase after similarly sized butterflies, presumably in search of potential mates. Adults perch on low vegetation with their wings held partially open. Adults visit flowers freely.

LITERATURE RECORD: Paulding County (Price, 1970).

Atlides halesus halesus (Cramer, 1777). Great Purple Hairstreak. Plate 21.

Fig. 8.147 *Atlides halesus*.

STATUS: Stray; rare. Only one specimen of this species is known from Ohio. Because the hostplant is locally common along the Ohio River, this species could be a very rare resident.

DISTRIBUTION/RANGE: In the eastern United States, this species ranges from the Gulf States north into Missouri, Illinois, Kentucky, and New Jersey (Opler and Krizek, 1984). The single Ohio record is from Avondale, Hamilton County (Figure 8.147). Ohio is on the extreme northern edge of this butterfly's range.

HABITAT: Where it is resident, this butterfly occurs in association with moist lowland forests, where its parasitic hostplant, mistletoe, grows on oak trees. In Ohio, this habitat type is most frequent along the Ohio River (Cusick and Silberhorn, 1977). Adults are usually encountered as they visit nectar sources.

HOSTPLANT(S): Not known in Ohio. The only known hostplants for this butterfly are mistletoes (*Phoradendron* spp.) (Pyle, 1981). The only mistletoe in Ohio (*P. flavescens* [Pursh] Nutt.), which is used as a host in other areas, occurs in at least 14 southern Ohio counties (Braun, 1961).

ADULT ENERGY RESOURCES: Goldenrod (*Solidago* sp.) (Dury, 1900).

FLIGHT PERIOD: The single Ohio record is dated 24 September 1871. Where resident, there are usually two or three broods. It is unknown whether or not this species reproduces in Ohio.

GENERAL COMMENTS: Although Dury (1900) stated that he collected his only specimen (a female) in September 1885, the label on the female that we located reads 24 September 1871. Because this earlier date supports a September 1871 date mentioned in Dury's personal notes, we believe that the published date (1885) is in error. The single specimen is deposited with Dury's collection in the Cincinnati Museum of Natural History.

This large hairstreak should be watched for in southern Ohio where mistletoe is common. There have been no recent attempts to locate this species in Ohio, and thus it is possible that it could be a resident along the Ohio River.

The flight of this species is very erratic and rapid. Adults are strongly attracted to flowers.

Harkenclenus titus titus (Fabricius, 1793)/***mopsus*** (Hübner, 1818). Coral Hairstreak. Plate 22.

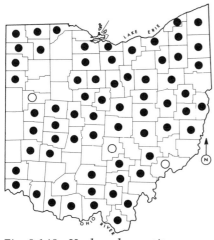

Fig. 8.148 *Harkenclenus titus.*

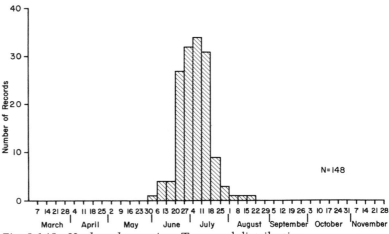

Fig. 8.149 *Harkenclenus titus*-Temporal distribution.

STATUS: Resident; uncommon to common.

DISTRIBUTION/RANGE: Statewide (Figure 8.148).

HABITAT: This species occurs in a variety of open areas such as old fields, neglected pastures, prairies, brushy wet meadows, powerline cuts, and along railroad rights-of-way and roadsides.

HOSTPLANT(S): Not known in Ohio. Wild black cherry (*Prunus serotina* Ehrh.), choke cherry (*Prunus virginiana* L.), and wild plums (*Prunus* spp.) are the reported hostplants throughout the eastern United States (Opler and Krizek, 1984). All of these members of the Rosaceae are common throughout Ohio (Braun, 1961).

ADULT ENERGY RESOURCES: Red clover (*Trifolium pratense* L.), common milkweed (*Asclepias syriaca* L.), butterfly-weed (*Asclepias tuberosa* L.), oxeye daisy (*Chrysanthemum leucanthemum* L.), yarrow (*Achillea millefolium* L.), and Indian hemp (*Apocynum cannabinum* L.). This butterfly is particularly fond of butterfly-weed, so much so that it will practically ignore all other flowers when this plant is present and in bloom.

FLIGHT PERIOD: One brood, peaking in late June and early July (Figure 8.149). Extreme dates range from 1 June to 17 August.

SIMILAR SPECIES: Although *H. titus* can potentially be confused with all of the *Satyrium* species, the ventral wing surfaces are distinctive. *Harkenclenus titus* lacks tails, and has bright orange submarginal bands on the ventral hindwings that separate it from all other species.

GENERAL COMMENTS: Although this species is found statewide, it usually occurs at low densities, and is not often seen in large numbers. The best way to locate this species is to check blooming heads of butterfly-weed, which are very attractive to this butterfly. When population densities are high, individual flowers of this species may have over 10 adults on them at any given moment.

Adults are rapid and erratic fliers. Males perch on top of shrubs and small trees that are as much as five meters in height, and fly out to investigate passing objects. Both sexes are most easily observed when visiting nectar sources.

Ohio is located in a blend zone between two weakly developed clinal subspecies. In northern Ohio, individuals are closest to *H. t. titus* but specimens from unglaciated Ohio resemble *H. titus mopsus. Harkenclenus t. titus* is darker ventrally and lacks white scaling around the black spots on the ventral hindwings; *H. titus mopsus* is paler ventrally and has the black spots on the ventral hindwings surrounded by white scaling. Populations in central Ohio are variable, whereas populations in extreme southern and northern Ohio seem phenotypically stable.

LITERATURE RECORDS: Auglaize (Hoying, 1975), Washington, and Fairfield (Albrecht, 1982) Counties.

Satyrium acadica acadica (W. H. Edwards, 1862). Acadian Hairstreak. Plate 22.

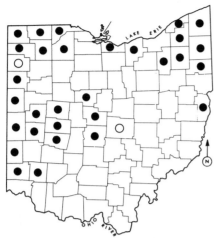

Fig. 8.150 *Satyrium acadica.*

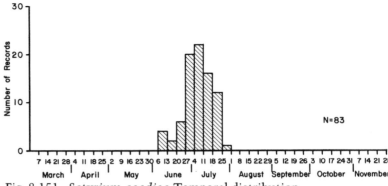

Fig. 8.151 *Satyrium acadica*-Temporal distribution.

STATUS: Resident; rare to uncommon. This species is most frequently encountered in northern Ohio, where it can be locally common. Near the glacial border, populations are rarer and generally occur at lower densities.

DISTRIBUTION/RANGE: Northern and western Ohio; this butterfly is virtually absent from unglaciated Ohio (Figure 8.150). Ohio populations are at the southern extreme of this species' range in the midwest.

HABITAT: This species is always associated with wetlands where willows (*Salix* spp.) are common. In northern Ohio, *S. acadica* inhabits a variety of wetland types including roadside ditches, wet old fields, sedge meadows, marshes, fens, swamps, stream bottoms, and bogs. In central Ohio, this species is more localized and usually occurs in and adjacent to undisturbed fens, sedge meadows, and swamps. In southwestern Ohio, it has been found in association with stream bottoms (Robert L. Langston, pers comm, 1988).

HOSTPLANT(S): In Ohio, *S. acadica* is strongly associated with willows (*Salix* spp.) and oviposition has been observed on black willow (*Salix nigra* Marsh.) (David K. Parshall, pers comm, 1987). Willows are the only reported hostplants throughout this butterfly's range (Opler and Krizek, 1984).

ADULT ENERGY RESOURCES: Common milkweed (*Asclepias syriaca* L.), swamp milkweed (*Asclepias incarnata* L.), butterfly-weed (*Asclepias tuberosa* L.), dogbanes (*Apocynum* spp.), Indian hemp (*Apocynum cannibium* L.), and thistles (*Cirsium* spp.).

FLIGHT PERIOD: One brood, peaking in late June and early July (Figure 8.151). Extreme dates range from 7 June to 25 July.

SIMILAR SPECIES: Although this species can be confused with other *Satyrium* species and *Harkenclenus titus*, the pale gray ventral wing surfaces of *S. acadica* will easily identify it.

GENERAL COMMENTS: This hairstreak is closely associated with wetlands which support abundant willows. Within wetlands, this butterfly is most often seen perching on willow leaves, tall sedges, and other plants, or visiting flowers such as dogbane. Populations usually occur at low densities, but occasionally this species can be locally abundant. In central and southwest Ohio, populations are extremely localized. Further collecting will probably result in the discovery of new county records in these areas.

The flight of this species is fast and erratic, and is often difficult to follow visually. Males perch at heights of one to two meters, and dart out to investigate other hairstreaks. However, male *S. acadica* do not seem as active in this pursuit as other hairstreak species. Adults are avid flower visitors, and are easily observed while they are feeding.

LITERATURE RECORDS: Paulding (Price, 1970), and Licking (Albrecht, 1982) Counties.

Satyrium edwardsii (Grote & Robinson, 1867). Edwards' Hairstreak. Plate 22.

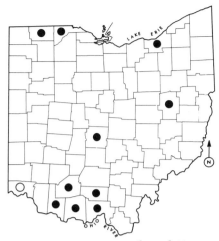

Fig. 8.152 *Satyrium edwardsii.*

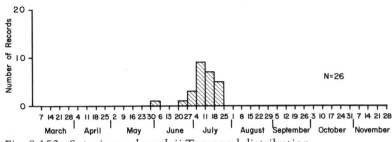

Fig. 8.153 *Satyrium edwardsii*-Temporal distribution.

STATUS: Resident; rare. Populations of this species are extremely localized, but usually occur at high densities.

DISTRIBUTION/RANGE: Our records are scattered statewide, but the vast majority are from the Oak Openings of Lucas County (Figure 8.152). Viable populations are known only from the Oak Openings of Lucas and Fulton Counties, and from the extreme southern portion of the State.

HABITAT: In the Oak Openings this species occurs in oak savannas. The southern Ohio populations inhabit xeric prairies and ridge top communities containing numerous prairie species. In both regions of the State where viable populations still exist, habitats are characterized by xeric conditions and abundant prairie forbs (Shuey, Iftner, and Calhoun, 1985[86]). Nothing is known about the habitats in the remaining counties.

HOSTPLANT(S): Although no hostplant has been recorded in Ohio, in the Oak Openings this species is closely associated with stands of stunted oaks, especially black oak (*Quercus velutina* Lam.). Oaks are also common at all the southern Ohio population localities. Oaks are the only confirmed hostplants throughout this butterfly's range (Opler and Krizek, 1984).

In Michigan, *S. edwardsii* is myrmecophilic with the ant species *Formica integra* Nylander (Webster and Nielsen, 1984). Because the habitats that were studied in Michigan are nearly identical to habitats in the Oak Openings, it is very probable that *S. edwardsii* is associated with this ant species in northwestern Ohio.

ADULT ENERGY RESOURCES: Common milkweed (*Asclepias syriaca* L.) and butterfly-weed (*Asclepias tuberosa* L.).

FLIGHT PERIOD: One brood, peaking in early July (Figure 8.153). Extreme dates range from 2 June to 24 July.

SIMILAR SPECIES: All *Satyrium* species, but especially *S. calanus falacer* and *S. caryaevorum. Satyrium edwardsii* can be separated from all other *Satyrium* species by the combination of its light gray ventral ground color, the postmedial band which is broken into separate black spots that are surrounded by a white ring, and the presence of a orange spot on the dorsal hindwing. The male genitalia of *S. edwardsii* will easily separate it from *S. caryaevorum* but they are less helpful in separating *S. edwardsii* from *S. calanus falacer.*

GENERAL COMMENTS: Although Price (1970) erroneously reported this species as being common throughout northwestern Ohio, and Albrecht (1982) included scattered records throughout the State, *S. edwardsii* is really known from just a few localities. Active populations are currently known from only two areas of the State, the Oak Openings of northwest Ohio and a few counties in the extreme southern portion of the State. It is probably more widespread in southern Ohio than our records indicate, and collectors should watch for it in likely habitats, especially along ridge tops in southern Ohio.

If this butterfly is dependent upon an ant for its survival as we suspect, then soil type could indirectly influence the distribution of *S. edwardsii*. Although we know nothing about the habitat requirements of the ant species, the known habitats of *S. edwardsii* in Ohio share several similarities. In both southern and northwestern Ohio, habitats which support this butterfly are xeric, open, and characterized by herbaceous prairie plants. Consequently, this butterfly could be a useful indicator of unique habitats.

Populations of this species are very localized, and adults are closely associated with small oak trees. Both males and females perch on oaks, and can be flushed by jarring the trees. In the Oak Openings, populations usually attain high densities. Males fly out from their perches to investigate passing objects, presumably as part of their mate-locating behavior. Groups of males chasing each other in what often resembles a fight, frequently spiral over the tops of small oaks. Both sexes visit flowers freely, and under high densities, 10-20 may occupy the same milkweed bloom. The flight of this species is fast and very erratic, and is usually difficult to follow with the eye.

LITERATURE RECORD: Hamilton County (Wyss, 1932).

This species has erroneously been reported from a number of counties (see Shuey, Iftner, and Calhoun, 1985[86]). Records listed by Price (1970) for Allen, Defiance, Putnam, Paulding, Van Wert, and Williams Counties were all based on misidentified females of *S. calanus falacer* and *S. caryaevorum*. A record listed by Albrecht (1982) from Greene County was based on a misidentified female *S. calanus falacer*. This species was also mistakenly reported from Vinton County (Lepidopterists' Society, 1972).

Satyrium calanus falacer (Godart, 1824). Banded Hairstreak. Plate 22.

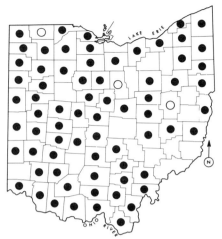

Fig. 8.154 *Satyrium calanus.*

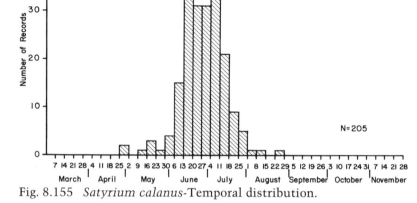

Fig. 8.155 *Satyrium calanus*-Temporal distribution.

STATUS: Resident; uncommon to common.

DISTRIBUTION/RANGE: Statewide (Figure 8.154).

HABITAT: This species is encountered primarily in openings in oak-hickory forests. Other habitats in which it may be found include prairies, oak savannas, old fields, and occasionally residential areas.

HOSTPLANT(S): In Ohio, this species has been found and reared on white oak (*Quercus alba* L.). Other reports include oaks (*Quercus* sp.) (Pilate, 1882) and walnut (*Juglans* sp.) (William N. Tallant, unpublished notes, 1886). It is also associated with shagbark and bitternut hickories (*Carya ovata* [Mill.] K. Koch and *C. cordiformis* [Wang.] K. Koch). Species of the beech (Fagaceae) and walnut (Juglandaceae) families are the primary hostplants throughout the range of this butterfly (Opler and Krizek, 1984).

ADULT ENERGY RESOURCES: Common milkweed (*Asclepias syriaca* L.), swamp milkweed (*Asclepias incarnata* L.), ironweed (*Vernonia* sp.), dogbane (*Apocynum* sp.), white sweet clover (*Melilotus alba* Desr.), red clover (*Trifolium pratense* L.), New Jersey tea (*Ceanothus americanus* L.), elderberry (*Sambucus canadensis* L.), thistles (*Cirsium* spp.), staghorn sumac (*Rhus typhina* L.), and cinquefoil (*Potentilla* sp.). Price (1970) also lists butterfly-weed (*Asclepias tuberosa* L.).

FLIGHT PERIOD: One brood, peaking in late June and early July (Figure 8.155). Extreme dates range from 25 April (early) to 22 August.

SIMILAR SPECIES: All *Satyrium* species (see *S. edwardsii*), but especially *S. caryaevorum*. Many specimens, males in particular, of these two species cannot be determined reliably without examining their genitalia. However, three traits will separate most specimens of these species. *Satyrium caryaevorum* has a large ventral hindwing anal blue spot that usually extends far beyond the adjacent orange crescents. In *S. calanus falacer*, this blue spot is only slightly larger than the adjacent orange crescents. The postmedial ventral forewing bands are nearly always offset in *S. caryaevorum*, whereas they are usually continuous in *S. calanus falacer*. Finally, the ventral ground color of *S. caryaevorum* is brownish gray and that of *S. calanus falacer* is slate gray.

GENERAL COMMENTS: This is the most common species of *Satyrium* in Ohio. Depending on the habitat, it often occurs with *S. caryaevorum* and *S. edwardsii*, two species with which it is easily confused. Because of its greater abundance, these other two species are often overlooked because they are difficult to identify in the field. Because *S. calanus falacer* apparently uses both oaks and hickories as hostplants, it is widespread throughout the State, and can even be found in residential areas. Populations tend to fluctuate, so this species can be abundant one year, and uncommon the next.

The flight of this species is fast and erratic. Adults are most often encountered while they are at flowers and while they are flying around or perching on their hostplants. Males perch on sunlit leaves, and dart out at other hairstreaks. After the chase, males usually return to their original perches. Males can be flushed into view by jarring small trees in sunlit clearings.

Satyrium boreale (Lafontaine, 1970), originally described as a distinct species, but now regarded as a form of *S. calanus falacer* (Gall, 1976), has been reported from Ohio (Lafontaine, 1970).

LITERATURE RECORDS: Fulton, Richland, and Tuscarawas Counties (Albrecht, 1982).

Satyrium caryaevorum (McDunnough, 1942). Hickory Hairstreak. Plate 22.

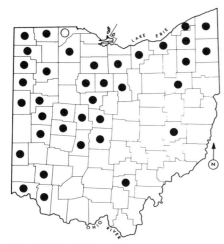

Fig. 8.156 *Satyrium caryaevorum.*

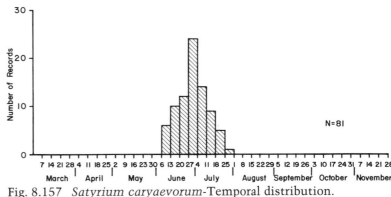

Fig. 8.157 *Satyrium caryaevorum*-Temporal distribution.

STATUS: Resident; rare. Populations of this species are localized and usually occur at low densities.

DISTRIBUTION/RANGE: Statewide, although most of our records are from glaciated regions (Figure 8.156).

HABITAT: This species is found primarily in deciduous forests where hickories are present, and in adjacent open areas such as forest margins and sunlit clearings. It is often associated with stands of younger trees. This species is occasionally found in residential areas and parks where hickories are used as landscape trees.

HOSTPLANT(S): In Ohio, this species has been found and reared on black walnut (*Juglans nigra* L.) (John W. Peacock, pers comm, 1987) and observed ovipositing on shagbark hickory (*Carya ovata* [Mill.] K. Koch) (David K. Parshall, pers comm, 1987). Adults are most often found in association with shagbark and bitternut hickories (*Carya ovata* [Mill.] K. Koch and *C. cordiformis* [Wang.] K. Koch). Hickories are the primary hosts throughout this hairstreak's range (Opler and Krizek, 1984).

ADULT ENERGY RESOURCES: Common milkweed (*Asclepias syriaca* L.), Indian hemp (*Apocynum cannabinum* L.), dogbane (*Apocynum* sp.), Canada thistle (*Cirsium arvense* [L.] Scop.), white sweet clover (*Melilotus alba* Desr.), and wild carrot (*Daucus carota* L.). Price (1970) also lists daisy fleabane (*Erigeron strigosus* Muhl.).

FLIGHT PERIOD: One brood, peaking in late June and early July (Figure 8.157). Extreme dates range from 8 June to 27 July.

SIMILAR SPECIES: See *Satyrium edwardsii* and *S. calanus falacer*. The male genitalia of *S. caryaevorum* are distinctive, and examination of these structures is the surest way to determine this species.

GENERAL COMMENTS: This species is probably more widespread than our records suggest, especially in southern Ohio where oak-hickory forests are common. *Satyrium caryaevorum* is easily overlooked because of its close resemblance to *S. calanus falacer*, which is usually much more common.

Adults are most often encountered when they are visiting nectar sources. They can also be flushed from their perches by tapping upon young hickories. Males perch on sunlit leaves and fly out at passing objects, often becoming involved in spiraling chases with other males. Male *S. caryaevorum* usually return to their original perches, which seem to be higher in the trees than the perches of *S. calanus falacer*. The flight of *S. caryaevorum* is fast and erratic.

LITERATURE RECORD: Lucas County (Price, 1970).

Satyrium liparops strigosum (Harris, 1862). Striped Hairstreak. Plate 22.

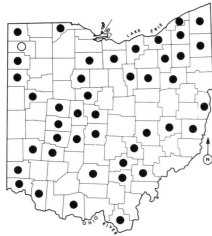

Fig. 8.158   *Satyrium liparops.*

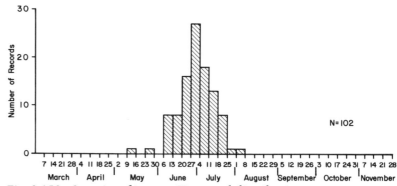

Fig. 8.159   *Satyrium liparops*-Temporal distribution.

STATUS: Resident; uncommon to rare. This species is usually encountered as single individuals or in low numbers.

DISTRIBUTION/RANGE: Statewide (Figure 8.158).

HABITAT: This butterfly occurs in a wide variety of open and forested situations. It is found in deciduous forests and associated openings, in brushy fields containing hawthorn and oak thickets, along overgrown fence rows and in wetlands such as bogs, sedge meadows, and swamps.

HOSTPLANT(S): In Ohio, this species has been reared on crabapple (*Malus* sp.), common choke cherry (*Prunus virginiana* L.), and plum (*Prunus* sp.). It has also been found in association with hawthorn (*Crataegus* spp.) and several blueberry species (*Vaccinium* spp.). Oaks (*Quercus* spp.) may also be hostplants because many captures occur in oak forests, where other potential hostplants are absent. Members of the rose (Rosaceae) and heath (Ericaceae) families are the primary hosts throughout eastern North America, although oaks (*Quercus* spp.), willows (*Salix* spp.), and American hornbeam (*Carpinus caroliniana* Walt.) are also used (Opler and Krizek, 1984).

ADULT ENERGY RESOURCES: Common milkweed (*Asclepias syriaca* L.), Indian hemp (*Apocynum cannabinum* L.), and cinquefoil (*Potentilla* sp.).

FLIGHT PERIOD: One brood, peaking in early July (Figure 8.159). Extreme dates range from 15 May to 1 August.

SIMILAR SPECIES: The ventral wing pattern will easily distinguish *S. liparops* from the other *Satyrium* species.

GENERAL COMMENTS: Although this species feeds on a wide variety of hostplants and occurs throughout the State in a wide variety of habitats, it is generally rare and very localized. Most adults are encountered as lone individuals, although occasionally several can be seen at some localities in good years. Like most hairstreaks, populations of *S. liparops* seem to fluctuate, and it can be locally common one year and rare to seemingly absent the next. *Satyrium liparops* is easily overlooked in the field because it usually flies with the much more abundant *S. calanus falacer*.

Adults are usually found perching on the sunlit leaves of shrubs and small trees or while visiting flowers. Males fly out from their perches and chase other males in spiraling flights. The flight is rapid and erratic.

Although wing pattern variation is rare in this species, occasional specimens have been found with orange patches on the dorsal wing surfaces, which vaguely resemble the southern nominate subspecies, *Satyrium l. liparops* (LeConte, 1833).

Henninger (1910) incorrectly associated the subspecies name *strigosum* with *S. calanus*.

LITERATURE RECORD: Defiance County (Price, 1970).

Calycopis cecrops (Fabricius, 1793). Red-banded Hairstreak. Plate 22

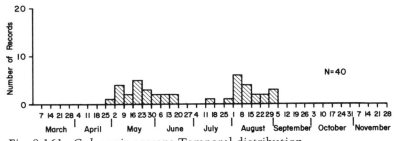

Fig. 8.161 *Calycopis cecrops*-Temporal distribution.

Fig. 8.160 *Calycopis cecrops*.

STATUS: Resident; rare to uncommon. Populations are localized and usually occur at low densities.

DISTRIBUTION/RANGE: Southern Ohio (Figure 8.160). Ohio populations represent the northern range limit of this species. Most of our records are from the southeastern corner of the State.

HABITAT: This species is usually associated with open brushy habitats such as woodland borders, forest clearings, powerline cuts, xeric prairies, and old fields.

HOSTPLANT(S): Although this species is usually closely associated with dwarf sumac (*Rhus copallina* L.) in Ohio, David K. Parshall (pers comm, 1987) has observed oviposition on staghorn sumac (*Rhus typhina* L.). These are the primary hostplants in the eastern United States (Opler and Krizek, 1984).

ADULT ENERGY RESOURCES: Staghorn sumac (*Rhus typhina* L.) and New Jersey tea (*Ceanothus americana* L.). Adults also use damp soil and mud.

FLIGHT PERIOD: Two, possibly three broods, with peaks in May and August (Figure 8.161). Extreme dates range from 29 April to 2 September.

GENERAL COMMENTS: As with most hairstreaks, this species is probably more widespread than our records indicate. Its sumac hostplants, *Rhus copallina* L. and *R. typhina* L., are common throughout southern Ohio, and *C. cecrops* should be continuously distributed through the region. Populations of this hairstreak are usually localized around stands of dwarf sumac and adults occur at low densities. Occasionally this species can be locally common.

The flight of this species is fast and erratic. Adults are usually observed perching on sunlit vegetation or while visiting flowers. Adults generally do not stray far from stands of their hostplants.

Adults are sexually dimorphic. Females usually have more blue pattern dorsally than do the males. Ohio specimens tend to be smaller than specimens from farther south.

LITERATURE RECORDS: None.

Mitoura gryneus gryneus (Hübner, 1819). Olive Hairstreak. Plate 23.

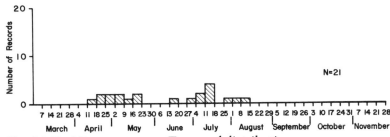

Fig. 8.163 *Mitoura gryneus*-Temporal distribution.

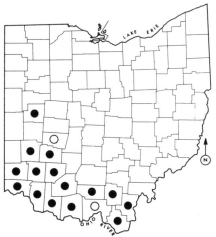

Fig. 8.162 *Mitoura gryneus*.

STATUS: Resident; rare. Populations are highly localized.

DISTRIBUTION/RANGE: Southern Ohio (Figure 8.162). Most of our records are from the southwestern corner of the State.

HABITAT: This species is associated with habitats that form over alkaline soils and which support red cedar (*Juniperus virginiana* L.) such as dry hillsides, rocky outcrops, bluffs, xeric prairies, and old fields. It can also be found in habitats where this tree has spread from plantings such as old cemeteries.

97

HOSTPLANT(S): Although no hostplant has been recorded for Ohio, populations are closely associated with stands of red cedar (*Juniperus virginiana* L.). This tree is the only known hostplant in eastern North America (Opler and Krizek, 1984).

ADULT ENERGY RESOURCES: Field pepper-grass (*Lepidium campestre* [L.] R. Br.), redbud (*Cercis canadensis* L.), dogwood (*Cornus* sp.), winter cress (*Barbarea vulgaris* R. Br.), pussy-toes (*Antennaria* sp.), and ragwort (*Senecio* sp.).

FLIGHT PERIOD: Two broods, peaking in late April-early May, and July-early August (Figure 8.163). Extreme dates range from 17 April to 8 August.

SIMILAR SPECIES: None.

GENERAL COMMENTS: This unique hairstreak occurs as localized populations, always in close association with its hostplant, red cedar. Populations can be difficult to locate and apparently do not occur in most stands of red cedar. Even where populations do occur, the protective coloration of this butterfly and the brief flight period often make it difficult to locate in the field. However, although *M. gryneus* is generally considered a rare species in the State, it is sometimes locally common at the correct time of year. Populations fluctuate from year to year.

This species is most often encountered in open stands of medium-sized (5-8m) red cedar with, or near, abundant nectar resources. Adults generally perch on the red cedar, and are best found by tapping or shaking the trees. Flushed adults generally return to the vicinity of their original perches, which can be quite high in the tree. Because the perches are often well out of net reach, an extension net is often needed to capture this species. Adults are sometimes observed in chases which spiral around the tops of the hostplants. The flight of this species is fast and erratic, and is difficult to follow with the eye.

Mitoura gryneus has undoubtedly benefited from the recent spread of its hostplant, and is probably more widespread and abundant in Ohio now than it was before European settlement. Originally, red cedar was probably a minor component of the forests of Ohio, and was probably restricted to poor alkaline soils in south-central and southwestern Ohio, and to Cedar Point and the Lake Erie islands of Erie County. As the original forest was cleared and then allowed to regenerate through succession, red cedar quickly spread into old field communities throughout the southwestern quarter of the State. Today red cedar is very common in young second growth communities, especially around xeric prairies. Although red cedar is found throughout the State, most of this wide distribution is the result of naturalization from home sites and cemeteries where this tree is used as an ornamental. Even though *M. gryneus* has the potential to occur statewide, most populations are probably limited to the southern portion of the State. Searches for this butterfly should be concentrated in southern Ohio where red cedar is most abundant, and possibly in Erie County, especially Cedar Point and the Lake Erie islands, where red cedar is also native. An individual of this species was observed, but not collected, on Kelleys Island, Erie County (Nault et al, 1989). It is possible that this butterfly is occasionally transplanted to new areas along with red cedar plantings.

This hairstreak has two seasonal phenotypes. Individuals from the spring brood are lighter and tend to have expanded orange pattern elements dorsally. The summer brood individuals are more subdued in color.

Two bilateral gynandromorphs of *M. gryneus* have been captured in Adams County (Shuey, 1984; David K Parshall, pers comm, 1989).

LITERATURE RECORDS: Clark and Scioto Counties (Albrecht, 1982).

Incisalia augustus croesioides Scudder, 1876. Brown Elfin. Plate 23.

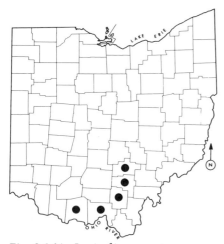

Fig. 8.164 *Incisalia augustus*.

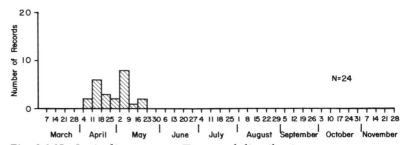

Fig. 8.165 *Incisalia augustus*-Temporal distribution.

STATUS: Resident; rare. Populations of this species are closely associated with the hostplant, and are extremely localized.

DISTRIBUTION/RANGE: This species is currently known from the southern-most portion of unglaciated Ohio (Figure 8.164). It is most frequently collected in Shawnee State Forest, Scioto County, where it is locally common.

HABITAT: This butterfly is usually found along cuts (roads and powerlines) that parallel or cross xeric, wooded ridges which support mountain laurel (*Kalmia latifolia* L.) and blueberries (*Vaccinium* spp.). Habitats which support this butterfly usually have southwestern exposures.

HOSTPLANT(S): This species has been found and reared on mountain laurel (*Kalmia latifolia* L.) (John S. Thomas, pers comm, 1985). Other species of heaths, such as blueberries and huckleberries (*Vaccinium* spp.), serve as hosts in other regions (Opler and Krizek, 1984) and may serve as additional hosts in Ohio.

ADULT ENERGY RESOURCES: Trailing arbutus (*Epigaea repens* L.) and blueberries (*Vaccinium* sp.). Adults have also been observed probing moist soil and mud.

FLIGHT PERIOD: One brood, peaking in late April and early May (Figure 8.165). Extreme dates range from 5 April to 18 May.

SIMILAR SPECIES: All *Incisalia* species are similar, but the chestnut brown ventral wing color will separate *I. augustus* from the other Ohio species.

GENERAL COMMENTS: This butterfly is extremely local, and is seldom found far from stands of mountain laurel. This, plus its early flight period have contributed to its being overlooked by most collectors. During the last few years, as its behavior and habitat requirements have become better understood, several additional populations have been discovered. Nonetheless, this is still the rarest extant *Incisalia* in southern Ohio.

To date, most reports of this species have come from Shawnee State Forest in Scioto County. Here, males have been observed in swirling chases over mountain laurel, or perching on the hostplant and adjacent plants, bare rocks, and gravel. In other areas of the State, where this butterfly occurs at lower densities, adults are best located by tapping the hostplant and flushing the adults from their perches.

This butterfly is probably more widespread than our records indicate. Mountain laurel is widespread and locally common throughout southern Ohio, and *I. augustus* should be associated with this plant throughout this area. This butterfly may also occur in the bogs of northeastern Ohio. Similar bog habitats in neighboring states support this species. Attempts to find populations in Ohio bogs have been unsuccessful.

Much more information remains to be learned about the habitat requirements of this butterfly. Many habitats which seem ideal have not produced this species, while nearby areas support populations. From our casual observations, it seems likely that exposure to the sun and the amount of tree cover may play as important a role in the distribution of this species as does the presence of the hostplant.

The flight of this species is low and erratic but is not especially rapid. Only when adults are disturbed do they fly rapidly. Except when involved in chases, adults fly only short distances before settling.

LITERATURE RECORDS: None.

Incisalia irus irus (Godart, 1824). Frosted Elfin. Plate 23.

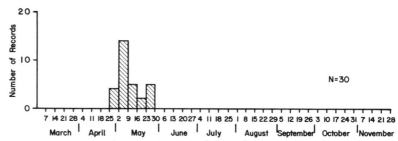

Fig. 8.167 *Incisalia irus*-Temporal distribution.

Fig. 8.166 *Incisalia irus*.

STATUS: Resident; rare and endangered. Very few populations of this butterfly are known in Ohio. This is the rarest elfin in Ohio.

DISTRIBUTION/RANGE: Except for two records from Cincinnati (Hamilton County), all of the known records have come from the Oak Openings of Lucas County (Figure 8.166). All of the known viable populations are restricted to the Oak Openings.

HABITAT: In the Oak Openings, this species is limited to dune communities and oak savannas where lupine (*Lupinus perennis* L.) is common. In Hamilton County, this species was probably associated with prairies.

HOSTPLANT(S): In the Oak Openings, this species oviposits on the flowers of lupine (*Lupinus perennis* L.). The larvae feed on the flowers and developing seed pods of this plant. Lupine is most commonly encountered in the Oak Openings region of Lucas, Wood, and Henry Counties. In southern Ohio, where lupine is absent, *I. irus* probably used a species of false-indigo (*Baptisia* sp.) as the host. Lupine and false-indigos are the primary hostplants in the eastern United States (Opler and Krizek, 1984).

ADULT ENERGY RESOURCES: Lupine (*Lupinus perennis* L.).

FLIGHT PERIOD: One brood, peaking in May (Figure 8.167). Extreme dates range from 27 April to 26 May.

SIMILAR SPECIES: *Incisalia henrici* is very similar to this species. In most cases, geography will separate these species in Ohio, because the known distributions of viable populations do not overlap. *Incisalia irus* can be identified by the presence of a male stigma on the dorsal forewing and by the presence of a submarginal "thecla spot" on the ventral hindwing of both sexes. Both of these characters are absent in *I. henrici*.

GENERAL COMMENTS: During the dust bowl years of the 1930's, this butterfly was very common and widespread in the Oak Openings (John S. Thomas, pers comm, 1986). Since that period, *I. irus* has steadily declined and several recently active populations have become extinct within the last few years (Price, 1970; Thomas W. Carr, pers comm, 1985). Today, this species is known from only a few populations in and around the Oak Openings Metropark system, and all of the known populations occupy very small tracts of habitat (less than 1 hectare).

The decline of this elfin is best attributed to changes in land use patterns. The Oak Openings ecosystem was originally a complex array of habitat types in which fire played an important role. Open habitats were originally maintained by occasional fires , which killed woody plants while favoring fire-adapted dune and savanna communities. Very recently, there has been a regime of fire suppression in the Oak Openings, which has allowed woody plants to invade open habitats. Thus, the unique botanical communities which gave the region its name, are being lost to forest invasion which shades out many of the unique plant species. The majority of habitats containing *I. irus* populations were purchased years ago by the Oak Openings Metropark system because of their unique botanical communities. Unfortunately, these communities were protected by benign neglect, and no active management was implemented to protect these communities from becoming overgrown through succession. Periodic disturbance is essential for the perpetuation of lupine, without which the more persistent woody plants will prevail. As a result, many of the populations of *I. irus* became extinct. Recently, The Nature Conservancy has begun an aggressive program of habitat management which, with the cooperation of the Metropark system, may restore many of the dune and savanna communities to their original condition. If this program is successful, all of the lupine feeding butterflies (*I. irus, Lycaeides melissa samuelis,* and *Erynnis persius*) should benefit greatly.

Although Dury (1900) included *I. irus* on a list of species from Cincinnati, most lepidopterists through the years have considered this to be a misidentification of *I. henrici.* However, a lone specimen collected in 1937 and deposited in the Cincinnati Museum of Natural History has validated this report. Nothing is known about these Hamilton County populations, but the urbanization of this area has presumably extirpated any populations in the immediate vicinity of Cincinnati.

This species could also be found in northeastern Ohio because lupine is found in a few scattered locations in Ashtabula and Summit Counties. These areas have not been adequately checked for the presence of lupine-feeding butterflies.

Adults are closely associated with their hostplants, and are seldom found far from them. In the Oak Openings, they usually rest on lupine leaves and flowers. The flight of this species is low and relatively slow for a hairstreak. However, the dark pattern and the erratic nature of the flight make adults difficult to follow visually.

LITERATURE RECORDS: None.

Incisalia henrici henrici (Grote & Robinson, 1867). Henry's Elfin. Plate 23.

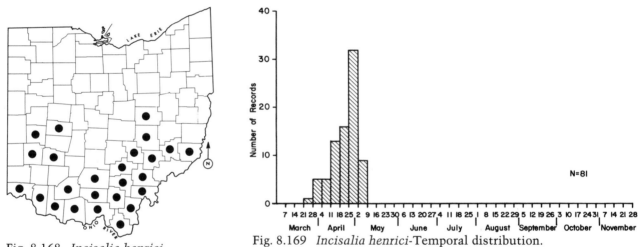

Fig. 8.168 *Incisalia henrici.*

Fig. 8.169 *Incisalia henrici*-Temporal distribution.

STATUS : Resident; rare to common. This species is most frequently encountered in the extreme southern counties of Ohio, where it is locally common. It becomes increasingly uncommon northward, and is rarely encountered in the northernmost counties of its Ohio range.

DISTRIBUTION/RANGE: This species is confined to the southern half of the State (Figure 8.168).

HABITAT: This elfin is most frequently encountered along woodland edges where redbud (*Cercis canadensis* L.) is common. Typical habitats include powerline cuts, woodland openings, roads through woodlands, and xeric prairies surrounded by shrubby cedar glades.

HOSTPLANT(S): In Ohio, this species has been found and reared on redbud (*Cercis canadensis* L.) (Horatio T. Enterline and David K. Parshall, pers comm, 1987). Females oviposit on the flowers and emerging leaf buds of redbud, and the larvae feed on the flowers, developing seed pods, and leaves. Although this butterfly is almost always associated with redbud, it may use other hostplants as well. Maple-leaf viburnum (*Viburnum acerifolium* L.), wild plum (*Prunus* sp.), and huckleberries and blueberries (*Vaccinium* spp.) are reported hostplants in adjacent states (Shapiro, 1966; Nielsen, 1985).

ADULT ENERGY RESOURCES: Redbud (*Cercis canadensis* L.) and fleabane (*Erigeron* sp.). Adults also imbibe moisture from damp spots on roads and trails.

FLIGHT PERIOD: One brood, peaking in late April and early May (Figure 8.169). Extreme dates range from 26 March to 5 May.

SIMILAR SPECIES: See *Incisalia irus.*

GENERAL COMMENTS: Although this species is usually considered one of the rarest elfins in eastern North America (eg Klots, 1951), this is the most common elfin in Ohio, particularly in the extreme southern portion of the State, where it can be locally common. This is one of the first species on the wing each spring, and populations peak simultaneously with the showy blooms of the hostplant, redbud (*Cercis canadensis* L.). During years of high population densities, it is not unusual to see dozens of individuals flying around redbud trees or sipping moisture from damp areas along gravel roads, particularly in Lawrence and Scioto Counties. This species is probably more widespread than our records indicate, and it should be looked for wherever redbud is common.

Populations of this elfin tend to be quite localized, and adults usually remain in the vicinity of redbud stands. Adults are frequently observed feeding at the flowers of redbud or resting on moist soil. Males perch on the tips of twigs, and chase after other elfins as they fly past. The flight of this species is fast and erratic, and is sometimes difficult to follow visually. When resting, adults rub their hindwings together in an alternating pattern.

LITERATURE RECORDS: None.

Incisalia niphon niphon (Hübner, 1823). Pine Elfin. Plate 23.

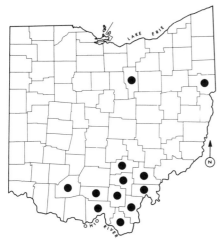

Fig. 8.170 *Incisalia niphon*.

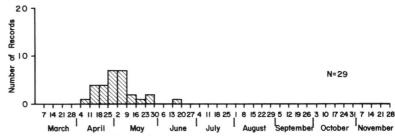

Fig. 8.171 *Incisalia niphon*-Temporal distribution.

STATUS: Resident; rare. This species occurs in localized populations and usually occurs at low densities.

DISTRIBUTION/RANGE: Most of our records are from the southern portion of unglaciated Ohio, where hard pines are native (Figure 8.170). However, a recent single record from Mohican State Forest, Ashland County indicates that it could occur wherever hard pines have been planted.

HABITAT: This elfin inhabits mixed pine-oak woodlands, hard pine plantings, and nearby open areas. Adults occasionally wander into fields to visit nectar sources.

HOSTPLANT(S): Although no hostplant has been recorded in Ohio, this species is closely associated with native and planted stands of hard pines such as pitch pine (*Pinus rigida* Mill.), shortleaf pine (*Pinus echinata* Mill.), and scrub pine (*Pinus virginiana* Mill.). Most populations have been found in association with young trees ranging from three to eight meters in height. Numerous species of hard pines serve as the hostplants throughout this butterfly's range (Opler and Krizek, 1984). It is also possible that this species could use white pine (*Pinus strobus* L.) as a host in northern Ohio.

ADULT ENERGY RESOURCES: Redbud (*Cercis canadensis* L.), dandelion (*Taraxacum officinale* Weber), winter-cress (*Barberia vulgaris* R.Br.), and pussy-toes (*Antennaria* sp.). Adults also probe damp soil, damp gravel, and mud.

FLIGHT PERIOD: One brood, peaking in late April and early May (Figure 8.171). Extreme dates range from 7 April to 15 June. This species flies later in the spring than the other *Incisalia* species.

SIMILAR SPECIES: The ventral wing surfaces will separate this elfin from all other hairstreaks.

GENERAL COMMENTS: This species is usually found as solitary individuals, or in low numbers. Most adults are found in close association with hard pines and can be found visiting flowers (especially pussy-toes), imbibing moisture from damp areas along roads and trails, or perched on pines or adjacent vegetation. Females are most often located by jarring them from their perches on young pines.

This elfin is undoubtedly more widespread then our records indicate, and it should occur throughout the eastern and southern hill country of Ohio where hard pines are native. The single record from north-central Ohio is intriguing. White pine (*Pinus strobus* L.) is native at the collection locality, Mohican State Forest, and this may indicate that *I. niphon* uses this soft pine as a hostplant. Conversely, hard pines have been planted extensively throughout Mohican State Forest, and a population of *I. niphon* may have been introduced with the plantings, or somehow become established since the planting of pines. Both scenarios indicate that this butterfly could be widely distributed throughout the State, and should be searched for wherever pines have been planted or are native.

The flight of this elfin is not as fast as other hairstreaks, although disturbed individuals are capable of wildly erratic escapes into the tree tops. Males perch on pines and dart out at passing objects and the spiraling chases of males are sometimes observed. When resting, this species often rubs its hindwings together in an alternating up and down fashion.

LITERATURE RECORDS: None.

Fixsenia ontario ontario (W. H. Edwards, 1868). Northern Hairstreak. Plate 23.

Fig. 8.172 *Fixsenia ontario.*

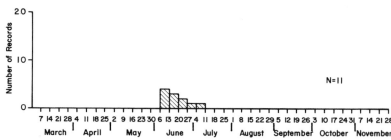

Fig. 8.173 *Fixsenia ontario*-Temporal distribution.

STATUS: Resident; rare. This species is rarely and sporadically encountered and is usually found as isolated individuals.

DISTRIBUTION/RANGE: Our records are scattered throughout the western half of the State, and most of the records are clustered in west-central Ohio (Figure 8.172). This species may occur throughout the State, but might be overlooked because of its rarity and similarity to other, more common hairstreaks.

HABITAT: This species is usually found in open areas such as fields, roadsides, sedge meadows, and fens that border oak forests. Some of the Ohio habitats for this species are upland forests, but the majority of the specimens have been collected adjacent to swamp forests.

HOSTPLANT(S): Although no hostplant has been recorded in Ohio, this species is usually associated with oaks (*Quercus* spp.), particularly wetland species such as swamp white oak (*Quercus bicolor* Willd.), black oak (*Quercus velitina* Lam.), and red oak (*Quercus rubra* L.), as well as white oak (*Quercus alba* L.) (David K. Parshall, pers comm, 1987). Oaks are the only known hosts of this butterfly (Opler and Krizek, 1984).

ADULT ENERGY RESOURCES: Indian hemp (*Apocynum cannabinum* L.), dogbane (*Apocynum* sp.), and Canada thistle (*Cirsium arvense* [L.] Scop.).

FLIGHT PERIOD: One brood, peaking in June (Figure 8.173). Extreme dates range from 30 April (early) to 4 July. This species flies earlier in the season than do the *Satyrium* species.

SIMILAR SPECIES: This species can be confused with several *Satyrium* species and with *Strymon melinus*. All *Satyrium* species have a dark bar at the end of the cell on the ventral forewing that is absent in *F. ontario*. *Strymon melinus* is slate gray dorsally, whereas *F. ontario* is brown.

GENERAL COMMENTS: This hairstreak may spend most of its time perched high in trees, only occasionally dropping to ground level to feed at flowers. Most of the known Ohio specimens were collected in the late afternoon (1600 to 2000 hrs) from flowers, primarily dogbane (*Apocynum* sp.), in sedge meadows adjacent to oak forests (David K. Parshall, pers comm, 1987). The rarity of this hairstreak in collections may be more a reflection of the brief periods of time it spends near the ground, rather than a measure of its actual abundance. Because this hairstreak tends to fly earlier in the season than the *Satyrium* species with which it is easily confused, collectors should closely examine all hairstreaks during June and early July.

Roger S. Boone (pers comm, 1985) collected an individual of this species at a mercury vapor light used to collect night flying insects.

Some authors consider the southern hairstreak (*Fixsenia favonius* [J. E. Smith, 1797]) and the northern hairstreak (*F. ontario*) to represent races of a single species. If future research determines this to be true, Ohio populations should be referred to as *F. favonius ontario*. See Chapter 10 for a discussion of erroneous records of *F. favonius* from Ohio.

Parrhasius m-album m-album (Boisduval & LeConte, 1833). White M Hairstreak. Plate 23.

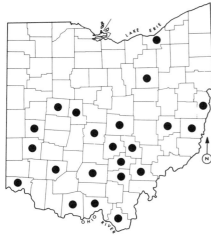

Fig. 8.174 *Parrhasius m-album.*

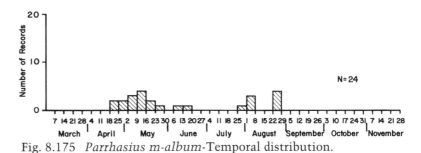

Fig. 8.175 *Parrhasius m-album*-Temporal distribution.

STATUS: Resident; rare. This species is usually encountered as solitary individuals.

DISTRIBUTION/RANGE: Ohio records are scattered throughout the southern two-thirds of the State with most records coming from unglaciated Ohio (Figure 8.174). This species is certainly more continuously distributed than our records indicate.

HABITAT: This butterfly is usually found in open areas associated with mesic woodlands such as gravel roads, fields, and clearings.

HOSTPLANT(S): In Ohio, this species has been found and reared on linden (*Tilia* sp.) (Pilate, 1906). Oaks (*Quercus* spp.) are also probably used, as they are the primary hostplants throughout this butterfly's range (Opler and Krizek, 1984).

ADULT ENERGY RESOURCES: Indian hemp (*Apocynum cannabinum* L.), common milkweed (*Asclepias syriaca* L.), Canada thistle (*Cirsium arvense* [L.] Scop.), dandelion (*Taraxacum officinale* Weber), pussy-toes (*Antennaria* sp.), fleabane (*Erigeron* sp.), and brambles (*Rubus* sp.). Pilate (1880) also lists goldenrod (*Solidago* sp.).

FLIGHT PERIOD: Two broods, peaking in May and again in August (Figure 8.175). Extreme dates range from 20 April to 27 August. Individuals from the spring brood are more frequently observed than individuals from the summer brood.

SIMILAR SPECIES: None.

GENERAL COMMENTS: This spectacular, metallic blue (rarely dark violet) species is another hairstreak that is rarely encountered. When found it is usually as solitary individuals at flowers. Little is known about the ecology or life history of this species, but it seems likely that adults spend much of their time perched high in trees and seldom come to ground level. Several specimens have been collected after flying directly downward from trees and alighting on flowers. This possible canopy association may account for its apparent rarity. This hairstreak is probably overlooked in many areas.

The flight of this species is fast and erratic, and flying individuals are difficult to follow visually. Although some adults have been observed perched on foliage, most are observed while they are visiting flowers.

LITERATURE RECORDS: None.

Strymon melinus humuli (Harris, 1841). Gray Hairstreak. Plate 24.

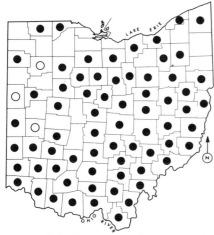

Fig. 8.176 *Strymon melinus.*

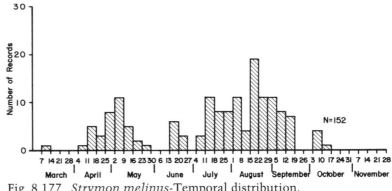

Fig. 8.177 *Strymon melinus*-Temporal distribution.

STATUS: Resident; uncommon to common. This butterfly is most frequently encountered in the southern half of the State. It becomes less common northward.

DISTRIBUTION/RANGE: Statewide (Figure 8.176).

HABITAT: This butterfly occurs in a wide variety of habitats. It can be found along woodland trails and roads, in old fields, prairies, vacant lots, pastures, gardens, and many other open habitats.

HOSTPLANT(S): Throughout its range, the gray hairstreak uses a tremendous variety of plants in over 20 families (Howe, 1975). In Ohio, this species has been found and/or reared on pods of the garden pea (*Lathyrus latifolius* L.), pods of garden beans (*Phaseolus vulgaris* L.) (Webster, 1899), and on the leaves and flowers of wild senna (*Cassia hebecarpa* Fern). Larvae have also been found on corn silk (*Zea mays*) (Webster, 1900) and adults have been found in association with hops (*Humulus* sp.) (Kirtland, 1854a) and *Desmodium* sp. (Robert Dirig, pers comm, 1988). Legumes and mallows are the primary hostplants of this butterfly (Opler and Krizek, 1984). South of Ohio, this species can become a pest of beans and hops.

   Young larvae feed primarily on the flowers and seed pods of the hostplant. Older larvae will also feed on the leaves.

ADULT ENERGY RESOURCES: Red clover (*Trifolium pratense* L.), alfalfa (*Medicago sativa* L.), redbud (*Cercis canadensis* L.), common milkweed (*Asclepias syriaca* L.), coneflower (*Rudbeckia laciniata* L.), Canada thistle (*Cirsium arvense* [L.] Scop.), horseweed (*Erigeron canadensis* L.), wing-stem (*Verbesina alternifolia* [L.] Britt.), and cinquefoil (*Potentilla* sp.). This butterfly also visits damp soil and mud.

FLIGHT PERIOD: Three, possibly four broods, with peaks in May, July, and August (Figure 8.177). Extreme dates range from 8 March to 10 October.

SIMILAR SPECIES: See *Fixsenia ontario*.

GENERAL COMMENTS: This is one of our most common hairstreaks. Although it is widespread, it is seldom encountered in large numbers. Population densities fluctuate, and occasionally it is locally common.

   Adults are most often encountered as they visit flowers or while they are perching on trees and shrubs. Males dart out from their perches at passing objects, presumably as part of their mate location behavior and often participate in spiraling chases with other males. These behaviors suggest that males are territorial (Alcock and O'Neill, 1987). The flight of this species is fast and erratic, and adults often circle their chosen landing spot before settling. When resting, adults rub their hindwings together in an alternating pattern.

   There is seasonal polyphenism in this species. Spring brood individuals are smaller and darker than individuals from later generations. A suffused 'heathi'-type aberration is also known from Ohio.

LITERATURE RECORDS: Putnam, (Price, 1970), Mercer (Webster, 1899), and Miami (Studebaker and Studebaker, 1967) Counties.

Erora laeta (W. H. Edwards, 1862). Early Hairstreak. Plate 24.

Fig. 8.178 *Erora laeta*.

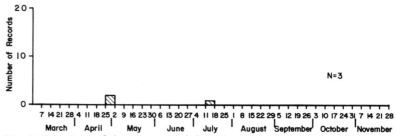

Fig. 8.179 *Erora laeta*-Temporal distribution.

STATUS: Resident; rare. Although we have only three records for this species in Ohio, two captures, many years apart at Fort Hill State Memorial, Highland County, indicate that a population exists at this site.

DISTRIBUTION/RANGE: This species is known from only two localities in Ohio: Fort Hill State Memorial, Highland County and Brecksville, Cuyahoga County (Figure 8.178). Ohio is on the extreme western edge of the Appalachian distribution of this species (Opler and Krizek, 1984), and is far removed from its primary range.

HABITAT: In Cuyahoga County, *E. laeta* was collected in a clearing within a beech forest (Lepidopterists' Society, 1977; Gary Meszaros, pers comm, 1988), whereas in Highland County it was captured along trails through rich deciduous forest (Potter and Thomas, 1970; David K. Parshall, pers comm, 1987). In other areas, this butterfly is usually encountered along trails through beech-maple forests (Opler and Krizek, 1985).

HOSTPLANT(S): Not known in Ohio. The only reported hostplants for this species are American beech (*Fagus grandifolia* Ehrh.) and beaked hazelnut (*Corylus cornuta* Marsh) (Klots and dos Passos, 1982). In Kentucky, oaks (*Quercus* spp.) are suspected hosts because *E. laeta* is found in areas which do not support the reported hostplants (Loren D. Gibson, pers comm, 1986).

ADULT ENERGY RESOURCES: Spring beauty (*Claytonia virginica* L.). Adults also visit damp soil.

FLIGHT PERIOD: Two broods, flying in late April-early May, and July (Figure 8.179). Extreme dates range from 25 April to 13 July.

SIMILAR SPECIES: None.

GENERAL COMMENTS: This is the rarest and most poorly understood of our resident hairstreaks. All of the known specimens have been collected while they were resting on damp soil or visiting flowers. It has been suggested that this species spends the majority of its time in the forest canopy, and seldom drops to ground level where it can be observed (Klots and dos Passos, 1982; Opler and Krizek, 1984). If this is the case, this species is probably more widespread in Ohio than the records indicate, and the rarity of this species is a behavioral artifact that may not reflect its true abundance in nature. As Klots (1951) suggested, this species ... "should be sought (and never expected)" ... in almost any forested habitat.

This hairstreak often seems oblivious to its surroundings as it imbibes moisture or nectar, and as a result, can be observed closely. This behavior has probably added to the likelihood of overlooking the species, because it does not readily fly when approached. The pale green ventral wing surfaces also allow it to blend into its surroundings. The flight of this species, especially males, is rapid and erratic (Bowers, 1978; Loren D. Gibson, pers comm, 1986).

LITERATURE RECORDS: None.

Hemiargus isola alce (W. H. Edwards, 1871). Reakirt's Blue. Plate 24.

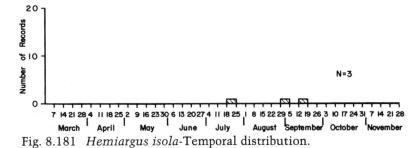

Fig. 8.181 *Hemiargus isola*-Temporal distribution.

Fig. 8.180 *Hemiargus isola*.

STATUS: Irregular immigrant; rare.

DISTRIBUTION/RANGE: This species is primarily a resident of the Southwest. It annually wanders northward into the Plains States, and on rare occasions reaches Ohio, Indiana, and Michigan (Opler and Krizek, 1984). In Ohio, this species is known only from Hamilton and Lucas Counties (Figure 8.180).

HABITAT: In the Oak Openings, Lucas County, several individuals were captured in very barren dune communities (Rawson and Thomas, 1939; John S. Thomas, pers comm, 1985). It should be watched for in almost any open habitat, but particularly old fields, alfalfa and clover fields, and prairies.

HOSTPLANT(S): Not known in Ohio. In other regions, this species uses a wide variety of legumes, including alfalfa (*Medicago sativa* L.) (Opler and Krizek, 1984).

ADULT ENERGY RESOURCES: None recorded for Ohio.

FLIGHT PERIOD: This species may produce one or more broods in Ohio (Rawson and Thomas, 1939), but our data are inconclusive (Figure 8.181). Extreme dates range from 24 July to 18 September.

SIMILAR SPECIES: Although this species is superficially similar to *Everes comyntas* and *Celastrina ladon*, *H. isola* is easily recognized by the row of submarginal spots on the ventral forewings.

GENERAL COMMENTS: This species has only been encountered three times in Ohio. Two individuals were collected near Cincinnati in 1901 and 1937, and George Rawson and John Thomas collected three specimens over a two-day period in Lucas County in 1939. The concentration of specimens collected in Lucas County indicates that a temporary breeding colony must have been established at that time. Remington (1942) believed that *H. isola* can establish temporary populations anywhere there are suitable hostplants. These populations certainly cannot survive Ohio's winters.

This blue probably reaches Ohio more frequently than our records would suggest. Because of its small size, and general similarity to other blues, *H. isola* is probably overlooked. Observers searching for this species should examine every blue butterfly they encounter during the late summer.

LITERATURE RECORDS: None.

Everes comyntas comyntas (Godart, 1824). Eastern Tailed Blue. Plate 24.

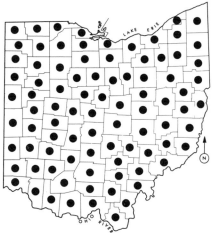

Fig. 8.182 *Everes comyntas.*

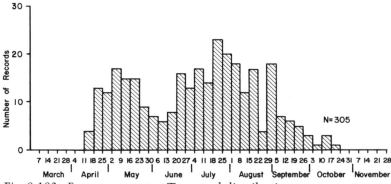

Fig. 8.183 *Everes comyntas*-Temporal distribution.

STATUS: Resident; common.

DISTRIBUTION/RANGE: Statewide (Figure 8.182). This species is known from all 88 counties.

HABITAT: This species occurs in any open habitat where suitable legume hostplants grow. Typical habitats include alfalfa and clover fields, soybean fields, roadsides, railroad rights-of-way, old fields, vacant lots, prairie remnants, lawns, and gardens. In early spring this species can also be found in forested areas.

HOSTPLANT(S): Not known in Ohio. Many different legumes are used throughout this blue's range (Opler and Krizek, 1984). Many of the legumes listed as adult energy resources may serve as hostplants.

ADULT ENERGY RESOURCES: Lupine (*Lupinus perennis* L.), red clover (*Trifolium pratense* L.), white clover (*Trifolium repens* L.), alfalfa (*Medicago sativa* L.), yellow sweet clover (*Melilotus officinalis* [L.] Lam.), white sweet clover (*Melilotus alba* Desr.), soybeans (*Glycine max* [L.] Merr.), shrubby cinquefoil (*Potentilla fructicosa* L.), blue vervain (*Verbena hastata* L.), Indian hemp (*Apocynum cannabinum* L.), butterfly-weed (*Asclepias tuberosa* L.), peppermint (*Mentha piperita* L.), common boneset (*Eupatorium perfoliatum* L.), asters (*Aster* spp.), and brambles (*Rubus* sp.). This butterfly is an avid visitor to damp soil, damp gravel, and damp sand.

FLIGHT PERIOD: Many overlapping broods throughout the summer. Although it is difficult to tell from the histogram (Figure 8.183), there are between three and five generations per year. Extreme dates range from 12 April to 18 October.

SIMILAR SPECIES: Although this species is vaguely similar to other species of blues, the presence of tails will easily separate *E. comyntas*.

GENERAL COMMENTS: This is one of Ohio's most common butterflies, and is well adapted to the wide variety of habitats that result from human disturbance. Populations often reach high densities, and hundreds of individuals may be seen in certain habitats in late summer.

There is marked seasonal polyphenism and individual variation in this species. The spring brood is usually characterized by small adults relative to later generations. However, individuals vary in size within each brood, and it is common to find a two-fold size difference in adults flying in the same field. Spring brood females have expanded blue pattern elements relative to later generations, but spring brood males generally have less blue than later generations. In both sexes, the spring brood tends to be paler ventrally than individuals found later in the season.

The flight of this butterfly is erratic but not as swift as in the hairstreaks. Adults usually fly close to the ground, and because of their dark appearance, can be difficult to follow visually. When perching, the wings are held above the body vertically or at a 45° angle. When resting, adults often rub their hindwings together in an alternating pattern.

Leland L. Martin (pers comm, 1988) has observed in this species a curious circular courtship display which both sexes perform on the upper surfaces of leaves.

LITERATURE RECORDS: None.

Celastrina ladon ladon (Cramer, 1780). Spring Azure. Plate 24.

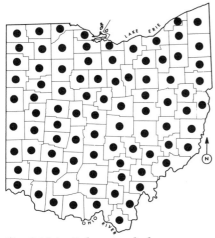

Fig. 8.184 *Celastrina ladon.*

STATUS: Resident; common.

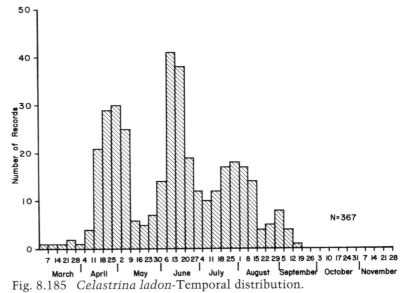

Fig. 8.185 *Celastrina ladon*-Temporal distribution.

DISTRIBUTION/RANGE: Statewide (Figure 8.184). This species has been recorded from all 88 counties.

HABITAT: This butterfly is most often associated with deciduous forests and adjacent open areas. It is also occasionally encountered in old fields, brushy fields, swamps, and, to some extent, urban habitats such as parks and gardens. Spring brood individuals are more closely associated with forests than are individuals from the later broods.

HOSTPLANT(S): In Ohio, larvae have been found on flowering dogwood (*Cornus florida* L.) (Studebaker and Studebaker, 1967). Females have been observed ovipositing on wing-stem (*Verbesina alternifolia* [L.] Britt.) and gray dogwood (*Cornus racemosa* Lam.). Throughout eastern North America, this species uses a wide variety of hostplants from several families (Opler and Krizek, 1984). In Michigan, the larvae are usually tended by ants (Harvey and Webb, 1980).

ADULT ENERGY RESOURCES: Redbud (*Cercis canadensis* L.), white clover (*Trifolium repens* L.), yellow sweet clover (*Melilotus officinalis* [L.] Lam.), wild carrot (*Daucus carota* L.), wild parsnip (*Pastinaca sativa* L.), narrowleaf dogwood (*Cornus obliqua* Raf.), flowering dogwood (*Cornus florida* L.), early saxifrage (*Saxifraga virginiensis* Michx.), wing-stem (*Verbesina alternifolia* [L.] Britt.), common boneset (*Eupatorium perfoliatum* L.), New Jersey tea (*Ceanothus americanus* L.), violet (*Viola* sp.), pussy-toes (*Antennaria* sp.), staghorn sumac (*Rhus typhina* L.), hawthorn (*Crataegus* sp.), rhubarb (*Rheum officinale* Baill.), blackberry (*Rubus* sp.), and a wide variety of garden flowers. This species also imbibes moisture from mud, soil wetted with urine, feces, and carrion such as dead crayfish and amphibians. *Celastrina ladon* is often found, especially in spring, congregating in large numbers around mud puddles.

FLIGHT PERIOD: Three to four overlapping broods throughout the summer (Figure 8.185). Extreme dates range from 4 March to 12 September.

SIMILAR SPECIES: *Celastrina ladon* is very similar to the other *Celastrina* species. However, *C. ebenina* males are easily identified by their sooty black dorsal color, which is unique. Female *C. ebenina* have wide, dark dorsal hindwing margins and black scaling on the dorsal wing veins. In *C. ladon*, both of these traits are absent.

Celastrina ladon also is very similar to the larger *C. neglecta-major*, and these two species are difficult to separate. Ventrally, *C. ladon* usually has a well defined black spot pattern, whereas in *C. neglecta-major* these spots are greatly reduced, and the ventral wing surfaces seem almost white. The forewing fringe of *C. ladon* is plain, but in *C. neglecta-major* the fringe is checkered. Finally, the black margin on the dorsal forewing of *C. ladon* is widened at the apex, but in *C. neglecta-major* the black margin is the same width along its length. Note the flight period of *C. neglecta-major* before considering this determination for questionable specimens. Confusing specimens that fall well out of *C. neglecta-major*'s flight period are probably referable to the summer broods of *C. ladon* that have a washed-out appearance. If in doubt, have an expert identify the specimens.

GENERAL COMMENTS: *Celastrina ladon*, with its numerous variations and forms, is a very complicated species that is not yet fully understood. Prior to 1970, most experts agreed that one species of *Celastrina* occurred in North America: now three species are recognized. Current research suggests that several additional sibling species are still included within the *C. ladon* complex, and it is likely that additional species occur in Ohio (David M. Wright, pers comm, 1987). When current studies are completed, four or more species could be recognized as occurring in Ohio. In addition to the problems associated with sibling species, taxonomists have disagreed about the correct name for this species. In the past, this species was called *Celastrina argiolus* L., but current thinking limits this name to European populations, and *C. ladon* is used for populations occurring in North America.

In Ohio, *C. ladon* is multiple brooded, and produces up to four broods per year. Later broods tend to be less common than the spring brood. There are two seasonal phenotypes. Individuals of the spring brood, form 'violacea' (W. H. Edwards, 1866), are smaller and darker than individuals of subsequent broods, form 'neglecta' (W. H. Edwards, 1862). Spring individuals with wide submarginal bands on both wings (form 'marginata' W.H. Edwards, 1883), are rare in Ohio, but have been recorded from several counties (Morrow, Lake, Cuyahoga, and Williams Counties). In Ohio, this form is best considered an extreme expression of the form 'violacea' (David M. Wright, pers comm, 1989).

Henninger (1910) reported *"Lycaena pseudargiolus lucia"* from Seneca County, presumably in reference to the northern "subspecies" *C. ladon lucia* (W. Kirby, 1837). This single brooded "subspecies" is characterized by large dark patches on the ventral hindwings. We have not seen any Ohio material representing *C. ladon lucia*, but this "subspecies" could occur in extreme northern Ohio.

Although *C. ladon* is not as abundant as *Everes comyntas*, *C. ladon* is by far the most conspicuous blue in Ohio. It is one of the first species to fly each spring, and is a common sight before most spring flowers are in bloom. The flight of this species is not particularly rapid, but it is erratic. Adults fly from ground level to tree top height, and adults tend to fly over obstacles rather than through or around them. They are often observed flying around and settling on the tops of bushes and shrubs. Adults are avid flower and mud puddle visitors.

LITERATURE RECORDS: None.

Celastrina neglecta-major Tutt, 1908. Appalachian Blue. Plate 24.

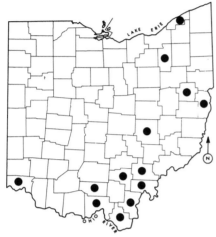

Fig. 8.186 *Celastrina neglecta-major.*

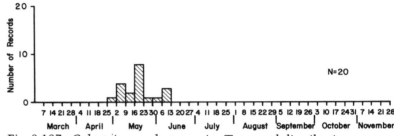

Fig. 8.187 *Celastrina neglecta-major*-Temporal distribution.

STATUS: Resident; rare. Populations of this species tend to be localized and usually occur at low densities.

DISTRIBUTION/RANGE: This species is primarily a resident of the Allegheny Plateau Section of Ohio (Figure 8.186). Most of our records are from the southeastern corner of the State.

HABITAT: This butterfly is usually found in cool, moist ravines, or along roads and streams that cut through mesic deciduous forest. It is occasionally collected in ridgetop woodland clearings. *Celastrina neglecta-major* often occurs in the same habitats that support *C. ebenina*.

HOSTPLANT(S): Not known in Ohio. In Virginia, this species has been reared on black cohosh (*Cimicifuga racemosa* [L.] Nutt.), a plant with which *C. neglecta-major* is often associated (Warren H. Wagner, pers comm, 1986). It has also been associated with maple-leaved viburnum (*Viburnum acerifolium* L.) in the Delaware Valley (Shapiro, 1966). Both of these plant species are common and widespread throughout unglaciated Ohio (Cusick and Silberhorn, 1977).

ADULT ENERGY RESOURCES: Sweet cicely (*Osmorhiza* sp.), blackberry (*Rubus* sp.), and gray dogwood (*Cornus racemosa*). This species also takes moisture from damp soil and sand, mud, and soil moistened with urine.

FLIGHT PERIOD: One brood, peaking in May (Figure 8.187). Extreme dates range from 28 April to 11 June.

SIMILAR SPECIES: See *C. ladon*.

GENERAL COMMENTS: This butterfly has often been considered to represent a large form of *C. ladon*, and only recently has biological evidence confirmed its specific status. It is now known that the pupae of *C. neglecta-major* enter diapause and do not emerge until the following spring: diapause is facultative in *C. ladon*, and several generations are produced throughout the summer. *Celastrina ladon* uses a wide variety of hostplants throughout the season. We suspect that populations of *C. neglecta-major* are monophagous.

The flight period of *C. neglecta-major* is temporally displaced from the flight periods of *C. ladon*. Generally, the first fresh adults of *C. neglecta-major* emerge after the peak of the spring brood of *C. ladon* has passed, and only a few worn individuals of *C. ladon* remain. Adults of *C. neglecta-major* fly for approximately two weeks, and after the population declines to a few worn individuals, the first summer brood of *C. ladon* begins to emerge. It is not unusual to see males of both species imbibing moisture together along woodland roads in southern Ohio.

Because populations are localized and occur at low densities, and because this species so closely resembles the ubiquitous *C. ladon*, *C. neglecta-major* tends to be overlooked or ignored by many lepidopterists. When flying, *C. neglecta-major* appears to be larger then *C. ladon*. The flight of *C. neglecta-major* is more direct and rapid than the flight of *C. ladon*. In southern Ohio, populations of *C. neglecta-major* often occupy the same habitats as *C. ebenina*, which can often be used as a potential indicator for the possible occurrence of *C. neglecta-major* later in the season.

LITERATURE RECORDS: None.

Celastrina ebenina Clench, 1972. Dusky Blue. Plate 24.

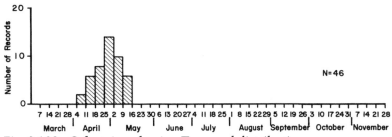

Fig. 8.189 *Celastrina ebenina*-Temporal distribution.

Fig. 8.188 *Celastrina ebenina*.

STATUS: Resident; rare to uncommon. Populations of this butterfly are localized, but sometimes attain high densities.

DISTRIBUTION/RANGE: This butterfly occurs throughout much of unglaciated Ohio (Figure 8.188).

HABITAT: This species is usually found in cool, moist ravines that cut through mature mesic woodlands. It is also occasionally encountered on wooded ridgetops.

HOSTPLANT(S): In Ohio, larvae have been found and reared on goats-beard (*Aruncus dioicus* [Walt.] Fern), the only reported hostplant (Wagner and Mellichamp, 1978). This plant is widespread and common in unglaciated Ohio (Cusick and Silberhorn, 1977).

ADULT ENERGY RESOURCES: Males imbibe moisture from patches of damp soil and gravel.

FLIGHT PERIOD: One brood, peaking in late April and early May (Figure 8.189). The first males appear each spring a few days after *C. ladon* begins its spring flight. A rare partial second brood of *C. ebenina* has been observed in Kentucky (Richard A. Henderson, pers comm, 1981). Extreme dates in Ohio range from 5 April to 11 May.

SIMILAR SPECIES: See *C. ladon.*

GENERAL COMMENTS: Populations of this butterfly are localized, and adults seldom stray far from stands of the hostplant. Males are usually encountered as they patrol through ravines and along hillsides or while they perch on the dried hostplant remnants from previous seasons. Males are also commonly observed imbibing moisture from moist soil and gravel. Females are more often observed flying near the hostplants. Because of their blue color pattern, females are difficult to separate from *C. ladon* in flight, and are easily overlooked.

Contrary to the typical sexual dimorphism in *Celastrina,* the females of *C. ebenina* have expanded blue patterns relative to the males. The males of *C. ebenina* were originally interpreted by William H. Edwards as dark form females of *C. ladon.* Only after Clench (1972) encountered a population of *C. ebenina* in Vinton County, Ohio, were the sexes correctly associated with each other and described as a new species. The ecology of the same Vinton County population was later briefly studied by Wagner and Showalter (1976).

The history of this species illustrates how easily certain species can be overlooked. Although occasional specimens were collected prior to Clench's (1972) work, they were considered as rare aberrations of the ubiquitous *C. ladon.* Once Clench correctly determined the specific status of *C. ebenina,* collectors actively searched for the species, and it was found to be locally common in several previously well-collected localities. Apparently, collectors had ignored this species historically, unable to distinguish it in flight from *C. ladon,* which they considered to be too common to collect. Males of *C. ebenina* often gather with numbers of male *C. ladon* at damp soil in spring. When disturbed into flight, the *C. ebenina* resemble dark shadows among the many blue *C. ladon.*

The flight of *C. ebenina* is fairly fast and direct, and is usually within one meter of the ground. Males can be difficult to follow visually because their dark pattern allows them to blend in with their background while they are flying. Populations can easily be located by examining flowers of the hostplant in June for the presence of larvae.

A bilateral gynandromorph was collected in Athens County (Shuey and Peacock, 1985).

Recently, there has been some controversy concerning the use of the name *Celastrina nigra* (W.H. Edwards, 1884) for this species (see Ferris, 1989).

LITERATURE RECORD: Wyss (1932) refers to a black form of *C. ladon,* alluding to its presence in the vicinity of Cincinnati, Hamilton County. Because *C. ebenina* was until recently considered a melanic form of *C. ladon,* this record is best placed as *C. ebenina.*

Glaucopsyche lygdamus lygdamus (Doubleday, 1841). Silvery Blue. Plate 25.

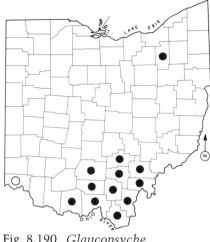

Fig. 8.190 *Glaucopsyche lygdamus.*

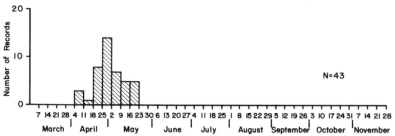

Fig. 8.191 *Glaucopsyche lygdamus*-Temporal distribution.

STATUS: Resident; rare to uncommon. Populations of this species are very localized.

DISTRIBUTION/RANGE: With the exception of one old record from Summit County in northeastern Ohio, all of our records are from the southern unglaciated portion of the State (Figure 8.190).

HABITAT: This species is usually found in or near openings within deciduous upland and bottomland forests where wood vetch (*Vicia caroliniana* Walt.) grows. Typical openings include powerline cuts, roadsides, clearings, and prairies.

HOSTPLANT(S): In Ohio, larvae of this species have been found in association with ants on wood vetch (*Vicia caroliniana* Walt.). Wood vetch is the only confirmed hostplant of *G. l. lygdamus* (Opler and Krizek, 1984).

Because larvae are attended by ants, larvae of this butterfly are most easily located by searching for ants on the hostplant.

ADULT ENERGY RESOURCES: Wood vetch (*Vicia caroliniana* Walt.), white clover (*Trifolium repens* L.), spring beauty (*Claytonia virginica* L.), and fleabane (*Erigeron* sp.). Adults also imbibe moisture from damp soil and mud.

FLIGHT PERIOD: One brood, peaking in late April and early May (Figure 8.191). Extreme dates range from 4 April to 20 May.

SIMILAR SPECIES: None.

GENERAL COMMENTS: This blue is one of the earliest butterflies to appear each spring, and often flies with *Celastrina ladon, C. ebenina,* and *C. neglecta-major.* Populations of *G. lygdamus* are closely associated with stands of the hostplant, and adults seldom wander far from these plants. Although this species usually occurs at low densities, it experiences population fluctuations and may become locally common in some years.

This blue is probably more widespread in Ohio than our records indicate. The hostplant, wood vetch (*Vicia caroliniana* Walt.) is widespread throughout eastern and southern Ohio, but tends to grow in localized populations. *Glaucopsyche lygdamus* should be found in association with this plant throughout Ohio. Those collectors seeking this butterfly should search first for the localized hostplant populations, and then for the butterfly.

Adults of this species have a low, rapid, and direct flight. Males patrol areas near stands of the hostplant, and because of their iridescent blue color, are easily recognized on the wing. Females often rest on or near the hostplant, and, because of their more subtle blue color are more difficult to separate from other species of blues while in flight. Adults are commonly observed visiting nectar sources, especially the flowers of the hostplant.

A second subspecies, *Glaucopsyche lygdamus couperi* Grote, 1873, could also occur in the prairies of western Ohio. It has been recorded in counties that border Ohio in both Michigan (Moore, 1960) and Indiana (Shull, 1987). It should be watched for in areas that support viney peavine (*Lathyrus venosus* Muhl.), the hostplant of this subspecies. Habitats which might support this butterfly include prairie remnants along highways, airports, and railroad tracks. Similar habitats in the Oak Openings of northwestern Ohio should be investigated for this butterfly.

An aberration lacking the ventral hindwing spots was collected in Meigs County (Calhoun, 1987[88]).

LITERATURE RECORDS: Hamilton County (Dury, 1878; Hine, 1898a, 1898b; Wyss, 1932).

Lycaeides melissa samuelis Nabokov, 1944. Karner Blue, Melissa Blue. Plate 25.

Fig. 8.192 *Lycaeides melissa.*

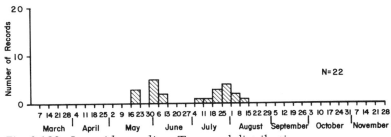

Fig. 8.193 *Lycaeides melissa*-Temporal distribution.

STATUS: Resident; rare and endangered. At present, there are no known viable populations in Ohio.

DISTRIBUTION/RANGE: This species is known only from the Oak Openings of Lucas County (Figure 8.192). Ohio populations are part of a widely scattered set of population isolates that stretch from southern Wisconsin and northern Indiana to New York.

HABITAT: This species is restricted to sandy soils where the hostplant, lupine (*Lupinus perennis* L.) is common. Typical habitats include dune communities and oak savannas.

HOSTPLANT(S): In Ohio, larvae have been found on lupine (*Lupinus perennis* L.). Lupine is the only recorded hostplant of *L. melissa samuelis* (Opler and Krizek, 1984). Lupine is a potentially threatened plant in Ohio (Cooperrider, 1982).

ADULT ENERGY RESOURCES: Lupine (*Lupinus perennis* L.) and false-indigo (*Baptisia tinctoria* [L.] R. Br.).

FLIGHT PERIOD: Two broods, peaking in late May-early June, and again in late July (Figure 8.193). Extreme dates range from 18 May to 12 August.

GENERAL COMMENTS: Although once widespread and common throughout the Oak Openings of Lucas County (Price, 1970; John S. Thomas, pers comm, 1987), this species is on the verge of extirpation from Ohio. Only three small populations were known and less than five adults were sighted per year during 1986-88. Although recent Ohio populations occurred at low densities (Shuey, Calhoun, and Iftner, 1987), healthy populations in Michigan maintain high densities, and are usually locally abundant when found. Price (1970) noted population fluctuations during his experiences in the Oak Openings.

The decline of this butterfly is probably attributable to uncontrolled succession in its specialized habitat, the result of fire suppression. This butterfly requires relatively large stands of the hostplant, lupine. As succession proceeds, woody plants shade the lupine, which apparently renders the lupine unsuitable for oviposition. As the size of the lupine stands decrease through succession, local populations of *L. melissa samuelis* become extinct. Of the three lupine-feeding butterflies (*L. melissa samuelis, Incisalia irus*, and *Erynnis persius*), *L. melissa samuelis* is the most susceptible to habitat shading, and the first to become locally extinct. (See GENERAL COMMENTS under *Incisalia irus* for additional information about lupine-feeding butterflies.)

Given the highly localized nature of populations of this butterfly, additional unknown populations may exist in the Oak Openings. Sizable populations of lupine still survive in the area, which may support the butterfly. A recent joint initiative by the Toledo Metropark system and The Nature Conservancy to survey these stands of lupine for the presence of lupine-feeding butterflies should increase the number of known populations of all three lupine-feeding species. Because lupine also occurs in northeastern Ohio, there is a slight possibility that *L. melissa samuelis* also occurs in this area.

Adults tend to remain close to the hostplant, and are often encountered while they are perching or taking nectar on lupine. Males patrol areas adjacent to the hostplant. The flight of this butterfly is weak and usually less than one-half meter above the ground.

LITERATURE RECORDS: None.

A record from Summit County (Albrecht, 1982) is based on a misidentified series of *Glaucopsyche lygdamus.*

Family RIODINIDAE-Metalmarks

Calephelis borealis (Grote & Robinson, 1866). Northern Metalmark. Plate 25.

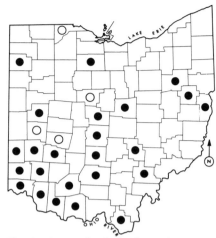

Fig. 8.194 _Calephelis borealis._

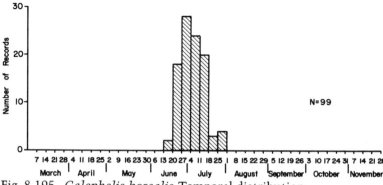

Fig. 8.195 _Calephelis borealis_-Temporal distribution.

STATUS: Resident; rare. This species is most often encountered in the southern half of the State, and becomes increasingly rare northward. Price (1970) knew of only one population in northwestern Ohio.

DISTRIBUTION/RANGE: Although most Ohio records are from the southern portion of the State (Figure 8.194), this species is probably more widely distributed. Populations are widely scattered and very localized.

HABITAT: This butterfly is usually found in xeric, open woodlands and adjacent open areas such as clearings, xeric prairies, and powerline cuts. In southern Ohio, populations are generally found on south to southeast facing slopes and road banks that cut through these habitats.

HOSTPLANT(S): In Ohio, this species has been found and reared on ragwort (_Senecio obovatus_ Muhl.) (Randle, 1953). Ragwort is the only verified hostplant (Opler and Krizek, 1984).

ADULT ENERGY RESOURCES: Butterfly-weed (_Asclepias tuberosa_ L.), white sweet clover (_Melilotus alba_ Desr.), black-eyed Susan (_Rudbeckia hirta_ L.), and fleabane (_Erigeron_ sp.).

FLIGHT PERIOD: One brood, peaking in late June and early July (Figure 8.195). Extreme dates range from 13 June to 31 July.

SIMILAR SPECIES: This species is almost indistinguishable from _C. muticum_. Perhaps the simplest method for separating these species in Ohio is habitat. _Calephelis borealis_ occurs in upland habitats. _Calephelis muticum_ is restricted to wetlands. Morphologically, _C. borealis_ tends to be larger, darker dorsally, and to have more rounded forewings than _C. muticum_. The silver markings on the ventral forewings of _C. borealis_ tend to be rectangular and connected, whereas in _C. muticum_ these spots are more square and separated.

GENERAL COMMENTS: _Calephelis borealis_ has often been confused with _C. muticum_, a closely related and very similar species. Even Klots (1951) erroneously considered Ohio records of _C. borealis_ to represent _C. muticum_. However, these two species are ecologically and morphologically distinct and, of the two, _C. borealis_ is by far the more widespread and common in Ohio.

Populations of _C. borealis_ are widely separated and are usually intensely localized, often inhabiting areas of a few square meters. Adults are closely associated with stands of the hostplant, and seldom stray far from them, even when visiting nectar sources. Although populations usually occur at low densities, this butterfly is occasionally locally common.

Very moth-like in its habits, this butterfly is usually found perching on the upper and undersides of leaves with its wings held out horizontally from the body. Even when on flowers, the wings are held in this position. The flight of this butterfly is weak and fluttery, and it can easily be mistaken for a moth. When disturbed, adults usually fly short distances and settle on the underside of nearby leaves.

Because of its localized populations and peculiar flight habits, this species is easily overlooked. The best method of discovering populations of this butterfly is to locate stands of the hostplant (ragwort) in the spring when it is in bloom, and then return during the flight period. Disturbing low growing foliage near the ragwort will occasionally flush individuals of _C. borealis_. Because adults are avid flower feeders, they may also be found visiting nearby nectar sources.

LITERATURE RECORDS: Lucas (Price, 1970), Miami (Studebaker and Studebaker, 1967), Marion, and Clark (Albrecht, 1982) Counties.

Calephelis muticum McAlpine, 1937. Swamp Metalmark. Plate 25.

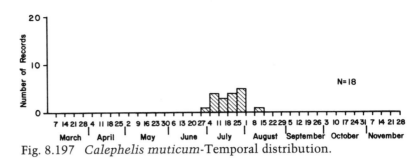

Fig. 8.197 *Calephelis muticum*-Temporal distribution.

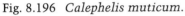

Fig. 8.196 *Calephelis muticum.*

STATUS: Resident; rare and endangered. Only two active populations are known.

DISTRIBUTION/RANGE: This butterfly has only been reported from Champaign and Logan Counties (Figure 8.196). Ohio records represent the eastern limit of this species' range.

HABITAT: This butterfly is restricted to open fen meadows and usually occupies a small fraction of each wetland. Fens are the typical habitat for this species in the Great Lakes Region.

HOSTPLANT(S): Although no hostplant has been recorded for Ohio, this species is closely associated with swamp thistle (*Cirsium muticum* Michx.). Swamp thistle and roadside thistle (*Cirsium altissimum* [L.] Spreng.) are the only reported hosts (Opler and Krizek, 1984).

ADULT ENERGY RESOURCES: Shrubby cinquefoil (*Potentilla fruticosa* L.).

FLIGHT PERIOD: One brood, peaking in July (Figure 8.197). Extreme dates range from 28 June to 10 August. In Ohio, there is no indication of the second brood which occurs in western Kentucky.

SIMILAR SPECIES: See *C. borealis.*

GENERAL COMMENTS: This species is very similar to *C. borealis*, and it was not until 1937, when *C. muticum* was named, that the differences between the two species were noted. Although the two species can be separated by physical characters, they are most easily separated by habitat type. *Calephelis muticum* is restricted to fens, whereas *C. borealis* inhabits upland woodlands and clearings.

Previous confusion over the ranges of *C. borealis* and *C. muticum* led to the popular belief (eg Klots, 1951) that all Ohio *Calephelis* specimens were referable to *C. muticum*. As a result, reviewers of Hoying's (1975) manuscript changed his listing of *C. borealis* to *C. muticum*, although his original determination was correct.

This butterfly has probably been severely impacted by habitat modification. Most of Ohio's fens have been entirely or partially drained for agricultural purposes, and undoubtedly some populations of *C. muticum* have been eliminated by these activities. For example, one fen from which this butterfly has been collected, Kaiser Lake State Park, Champaign County, was flooded to form a reservoir for the Ohio canal system. The current status of *C. muticum* at this locality is unknown, but certainly the flooding of this habitat did not enhance it.

Today this species has declined to the point where only two small populations are currently known. The better known of these occurs at Cedar Bog State Memorial, Champaign County (Albrecht, 1974). A pair of *C. muticum* specimens from this locality was designated as paratypes by McAlpine (1937) in his original description of this species.

Populations of this butterfly usually occur at very low densities and are extremely localized, usually occupying one or two hectares. Populations are easy to overlook, and most populations have probably escaped the attention of collectors. Because the hostplant occurs throughout the State in moist alkaline habitats, this butterfly could be more widespread than our records indicate. It is undoubtedly present in other small fens in the Teays River Valley, particularly those in Champaign and Logan Counties. It may also occur in north-central Ohio where the hostplant is still relatively common. It is also remotely possible that populations of *C. muticum* could inhabit low, poorly drained meadows in southwestern Ohio. It has been found in similar areas in north central Kentucky (Covell et al, 1979).

Because populations are so localized and generally contain very few adults, this butterfly may be very susceptible to collecting pressure. Collectors encountering this species should limit the number of adults captured, especially females.

This butterfly is generally inactive and is very moth-like in behavior. Adults are usually found resting on foliage near the hostplant or visiting the flowers of shrubby cinquefoil. Adults are sometimes flushed from their resting places on the undersides of leaves as one walks through their habitat. The flight of this species is very weak and fluttery, and usually just above the tops of the wetland plants. Both sexes tend to fly only short distances before settling. Adults rest with their wings held out horizontally.

This species has been attracted to ultraviolet lights used to attract moths (J. Richard Heitzman, pers comm, 1986). Additional Ohio populations may be discovered using this technique.

LITERATURE RECORDS: None.

Literature records from Clermont (Albrecht, 1982-miscited as Hamilton County by Shuey, Calhoun, and Iftner [1987]), Seneca (Porter, 1965), and Shelby Counties (Hoying, 1975) are based upon misdeterminations. Ehrlich and Ehrlich (1961) reported this species from near Cincinnati, but this was probably a poor geographic reference to the Cedar Bog population.

Family LIBYTHEIDAE-Snouts

Libytheana bachmanii bachmanii (Kirtland, 1851). Eastern Snout Butterfly. Plate 25.

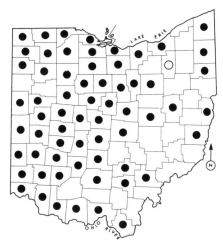

Fig. 8.198 *Libytheana bachmanii.*

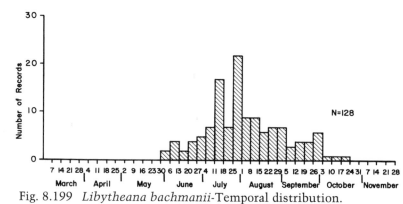

Fig. 8.199 *Libytheana bachmanii*-Temporal distribution.

STATUS: Uncertain, either a regular immigrant or a resident; uncommon to rare.

DISTRIBUTION/RANGE: Statewide (Figure 8.198). This butterfly is most frequently encountered in the glaciated counties of western Ohio. It is relatively rare elsewhere.

HABITAT: This species is found in and adjacent to mesic woodlands, along streams and rivers through flood plain forests, near swamps and ponds, and in brushy fields where the hostplant occurs.

HOSTPLANT(S): Although no hostplant has been recorded in Ohio, *L. bachmanii* is closely associated with hackberry (*Celtis occidentalis* L.). Dwarf hackberry (*Celtis tenuifolia* Nutt.) may also be used in southern Ohio. Hackberries (*Celtis* spp.) are the only recorded hostplants (Opler and Krizek, 1984).

ADULT ENERGY RESOURCES: Common milkweed (*Asclepias syriaca* L.), Indian hemp (*Apocynum cannabinum* L.), wild carrot (*Daucus carota* L.), common boneset (*Eupatorium perfoliatum* L.), bur-marigold (*Bidens aristosa* [Michx.] Britt.), small white aster (*Aster vimineus* Lam.), buttonbush (*Cephalanthus occidentalis* L.), Canada thistle (*Cirsium arvense* [L.] Scop.), hoary alyssum (*Berteroa incana* [L.] DC.), and shrubby cinquefoil (*Potentilla fruticosa* L.). Bubna (1897) also lists blackberry (*Rubus* sp.). This butterfly also imbibes moisture from damp soil and mud.

FLIGHT PERIOD: Although not obvious on the histogram, this species produces at least two broods a year (Figure 8.199). Extreme dates range from 30 May to 19 October.

GENERAL COMMENTS: This butterfly is a unique species that is easily recognized by its squared-off forewings and extremely long labial palpi which resemble a beak-like snout. Widespread but uncommon, populations fluctuate from year to year. Populations are usually very localized and are found in close association with stands of hackberry trees. *Libytheana bachmanii* is often associated with *Asterocampa celtis* and *A. clyton,* two other butterflies which also use hackberry trees as their hostplants.

 The status of this butterfly in Ohio is uncertain. Opler and Krizek (1984) consider this species to be a resident only in the middle and lower South, and consider Ohio specimens to represent immigrants. However, this species occurs consistently from year to year at many southern Ohio localities, suggesting that it may be a resident in that part of the State. Populations in the northern portion of the State are probably established yearly by immigrants.

 Although this butterfly is occasionally observed visiting flowers, it is most often encountered while it is visiting damp soil and sand along streams, rivers, and gravel roads. Males seem territorial and will investigate intruders by flying out from their leaf and twig perches. The flight is swift and erratic and can be difficult to follow. When perched on twigs, the ventral wing surfaces give this butterfly a dead leaf appearance.

 There are two phenotypes of *L. bachmanii.* The form 'kirtlandi' (Field, 1938) has the hindwing pattern nearly uniform dark violet-gray with little mottling. The other phenotype is much lighter ventrally, and is heavily mottled with tan and brown.

 This species was first described by Jared P. Kirtland (1851b) from a specimen collected in Mahoning County, and is the only butterfly described by an Ohio resident from Ohio material. In honor of Kirtland's description, the logo of The Ohio Lepidopterists features a reproduction of the original woodcut of this butterfly which appeared in Kirtland's description.

LITERATURE RECORDS: Summit County (Claypole, 1897).

114

Family HELICONIIDAE-Heliconians

Agraulis vanillae nigrior **Michener, 1942.** Gulf Fritillary. Plate 25.

Fig. 8.200 *Agraulis vanillae.*

STATUS: Stray or irregular immigrant; rare. This species has only rarely been recorded from Ohio. Only a single Ohio specimen with complete data is known to exist.

DISTRIBUTION/RANGE: In the eastern United States, this butterfly is a resident only in the lower Gulf States. Periodically, this species wanders northward, and on rare occasions reaches states as far north as Minnesota, Wisconsin, Ohio, Pennsylvania, and New York (Opler and Krizek, 1984). Temporary breeding populations have been reported as far north as Missouri (Heitzman and Heitzman, 1987), Illinois (Irwin and Downey, 1973), Virginia (Clark and Clark, 1951), and Kentucky. Ohio records are from Hamilton (A. Wyss, 1931; 1932) Morrow, and Adams Counties (Figure 8.200). (The Adams County record was reported too late to appear on the distribution map for this species).

HABITAT: Where this species is resident, it frequents a variety of open habitats such as old fields, pastures, forest margins, and gardens. The Morrow County individual was captured in a hay field (John S. Gill, pers comm, 1987). The Adams County individual was captured in a ridgetop xeric prairie opening.

HOSTPLANT(S): In Ohio, a larva was found and reared on yellow passion flower (*Passiflora lutea* L.), a plant found throughout much of southeastern Ohio (Cusick and Silberhorn, 1977). The primary hostplant of this species in the eastern United States is maypop (passion flower, *Passiflora incarnata* L.) (Opler and Krizek, 1984). This plant occurs in at least two southern Ohio counties (Cusick and Silberhorn, 1977).

ADULT ENERGY RESOURCES: None recorded for Ohio.

FLIGHT PERIOD: Albert Wyss (1931) reports a capture of this species from Cincinnati on 17 August 1929. The Morrow County specimen was captured in the summer of 1944 (John S. Gill, pers comm, 1987).

SIMILAR SPECIES: None.

GENERAL COMMENTS: This species may occur in Ohio more frequently than the few records suggest. It should be watched for in open areas during the late summer and early autumn, especially in southern Ohio. A single adult was reared (and subsequently released) from a larva found at Lynx Prairie, Adams County, in July 1990 (Whan, 1990). This suggests that *A. vanillae* has the potential to establish temporary breeding populations in Ohio. Evidence from Kentucky (Charles V. Covell, Jr., pers comm, 1989) indicates that *A. vanillae* is capable of reproducing more often in our area, and stands of the hostplant should be watched for this butterfly. This species cannot survive Ohio's winters.

The flight of this species is rapid and usually within one meter of the ground. Adult *A. vanillae* are avid flower visitors. Despite its general resemblance to *Euptoieta claudia* and several *Speyeria* species, *A. vanillae* is easily recognized while in flight by its unique wing shape and bright ventral wing pattern.

LITERATURE RECORDS: Hamilton County (A. Wyss, 1931; 1932).

Family NYMPHALIDAE-Brushfoots

Euptoieta claudia (Cramer, 1775). Variegated Fritillary. Plate 26.

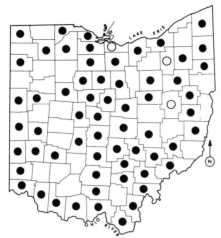

Fig. 8.201 *Euptoieta claudia.*

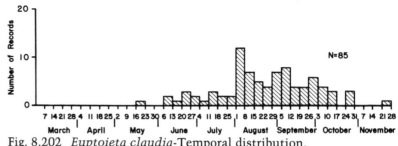

Fig. 8.202 *Euptoieta claudia*-Temporal distribution.

STATUS: Regular immigrant; uncommon to rare. This species is most frequently encountered in southern Ohio. Adults of this species may occasionally survive mild winters in the extreme southern portion of the State.

DISTRIBUTION/RANGE: In the eastern United States, this species is a resident of the southern Atlantic and Gulf States. Each year this butterfly wanders northward reaching states as far north as Minnesota and Michigan (Opler and Krizek, 1984). Although our records are scattered statewide, this butterfly is most often reported from the southern half of the State (Figure 8.201).

HABITAT: This species is usually found in open disturbed areas such as clover fields, alfalfa fields, pastures, old fields, waste areas, and along roadsides. It is also occasionally found in gardens and in urban areas.

HOSTPLANT(S): In Ohio, ova of this species have been found and reared on field pansy (*Viola raffinesqueii* Green). It has also been observed ovipositing on other species of violets (*Viola* spp.) as well. Plantain (*Plantago* sp.), purslane (*Portulaca* sp.), passion flower (*Passiflora* spp.), stonecrop (*Sedum* sp.), moonseed (*Menispermum* sp.), and May-apple (*Podophyllum peltata* L.) are other frequently reported hostplants (Howe, 1975; Opler and Krizek, 1984). All of these plants occur in Ohio (Weishaupt, 1971).

ADULT ENERGY RESOURCES: Alfalfa (*Medicago sativa* L.), red clover (*Trifolium pratense* L.), common milkweed (*Asclepias syriaca* L.), dogbane (*Apocynum* sp.), ironweed (*Vernonia* sp.), common boneset (*Eupatorium perfoliatum* L.), bur-marigold (*Bidens aristosa* [Michx.] Britt.), asters (*Aster* spp.), fleabane (*Erigeron* sp.), thistles (*Cirsium* spp.), and various garden flowers. This butterfly also imbibes moisture from damp soil and mud.

FLIGHT PERIOD: One to three broods, depending upon how early in the season adults become established (Figure 8.202). Extreme dates range from 22 May to 22 November.

SIMILAR SPECIES: None.

GENERAL COMMENTS: This is a southern species that regularly wanders into Ohio, and during typical years is first seen in June and July. Populations fluctuate greatly from year to year, and reach their highest densities during late summer. Although this species occurs sporadically over most of the State, it can be found almost every year along the Ohio River, where it is often locally common.

The flight of this species is fast, darting, and usually within one meter of the ground. Adults are extremely wary, and can be difficult to approach. Fortunately, adults are avid flower visitors, and can be easily observed at flowers, especially in clover and alfalfa fields. Adults also perch on exposed soil and herbaceous plants.

This butterfly exhibits extreme size variation. It is not uncommon to find females flying with males that are only half their size.

LITERATURE RECORDS: Summit (Claypole, 1897; Hine, 1898a) Tuscarawas (Albrecht, 1982), and Erie (Henninger, 1910) Counties.

Speyeria diana (Cramer, 1775). Diana. Plate 26.

Fig. 8.203 *Speyeria diana.*

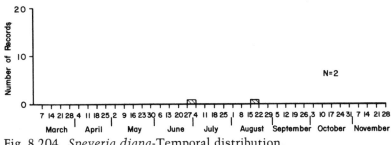

Fig. 8.204 *Speyeria diana*-Temporal distribution.

STATUS: Resident; rare, extirpated. There are very few Ohio records with complete data for this species.

DISTRIBUTION/RANGE: Most of our records are from southern Ohio, with the majority of these records coming from the vicinity of Cincinnati in Hamilton County. In addition to the records plotted on Figure 8.203, there are two specimens in the Carnegie Museum of Natural History that are simply labeled "S. Ohio" and "S.E. Ohio". The records from Franklin and Medina Counties probably represent strays. Ohio lies at the northern range limit for this species.

HABITAT: This species usually inhabits hilly and mountainous areas supporting mature hardwood forests. Adults are usually restricted to forests and adjacent clearings such as meadows and roadsides.

HOSTPLANT(S): Not known in Ohio. Although the natural hostplants have never been reported, larvae will feed on violets (*Viola* spp.) in captivity (Opler and Krizek, 1984).

ADULT ENERGY RESOURCES: None recorded for Ohio.

FLIGHT PERIOD: This species produces one brood per year (Figure 8.204). Extreme dates range from 29 June to 17 August.

SIMILAR SPECIES: Females of *S. diana* are similar to *Limenitis arthemis astyanax*, but use of the plates will allow easy separation of these two species.

GENERAL COMMENTS: Originally, this species was probably resident throughout the southern portion of the State. However, the widespread deforestation for iron smelting and agriculture that took place during the late 1800's and early 1900's probably eliminated most of the populations in Ohio. Although some populations of *S. diana* survived this period, at least around Cincinnati, the continuing elimination of the remaining forests for agriculture and urban expansion eventually resulted in the extinction of this species in Ohio. This butterfly was probably still resident in the Cincinnati area as late as the 1930's (Wyss, 1932; and Charles Oehler, pers comm, 1986).

Although *S. diana* has experienced similar declines throughout its original range, it is now staging a comeback. As second growth forests have begun to mature, this butterfly is re-establishing itself in many areas from which it had been eliminated (Hammond and McCorkle, 1983[84]). Thomas J. Allen (pers comm, 1986) has observed the re-appearance of this species in several areas of West Virginia. It is possible that this butterfly will eventually be rediscovered in Ohio as it continues to expand its range. Collectors should watch for this species in July and August in the mature woodlands of Wayne National Forest and Shawnee State Forest of southern Ohio.

This species is sexually dimorphic, and the sexes are dissimilar enough that they could be mistaken for distinct species. The male displays a fairly typical orange fritillary pattern whereas the female is black with blue marginal patterns on the dorsal wing surfaces. The female is assumed to mimic *Battus philenor*, a species that is distasteful to predators. Hence, some predators may confuse females of *S. diana* with *B. philenor*, giving the *S. diana* females a measure of protection.

The flight of this species is strong and direct, but not particularly rapid unless alarmed. Adults are strongly attracted to flowers, especially common milkweed (*Asclepias syriaca* L), butterfly-weed (*Asclepias tuberosa* L.), and Joe-Pye weed (*Eupatorium purpureum* L.).

LITERATURE RECORDS: Medina County (Hine, 1898a; 1898b).

117

Speyeria cybele cybele (Fabricius, 1775). Great Spangled Fritillary. Plate 26.

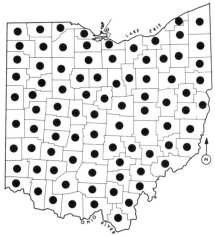

Fig. 8.205 *Speyeria cybele.*

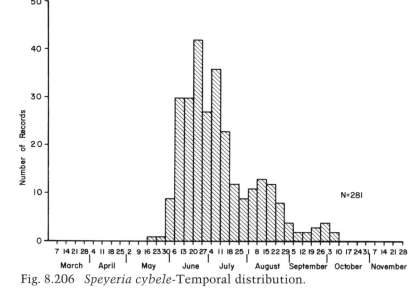

Fig. 8.206 *Speyeria cybele*-Temporal distribution.

STATUS: Resident; common.

DISTRIBUTION/RANGE: Statewide (Figure 8.205). This species has been recorded from all 88 Ohio counties.

HABITAT: This butterfly is found in open woodlands and in associated open areas such as pastures, prairies, clover fields, alfalfa fields, roadsides, and gardens. This species is often encountered visiting flowers far from woodlands.

HOSTPLANT(S): In Ohio, larvae of this species have been found and reared on violets (*Viola* spp.) (Clement W. Baker, unpublished notes; David K. Parshall, pers comm, 1987). This butterfly uses various species of violets as hostplants (Opler and Krizek, 1984).

ADULT ENERGY RESOURCES: Common milkweed (*Asclepias syriaca* L.), swamp milkweed (*Asclepias incarnata* L.), butterfly-weed (*Asclepias tuberosa* L.), Indian hemp (*Apocynum cannabinum* L.), red clover (*Trifolium pratense* L.), alfalfa (*Medicago sativa* L.), teasel (*Dipsacus sylvestris* Huds.), buttonbush (*Cephalanthus occidentalis* L.), bull thistle (*Cirsium vulgare* [Savi] Tenore), Canada thistle (*Cirsium arvense* [L.] Scop.), field thistle (*Cirsium discolor* [Muhl.] Spreng.), ironweed (*Vernonia* sp.), black-eyed Susan (*Rudbeckia hirta* L.), spotted Joe-Pye weed (*Eupatorium maculatum* L.), oxeye daisy (*Chrysanthemum leucanthemum* L.), wild bergamot (*Monarda fistulosa* L.), and St. John's-wort (*Hypericum* sp.). Adults have also been observed visiting carrion, damp soil, and damp sand.

FLIGHT PERIOD: One generation, peaking in late June-early July (Figure 8.206). Extreme dates range from 5 April (unusually early) to 30 October.

SIMILAR SPECIES: This species can be confused with both *S. aphrodite* and *S. atlantis. Speyeria cybele* lacks the black spot below the discal cell that is usually present on both *S. aphrodite* and *S. atlantis.* Ventrally, the submarginal hindwing buff band is much wider in *S. cybele* than in *S. aphrodite* or *S. atlantis;* this band is often entirely absent in *S. aphrodite. Speyeria cybele* is usually larger than the other two species as well.

GENERAL COMMENTS: This is the most common fritillary in Ohio. Although this species may have declined in overall abundance in recent years (Price, 1970), it is still a common sight throughout the State.

The flight of this species is rapid and is usually within two meters of the ground. Males patrol, presumably to locate mates, and seem to follow set "routes" around fields. Both sexes are avid flower visitors and are easily observed while they perch on favored flowers.

Speyeria cybele often occurs in the same habitats as does *S. aphrodite*, a species with which it is easily confused. Throughout its Ohio range, *S. cybele* is the more abundant of the two species.

This species is extremely variable. Both sexes, but especially females, vary greatly in color, and can range from pale buff individuals which sometimes resemble the northern subspecies, *S. cybele krautwurmi* (Holland, 1931), to individuals that are aberrantly melanic (*S. cybele* form 'baal' [Strecker, 1878], type locality Toledo, Lucas County, Ohio). Adults are also variable in size.

Speyeria aphrodite aphrodite **(Fabricius, 1787)/*alcestis* (W. H. Edwards, 1877).** Aphrodite Fritillary.
Plate 27.

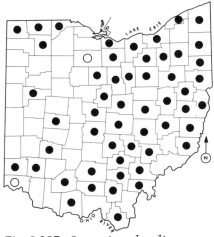

Fig. 8.207 *Speyeria aphrodite.*

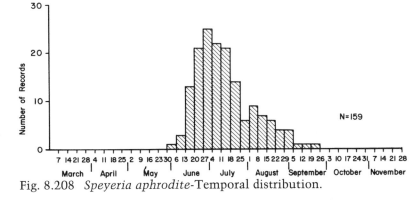

Fig. 8.208 *Speyeria aphrodite*-Temporal distribution.

STATUS: Resident; rare to common. This species is most common in northern and southeastern Ohio. There are very few records from the southwestern and west-central regions of the State.

DISTRIBUTION/RANGE: Statewide (Figure 8.207).

HABITAT: This species is most often encountered in open woodlands, wet meadows, prairies, and along roadsides. It will also venture into alfalfa and clover fields to visit nectar sources.

HOSTPLANT(S): In Ohio, larvae of this species have been found and reared on violets (*Viola* sp.) (Clement W. Baker, unpublished notes). Throughout its range, this butterfly uses a variety of violets (Opler and Krizek, 1984).

ADULT ENERGY RESOURCES: Common milkweed (*Asclepias syriaca* L.), butterfly-weed (*Asclepias tuberosa* L.), Indian hemp (*Apocynum cannabinum* L.), red clover (*Trifolium pratense* L.), Canada thistle (*Cirsium arvense* [L.] Scop.), bull thistle (*Cirsium vulgare* [Savi] Tenore), ironweed (*Vernonia* sp.), oxeye daisy (*Chrysanthemum leucanthemum* L.), orange hawkweed (*Hieracium aurantiacum* L.), and blazing-star (*Liatris* sp.).

FLIGHT PERIOD: One brood, peaking in late June and early July (Figure 8.208). Extreme dates range from 3 June to 20 September.

SIMILAR SPECIES: See *S. cybele. Speyeria aphrodite* can also be confused with *S. atlantis.* The ventral hindwing ground color of *S. aphrodite* is dark reddish-brown, whereas the ground color of *S. atlantis* is purple-brown. The outer margin of the forewing of *S. atlantis* is generally darker than that of *S. aphrodite. Speyeria aphrodite* is generally larger than *S. atlantis.*

GENERAL COMMENTS: Although this species is widespread, it is less common and more localized than *S. cybele. Speyeria aphrodite* may have been more common in the past. Wyss (1932) noted the apparent decline of this species in southwestern Ohio during the early part of this century. Today, this species is rare throughout the western half of the State. As with other species of *Speyeria, S. aphrodite* experiences periodic population fluctuations.

The habits of *S. aphrodite* are very similar to those of *S. cybele*, and on the wing, these two species are easily confused. Always less numerous, *S. aphrodite* may be overlooked where it occurs with *S. cybele*. The flight of *S. aphrodite* is rapid and erratic. Adults are avid flower visitors and can be closely observed while they probe flowers.

Two putative "subspecies" of *S. aphrodite* occur in Ohio, with overlap and intergradation of the forms occurring in northern Ohio. *Speyeria a. aphrodite* is the most common form and is found statewide. Specimens resembling *S. aphrodite alcestis* comprise a small percentage of the specimens found in the northern two tiers of counties. Moeck (1957) exaggerated when he remarked that *S. aphrodite alcestis* occurs "especially in the lush grasslands of Ohio". The two "subspecies" are best separated by the amount of reddish-brown that extends into the buff submarginal band on the ventral hindwings. In *S. a. aphrodite* this reddish-brown scaling only partially invades the buff submarginal band, but in *S. aphrodite alcestis* it totally obliterates the buff band. In northern Ohio, intergradation between these two forms is common, and it is sometimes difficult to find specimens that fit the description of either form perfectly. At best, these two subspecies are weakly differentiated in northern Ohio, and illustrate well the inherent difficulties associated with the identification of clinal subspecies.

A dark aberration 'bakeri' (A. H. Clark, 1932) was named in honor of Clement W. Baker, who collected the type specimen in Waynesburg, Stark County, Ohio.

LITERATURE RECORDS: Hamilton (Dury, 1878; Hine, 1898a; Wyss, 1932) and Seneca (Henninger, 1910) Counties.

Speyeria idalia (Drury, 1773). Regal Fritillary. Plate 27.

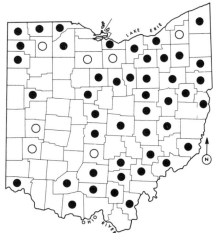

Fig. 8.209 *Speyeria idalia.*

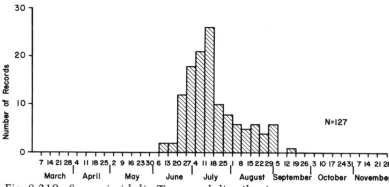

N=127

Fig. 8.210 *Speyeria idalia*-Temporal distribution.

STATUS: Resident; rare to uncommon (potentially endangered). Populations of this species are localized, but adults are sometimes common within limited areas.

DISTRIBUTION/RANGE: Statewide (Figure 8.209). Records of this butterfly are scattered throughout the State, but the majority of recent records have come from the Unglaciated Allegheny Plateau. There are also a few recent records from several north-central counties. Records from western Ohio are few.

HABITAT: In southeastern Ohio, this butterfly occurs in wet fields, pastures, and along roadsides, but usually near a woodland border. In northern Ohio, this species primarily inhabits mesic prairies which grade into wetlands. This butterfly will wander into clover and alfalfa fields, and along roadsides, in search of nectar sources.

HOSTPLANT(S): In Ohio, larvae have been found and reared on birdsfoot violet (*Viola pedata* L.) (Ray W. Bracher, pers comm, 1987). Because birdsfoot violet is not found in many areas which support this butterfly, other violets are undoubtedly used. Violets are the only recorded hosts of this butterfly (Opler and Krizek, 1984).

During the 1930's, Clement W. Baker and Ray W. Bracher collected the nocturnal larvae of this species by placing weighted down linen sheets over stands of violets. The sheets were put in place in the evenings, and checked the following morning for larvae (Ray W. Bracher, pers comm, 1987).

ADULT ENERGY RESOURCES: Common milkweed (*Asclepias syriaca* L.), butterfly-weed (*Asclepias tuberosa* L.), red clover (*Trifolium pratense* L.), alfalfa (*Medicago sativa* L.), thistles (*Cirsium* spp.), yarrow (*Achillea millefolium* L.), and ironweed (*Vernonia* sp.). This species has also been reported on self-heal (*Prunella vulgaris* L.), sumac (*Rhus* sp.), swamp milkweed (*Asclepias incarnata* L.), green milkweed (*Asclepias viridiflora* Raf.), dogbane (*Apocynum androsaemifolium* L.) (Clement W. Baker, unpublished notes), and teasel (*Dipsacus* sp.) (Edward C. Welling, unpublished notes). This species also imbibes moisture from damp soil.

FLIGHT PERIOD: One brood peaking in early July (Figure 8.210). Extreme dates range from 9 June to 18 September.

GENERAL COMMENTS: This butterfly is another species that has been greatly affected by human activities. Once common throughout Ohio in suitable areas, this species has declined throughout much of the State, and has virtually disappeared from most of western Ohio. The prairies of west-central Ohio were eliminated so rapidly that very few records of *S. idalia* exist for this region. From the 1920's through the 1940's, this species remained common elsewhere, particularly in the northeastern corner of the State and in the Oak Openings where Clement W. Baker and J. Donald Eff collected long series of this species. Baker once collected 84 males in a two hour period and remarked that the species was "not so plentiful that year" (Clement W. Baker, unpublished notes). Since that period, this species has declined throughout most of its Ohio range. Loss of habitat to agriculture and urban growth as well as the increased use of herbicides have probably contributed to the decline of this species. Today, with the exception of a few localities in southern Ohio, there are few areas where this species is encountered with any regularity. Most encounters in northern Ohio are with lone individuals, which may represent adults that wander from nearby populations.

Populations of this butterfly are extremely localized and scattered, and population densities fluctuate from year to year. A few individuals of both sexes seem to wander away from each population in late summer. Males patrol large areas, in a low, rapid, and direct flight, chasing after the females that they encounter. It is possible to watch individual males for several hours as they repeatedly fly their circuitous routes. Females usually perch on low vegetation and fly less frequently than males. Members of this species can often be seen basking on low-growing vegetation with outstretched wings. Both sexes are avid flower visitors, and can be found clustered at stands of milkweed. Populations may be highly dependent upon local nectar resources and we have noticed the extinction of one population that coincided with the elimination of its milkweed nectar source.

This species is sexually dimorphic. Females are generally larger than males, and have two rows of white spots on the dorsal hindwings. In males, only the inner row of spots is white; the outer row is orange.

LITERATURE RECORDS: Henry, (Hine, 1898b), Montgomery (Kirtland, 1854a; Scudder, 1889), Pickaway (Bales, 1909), Seneca (Henninger, 1910; Porter, 1965), Geauga (Lepidopterists' Society, 1980), Huron (Lepidopterists' Society, 1979), and Miami (Studebaker and Studebaker, 1967) Counties.

Speyeria atlantis atlantis (W. H. Edwards, 1862). Mountain Silver-spot. Plate 27.

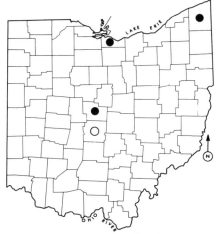

Fig. 8.211 *Speyeria atlantis*.

STATUS: Uncertain, either an irregular immigrant or a resident; rare. This species could be an irregular immigrant, but fresh individuals from Erie and Ashtabula Counties, and a short series from Erie County suggest that it is a possible resident. Individuals from central Ohio probably represent strays.

DISTRIBUTION/RANGE: *Speyeria atlantis* is primarily a species of the Canadian Life Zone. In eastern North America, this species occurs from the Maritime Provinces of Canada, west through southern Canada and the northern United States, and south in the mountains to Virginia (Opler and Krizek, 1984). Ohio records are primarily from the northeastern corner of the State (Figure 8.211), and represent a regional southern range limit for this species.

HABITAT: Although little is known about the habitat requirements of this butterfly within Ohio, it has been collected near Pennline Bog, Ashtabula County, a fen/woodland complex notable for its boreal plant communities. In adjacent states where this butterfly is resident, it is usually found in open mixed coniferous-deciduous forests and peatlands, where it is often seen visiting nectar sources along roads. Because this species is usually associated with botanical communities containing boreal elements, Ohio populations will probably be found in association with relict communities found in wetlands or in narrow river valleys in the northeastern corner of the State.

HOSTPLANT(S): Not known in Ohio. Violets (*Viola* spp.) are the only known hosts (Opler and Krizek, 1984).

ADULT ENERGY RESOURCES: None recorded for Ohio.

FLIGHT PERIOD: Populations adjacent to Ohio produce one brood per year. Extreme dates range from 28 June to 10 August.

SIMILAR SPECIES: See *S. cybele* and *S. aphrodite*.

GENERAL COMMENTS: The status of this species in Ohio is uncertain. It may stray into the State from adjacent areas, and/or it may be resident in the northeastern corner of the State. This corner of the State contains many community types which support northern plants found nowhere else in Ohio. *Speyeria atlantis* may be a part of one or more of these communities.

This species may occur more regularly than our records suggest. It is known from adjacent regions of Pennsylvania (Opler and Krizek, 1984) and should be searched for throughout the northeastern corner of Ohio. Because of its similarity to other *Speyeria* species, it may be overlooked by many observers. Those searching for this species in Ohio should examine every *Speyeria* they encounter, particularly in appropriate areas in northeastern Ohio.

Although it has a rapid flight, adults of *S. atlantis* are strongly attracted to nectar sources whereupon they are easily observed.

LITERATURE RECORDS: Franklin County (Hine, 1898a; b).

Although Albrecht (1982) reported this species from Morrow, Licking, and Guernsey Counties, we feel that these records are based upon misdeterminations, because searches of the collections that he reviewed failed to substantiate these records.

Boloria selene myrina (Cramer, 1777)/*nebraskensis* (Holland, 1928). Silver-bordered Fritillary. Plate 28.

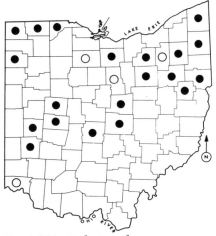

Fig. 8.212 *Boloria selene*.

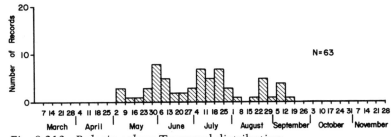

Fig. 8.213 *Boloria selene*-Temporal distribution.

STATUS: Resident; rare (threatened). Populations of this species are localized, but may occasionally reach high densities.

DISTRIBUTION/RANGE: Glaciated Ohio (Figure 8.212). Ohio represents the southern range limit for this species.

HABITAT: This species is most often encountered in moist open habitats such as sedge meadows, mesic prairies, and moist old fields. This butterfly will wander into drier open habitats in search of nectar sources.

HOSTPLANT(S): Although no hostplant has been recorded in Ohio, in the Oak Openings this butterfly is closely associated with lance-leaved violet (*Viola lanceolata* L.), a threatened species in Ohio (Cooperrider, 1982). Elsewhere, other violets are probably used because lance-leaved violets are not always found at localities where *B. selene* is found (Shuey, Calhoun, and Iftner, 1987). Violets are the only verified hostplants of this butterfly (Opler and Krizek, 1984).

ADULT ENERGY RESOURCES: Red clover (*Trifolium pratense* L.), alfalfa (*Medicago sativa* L.), common milkweed (*Asclepias syriaca* L.), butterfly-weed (*Asclepias tuberosa* L.), and purple coneflower (*Echinacea purpurea* L.). Adults also take moisture from damp soil and damp sand.

FLIGHT PERIOD: Three broods with peaks in late May-early June, July, and late August-early September (Figure 8.213). Extreme dates range from 8 May to 15 September.

SIMILAR SPECIES: This species is superficially similar to *B. bellona.* The presence of silver spots on the ventral hindwings of *B. selene* will distinguish it from *B. bellona.*

GENERAL COMMENTS: Once common throughout much of glaciated Ohio, this species has undergone a serious decline in abundance and distribution in recent years, probably because of habitat destruction (Shuey, Calhoun, and Iftner, 1987). All known extant populations occur in open mesic habitats, and the loss of these habitats due to draining for agriculture and urban expansion may have eliminated this species from most of the State. Today *B. selene* is most often encountered in the Oak Openings in northwestern Ohio and in wetlands of extreme northeastern Ohio. This butterfly could be extirpated from the State if wetlands continue to be destroyed.

Kohler (1977) recognized Ohio populations as transitional between two subspecies of *B. selene*. Populations in the northeastern corner of the State are referable to *B. selene myrina.* These populations are composed of small, dark individuals. Populations in central and west-central Ohio are composed of larger and lighter-colored individuals and are best referred to as *B. selene nebraskensis.* These populations are very rare, and may be on the verge of extinction. In northwestern Ohio, and areas between central Ohio and northeastern Ohio, populations which are intermediate between these subspecies are found. Intergradation between the two subspecies closely parallels environmental factors. *B. selene myrina* is usually associated with habitats found within forested regions, whereas *B. selene nebraskensis* is associated with habitats associated with prairies. Where these biomes meet and mix, intermediate populations of *B. selene* occur (Kohler, 1977). It is possible that *B. selene nebraskensis* is a xerothermic relict in Ohio. Most of the known populations were found in areas within the prairie peninsula, and it seems likely that populations of this butterfly became established during the period of prairie expansion several thousand years ago.

Most populations of this species are generally small and localized, with adults seldom straying far from their habitat, except to visit nectar sources. However, in the Oak Openings, where suitable habitats are found in many old fields, this butterfly is generally distributed and populations often attain high densities. Males patrol at a height of approximately one meter, presumably in search of females. The flight of this species is low and erratic. Populations of this species nearly always co-occur with the more common *B. bellona,* a species with which it can be confused. Collectors searching for *B. selene* should examine all *Boloria* encountered in mesic habitats.

LITERATURE RECORDS: Hamilton (Hine, 1898a), Richland (Kohler, 1977), Summit (Claypole, 1897; Hine, 1898a), and Seneca (Henninger, 1910) Counties.

Boloria bellona bellona (Fabricius, 1775). Meadow Fritillary. Plate 28.

Fig. 8.214 *Boloria bellona.*

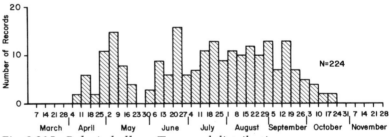

Fig. 8.215 *Boloria bellona*-Temporal distribution.

STATUS: Resident; common.

DISTRIBUTION/RANGE: Statewide (Figure 8.214).

HABITAT: This species inhabits a variety of open mesic habitats. Typical habitats include wet meadows, grassy fields, pastures, sedge meadows, prairies, fens, ditches, and pond and stream margins. Adults will wander into drier areas in search of nectar sources.

HOSTPLANT(S): In Ohio, this species has been observed ovipositing on violets (*Viola* sp.). Various species of violets are used as hostplants throughout the range of this species (Opler and Krizek, 1984).

ADULT ENERGY RESOURCES: Garlic-mustard (*Alliaria officinalis* Andrz.), violets (*Viola* spp.), alfalfa (*Medicago sativa* L.), red clover (*Trifolium pratense* L.), Indian hemp (*Apocynum cannabinum* L.), butterfly-weed (*Asclepias tuberosa* L.), self-heal

(*Prunella vulgaris* L.), teasel (*Dipsacus sylvestris* Huds.), dandelion (*Taraxacum officinale* Webr.), purple coneflower (*Echinacea purpurea* L.), black-eyed Susan (*Rudbeckia hirta* L.), oxeye daisy (*Chrysanthemum leucanthemum* L.), wing-stem (*Verbesina alternifolia* [L.] Britt.), Canada thistle (*Cirsium arvense* [L.] Scop.), thistles (*Cirsium* spp.), ironweed (*Vernonia* sp.), and goldenrod (*Solidago* sp.). Adults also imbibe moisture from damp soil and feces.

FLIGHT PERIOD: Two to three broods, with a possible fourth in some years. Populations peak in May, June, July, and September (Figure 8.215). Extreme dates range from 4 April to 21 October.

SIMILAR SPECIES: See *B. selene*.

GENERAL COMMENTS: This is our most common and widespread *Boloria* species. Generally distributed, this species can be expected to occur almost anywhere that moist, open habitats are found. It has adapted particularly well to human-made habitats, and as a result, is probably much more common and widespread today than it was in the past.

This species has spread far to the south of its original range, and is still apparently colonizing new areas in Illinois (Sedman and Hess, 1985), Missouri (Heitzman and Heitzman, 1987), and Kentucky (Charles V. Covell, Jr., pers comm, 1983). It is likely that this species did not originally occur in the southern portion of Ohio and only became established in this region in the mid 1800's. Dury (1878) noted that *B. bellona* was generally rare around Cincinnati, but today it is common in that area.

The behavior of *B. bellona* is very similar to that of *B. selene*, and these two species can be confused in habitats that support both species. Adults of *B. bellona* tend to fly within one meter of the ground. The flight is fairly rapid and erratic. Adults are avid flower visitors, and are best observed while they are visiting nectar sources.

Boloria bellona is phenotypically variable, and is especially variable in size. Wing pattern is also variable, and melanic individuals are sometimes encountered.

LITERATURE RECORDS: None.

Chlosyne nycteis nycteis (Doubleday & Hewitson, 1847). Silvery Checkerspot. Plate 28.

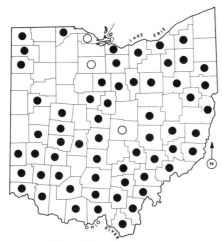

Fig. 8.216 *Chlosyne nycteis*.

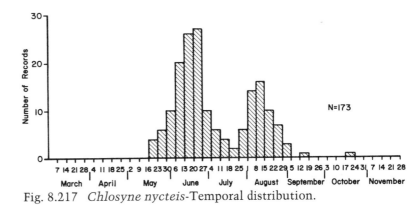

Fig. 8.217 *Chlosyne nycteis*-Temporal distribution.

STATUS: Resident; uncommon. This species is most often encountered in southern Ohio, where it can be locally common. Northward, this species becomes progressively more localized and uncommon.

DISTRIBUTION/RANGE: Statewide (Figure 8.216).

HABITAT: This species is usually found in open areas that border mesic deciduous forests. Typical habitats include forest margins and openings, mesic fields, and old fields. These habitats are often near streams and rivers.

HOSTPLANT(S): In Ohio, this species has been reared on wing-stem (*Verbesina helianthoides* Michx.) (Eugene Pilate, unpublished notes). Other composites are undoubtedly used as well. In the eastern United States, wing-stem is the most often reported hostplant, although sunflowers (*Helianthus* spp.), purple-stemmed aster (*Aster puniceus* L.), and sneezeweed (*Helenium autumnale* L.), are also used (Opler and Krizek, 1984). All of these plants occur in Ohio (Weishaupt, 1971).

ADULT ENERGY RESOURCES: Red clover (*Trifolium pratense* L.), white clover (*Trifolium repens* L.), oxeye daisy (*Chrysanthemum leucanthemum* L.), dandelion (*Taraxacum officinale* Webr.), Canada thistle (*Cirsium arvense* [L.] Scop.), ox-eye (*Heliopsis helianthoides* [L.] Sweet), fleabane (*Erigeron* sp.), common milkweed (*Asclepias syriaca* L.), wild parsnip (*Pastinaca sativa* L.), and winter cress (*Barbarea vulgaris* R. Br.). Adults also take moisture from damp soil, mud, urine, and fecal deposits.

FLIGHT PERIOD: Two broods with peaks in June and August (Figure 8.217). Extreme dates range from 11 May to 19 October. Henninger (1910) remarked that this species occurred as early as April in Seneca County.

SIMILAR SPECIES: This species is superficially similar to *C. harrisii* and the two *Phyciodes* species. *Chlosyne nycteis* lacks the reddish bands on the ventral hindwings that characterize *C. harrisii*. *Chlosyne nycteis* is larger and has a more pale and checkered ventral hindwing pattern than either *P. tharos* or *P. pascoensis*.

GENERAL COMMENTS: Although this species is widespread, it is seldom found in large numbers. Populations of this butterfly fluctuate from year to year, and can be locally common one year, and seemingly absent the next.

This species is most often encountered at flowers, or as it is perching on low vegetation, or while it is visiting moist soil. The flight is very direct and close to the ground. The flight of *C. nycteis* is very similar to *Phyciodes tharos*.

Adults are variable in size, and some females may be nearly twice as large as small males. There is also some variation in the black pattern elements on the dorsal wing surfaces.

LITERATURE RECORDS: Seneca (Henninger, 1910), Ottawa, and Licking (Albrecht, 1982) Counties.

Chlosyne harrisii harrisii (Scudder, 1864)/*liggetti* (Avinoff, 1930). Harris' Checkerspot. Plate 28.

Fig. 8.218 *Chlosyne harrisii.*

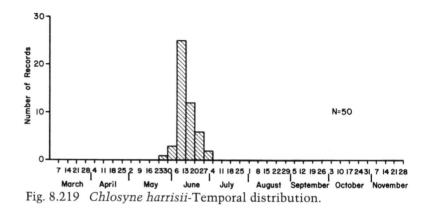

Fig. 8.219 *Chlosyne harrisii*-Temporal distribution.

STATUS: Resident; rare to uncommon. This species is most frequently encountered in northeastern Ohio, where it is occasionally locally common. It is extremely rare in the Oak Openings region, where it has not been observed in several years. Populations from southwestern Ohio have probably been extirpated.

DISTRIBUTION/RANGE: Although there are records from northwestern and southwestern Ohio, most of the records are from the northeastern corner of the State (Figure 8.218).

HABITAT: This species is usually associated with sedge meadows, mesic pastures, and mesic fields. Adults will wander into other nearby habitats in search of nectar sources.

HOSTPLANT(S): Not known in Ohio. Flat-topped white aster (*Aster umbellatus* Mill.) is the only known host of this butterfly (Opler and Krizek, 1984). This plant is common in many habitats which support *C. harrisii* in Ohio.

ADULT ENERGY RESOURCES: Orange hawkweed (*Hieracium aurantiacum* L.). Adults also imbibe moisture from damp soil, damp gravel, and mud.

FLIGHT PERIOD: One brood which peaks in June (Figure 8.219). Extreme dates range from 23 May to 16 September (unusually late).

SIMILAR SPECIES: See *C. nycteis*.

GENERAL COMMENTS: This species occurs in localized populations, and adults seldom stray far from their mesic habitat. It is probably more widespread in northeastern Ohio than our records indicate, but populations are easily overlooked because of their small size and the reluctance of many collectors to enter wetlands. Populations in other areas of the State have declined, probably as a result of wetland modification for agricultural and urban uses.

From the material that has been examined, it seems likely that two variable subspecies occur in Ohio. Because populations of this species are extremely variable, individual specimens are generally difficult to identify accurately to subspecies, but series of specimens can usually be placed based upon population trends. Populations in northeastern Ohio are referable to *C. harrisii liggetti*, which is characterized by its expanded melanic pattern elements on the dorsal wing surfaces and to a lesser extent ventrally. These populations have been recorded from a number of counties, and this is the most frequently encountered subspecies in the State. The limited material examined from northwestern Ohio seems to represent *C. h. harrisii*, which is characterized by not having expanded melanic pattern elements. Populations of this subspecies, which may have originally extended eastward to Seneca County (Henninger, 1910), have not been observed in several years, and this subspecies may be extirpated from Ohio. The single specimen from southwestern Ohio is not reliably referable to either subspecies. Although the Hamilton County record seems well out of the normal range of *C. harrisii*, it is supported by one extant specimen and literature reports (Dury, 1878; Wyss, 1930b). Scudder (1889) and Hine (1898a) reiterate Dury's report.

The presence of two subspecies of *C. harrisii* in Ohio is intriguing. It seems likely that these populations colonized the State via movements from separate directions. These two subspecies are clinal in nature, and Ohio populations probably represent two ends of a cline which wraps around Lake Erie. Because all populations of *C. harrisii* in Ohio are phenotypically variable, the subspecies found in the State are a population-level phenomenon, involving variations of gene frequencies. As such, populations in both northwestern and northeastern Ohio should be protected in order to preserve the genetic heterogeneity present within Ohio.

The flight of this species is low, near the ground cover, and is characterized by alternating periods of active flight and gliding. Most specimens encountered are flushed from their perches. Adults perch on sedges and other herbaceous plants with outstretched wings.

LITERATURE RECORD: Seneca County (Henninger, 1910).

Phyciodes tharos tharos (Drury, 1773). Pearl Crescent. Plate 28.

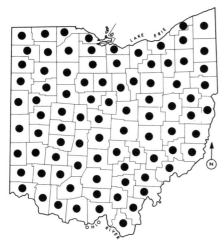

Fig. 8.220 *Phyciodes tharos.*

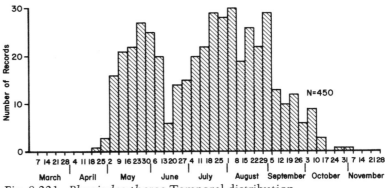

Fig. 8.221 *Phyciodes tharos*-Temporal distribution.

STATUS: Resident; common.

DISTRIBUTION/RANGE: Statewide (Figure 8.220). This species has been recorded from all 88 Ohio counties.

HABITAT: This species is ubiquitous in open areas which contain nectar resources. Typical habitats include old fields, pastures, vacant lots, lawns, waste areas, prairies, fens, sedge meadows, alfalfa and clover fields, lake margins, and open woodlands.

HOSTPLANT(S): Not known in Ohio. Throughout its range, this species uses several species of asters (*Aster* spp.), particularly those of the subgenus *Euaster* (Shapiro, 1974; Oliver, 1980). Asters are common and widespread in Ohio.

ADULT ENERGY RESOURCES: Alfalfa (*Medicago sativa* L.), red clover (*Trifolium pratense* L.), white clover (*Trifolium repens* L.), white sweet clover (*Melilotus alba* Desr.), black mustard (*Brassica nigra* [L.] Koch), field pepper-grass (*Lepidium campestris* [L.] R. Br.), bouncing-bet (*Saponaria officinalis* L.), shrubby cinquefoil (*Potentilla fructicosa* L.), cinquefoil (*Potentilla* sp.), brambles (*Rubus* sp.), pale touch-me-not (*Impatiens pallida* Nutt), wild carrot (*Daucus carota* L.), common milkweed (*Asclepias syriaca* L.), butterfly-weed (*Asclepias tuberosa* L.), Indian hemp (*Apocynum cannabinum* L.), peppermint (*Mentha piperita* L.), black-eyed Susan (*Rudbeckia hirta* L.), brown-eyed Susan (*Rudbeckia triloba* L.), wing-stem (*Verbesina alternifolia* [L.] Britt.), Jerusalem artichoke (*Helianthus tuberosa* L.), dandelion (*Taraxacum officinale* Webr.), horseweed (*Erigeron canadensis* L.), small white aster (*Aster vimineus* Lam.), asters (*Aster* spp.), Philadelphia fleabane (*Erigeron philadelphicus* L.), Canada thistle (*Cirsium arvense* [L.] Scop.), tall ironweed (*Vernonia altissima* Nutt), spotted Joe-Pye weed (*Eupatorium maculatum* L.), and common boneset (*Eupatorium perfoliatum* L.). Adults also take moisture from damp soil, sand and gravel, urine and fecal deposits, and carrion. This species is a common visitor to mud puddles.

FLIGHT PERIOD: Three to four broods per year, with peaks in May, July, and late August-early September (Figure 8.221). Extreme dates range from 18 April to 2 November.

SIMILAR SPECIES: See *Chlosyne nycteis.* This species is also extremely similar to *P. pascoensis.* In *P. pascoensis*, the thin linear markings on the ventral hindwings are usually pale orange whereas in *P. tharos* these markings are usually black. Similarly, *P. pascoensis* has a pale marginal patch surrounding the crescent spot on the ventral hindwing but in *P. tharos* the area surrounding the crescent spot is usually black. Dorsally, *P. pascoensis* has a more yellowish postmedial band on the forewings and a relatively clear, orange band on the hindwings (Paul A. Opler, pers comm, 1988). Although these two species can be distinguished by antennal club coloration in most regions (orange in *P. pascoensis*; black in *P. tharos),* this character is unreliable in Ohio. Questionable specimens should be determined by an authority.

Because *P. tharos* and *P. pascoensis* have only recently been recognized as distinct species (Oliver, 1980), reliable characters which separate these species over their entire ranges have not yet been discovered. They are genitalically similar, and both species are phenotypically variable.

GENERAL COMMENTS: This is one of Ohio's most common butterflies and is a familiar sight throughout the State in almost every open habitat. It is particularly abundant in old fields where there is a proliferation of nectar sources.

Males of this species seem very aggressive, and are often observed chasing other insects. This is probably an investigative behavior associated with mate location. The flight of this species is erratic and fairly rapid for its size. Adults alternate short periods of active flight with periods of gliding and usually fly close to the ground. When not patrolling, males are most often encountered while they visit flowers or moist soil. Both sexes perch with their wings held outstretched.

There are two phenotypes of this species, both of which are extremely variable. The cool weather form 'marcia' (W. H. Edwards, 1868), which occurs in the spring and rarely in the autumn, has dark brown and white markings on the ventral hindwings. The warm weather form 'morpheus' (Fabricius, 1775), which occurs in the summer, has more yellow or cream-colored ventral hindwings. Females of both forms are larger and more variable than males. The melanic aberration 'packardii'

Saunders, 1869, has been captured at various locations throughout the State. Many Ohio literature records of *Phyciodes batesii* (eg Strecker, 1878; Edwards, 1884; Maynard, 1891; Bales, 1909) are probably based upon variant phenotypes of *P. tharos*.

LITERATURE RECORDS: None.

Phyciodes pascoensis Wright, 1905. Northern Pearl Crescent. Plate 29.

Fig. 8.222 *Phyciodes pascoensis*.

STATUS: Resident; rare. Only two Ohio records, both males, are known to exist.

DISTRIBUTION/RANGE: This species is usually found in more northern and western areas. In the eastern United States, this species is found across the northern tier of states and in the Appalachian Mountains south to Virginia (Opler and Krizek, 1984). Ohio records are from Highland and Hamilton Counties (Figure 8.222) and may represent the southern range limit for the species in the Midwest.

HABITAT: Moist, open areas and brushy old fields on slopes near streams (Charles G. Oliver, pers comm, 1984). The Highland County record was taken in a brushy valley along a stream near Fort Hill State Memorial. Nothing is known about the Hamilton County habitat.

HOSTPLANT(S): Not known in Ohio. Although the natural hostplant is unknown, females will oviposit and larvae will develop on paniced aster (*Aster simplex* Willd.) in captivity (Opler and Krizek, 1984). Asters, including *Aster simplex*, are common in Ohio.

ADULT ENERGY RESOURCES: Damp soil.

FLIGHT PERIOD: Probably one brood. The two Ohio records are dated June 1937 and 30 May 1982.

SIMILAR SPECIES: See *P. tharos*.

GENERAL COMMENTS: *Phyciodes pascoensis* was only recently recognized as a species distinct from *P. tharos* (Oliver, 1980). So similar are these two species in appearance and habits, that even the authorities find it difficult to identify individual specimens. *Phyciodes pascoensis* undoubtedly occurs more frequently in Ohio than the two records indicate, and it should eventually be found in a wider area. Few collectors have actively searched for this butterfly in Ohio.

The flight of this species is close to the ground and is very similar to that of *P. tharos*.

Because *P. pascoensis* often looks like *P. batesii*, some of the numerous literature reports of *P. batesii* from Ohio (eg French, 1886; Henninger, 1910; Wyss, 1932;) may be based on specimens of *P. pascoensis*.

There has been much controversy concerning the correct name for this species. Authors have utilized at least four names in reference to this butterfly: *Phycoides tharos* "Type B," *P. pascoensis*, *P. selenis*, and *P. morpheus* (see Opler and Krizek, 1984; Scott, 1986).

LITERATURE RECORDS: None.

Euphydryas phaeton phaeton (Drury, 1773). Baltimore. Plate 29.

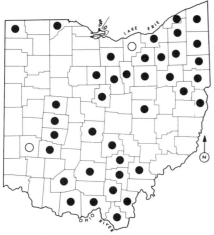

Fig. 8.223 *Euphydryas phaeton*.

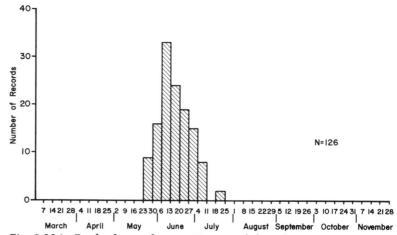

Fig. 8.224 *Euphydryas phaeton*-Temporal distribution.

STATUS: Resident; rare to uncommon. This species is most frequently encountered in the northeastern quarter of the State where wetlands are common. Westward and southward this species becomes increasingly uncommon. There are very few records from the northwestern corner of the State.

DISTRIBUTION/RANGE : Statewide (Figure 8.223).

HABITAT: This butterfly inhabits a variety of wet habitats. In northeastern Ohio this species occurs in fens, sedge meadows, mesic pastures and fields, and in other poorly drained areas. In southern Ohio it is found in fens, seeps, along lake margins, and assorted wet waste areas. It has also been found in a ridgetop clear-cut (John W. Peacock, pers comm, 1985). Solitary adults are occasionally observed far from potentially suitable habitats.

HOSTPLANT(S): The larval hostplants of this butterfly can be split into two groups: those upon which females oviposit and which serve as hosts until winter diapause, and those to which the larvae disperse in the spring. In Ohio, the primary oviposition substrate is turtlehead (*Chelone glabra* L.), although beardtongue (*Penstemon* sp.) has also been reported (Lepidopterists' Society, 1951). *Chelone glabra* is the primary oviposition substrate in the northeastern United States (Opler and Krizek, 1984). After diapause, wandering larvae have been found on many species of plants including *C. glabra*, wood betony (*Pedicularis canadensis* L.), and English plantain (*Plantago lanceolata* L.). In addition, larvae have been successfully transferred from *C. glabra* and reared on pale plantain (*Plantago rugelii* Dcne.).

Prior to diapause, larvae feed gregariously in communal webs constructed on the hostplant. Larvae overwinter in leaf litter at the base of the hostplant. Upon emergence in the spring, the larvae wander from their original host and feed as solitary individuals.

ADULT ENERGY RESOURCES: Common milkweed (*Asclepias syriaca* L.), butterfly-weed (*Asclepias tuberosa* L.), dogbane (*Apocynum* sp.), black-eyed Susan (*Rudbeckia hirta* L.), oxeye daisy (*Chrysanthemum leucanthemum* L.), and star-thistle (*Centaurea* sp.). This species is also attracted to damp soil, mud, and feces.

FLIGHT PERIOD: One brood which peaks in early June (Figure 8.224). Extreme dates range from 23 May to 22 July.

GENERAL COMMENTS: Populations of this species are usually very localized, but it can be quite common in the proper habitat. Adults tend to remain in close proximity to the primary hostplant, which like the butterfly, occurs in localized populations. Although widespread, this butterfly is best sought in the northeastern corner of the State where it occurs in many wetland habitats. Elsewhere, populations are widely separated.

Although adults fly with rapid wing beats, the flight itself in not particularly fast. Normal active flight, which is usually interspersed with periods of gliding, is usually low to the ground and just above the tops of the surrounding vegetation. When disturbed, males have been observed to fly upwards rapidly to a height of approximately six meters before returning to the ground. Females are weak fliers, and are generally less active than males. Both sexes perch on shrubs, sedges, and grasses with their wings held outstretched. Adults can be easily observed while they are visiting flowers.

This butterfly is phenotypically variable. The amount of red and white spotting on the dorsal forewings varies greatly from individual to individual, and extreme individuals which are almost completely black have been recorded. The bright red, white, and black color pattern is thought to be aposomatic. Birds find adults of this butterfly to be distasteful, and the bright pattern serves as an easily learned warning pattern that advertises this butterfly's unpalatability (Bowers, 1980).

LITERATURE RECORDS: Montgomery (Kirtland, 1854a) and Lorain (Lepidopterists' Society, 1968) Counties.

Polygonia interrogationis (Fabricius, 1798). Question Mark. Plates 29 and 30.

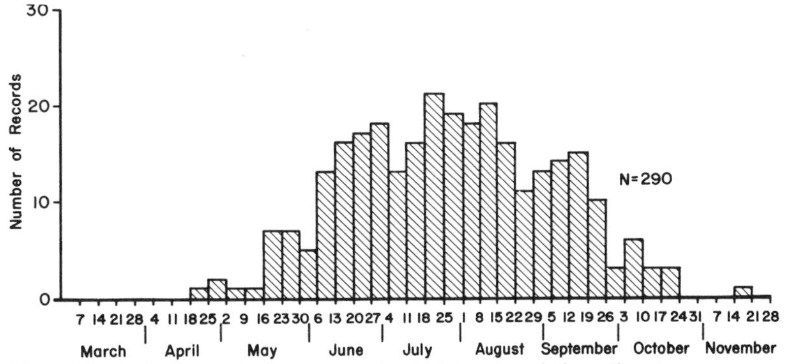

Fig. 8.226 *Polygonia interrogationis*-Temporal distribution.

Fig. 8.225 *Polygonia interrogationis*.

STATUS: Resident; uncommon to common.

DISTRIBUTION/RANGE: Statewide (Figure 8.225).

HABITAT: This species is most often associated with deciduous woodlands and adjacent openings. It is also found in a variety of open and disturbed habitats when hostplants or adult resources are available. Typical open habitats include prairies, old fields, shrubby fence rows, orchards, parks, and residential areas. This species is not as limited to forested habitats as are the other *Polygonia* species.

HOSTPLANT(S): In Ohio, this species has been found and reared on Siberian elm (*Ulmus pumila* L.) (John W. Peacock, pers comm, 1987), slippery elm (*Ulmus rubra* Muhl.), and American elm (*Ulmus americana* L.). It has also been reported on hackberry (*Celtis occidentalis* L.) (Pilate, 1882; Studebaker and Studebaker, 1967) and hop (*Humulus* sp.) (Kirtland, 1854a). Elms are the primary hostplants in Ohio. In other parts of its range, this butterfly uses a number of other hostplants, including nettles (*Urtica* spp.) (Opler and Krizek, 1984).

ADULT ENERGY RESOURCES: Red clover (*Trifolium pratense* L.), dogwood (*Cornus obliqua* Raf.), common milkweed (*Asclepias syriaca* L.), and asters (*Aster* spp.). Adults also visit damp soil, damp sand, tree sap, rotting fruit, carrion, and feces. Fermenting tree sap and rotting fruit are the primary adult energy resources. This species also gathers at mud puddles.

FLIGHT PERIOD: Two broadly overlapping broods, with the autumn brood entering reproductive diapause and overwintering (Figure 8.226). Extreme dates range from 23 April to 19 November.

SIMILAR SPECIES: Although *P. interrogationis* is superficially similar to the other species of *Polygonia*, it can be easily distinguished by its longer tails, its more falcate forewing apexes, and its two-part silver "question-mark" on the ventral hindwing.

GENERAL COMMENTS: This is the largest and most common of Ohio's *Polygonia* species. Generally distributed, it is a familiar sight along woodland roads where adults are often seen basking in sunlit patches or imbibing moisture from damp soil. Because the species overwinters as an adult, it is often active in the very early spring before the flowers have bloomed and before most other butterflies have emerged. Adults are occasionally seen flying about during warm winter days.

Males seem quite aggressive, and often fly out from their perches after other butterflies, probably as part of their mate-locating behavior. Males may be somewhat territorial, as they often return to their original perch after a chase. Adults perch on tree trunks, low vegetation, and on the ground with their wings held together or outstretched. The ventral wing surfaces are cryptic, and when the wings are held over the body, this butterfly resembles a dead leaf. The flight of this species is usually fast and erratic. Adults often circle around before landing on sunlit perches. This species has been observed accompanying groups of migrating *Vanessa cardui* through west-central Ohio (Hoying, 1968).

As with the other *Polygonia*, adults of this species prefer visiting fermenting tree sap and rotting fruit to flowers, and are often common in areas where these resources are found. Adults may become intoxicated while feeding, especially at sap flows, and can occasionally be observed very closely or even touched by hand. Because adults are fond of rotting fruits, adults can be attracted to fermenting bait mixtures placed out by collectors.

This species is sexually dimorphic. Males are smaller and have more mottled and striated ventral wing surfaces than do the females, which have relatively plain ventral wing surfaces. In addition, both sexes have two seasonal phenotypes. The summer form 'umbrosa' (Lintner, 1869), is the darker of the two forms, and possesses black dorsal hindwings. The autumn (winter) form (formerly known as 'fabricii' [W. H. Edwards, 1870]), is much more brightly colored and has reddish dorsal hindwings. This form also has longer tails, and a more distinctive violet hindwing fringe. The summer form is the more frequently encountered.

LITERATURE RECORDS: None.

Polygonia comma (Harris, 1842). Comma. Plates 30 and 31.

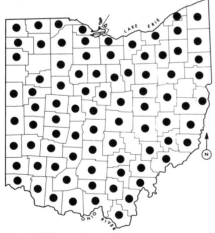

Fig. 8.227 *Polygonia comma*.

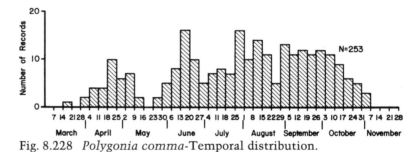

Fig. 8.228 *Polygonia comma*-Temporal distribution.

STATUS: Resident; uncommon to common.

DISTRIBUTION/RANGE: Statewide (Figure 8.227).

HABITAT: This species is most often associated with deciduous forests and adjacent open areas. It can also be found in a variety of open and disturbed habitats such as old fields, parks, residential areas, and orchards.

HOSTPLANT(S): In Ohio, larvae of this species have been recorded on nettles (*Urtica* sp.), elm (*Ulmus* sp.), American elm (*Ulmus americana* L.), and hop (*Humulus* sp.) (Kirtland, 1854a; Pilate, 1882; Hine, 1898b). These plants are the primary hosts for this butterfly (Opler and Krizek, 1984).

ADULT ENERGY RESOURCES: Common boneset (*Eupatorium perfoliatum* L.) and blackberry (*Rubus* sp.). Adults also imbibe moisture from damp soil, damp sand, tree sap, rotting fruit, and feces. Fermenting tree sap and rotting fruit are the primary adult energy resources.

FLIGHT PERIOD: Two, possibly three broadly overlapping broods (Figure 8.228). Adults of the autumn brood overwinter in reproductive diapause. Extreme dates range from 15 March to 5 November.

SIMILAR SPECIES: See *P. interrogationis*. *Polygonia comma* can also be confused with *P. progne*. In *P. comma*, the ventral wing surfaces are brown but in *P. progne* they are dark gray. The silver "comma" on the ventral hindwing is more smoothly rounded

("C"-shaped) in *P. comma*, whereas it is more angled ("V"-shaped) in *P. progne*. The ends on the silver "comma" recurve in *P. comma* but they taper to a point in *P. progne*.

GENERAL COMMENTS: Because this species overwinters as adults in reproductive diapause, it is one of the first species on the wing in early spring. It may even be found flying about during warm winter days when patches of snow are still on the ground. Although it is found throughout the State, it is more closely restricted to forested areas than is the more common *P. interrogationis*.

Males of *P. comma* seem aggressive, and will fly out from their perches and chase passing butterflies, dragonflies, and even birds. This behavior is probably investigative, and functions as mate-locating behavior. Males may be somewhat territorial, as they often return to their original perch after a chase. Both sexes are commonly encountered along woodland roads, where they bask with wings outstretched or imbibe moisture from damp areas. During the early evening and late morning hours adults can be found perched on foliage in small sunlit patches. This species is extremely wary, and can be difficult to approach. The flight is fast and erratic, and when disturbed, individuals fly off rapidly to the tops of nearby trees.

Like all *Polygonia* species, *P. comma* is only occasionally found visiting flowers. Adults use tree sap and fermenting fruits as their primary energy resources, and can be attracted to fermenting bait mixtures placed out by collectors. When feeding at sap flows, adults usually feed in a head-down position.

This species exhibits two types of wing pattern variations. First, it is sexually dimorphic, with females being more plainly patterned ventrally than males. Females are also usually larger than males. Secondly, like all *Polygonia* species, *P. comma* has two seasonal phenotypes. The summer form 'dryas' (W. H. Edwards, 1870), is the darker of the two forms, and adults of this form have almost totally black dorsal hindwings. The autumn form (formerly known as 'harrisii' [W. H. Edwards, 1873]), is much brighter, and has reddish dorsal hindwings. The summer form is most often encountered in the field. The ventral wing pattern is cryptic, and when the wings are held together over the body this species resembles a dead leaf.

LITERATURE RECORDS: None.

Polygonia progne progne (Cramer, 1776). Gray Comma. Plate 31.

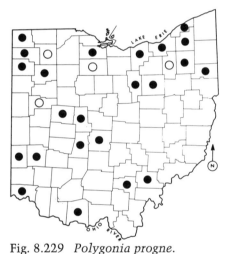

Fig. 8.229 *Polygonia progne*.

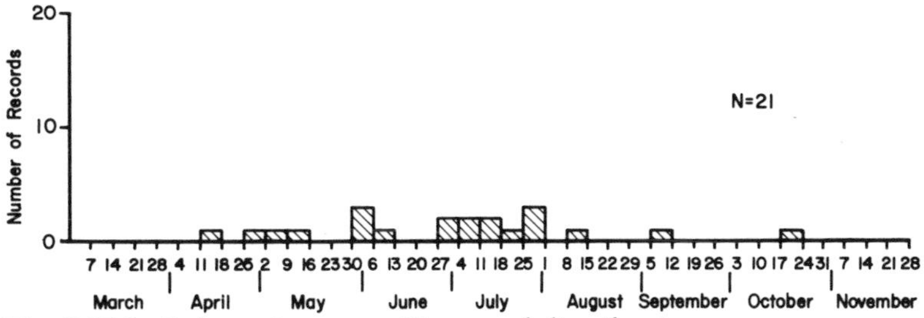

Fig. 8.230 *Polygonia progne*-Temporal distribution.

STATUS: Resident; rare. Populations of this species are extremely localized and are usually widely separated.

DISTRIBUTION/RANGE: Statewide (Figure 8.229).

HABITAT: This species is associated with mesic to wet deciduous woodlands such as swamps and bottomland forests.

HOSTPLANT(S): Although no hostplant has been recorded in Ohio, this species is associated with elms (*Ulmus* sp.) (Kirtland, 1854a) and gooseberries (*Ribes* spp.). Gooseberries and currents (*Ribes* spp.) are the primary hostplants for this butterfly (Opler and Krizek, 1984). These plants are common throughout Ohio.

ADULT ENERGY RESOURCES: Teasel (*Dipsacus sylvestris* Huds.). Tree sap and rotting fruit are the primary adult energy resources for this species. Adults also feed on feces and moist soil.

FLIGHT PERIOD: Two broadly overlapping broods (Figure 8.230). Adults of the autumn brood overwinter in reproductive diapause. Extreme dates range from 14 April to 20 October.

SIMILAR SPECIES: See *P. interrogationis* and *P. comma*.

GENERAL COMMENTS: Although Dury (1878) and Hine (1898a) considered this species to be common, very little is known about the biology of this rare Ohio resident. Normally found along the edges of wet to swampy woodlands, this species is usually encountered as lone individuals or in very low numbers. This is the rarest and most habitat-restricted *Polygonia* in Ohio.

Adults are most active in the late afternoon (1600-1800 hrs.), when they may be observed flying or basking along forest margins, trails, and roads that have west-facing exposures. Perching adults may either hold their wings outstretched or closed. When the wings are closed, the cryptic ventral wing surfaces give this butterfly the appearance of a dead leaf. The flight is not as fast as in the other *Polygonia* species, although it is still quite rapid and erratic. Adults are very wary, and are difficult to approach.

Because adults are primarily attracted to tree sap, rotting fruit, and feces, this species can be attracted to fermenting bait mixtures placed out by collectors.

Like all *Polygonia* species, *P. progne* has two seasonal phenotypes. The summer form 'l-argenteum' Scudder, 1875, is the darker of the two forms and has blackish dorsal hindwings. The autumn form is much brighter and has orange-washed dorsal hindwings.

LITERATURE RECORDS: Henry (Hine, 1898a), Auglaize (Williamson, 1905), Summit (Claypole, 1897), and Seneca (Henninger, 1910) Counties.

Porter (1965) listed this species from Seneca County, but his record was based on a misdetermined specimen of *P. comma*.

Nymphalis vau-album j-album (Boisduval & LeConte, 1833). Compton Tortoise Shell. Plate 31.

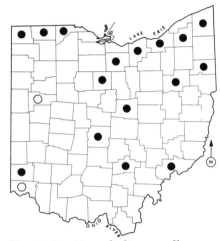

Fig. 8.231 *Nymphalis vau-album*.

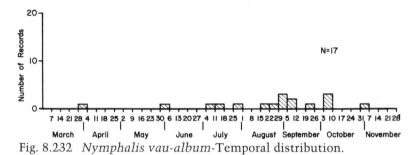

Fig. 8.232 *Nymphalis vau-album*-Temporal distribution.

STATUS: Irregular immigrant; rare.

DISTRIBUTION/RANGE: In eastern North America, this species is primarily a resident of Canadian Zone habitats. It periodically wanders southward, and is occasionally found in states as far south as Missouri, Ohio, Maryland, and even Florida (Opler and Krizek, 1984). Although Ohio records are distributed statewide, this species is most frequently encountered in the northern counties of the State (Figure 8.231).

HABITAT: Where this species is a resident, it occurs in deciduous and coniferous forests. Most Ohio specimens have been taken near forested areas.

HOSTPLANT(S): Not known in Ohio. Willows (*Salix* spp.), birches (*Betula* spp.), and aspen (*Populus* spp.) are the primary hostplants where this species is a permanent resident (Opler and Krizek, 1984).

ADULT ENERGY RESOURCES: In Ohio, adults have been found visiting rotting fruit and damp soil. This species is also attracted to tree sap and carrion.

FLIGHT PERIOD: There are no reports of this species reproducing in Ohio, but in northern Michigan this butterfly produces one generation per year (Figure 8.232). Adults emerge in July and August, overwinter, and survive until the next spring (Mogens C. Nielsen, pers comm, 1986). Extreme dates for Ohio specimens range from 28 March to 31 October.

SIMILAR SPECIES: None.

GENERAL COMMENTS: This butterfly is another rare visitor to our State, and is infrequently encountered by resident lepidopterists. Most Ohio records probably coincide with population outbreaks that have occurred further north because this species is most migratory during years of abnormally high abundance (Shapiro, 1966). Although there is no evidence that this species has ever reproduced in Ohio, overwintering individuals do have the potential to establish temporary colonies. This species probably occurs more frequently in Ohio than our records indicate, especially in the northeastern corner of the State.

Adults of this species are extremely wary, and can be difficult to approach. Adults are usually encountered as solitary individuals while they perch on gravel roads through forested areas, or while they visit fermenting fruit, particularly rotting apples (Price, 1970). Kirtland (1854a) often found this species visiting rotting apples around cider mills. Because it is attracted to fermenting fruits, this species can be attracted to fermenting bait mixtures.

The flight of this species is generally swift and erratic, although adults circle slowly before settling. Adults often perch head down on tree trunks with their wings held together over their body. When their wings are closed, the cryptic ventral wing pattern resembles a dead leaf. Adults usually overwinter in hollow logs, under stones, in barns, and in other similar sheltered locations. Edward S. Thomas (1981) once found an individual of this species overwintering under the blankets of a bed in a cabin in Richland County.

LITERATURE RECORDS: Auglaize (Williamson, 1905) and Hamilton Counties (Hine, 1898a).

Nymphalis antiopa antiopa (Linnaeus, 1758). Mourning Cloak. Plate 32.

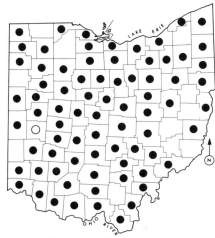

Fig. 8.233 *Nymphalis antiopa*.

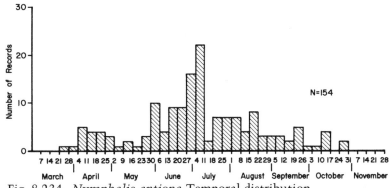

Fig. 8.234 *Nymphalis antiopa*-Temporal distribution.

STATUS: Resident; uncommon.

DISTRIBUTION/RANGE: Statewide (Figure 8.233).

HABITAT: This species is most often encountered in or near deciduous forests, and along streams and rivers. It is also found in orchards and residential areas when suitable hostplants and adult energy resources are available.

HOSTPLANT(S): In Ohio, this species has been found and reared on black willow (*Salix nigra* Marsh), weeping willow (*Salix babylonica* L.), Siberian elm (*Ulmus pumila* L.), and American elm (*Ulmus americana* L.) (John W. Peacock, pers comm, 1987). Larvae have been observed on cottonwood (*Populus deltoides* Marsh). Kirtland (1854a) also reports Lombardy poplar (*Populus nigra* L.) as a host. This butterfly occasionally becomes a pest on trees such as elms (Anonymous, 1887). Willows, elms, birches (*Betula* spp.), cottonwood, aspens (*Populus* spp.), and hackberries (*Celtis* spp.) are the usual hosts of this butterfly (Opler and Krizek, 1984). All of these trees are widespread in Ohio.

ADULT ENERGY RESOURCES: Common milkweed (*Asclepias syriaca* L.). The primary energy resources for this butterfly are fermenting tree sap and rotting fruit. Adults have also been observed visiting damp soil and sand.

FLIGHT PERIOD: This species produces a single brood, with adults emerging in June and July (Figure 8.234). Adults overwinter in reproductive diapause. Opler and Krizek (1984) consider this to be the longest lived butterfly (as adults) in North America. Extreme dates range from 26 March to 27 October.

GENERAL COMMENTS: This is one of the first butterflies to become active each spring, and may even fly on warm winter days when patches of snow are still present. In the spring, it is one of the most conspicuous butterflies in the forest as the worn survivors of the winter sail and swirl along trails and through openings. Population densities fluctuate, and at times this species may become locally common. During typical years, this species is usually encountered as solitary individuals or at low densities.

Adults are extremely wary, and will take to the wing in reaction to the slightest movement. The flight of this species is active and rapid, although it often glides in circles, especially before settling. Males fly out from their perches to investigate other passing objects, and may be somewhat territorial because they often return to their original perches. Adults perch and rest with their wings closed, but bask with their wings outstretched. Adults are frequently encountered at rotting fruit and fermenting tree sap, and can be attracted to fermenting bait mixtures.

Normally, this species is not variable, but extreme temperatures may induce aberrant phenotypes (Shapiro, 1970b). The aberration 'hygiaea' (Heydenreich, 1846), which has greatly expanded and smeary yellow wing borders is known from Stark County. An aberrant specimen approaching 'hygiaea' was reported from Granville, Licking County (Keil, 1915). Additional aberrations, including 'lintneri' (Fitch, 1856) have also been reported by Pilate (1882) and Scudder (1889).

LITERATURE RECORDS: Miami County (Studebaker and Studebaker, 1967).

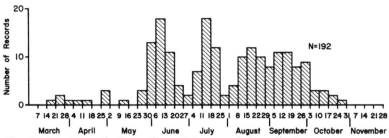

Nymphalis milberti milberti **(Godart, 1819).** Milbert's Tortoise Shell. Plate 32.

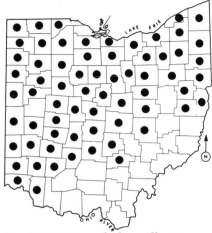

Fig. 8.235 *Nymphalis milberti.*

Fig. 8.236 *Nymphalis milberti*-Temporal distribution.

STATUS: Resident; rare to common. This species is most common in the northern half of the State, becoming uncommon to rare southward. There are very few records from southeastern Ohio.

DISTRIBUTION /RANGE: This species is primarily a resident in the northwestern two-thirds of the State, but may stray southward (Figure 8.235). Ohio represents the southern range limit for this species.

HABITAT: This species is usually found in open areas adjacent to mesic woodlands. Typical habitats include fens, wet pastures, old fields, waste areas, farm yards, woodland borders, and roadsides and stream banks through deciduous forests. This species is less restricted to forested habitats than the other *Nymphalis* species found in Ohio.

HOSTPLANT(S): In Ohio, this species has been found and reared on stinging nettles (*Urtica dioica* L. and *U. dioica* var. *procera* [Muhl.] Wedd.). Nettles are the only verified hosts of this butterfly (Opler and Krizek, 1984).

ADULT ENERGY RESOURCES: Red clover (*Trifolium pratense* L.), alfalfa (*Medicago sativa* L.), crown-vetch (*Coronilla varia* L.), common milkweed (*Asclepias syriaca* L.), swamp milkweed (*Asclepias incarnata* L.), ox-eye (*Heliopsis helianthoides* [L.] Sweet), wing-stem (*Verbesina alternifolia* [L.] Britt.), chicory (*Cichorium intybus* L.), horseweed (*Erigeron canadensis* L.), Canada thistle (*Cirsium arvense* [L.] Scop.), tall ironweed (*Vernonia altissima* Nutt), asters (*Aster* spp.), goldenrod (*Solidago* sp.), wild bergamot (*Monarda fistulosa* L.), spring beauty (*Claytonia virginica* L.), and squirrel-corn (*Dicentra canadensis* [Goldie] Walp.). Edward S. Thomas (unpublished notes) also reports willow (*Salix* sp.) as a nectar source. Adults also imbibe moisture from damp soil, damp sand, and rotting fruit.

FLIGHT PERIOD: Two broadly overlapping broods (Figure 8.236). Adults overwinter in reproductive diapause. This species has been recorded from every month of the year.

GENERAL COMMENTS: This species is most frequently encountered in northern Ohio, where it can often be observed in numbers while it visits mud puddles and nectar sources. Like all *Nymphalis* species, *N. milberti* overwinters as adults in reproductive diapause, and re-emerges early in the spring. Overwintering sites include hollow logs and farm buildings.

This species has probably increased in abundance with the onset of European land use patterns; most early authors (Kirtland, 1851a; Kirkpatrick, 1864; Claypole, 1897; Hine, 1898b; Henninger, 1910) allude to its scarcity. Hine (1898a) noted that this species was unknown south of Oberlin, Lorain County. Presently, *N. milberti* occurs with regularity over the northwestern two-thirds of the State. Populations of this species fluctuate greatly from year to year, and it can be locally abundant one year and seemingly absent the next. Populations are usually most common in mid to late summer.

The flight of this species is rapid and close to the ground. Adults are often wary and difficult to approach unless feeding. This species basks with outstretched wings, but usually feeds with the wings held together or only partially open. They are avid flower visitors, which is unlike the other *Nymphalis* species in Ohio. However, *N. milberti* is also attracted to rotting fruits and can be attracted to fermenting bait mixtures placed out by collectors.

The species is phenotypically variable, especially in the ratio of yellow, orange, and brown present on the dorsal wing surfaces. Occasionally specimens are found that possess large yellow bands on the dorsal wing surfaces, which superficially resemble the putative subspecies *N. milberti furcillata* (Say, 1825).

Vanessa virginiensis (Drury, 1773). American Painted Lady. Plate 32.

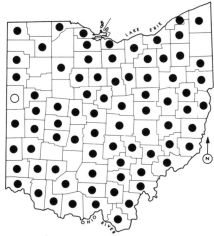

Fig. 8.237 *Vanessa virginiensis.*

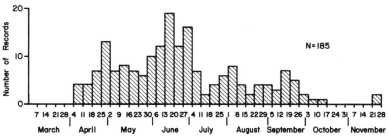

Fig. 8.238 *Vanessa virginiensis*-Temporal distribution.

STATUS: Resident; uncommon to common.

DISTRIBUTION/RANGE: Statewide (Figure 8.237).

HABITAT: This species primarily inhabits open areas, although it occasionally wanders into forested areas. Typical habitats include roadsides, pastures, old fields, vacant lots, river and stream banks, alfalfa and clover fields, gardens, forest openings, and woodland margins.

HOSTPLANT(S): In Ohio, this species has been found and reared on plantain-leaved everlasting (*Antennaria plantaginifolia* [L.] Hook.) (John W. Peacock, pers comm, 1987) and cudweed (*Gnaphalium* sp.) (Leland L. Martin, pers comm, 1988). Viper's bugloss (*Echium vulgare* L.), a member of the Boraginaceae, has also been reported (Pilate, 1882), but this hostplant requires confirmation. Plants of the everlasting tribe (Compositae) are the primary hostplants for this butterfly (Opler and Krizek, 1984).

ADULT ENERGY RESOURCES: Red clover (*Trifolium pratense* L.), alfalfa (*Medicago sativa* L.), Canada thistle (*Cirsium arvense* [L.] Scop.), thistles (*Cirsium* spp.), dandelion (*Taraxacum officinale* Webr.), common boneset (*Eupatorium perfoliatum* L.), goldenrod (*Solidago* sp.), asters (*Aster* spp.), marigold (*Tagetes* sp.), zinnias (*Zinnia* spp.), common milkweed (*Asclepias syriaca* L.), swamp milkweed (*Asclepias incarnata* L.), and redbud (*Cercis canadensis* L.). Adults are also attracted to fermenting tree sap, rotting fruit, damp soil, and damp sand.

FLIGHT PERIOD: Three, with an occasional fourth brood with peaks in late April-early May, June, August, and September (Figure 8.238). Extreme dates range from 7 April to 27 November. Both pupae and adults maybe able to survive Ohio's winters.

SIMILAR SPECIES: *Vanessa cardui. Vanessa virginiensis* has only two large postmedial ocelli on each ventral hindwing, whereas *V. cardui* has four or five small ocelli on the ventral hindwing.

GENERAL COMMENTS: Although this species is usually considered to be common, it is seldom found in very large numbers. Its occurrence is often sporadic, and population densities vary from year to year. This is one of the first butterflies to appear each spring.

The flight of this species is rapid, erratic, and usually within one-half meter of the ground. Adults are often wary, and may be difficult to approach unless they are feeding. Adults are usually encountered while basking on patches of exposed soil or while visiting flowers. Adults bask with their wings outstretched, but feed with their wings held together or only partially open. Adults can be attracted to fermenting fruit mixtures placed out by collectors.

Unlike other *Vanessa* species in Ohio, *V. virginiensis* is only occasionally migratory. This is the most frequently encountered of the two painted lady species in Ohio.

This species is also known as the hunter's butterfly, a reflection of the time when this species' Linnaean binomial was *Vanessa huntera* (Fabricius, 1775).

LITERATURE RECORDS: Mercer County (Price, 1970).

Vanessa cardui (Linnaeus, 1758). Painted Lady. Plate 32.

Fig. 8.239 *Vanessa cardui.*

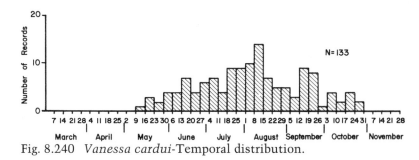

Fig. 8.240 *Vanessa cardui*-Temporal distribution.

STATUS: Irregular immigrant; rare to common. This species is very sporadic in occurrence.

DISTRIBUTION/RANGE: This species occurs throughout Africa, Asia, Europe, North America, and Central America. In the western Hemisphere, it is a permanent resident only in Mexico and Central America. This species periodically spreads northward from the deserts of northern Mexico and may range as far as Alaska and the Northwest Territories of Canada (Williams, 1970; Myers, 1985). Ohio records are distributed statewide (Figure 8.239).

HABITAT: This species can be encountered in any open habitat that contains nectar sources. During years when it is abundant, it occasionally wanders into woodlands.

HOSTPLANT(S): In Ohio, this species has been found and reared on Canada thistle (*Cirsium arvense* [L.] Scop.) (Price, 1970) and bull thistle (*Cirsium vulgare* [Savi] Tenore) (John W. Peacock, pers comm, 1987). Larvae have also been found on hollyhock (*Althaea rosea* Cav.) (Ray W. Bracher, pers comm, 1987). This butterfly uses a wide variety of hostplants in the Compositae, Boraginaceae, Malvaceae, and Fabaceae (Opler and Krizek, 1984).

ADULT ENERGY RESOURCES: Red clover (*Trifolium pratense* L.), alfalfa (*Medicago sativa* L.), wild carrot (*Daucus carota* L.), common milkweed (*Asclepias syriaca* L.), Canada thistle (*Cirsium arvense* [L.] Scop.), bull thistle (*Cirsium vulgare* [Savi] Tenore), tall ironweed (*Vernonia altissima* Nutt), common boneset (*Eupatorium perfoliatum* L.), goldenrod (*Solidago* sp.), asters (*Aster* spp.), dandelion (*Taraxacum officinale* Webr.), spotted Joe-Pye weed (*Eupatorium maculatum* L.), zinnias (*Zinnia* spp.), and marigold (*Tagetes* sp.). This species has also been observed feeding on rotting fruit, and at moist areas along roadsides and motor oil stains on pavement.

FLIGHT PERIOD: One to three broods, depending on how early in the season this species becomes established (Figure 8.240). Extreme dates range from 11 May to 27 October.

SIMILAR SPECIES: See *V. virginiensis.*

GENERAL COMMENTS: This species is probably the most widely distributed butterfly in the world, and is known for its large periodic migrations. In Ohio, this species is sporadic and ranges in abundance from being extremely rare or absent in most years, to occasionally being one of the most common species in the State. The abundance of this butterfly in Ohio depends directly upon the success of immigrating females, and years of high abundance can usually be traced to favorable conditions during the late spring and early summer in the areas between Ohio and Mexico. Movements in and through Ohio are generally unidirectional, and the influx generally flows in a northeasterly direction. Hoying (1968) noted a migration in west-central Ohio in which 20 to 25 individuals passed by per hour. During this migration, the adults flew in a straight line, flying over obstacles rather than around them. Once this butterfly arrives in Ohio, it is capable of reproducing, but it does not survive Ohio's winters. In Ohio, populations usually peak in late summer.

A number of years with notable occurrences of this species have been recorded. This first was recorded by Edward Doubleday (Doubleday et al, 1846-1850), who noted that he saw "literally tens of thousands on the thistles by the roadsides" during his visit to Ohio in 1837. Other years of extreme abundance have occurred in 1896 (Bubna, 1897), 1942-43 (Price, 1970), 1949 (Lepidopterists' Society, 1949b), 1966 (Hoying, 1968), 1983, and 1988.

There is some phenotypic variation in this species. The migrating adults seen early in the season are usually smaller and more darkly patterned than adults found later in the year. An abberation of this species, 'ate' (Strecker 1878) was described from a specimen collected in Summit County, Ohio, probably by Edward W. Claypole.

The flight of this species is very fast and erratic. Adults often bask on exposed patches of soil. They can be very wary and difficult to approach. However, both sexes are highly attracted to flowers where they can be easily observed.

This butterfly is also known as the thistle butterfly or the cosmopolitan.

LITERATURE RECORDS: Van Wert and Williams Counties (Price, 1970).

Vanessa atalanta rubria (Fruhstorfer, 1909). Red Admiral. Plate 33.

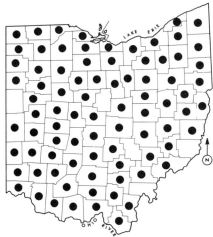

Fig. 8.241 *Vanessa atalanta*.

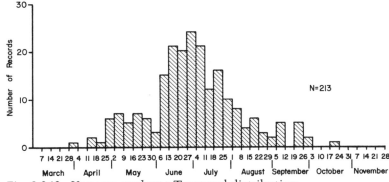

Fig. 8.242 *Vanessa atalanta*-Temporal distribution.

STATUS: Resident; uncommon to common.

DISTRIBUTION/RANGE: Statewide (Figure 8.241).

HABITAT: This species inhabits open areas near mesic deciduous forests. It is most frequently encountered along forest margins and roads, in old fields and shrubby wetlands, but it is also frequent in hay fields, parks, gardens, and orchards.

HOSTPLANT(S): In Ohio, this species has been found and reared on nettles (*Urtica* sp.) (Studebaker and Studebaker, 1967; John W. Peacock and Ray W. Bracher, pers comm, 1987) and pellitory (*Parietaria pennsylvanica* Muhl.) (Joseph E. Riddlebarger, pers comm, 1988). Nettles (Urticaceae) are the primary hostplants for this butterfly (Opler and Krizek, 1984).

ADULT ENERGY RESOURCES: Alfalfa (*Medicago sativa* L.), red clover (*Trifolium pratense* L.), crown-vetch (*Coronilla varia* L.), wild carrot (*Daucus carota* L.), teasel (*Dipsacus sylvestris* Huds.), common milkweed (*Asclepias syriaca* L.), common boneset (*Eupatorium perfoliatum* L.), goldenrod (*Solidago* sp.), dame's rocket (*Hesperis matronalis* L.), and bouncing-bet (*Saponaria officinalis* L.). Adults also take moisture from fermenting tree sap, rotting fruit, feces, and damp soil.

FLIGHT PERIOD: Two, possibly three broods, with major peaks in May and late June-early July (Figure 8.242). Extreme dates range from 2 February to 21 October.

GENERAL COMMENTS: Population densities of this species fluctuate greatly from year to year. It is likely that years with high population densities are the result of overwintering populations that have been supplemented by migrants from the south. Large numbers of this species were observed "very noticeably moving northward" through Ohio in May 1975 (Lepidopterists' Society, 1976).

The flight of this species is fast and erratic. Males perch head downward on tree trunks, exposed leaves, and on the corners and sides of buildings. Males dart out from their perches at almost any passing object including other species of butterflies, dragonflies, and even birds. Adults bask on exposed patches of soil and on roads. Both sexes are wary and can be difficult to approach. However, they are strongly attracted to flowers where they are easily observed while they are feeding. Adults are also attracted to fermenting tree sap and fruit, and can be collected at fermenting bait mixtures.

This species has two seasonal phenotypes. Individuals from the spring brood are smaller and less brightly colored than individuals from the summer brood. The red dorsal forewing band is often broken on individuals of the summer brood.

Junonia coenia Hübner, 1822. Buckeye. Plate 33.

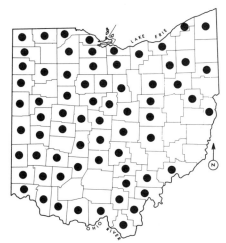

Fig. 8.243 *Junonia coenia*.

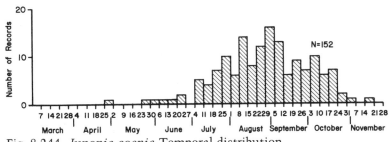

Fig. 8.244 *Junonia coenia*-Temporal distribution.

STATUS: Regular immigrant; rare to uncommon.

DISTRIBUTION/RANGE: In the eastern United States, this species is a permanent resident only in the extreme South. Each year this species wanders northward, often reaching areas as far north as Minnesota, Michigan, and Maine (Opler and Krizek, 1984). Ohio records are statewide in occurrence (Figure 8.243).

HABITAT: This species is most frequently encountered in open areas characterized by low vegetation and exposed patches of soil. Typical habitats include old fields, pastures, vacant lots, clover and alfalfa fields, railroad rights-of-way, and open areas along rivers and streams.

HOSTPLANT(S): In Ohio, this species has been found and reared on English plantain (*Plantago lanceolata* L.). Members of the plantain (Plantaginaceae), acanthus (Acanthaceae), snapdragon (Scrophulariaceae), and vervain families (Verbenaceae) are the primary hostplants of this butterfly (Opler and Krizek, 1984). These plants are widespread in Ohio.

ADULT ENERGY RESOURCES: Red clover (*Trifolium pratense* L.), alfalfa (*Medicago sativa* L.), wild carrot (*Daucus carota* L.), blazing-star (*Liatris spicata* [L.] Willd.), swamp milkweed (*Asclepias incarnata* L.), common boneset (*Eupatorium perfoliatum* L.), asters (*Aster* spp.), sunflower (*Helianthus decapetalus* L.), and ironweed (*Vernonia* sp.). This species also imbibes moisture from damp soil, damp sand, and rotting fruit.

FLIGHT PERIOD: One to three broods, depending on how early in the season this species becomes established (Figure 8.244). Extreme dates range from 26 April to 29 November.

GENERAL COMMENTS: This species does not normally overwinter in Ohio, and must re-establish itself yearly from populations farther south. The general abundance of this species varies greatly from year to year, and it may be common one year and absent the next. Although this species occurs statewide, it is most often encountered in the southern half of the State, particularly in the counties along the Ohio River. Populations are often localized and small, but sometimes attain high densities in very small areas. This butterfly is most common in late summer.

The flight of this species is fast and irregular, and usually occurs within one-half meter of the ground. Adults are most often encountered while they patrol open areas or as they perch with outstretched wings on exposed soil. Males seem very aggressive, and will chase after almost any object that flies past. Males may be territorial, because they usually return to the vicinity of their original perches. Adults are quite wary and can be very difficult to approach unless they are visiting flowers.

This species is variable in size and color. Early season adults are smaller and have a lighter ventral color pattern than adults occurring later in the season. In the autumn, adults may be found that have deep pink or reddish scaling on the ventral hindwings. This form, 'rosa' (Whittaker and Stallings, 1944), is most pronounced in the females. The size of the eye-spots on the dorsal hindwings is also quite variable.

LITERATURE RECORDS: None.

Limenitis arthemis arthemis (Drury, 1773)/*astyanax* (Fabricius, 1775). White Admiral/Red-spotted Purple. Plate 34.

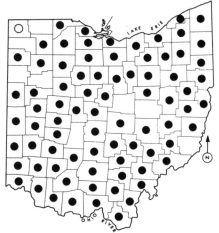

Fig. 8.245 *Limenitis arthemis*.

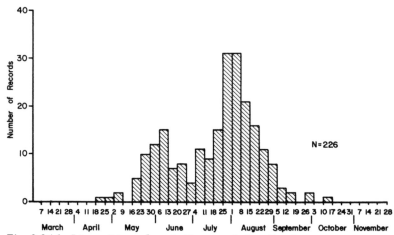

Fig. 8.246 *Limenitis arthemis*-Temporal distribution.

STATUS: Resident; uncommon to common.

DISTRIBUTION/RANGE: Statewide (Figure 8.245).

HABITAT: This species is most frequently found in and adjacent to deciduous forests. Typical habitats include forest openings, woodland borders, and areas along roads and railroad rights-of-way that cut through deciduous forests. This species also occurs in parks, gardens, and orchards.

HOSTPLANT(S): In Ohio, *L. arthemis astyanax* has been found and reared on wild black cherry (*Prunus serotina* Ehrh.). Although wild black cherry is the primary hostplant of *L. a. astyanax*, larvae will also feed on aspens and poplars (*Populus* spp.) and black oaks (*Quercus* spp.) (Opler and Krizek, 1984). These trees are all widespread in Ohio (Braun, 1967).

No hostplant has been recorded for *L. a. arthemis* in Ohio. Elsewhere, this subspecies uses birches (*Betula* spp.) and aspen (*Populus* spp.) as its primary hostplants (Opler and Krizek, 1984).

ADULT ENERGY RESOURCES: Wild black cherry (*Prunus serotina* Ehrh.) and dogwood (*Cornus obliqua* Raf.). Adults also visit rotting fruit, fermenting tree sap, carrion, soil dampened with urine, damp soil, and damp sand. This species is often observed congregating in large numbers at feces and around mud puddles.

FLIGHT PERIOD: Two broods, with peaks in late May-early June and late July-early August (Figure 8.246). Extreme dates range from 23 April to 10 October.

SIMILAR SPECIES: *Limenitis arthemis astyanax* is superficially similar to female *Speyeria diana*, but use of the plates will readily separate these two species.

GENERAL COMMENTS: Although several forms of this butterfly are found in Ohio, populations of only one subspecies, *L. arthemis astyanax*, are resident. This subspecies is characterized by black forewings with no hint of a white band. In the northern portion of the State, especially the northeastern corner, some populations show intergradation towards *L. a. arthemis*, which is characterized by broad white bands on both sets of wings. Individuals which closely resemble this subspecies have been recorded in Mahoning (Kirtland, 1854a; Scudder, 1889), Cuyahoga (Kirtland, 1854a; Scudder, 1889), Lorain (Hine, 1898a; 1898b), Seneca (Porter, 1965), Geauga, and Ashtabula Counties. Despite the appearance in Ohio of these *L. a. arthemis*-like individuals, there are no actual populations of this subspecies in the State. The regular appearance of these white-banded forms in populations that are predominately unbanded indicates that the genes which code for white bands are present at low frequencies in some populations. The appearance of white-banded individuals is the result of matings between individuals which carry these genes, but which may show little or no banding themselves. Thus, most *L. a. arthemis*-like individuals are intergrades that range from individuals that are partially banded to ones that seem identical to *L. a. arthemis*. The most common intergrade in collections is the form 'proserpina' (W. H. Edwards, 1865), which is characterized by possessing only a trace of the white band. This form has been found throughout northeastern Ohio and as far south as Gallia County. Form 'albofaciata' (Newcomb, 1907) possesses a more highly developed white band which extends across both sets of wings. This form is rare in Ohio collections and is known mostly from extreme northeastern Ohio. Specimens with the full white band of *L. a. arthemis* are extremely rare in Ohio, and may be represented by locally bred individuals as well as by strays from Pennsylvania.

Adult *L. arthemis astyanax* are presumed to be Batesian mimics of *Battus philenor*, a species which is known to be distasteful to vertebrate predators. By resembling *B. philenor*, *L. arthemis astyanax* probably gains some protection from predators which are unable to distinguish between these two butterflies. In more northern areas, where *B. philenor* does not occur, *L. arthemis* gains no protection from resembling this swallowtail, and populations possess the wide white bands which characterize *L. a. arthemis* (Platt and Brower, 1968). Because the adults of the two *L. arthemis* subspecies differ so radically in their wing patterns, they were long considered to be separate species.

In addition to the variation caused by intergradation, this species varies greatly in size. Females are usually much larger than males, and it is not unusual to find females flying with males half their size. Occasional individuals with green reflectance, form 'viridis' (Strecker, 1878), are also known from Ohio. Although no wild hybrids are known from Ohio, a male *L. archippus* was observed actively courting a female *L. a. astyanax* in Lorain County (Leland L. Martin, pers comm, 1988).

The flight of this species is leisurely, although when disturbed the flight can become rapid and erratic. Males perch on exposed leaves with partially outstretched wings and chase after passing objects, presumably in search of mates. Both sexes are wary and are often difficult to approach. However, they are attracted to fermenting tree sap, rotting fruit, and animal dung, where they can be easily observed. Adults can also be attracted to fermenting bait mixtures placed out by collectors.

LITERATURE RECORDS: Williams County (Price, 1970).

Limenitis archippus archippus (Cramer, 1776). Viceroy. Plate 33.

Fig. 8.247 *Limenitis archippus.*

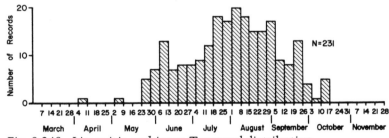

Fig. 8.248 *Limenitis archippus*-Temporal distribution.

STATUS: Resident; uncommon to common. Populations of this species are generally localized.

DISTRIBUTION/RANGE: Statewide (Figure 8.247).

HABITAT: This species is most frequently encountered in moist open habitats where small willows (*Salix* spp.) are common. Typical habitats include marshes, sedge meadows, fens, edges of ponds and lakes, and areas along streams, rivers, and drainage ditches. Adults occasionally stray into upland habitats.

HOSTPLANT(S): In Ohio, this species has been found and reared on cottonwood (*Populus deltoides* Marsh) (Pilate, 1882; John W. Peacock, pers comm, 1987), pussy willow (*Salix discolor* Muhl.) (Ray W. Bracher and Leland L. Martin, pers comm, 1987), black willow (*Salix nigra* L.), and apple (*Malus pumila* Mill.). Willows (*Salix* spp.) and poplars (*Populus* spp.) are the primary hostplants for this butterfly (Opler and Krizek, 1984).

A report of oak (*Quercus* sp.) (Kirtland, 1854a) is unlikely and requires confirmation.

ADULT ENERGY RESOURCES: Red clover (*Trifolium pratense* L.), wild carrot (*Daucus carota* L.), cow-parsnip (*Heracleum lanatum* Michx.), dogwood (*Cornus obliqua* Raf.), peppermint (*Mentha piperita* L.), teasel (*Dipsacus sylvestris* Huds.), common milkweed (*Asclepias syriaca* L.), swamp milkweed (*Asclepias incarnata* L.), coneflower (*Rudbeckia laciniata* L.), ox-eye (*Heliopsis helianthoides* [L.] Sweet), horseweed (*Erigeron canadensis* L.), Canada thistle (*Cirsium arvense* [L.] Scop.), bull thistle (*Cirsium vulgare* [Savi] Tenore), common boneset (*Eupatorium perfoliatum* L.), and goldenrod (*Solidago* sp.). Adults also feed at rotting fruit, carrion, feces, moist soil, and moist sand.

FLIGHT PERIOD: Two broods, with peaks in June and late July-August (Figure 8.248). Extreme dates range from 7 April (unusually early) to 14 October.

SIMILAR SPECIES: This species can be confused with *Danaus plexippus* and *Danaus gilippus*. However, *L. archippus* can be easily identified by the presence of a black postmedian line on the dorsal hindwing, which is absent in both species of *Danaus*. *Limenitis archippus* is usually smaller than both *Danaus* species.

GENERAL COMMENTS: The viceroy is perhaps the most famous example of Batesian mimicry in the animal kingdom. Because this species closely resembles *D. plexippus*, which is distasteful to predators (see GENERAL COMMENTS under *D. plexippus*), *L. archippus* is probably protected to a certain degree from predation. Predators, usually birds, which taste *D. plexippus* usually become sick from the chemicals that this butterfly sequesters as larvae from its milkweed (*Asclepias* spp.) hostplants. Birds conditioned by this experience avoid eating more *D. plexippus*. Because *L. archippus* so closely resembles *D. plexippus*, birds may be unable to distinguish between the two species, avoiding the edible *L. archippus*. In Florida, where the model *D. plexippus* is uncommon but is replaced by the darker *D. gilippus*, *L. archippus* has evolved a darker color which perfectly matches this model's ground color. However, a recent study (Ritland and Brower, 1991) concluded that *L. archippus* is also distasteful, implying that this species is actually a Müllerian co-mimic (rather than a Batesian mimic) of *D. plexippus* and *D. gilippus*.

Adults are usually encountered as they perch one to two meters above the ground on small trees and shrubs in wetlands, or as they rest on exposed soil. Males chase after other butterflies and even birds, apparently in search of potential mates. Males often return to their original perches, which suggests that they may be territorial. Although the flight of this species is similar to that of *D. plexippus*, *L. archippus*'s flight is readily distinguishable by its more rapid wing beats, and its long glides where the wings are held horizontally. In *D. plexippus*, the wings are held at an angle while gliding. *Limenitis archippus* is often wary, and adults can be difficult to approach.

Although there is little phenotypic variation in Ohio populations of this species, a specimen with dark forewings and light hindwings, which superficially resembles the subspecies *Limenitis archippus watsoni* dos Passos (1938) has been collected in Lorain County by Leland L. Martin. Although no wild hybrids are known from Ohio, a male *L. archippus* was observed actively courting a female *L. a. astyanax* in Lorain County (Leland L. Martin, pers comm, 1988).

LITERATURE RECORDS: Tuscarawas County (Albrecht, 1982).

Family APATURIDAE-Leaf Wing and Hackberry Butterflies

Anaea andria Scudder, 1875. Goatweed Butterfly. Plate 35.

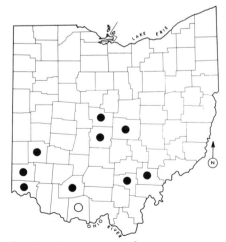

Fig. 8.249 *Anaea andria*.

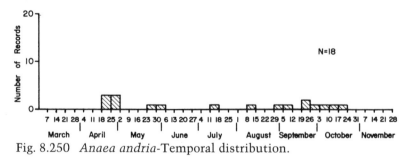

Fig. 8.250 *Anaea andria*-Temporal distribution.

STATUS: Irregular immigrant; rare.

DISTRIBUTION/RANGE: In the eastern United States, this species is a permanent resident from southwestern Illinois, south through Texas and the Mississippi River drainage (Opler and Krizek, 1984). This species periodically ranges eastward to Ohio and West Virginia. Ohio records are scattered throughout the southern half of the State (Figure 8.249). There are also unconfirmed records from Hancock and Fayette Counties.

HABITAT: This species is associated with old fields, open woodlands, forest margins, roadsides, and farmyards. Most recent Ohio sightings and captures have been in old fields and along forest margins.

HOSTPLANT(S): Not known in Ohio. Goatweeds (*Croton* spp.) are the only reported hostplants for this butterfly. In Missouri, this butterfly uses wooly croton (*Croton capitatus* Michx.) and prairie tea (*Croton monanthogynus* Michx.) (Heitzman and Heitzman, 1987). Both of these plants occur in Ohio (Weishaupt, 1971).

ADULT ENERGY RESOURCES: Spring beauty (*Claytonia virginica* L.). Elsewhere, the primary adult resources of this butterfly are fermenting tree sap, rotting fruit, feces, and damp soil.

FLIGHT PERIOD: Although the data are inconclusive, this species may have the potential to produce one to two broods in Ohio (Figure 8.250). Early spring dates may indicate that this species occasionally overwinters in Ohio. Extreme dates range from 19 March (Dury, 1898) to 20 October.

SIMILAR SPECIES: None.

GENERAL COMMENTS: Although this species has been recorded at scattered localities within Ohio, it has been found most frequently in the extreme southwestern corner of the State. This species is almost always encountered as solitary individuals. Adults probably occur more frequently than our records indicate, especially in southwestern Ohio. This immigrant has the potential to be found statewide, and should be sought along forest margins and in old fields during late summer and autumn.

There are two seasonal phenotypes, which are controlled by photoperiod length (Riley, 1980). Adults of the summer form 'andriaesta' F. Johnson and W. P. Comstock (1941) are paler and have a less produced forewing apex than adults of the winter form. This species is also sexually dimorphic, with females being paler and more heavily mottled than males. The ventral wing surfaces are cryptically patterned, and when at rest this butterfly closely resembles a dead leaf. In flight, *A. andria* resembles a species of *Polygonia*, but is brighter red dorsally.

The flight of this species is rapid, powerful, and erratic. Adults perch on twigs, fallen logs, rocks, and exposed soil with their wings held together. Adults are wary and are very difficult to approach. However, like most sap-feeding species, this butterfly can be attracted to fermenting bait mixtures placed out by collectors.

LITERATURE RECORDS: Adams County (Albrecht, 1982).

Asterocampa celtis celtis (Boisduval & LeConte, 1835). Hackberry Butterfly. Plate 35.

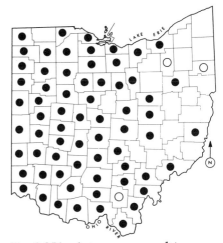

Fig. 8.251 *Asterocampa celtis*.

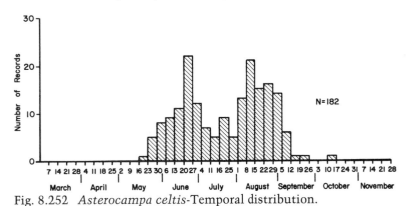

Fig. 8.252 *Asterocampa celtis*-Temporal distribution.

STATUS: Resident; uncommon to common. The frequency of this species parallels the abundance of its hostplant, *Celtis occidentalis* L. This butterfly is most frequently encountered in the western half of the State where the hostplant is most common.

DISTRIBUTION/RANGE: Statewide (Figure 8.251).

HABITAT: This species is found practically anywhere that hackberry trees (*Celtis* spp.) occur. Typical habitats include bottomland forests, mesic woodlands, areas along rivers and streams, railroad rights-of-way, roadsides, and fence rows.

HOSTPLANT(S): In Ohio, this species has been found and reared on hackberry (*Celtis occidentalis* L.) (Studebaker and Studebaker, 1967). This species may also use elms (*Ulmus* spp.) as secondary hosts in areas where hackberries are not found. Elms are also suspected hostplants in Illinois (Sedman and Hess, 1985). Hackberries are the primary hosts throughout this butterfly's range (Friedlander, 1986[87]).

ADULT ENERGY RESOURCES: Red clover (*Trifolium pratense* L.), common milkweed (*Asclepias syriaca* L.), and yellow sweet clover (*Melilotus officinalis* [L.] Lam.). The primary adult resources are fermenting tree sap, rotting fruit, feces, carrion, and damp soil. This butterfly will also land on humans, presumably to imbibe the salts present in perspiration.

FLIGHT PERIOD: Two broods, with peaks in June and August (Figure 8.252). Extreme dates range from 26 April (unusually early) to 16 October.

SIMILAR SPECIES: This species can be confused with *A. clyton*, but *A. celtis* has an eyespot on each forewing, which is absent in *A. clyton*. The light tan coloring of *A. celtis* will also separate it from the more orange *A. clyton*.

GENERAL COMMENTS: Populations of this species are usually localized, and are almost always associated with hackberry trees. Populations usually occur at moderate to high densities. Likewise, larvae can also be abundant and have been known to defoliate entire trees (Langlois, 1964). Langlois and Langlois (1964) reported that in the 1950's, this butterfly caused widespread damage to stands of hackberry trees on South Bass Island, Ottawa County. This defoliation caused the death of many trees, which resulted in the butterfly being rare on the island for several years afterward.

Males are by far more often observed than females, and are most frequently seen perching on or flying around the branches of hackberry trees. Males dart out from their perches at almost any passing object, presumably in an attempt to locate females. Interactions between males are common. Because males often return to their original perches after these chases, they may be territorial, defending small areas from other males. Typical male perches include tree trunks and leaves of the hostplant, nearby trees, buildings, fenceposts, and rocks. Males can even be coaxed to settle on or in an insect net. Males appear to be attracted to bright clothing (such as red or white) and will often settle on people. Males usually perch in a head-down position. Females apparently remain in the upper reaches of the hostplant, and are rarely encountered. Adults are sometimes wary and difficult to approach, but perching males are generally easy to observe. The flight of this species is fast and erratic, but adults usually settle after flying short distances.

Adults are active throughout the day, but there is often an increase of activity at dusk. Adults are often on the wing at sunset and adults have been collected at white lights and sugar-baited tree trunks after dark (Stehr, 1945). This species can be attracted to fermenting bait mixtures, which is the most reliable method to collect females (John W. Peacock, pers comm, 1989).

This species is sexually dimorphic. Females are larger and have broader and more rounded wings than males. Adults also exhibit some seasonal polyphenism, and first brood individuals tend to be smaller than individuals of the second brood.

LITERATURE RECORDS: Mahoning (Kirtland, 1854a), Jackson (Stehr, 1945) and Summit (Claypole, 1897) Counties.

Asterocampa clyton clyton (Boisduval & LeConte, 1835). Tawny Emperor. Plate 35.

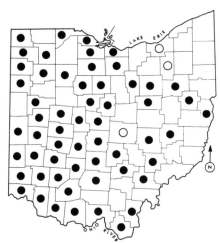

Fig. 8.253 *Asterocampa clyton.*

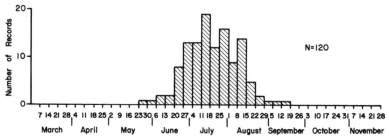

Fig. 8.254 *Asterocampa clyton*-Temporal distribution.

STATUS: Resident; rare to uncommon. Populations of this species are extremely localized and are most frequently encountered in southwestern Ohio. There are few records from the eastern third of the State.

DISTRIBUTION/RANGE: Statewide (Figure 8.253).

HABITAT: This species is found in association with hackberry trees (*Celtis* spp.). Typical habitats include bottomland forests, mesic deciduous forests, areas along streams and rivers, and open fields and yards where isolated trees occur. This butterfly is most often encountered along rights-of-way and other openings that transect forested habitats.

HOSTPLANT(S): In Ohio, this species has been found and reared on hackberry (*Celtis occidentalis* L.) (Studebaker and Studebaker, 1967; Charles Dury, unpublished notes). Various species of hackberries serve as the primary hosts for this butterfly (Friedlander, 1986[87]).

ADULT ENERGY RESOURCES: Common boneset (*Eupatorium perfoliatum* L.). The primary adult resources are fermenting tree sap, rotting fruit, feces, carrion, damp soil, and damp sand. This butterfly will also land on humans, presumably to imbibe the salts present in perspiration.

FLIGHT PERIOD: One brood, which peaks in July (Figure 8.254). Extreme dates range from 13 April (unusually early) to 15 September.

SIMILAR SPECIES: See *A. celtis*.

GENERAL COMMENTS: Populations of this butterfly are generally local, and are often closely associated with single hackberry trees. Populations often reach high enough densities to be considered locally common. Numbers of this species fluctuate from year to year, and this butterfly may seemingly be absent for several years from areas where populations were once known to exist. Of the two *Asterocampa* species, *A. clyton* is less frequently encountered, and in most areas, there seem to be far fewer populations of *A. clyton* than of *A. celtis*. However, many populations of *A. clyton* may be overlooked because of the close resemblance of this species to *A. celtis*.

The behavior of *A. clyton* is very similar to that of *A. celtis. Asterocampa clyton* males perch on leaves and tree trunks and dart out at almost any passing object, presumably as part of their mate locating behavior. Interactions between males are frequent.

140

Males often return to their original perches, which suggests that they are territorial. To a lesser extent than *A. celtis, A. clyton* males are attracted to bright clothing. Females are much less active than are males, and tend to remain closer to the hostplant. Females are infrequently encountered, and are uncommon in collections. The flight of this species is rapid and erratic.

This species is active late into the evening, and adults have been collected at night at white lights and at tree trunks sugared for moths (Stehr, 1945). Adults can be attracted to fermenting bait mixtures.

This species is polymorphic. Adults of the dark form 'proserpina' (Scudder, 1868) are characterized by darkened dorsal hindwings with obscured black markings. The light form has tawny dorsal hindwings with well defined pattern elements. Both forms occur in the same brood. The sexes are also dimorphic, with the females being larger, and having broader and more rounded wings than the males.

LITERATURE RECORDS: Cuyahoga (Bubna, 1897), Summit (Claypole, 1897) and Licking (Albrecht, 1982) Counties.

Family SATYRIDAE-Satyrs and Wood Nymphs

Enodia anthedon A. H. Clark, 1936. Northern Pearly Eye. Plate 36.

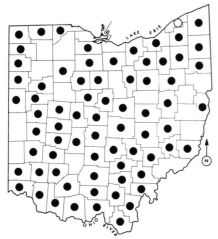

Fig. 8.255 *Enodia anthedon.*

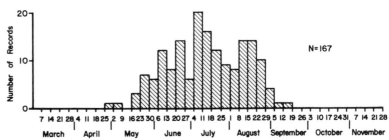

Fig. 8.256 *Enodia anthedon*-Temporal distribution.

STATUS: Resident; uncommon. Populations of this species are localized, but in some years may attain high densities, especially in southeastern Ohio. This species is most frequently encountered in the southern portion of the State. It becomes increasingly less common and more localized throughout the north.

DISTRIBUTION/RANGE: Statewide (Figure 8.255).

HABITAT: This species is most frequently encountered in mesic deciduous forests near streams. In northern Ohio it is often found in grassy swamps and along the shrubby perimeters of wetlands such as marshes, sedge meadows, and fens. This species seldom strays far from shaded habitats.

HOSTPLANT(S): In Ohio, this species has been found and reared on alta fescue grass (*Festuca arundinacea* (Schreb.) Wimmer). Various species of grasses including bottle-brush grass (*Hystrix patula* Moench), broadleaf uniola (*Uniola latifolia* Michx.), whitegrass (*Leersia virginica* L.), and plumegrass (*Erianthus* sp.) have also been recorded as hostplants in the eastern United States (Shapiro, 1974; Opler and Krizek, 1984; Heitzman and Heitzman, 1987). All of these grasses occur in Ohio (Weishaupt, 1985).

ADULT ENERGY RESOURCES: Fermenting tree sap, rotting fruit, feces, and damp soil are the primary adult resources. An individual was once collected while it was visiting a loaf of hot yeast bread that had been set out on a window sill to cool (Hine, 1898a; 1898b).

FLIGHT PERIOD: Throughout most of Ohio, this butterfly has two broods. In extreme northeastern Ohio, there may be only a single brood. In exceptional years, there may be three broods in the southern portion of the State. Peaks are in July and August (Figure 8.256). Extreme dates range from 26 April to 12 September.

SIMILAR SPECIES: This species is superficially similar to the two species of *Satyrodes* that occur in Ohio, but use of the plates will readily separate *E. anthedon*.

GENERAL COMMENTS: Until recently, this species was considered a subspecies of the more southern *Enodia portlandia* (Fabricius, 1781), and only recently was it realized that it is a distinct species (Heitzman and dos Passos, 1974). South of Ohio, these species occur sympatrically but do not interbreed.

The flight of the species is rapid and erratic, and usually within two meters of the ground. Males generally perch head down on tree trunks and leaves, and often fly out to chase other males. Males often return to their original perches, suggesting that they might be territorial. Adults rest with their wings together, although in the early morning they often bask with their wings held partially to completely open. Adults are active later into the evening than most butterflies, and have been attracted to mercury vapor lights at night. Both sexes are wary, and can be difficult to approach. Disturbed individuals often fly upwards into the trees or to new perches located deeper in their tangled habitat. Adults are strongly attracted to fermenting sap and rotting fruit, and can be attracted to fermenting bait mixtures.

LITERATURE RECORD: Lake County (Albrecht, 1982).

141

***Satyrodes eurydice eurydice* (Johansson, 1763).** Northern Eyed Brown. Plate 36.

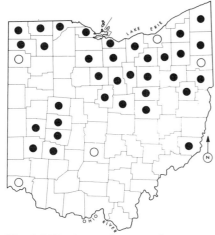

Fig. 8.257 *Satyrodes eurydice.*

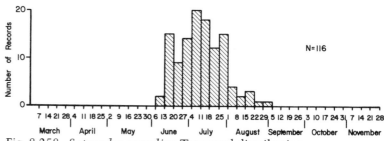

Fig. 8.258 *Satyrodes eurydice*-Temporal distribution.

STATUS: Resident; uncommon. Populations of this species are extremely localized and are most frequently encountered in the northeastern corner of the State, where wetlands are prevalent. Outside of this region, both the butterfly and its required habitat become more localized.

DISTRIBUTION/RANGE: This species is primarily restricted to glaciated Ohio (Figure 8.257).

HABITAT: *Satyrodes eurydice* is restricted to wetlands. It is most frequently encountered in sedge meadows, fens, and wet prairies, and is occasionally sighted in bog meadows. Adults occasionally wander into nearby upland habitats.

HOSTPLANT(S): In Ohio, this species has been found and reared on the sedges *Carex stricta* Lam. and *Carex lacustris* Willd. Studebaker and Studebaker (1967) also report finding larvae on "swamp grass", a probable reference to some *Carex* species. Sedges are the only known hostplants throughout this butterfly's range (Opler and Krizek, 1984).

ADULT ENERGY RESOURCES: Although this species is rarely observed at flowers, a male was observed visiting wild bergamot (*Monarda fistulosa* L.), at Marsh Lake, Steuben County, Indiana (approximately six kilometers from the Ohio border). This species has been collected at fermenting bait mixtures (David K. Parshall and Leroy C. Koehn, pers comm, 1988).

FLIGHT PERIOD: One brood, which peaks in July (Figure 8.258). The actual emergence period at some localities is often drawn out for several weeks. In some areas, the seemingly sudden appearence of newly emerged butterflies in August when worn adults are also present may indicate that more than one species is involved. Extreme dates range from 14 April (unusually early) to 4 September.

SIMILAR SPECIES: *Satyrodes eurydice* is very similar to *S. appalachia*. The most reliable character with which to separate these two species of *Satyrodes* is the configuration of the postmedial lines on the ventral wing surfaces. In *S. eurydice* these lines are jaggedly indented but in *S. appalachia* they are straighter and less wavy. On average, the ground color of both wing surfaces of *S. eurydice* is tan whereas in *S. appalachia* the ground color of both wing surfaces is gray-brown.

Perhaps the easiest way to separate these two species is based on habitat. *Satyrodes eurydice* is almost always found in open sunny wetlands whereas *S. appalachia* is usually found in shaded wetlands.

This species is also vaguely similar to *Enodia anthedon*, but use of the plates will readily separate these two species.

GENERAL COMMENTS: Until recently, it was widely assumed that there was only one species of *Satyrodes* in eastern North America. However, careful studies by Carde', Shapiro, and Clench (1970), led to the realization that there were two distinct phenotypes, both of which were often found at the same localities, but which were segregated by habitat type. They discovered that at several localities, *S. eurydice* was abundant in open sunny wetlands, but the very similar *S. appalachia* could be found only in the shaded confines of the shrubs that surrounded the wetlands. For over one hundred years, lepidopterists had been observing both species without noticing the subtle differences in color and pattern which corresponded to this habitat difference.

Before the massive drainage of Ohio's wetlands and mesic prairies occurred, this species was probably more widespread than it is today, particularly in western Ohio. Kirtland (1854a) noted that this species was "excessively abundant" in "the western prairies of Ohio". Today the species is restricted to the few fen and prairie remnants which still exist in this area. This butterfly is still fairly common in northeastern Ohio, where wetlands form a conspicuous element in the landscape.

The flight of this species is slow and erratic, and adults fly through or just above the tops of the sedges that dominate their habitat. Adults perch on sedges with their wings closed to slightly open. Males seem to alternate between patrolling and perching throughout the day.

This species is phenotypically variable. The ground color ranges from light tan to brown, and females are on average more lightly colored than males. Occasional specimens are pale enough to appear nearly white while in flight.

LITERATURE RECORDS: Although it is impossible to know whether unverifiable literature records refer to *S. eurydice* or to *S. appalachia*, we have included all such literature records here: Cuyahoga (Kirtland, 1854a; Kirkpatrick, 1864; Lepidopterists' Society, 1974), Mahoning (Kirtland, 1854a), Paulding (Price, 1970), Pickaway (Bales, 1909), and Hamilton (Hine, 1898b) Counties.

Records for Delaware County (Lepidopterists' Society, 1984) and Auglaize County (Hoying, 1975) were based upon misidentified specimens of *S. appalachia*.

Satyrodes appalachia leeuwi (Gatrelle & Arbogast, 1974). Appalachian Eyed Brown. Plate 36.

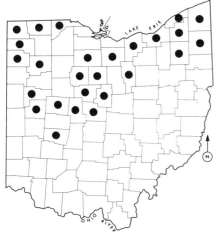

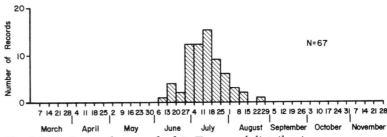

Fig. 8.260 *Satyrodes appalachia*-Temporal distribution.

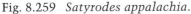

Fig. 8.259 *Satyrodes appalachia.*

STATUS: Resident; rare to uncommon. Although populations of this species tend to be localized, they can attain moderate densities.

DISTRIBUTION/RANGE: Primarily the northern glaciated counties of Ohio (Figure 8.259).

HABITAT: This species usually occurs in shaded wetlands with abundant sedges. Typical habitats include swamps, mesic woodlands, and the shrubby borders of fens and sedge meadows. Adults will occasionally stray into more open habitats.

HOSTPLANT(S): In Ohio, this species has been found and reared on the sedge, *Carex lacustris* Willd. However, several populations occur in habitats which do not support this sedge, and *S. appalachia* associates with, and probably uses other sedges such as *Carex squarrosa* L. and *Carex stricta* Lam. *Carex lacustris* is the only confirmed host in the northern portion of this butterfly's range (Opler and Krizek, 1984).

ADULT ENERGY RESOURCES: Fermenting tree sap and rotting fruit.

FLIGHT PERIOD: One brood, which peaks in late June-early July (Figure 8.260). Larvae reared under normal photoperiods, but under greenhouse conditions, produce a second brood with adults emerging in late summer. A second brood ocurrs in western Kentucky. Extreme dates range from 6 June to 23 August.

SIMILAR SPECIES: See *S. eurydice.*

GENERAL COMMENTS: Only recently was it realized that *S. appalachia* was phenotypically and ecologically different from *S. eurydice* (Carde', Shapiro, and Clench, 1970) (see GENERAL COMMENTS under *S. eurydice*). Thus, many of the older literature records for *S. eurydice* may actually refer to *S. appalachia*. For example, Hine (1898b) noted that *S. eurydice* "usually flies along streams in thickly wooded grounds," which suggests that he was actually referring to *S. appalachia*.

Like all wetland butterflies, this species was probably more widespread in the past than it is now. Populations were probably common throughout northwestern Ohio in the Black Swamp before it was drained. This swamp, which covered all or part of 10 counties was largely drained by the 1880's (Platt, 1987). Today, populations of *S. appalachia* as well as those of *Euphyes dukesi* are restricted to the isolated remnants of this once vast wetland. In other areas, the draining of isolated wetlands has undoubtedly resulted in the localized extinction of many populations. However, populations are often more common than some local collectors realize because there is a general reluctance to enter this butterfly's mosquito-infested habitat.

Unlike *S. eurydice*, which inhabits open wetlands, *S. appalachia* prefers shaded habitats, from which it seldom strays. Populations of these two species may occur in close proximity, but adults seldom interact because of their preferences for different solar intensities. A notable exception to this general rule occurs at Springville Fen State Nature Preserve, Clark County, where both species fly in an open fen meadow. In the northwestern quarter of the State, the presence of *S. appalachia* can be used as an indicator for potential populations of the wetland skipper, *Euphyes dukesi*.

The flight of *S. appalachia* is very similar to that of *S. eurydice*, although *S. appalachia* is much more difficult to follow in its shaded, forested habitat. Adults are wary, and are sometimes difficult to approach. Adults usually perch on sedges with their wings held together or partially open, but will occasionally land on tree trunks and branches. This species is attracted to fermenting tree sap and rotting fruit, and can be attracted to baits placed out by collectors.

LITERATURE RECORDS: None (see *S. eurydice*).

Cyllopsis gemma gemma (Hübner, 1808). Gemmed Satyr. Plate 36.

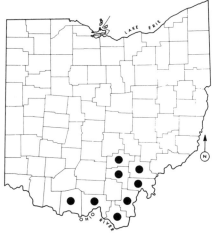

Fig. 8.261 *Cyllopsis gemma.*

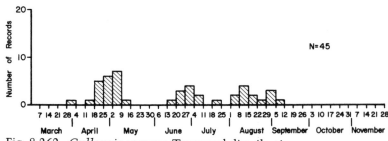

Fig. 8.262 *Cyllopsis gemma*-Temporal distribution.

STATUS: Resident; rare. Populations of this species are localized and usually occur at low densities.

DISTRIBUTION/RANGE: Southern Ohio (Figure 8.261). Ohio represents a northern range limit for this species.

HABITAT: This species is most often found on xeric ridgetops dominated by oak forests, and along trails and roads that traverse this habitat type. It is also occasionally found in shaded grassy clearings along streams in mesic valleys and ravines.

HOSTPLANT(S): Not known in Ohio. In other parts of its range, this butterfly is closely associated with Bermuda grass (*Cynodon dactylon* [L.] Pers.) (Opler and Krizek, 1984), a grass that is widespread in unglaciated Ohio (Cusick and Silberhorn, 1977). *Cyllopsis gemma* probably uses other grasses in Ohio as well, because Bermuda grass is not found at many sites which support populations of this butterfly.

ADULT ENERGY RESOURCES: Adults imbibe moisture from fermenting tree sap, rotting fruit, damp soil, and damp gravel. This species occasionally gathers at mud puddles.

FLIGHT PERIOD: Three broods with peaks in late April-early May, late June-early July, and August (Figure 8.262). Extreme dates range from 1 April to 8 September.

SIMILAR SPECIES: This species is superficially similar to other small satyrs, but referring to the plates will make its uniqueness obvious.

GENERAL COMMENTS: Although in areas south of Ohio this species inhabits moist grassy meadows and bottomland forests near streams (Opler and Krizek, 1984; Scott, 1986), in Ohio it is most often found on xeric ridges dominated by oak forests. This may indicate that Ohio populations are ecologically divergent from populations found in the heart of this species' range. Because the adults superficially resemble *Megisto cymela* and *Hermeuptychia sosybius*, species with which *C. gemma* often occurs, it may be easily overlooked. This species is probably more continuously distributed in southern Ohio than our records indicate.

   Although this species can exhibit a very erratic, side-to-side dancing flight when alarmed, its flight is usually slow and low to the ground. Adults are most often encountered flying along trails and woodland roads, or while they are imbibing moisture from damp areas. Because adults are attracted to fermenting tree sap and rotting fruit, they can be attracted to fermenting bait mixtures placed out by collectors.

LITERATURE RECORDS: None.

Hermeuptychia sosybius (Fabricius, 1793). Carolina Satyr. Plate 36.

Fig. 8.263 *Hermeuptychia sosybius.*

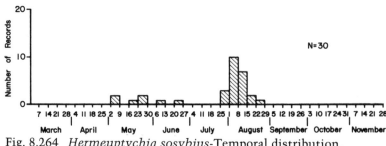

Fig. 8.264 *Hermeuptychia sosybius*-Temporal distribution.

STATUS: Resident; rare. This species is most often encountered in Lawrence and Gallia Counties, where populations can reach moderately high densities. Populations elsewhere in the State occur at low densities and are widely separated.

DISTRIBUTION/RANGE: Southern Ohio (Figure 8.263). Ohio represents a northern range limit for this species.

144

HABITAT: This species is most often encountered in grassy clearings near streams through deciduous forests, and along trails, roads, and powerline cuts through bottomland forests. It is also occasionally found in upland forests and ridgetop clearings.

HOSTPLANT(S): Not known in Ohio. Various grasses are used throughout the range of this butterfly (Opler and Krizek, 1984).

ADULT ENERGY RESOURCES: Fermenting tree sap, rotting fruit, and damp soil. Adults are occasionally found feeding at mud puddles.

FLIGHT PERIOD: Two broods with peaks in May and August (Figure 8.264). Extreme dates range from 4 May to 25 August.

SIMILAR SPECIES: *Megisto cymela* is superficially similar, but has ocelli on the dorsal wing surfaces. *Hermeuptychia sosybius* lacks dorsal ocelli and is usually smaller.

GENERAL COMMENTS: This species occurs as localized populations, and is seldom seen far from moist, shaded habitats. Because of its small size, and similarity to *M. cymela* and *Cyllopsis gemma*, species with which *H. sosybius* often occurs, it may be easily overlooked. This species is probably more continuously distributed in southern Ohio than our records indicate.

Although alarmed individuals fly erratically, the normal flight of this species is weak, slow, and close to the ground. Because of its small size and dark coloration, adults can be difficult to follow visually. Adults are most often encountered while they are perching on exposed soil, leaf litter, and low vegetation, with their wings held tightly closed. These butterflies often bask with closed wings, tilting their bodies so that the ventral surfaces of their wings receive direct sunlight.

Because adults are attracted to fermenting tree sap and rotting fruit, they can be attracted to fermenting bait mixtures placed out by collectors.

Some authors (eg Opler and Krizek, 1984) consider *H. sosybius* to be a subspecies of the more western and southern *Hermeuptychia hermes* (Fabricius, 1775).

LITERATURE RECORDS: None.
Henninger (1910) lists this species from Seneca County, but this record is undoubtedly based upon a misdetermined or mislabeled specimen. Seneca County lies far north of the normal range of this species.

Neonympha mitchellii mitchellii French, 1889. Mitchell's Satyr. Plate 36.

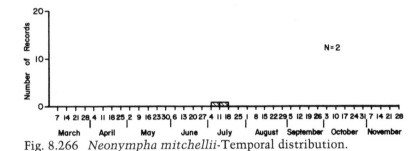

Fig. 8.266 *Neonympha mitchellii*-Temporal distribution.

Fig. 8.265 *Neonympha mitchellii*.

STATUS: Resident (probably extirpated); rare. This species has only been collected on three occasions in Ohio. It was last reported in 1950.

DISTRIBUTION/RANGE: This species is known from a few scattered locations in southern Michigan and northeastern Indiana, one site in Ohio, two sites in New Jersey, and one site in North Carolina. In Ohio, this species is only known from Streetsboro Fen in Portage County (Figure 8.265).

HABITAT: All of the known habitats for this species, including the Ohio site, are fens supporting lush stands of sedges (Shuey, 1985).

HOSTPLANT(S): Although no hostplant has been recorded in Ohio, Ohio specimens were taken is association with sedges ("swamp grasses") (*Carex* spp.) (Pallister, 1927). In Michigan, *N. mitchellii* has been reared on *Carex* and *Scirpus* (McAlpine, Hubbell, and Pliske, 1960). Females will oviposit on *Carex stricta* Lam. in captivity. It is assumed that some species of *Carex* is the natural host.

ADULT ENERGY RESOURCES: None recorded for Ohio.

FLIGHT PERIOD: One brood, which flies in early July (Figure 8.266). Extreme dates range from 4 July to 10 July.

SIMILAR SPECIES: This species is superficially similar to the other small satyrids in Ohio, but the continuous series of ocelli on the ventral wing surfaces make it easy to identify *N. mitchellii*.

GENERAL COMMENTS: This species was first reported from Ohio by Pallister (1927) who found it in numbers at Streetsboro Fen on 4 July 1926 and again on 10 July 1927. Since then, only one other record has been reported: 19 June 1950 (McAlpine, Hubbell, and Pliske, 1960). Recent attempts to rediscover this species in Streetsboro Fen and other fens in northeastern Ohio have been unsuccessful (Shuey et al, 1987; Shuey, Calhoun, and Iftner, 1987). It is possible that populations still survive in some of the unexplored fens of northeastern Ohio.

It seems likely that habitat destruction resulted in the extinction of the Streetsboro Fen population. When Pallister (1927) first encountered *N. mitchellii*, he described the habitat as a "vast swamp", but by the 1950's most of the fen had been converted to a truck farm. Today, much of the cultivated land has been allowed to revert to sedge meadow, but these areas support sedges that are unlikely hostplants for this butterfly. The core of the fen has never been manipulated and is preserved as Gott Fen State Nature Preserve. This small area has been repeatedly searched for the butterfly with no success.

It is possible that a population may once have occurred in Seneca County. Henninger (1910) reported *Neonympha areolatus* (J. E. Smith, 1797), a very closely related species. This area once had large expanses of wetlands, including some fens which might have supported populations of *N. mitchellii*. This population would have bridged the gap between Streetsboro Fen and the populations in Michigan and Indiana.

The flight of this species is weak and bouncy, and adults fly through the sedges rather than over them. Adults seldom fly far before settling on sedges or other vegetation. This butterfly is very delicately scaled, and adults lose their scales quickly in the field. They can become especially rubbed if captured in a coarse net.

LITERATURE RECORDS: None.

This species has been erroneously attributed to Lake County (Albrecht, 1982) and northwestern Ohio (Shapiro, 1970a).

Megisto cymela cymela (Cramer, 1777). Little Wood Satyr. Plate 36.

Fig. 8.267 *Megisto cymela*.

STATUS: Resident; common.

DISTRIBUTION/RANGE: Statewide (Figure 8.267).

HABITAT: This species is most often encountered in shaded habitats, such as forest margins, brushy meadows, and weedy fields.

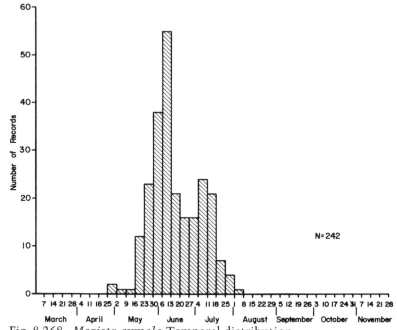

Fig. 8.268 *Megisto cymela*-Temporal distribution.

HOSTPLANT(S): Although no hostplant has been recorded in Ohio, this species has been found in association with Virginia wild-rye (*Elymus virginicus* L.). Various grasses, including orchard grass (*Dactylis glomerata* L.), which is common in Ohio (Braun, 1967), are used throughout this butterfly's range (Opler and Krizek, 1984).

ADULT ENERGY RESOURCES: The primary adult resources are fermenting tree sap, rotting fruit, and damp soil. Adults rarely visit flowers, but have been observed on common milkweed (*Asclepias syriaca* L.).

FLIGHT PERIOD: One bimodal brood with peaks in late May-early June and July (Figure 8.268). Extreme dates range from 7 March (unusually early) to 2 August.

SIMILAR SPECIES: This species is superficially similar to the other small satyrids, but the presence of ocelli on the dorsal wing surfaces will easily identify *M. cymela*.

GENERAL COMMENTS: Unlike most of Ohio's butterflies, this species prefers to fly in shaded situations. Adults are even active on overcast days and during periods of light rain. This is the most common of the small woodland satyrs in the State. Because *M. cymela* is so widespread and common, it often makes it difficult to locate populations of the very similar, but rarer species.

The flight of this species is close to the ground and bouncy, and it is very difficult to follow visually as it weaves through grasses or forest understory. When alarmed, its flight can become very rapid and erratic. Disturbed adults usually head into thickets, dense grass, or occasionally into the tree tops. Males patrol all day, presumably in search of females. When perching on sunlit leaves, adults hold their wings slightly open or they may bask with the wings held outstretched.

Both sexes are attracted to fermenting sap and rotting fruit, and can be attracted to baits placed out by collectors.

Megisto cymela may actually include two sibling species that are superficially so similar that they are indistinguishable by color pattern (Opler and Krizek, 1984). In Ohio, some populations seem to have two distinct emergences, the first in early June, the second in early July. The elapsed time between these two peaks is not sufficient for the production of an actual brood, indicating that two distinct genotypes may be involved. If this is the case, this bimodal emergence could be indicative of either a single species with multiple alleles controlling emergence, or of two sibling species which differ slightly in their seasonal periods of adult activity.

LITERATURE RECORDS: None.

Cercyonis pegala alope (Fabricius, 1793)/*nephele* (W. Kirby, 1837). Common Wood Nymph. Plate 37.

Fig. 8.269 *Cercyonis pegala.*

STATUS: Resident; uncommon to common.

DISTRIBUTION/RANGE: Statewide (Figure 8.269).

HABITAT: This species is found in a variety of habitats, including open woodlands, woodland margins, brushy old fields, pastures, wet meadows, prairies, and fens.

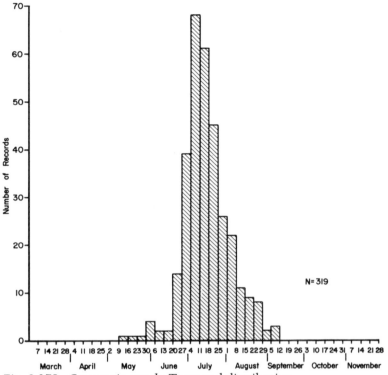

Fig. 8.270 *Cercyonis pegala*-Temporal distribution.

HOSTPLANT(S): Although no hostplant has been recorded in Ohio, larvae of this species have been found and reared on an unidentified species of grass (Studebaker and Studebaker, 1967). Purple-top (*Triodia flava* [L.] Smyth), a common plant in Ohio (Braun, 1967), is used in New York (Shapiro, 1974). Various species of grass are probably used throughout this butterfly's range.

ADULT ENERGY RESOURCES: Red clover (*Trifolium pratense* L.), wild carrot (*Daucus carota* L.), teasel (*Dipsacus sylvestris* Huds.), mountain-mint (*Pycnanthemum virginianum* [L.] Durand & Jackson), bull thistle (*Cirsium vulgare* [Savi] Tenore), Canada thistle (*Cirsium arvense* [L.] Scop.), tall ironweed (*Vernonia altissima* Nutt), black-eyed Susan (*Rudbeckia hirta* L.), butterfly-weed (*Asclepias tuberosa* L.), and wild bergamot (*Monarda fistulosa* L.). Fermenting tree sap and rotting fruit are also used.

FLIGHT PERIOD: One brood, which peaks in July (Figure 8.270). Extreme dates range from 10 May to 11 September.

SIMILAR SPECIES: None.

GENERAL COMMENTS: Two putative "subspecies" or forms of this butterfly occur in Ohio. In the southern quarter of the State, and in unglaciated regions, populations referable to *C. pegala alope* are found. These populations are characterized by the presence of large rectangular yellow or orange patches around the ocelli of the forewings. These populations generally occur in upland habitats such as scrubby old fields and along woodland margins. Throughout the remainder of Ohio, populations are intermediate between *C. pegala alope* and *C. pegala nephele*, which is a smaller, darker, northern subspecies that lacks the yellow patches on the forewings. In the southern portion of the intergrade area, 'alope'-like and 'nephele'-like populations occur sympatrically, with 'alope'-like populations occurring in upland habitats, and 'nephele'-like populations occurring in sedge meadows, wet prairies, and fens. Throughout the northern half of this intergrade area, darker 'nephele-like' populations become more frequent until they become dominant in the northern two tiers of counties. However, none of these populations are pure *C. pegala nephele*, and individuals with rudimentary orange forewing patches can be found. Because these two phenotypes seem to be associated with different habitat types, they may be environmentally controlled. This phenomenon deserves further investigation.

This species may be more common today than in the past. Many early collectors (eg Bubna, 1897; Bales, 1909) fail to mention the species in areas where it is now common, suggesting that it was either absent or extremely rare. Hine (1898a; 1898b) knew of only a few records for Ohio. The first collector who noted this species as common was Clement W. Baker (unpublished notes) in the 1930's. Because this species primarily inhabits open habitats, the apparent increase in abundance may be a reflection of the destruction of Ohio's forests at the turn of the century.

147

This butterfly has a low bouncing flight that is difficult to follow as it weaves through its habitat. Males patrol grassy areas for females. Adults perch on grass blades, twigs, and other low vegetation. When alarmed, the flight can be very rapid and erratic. Alarmed individuals usually fly into brushy areas or drop into the dense cover of grasses or sedges. In wooded areas, adults sometimes flee into the tops of trees. Because of its erratic flight, this species can be very difficult to pursue, especially when alarmed. However, adults are attracted to fermenting sap and rotting fruit, and can be easily observed at fermenting bait mixtures placed out by collectors.

A synonym of *C. pegala nephele*, *C. pegala borealis* F. Chermock (1929), was described from specimens collected in Trumbull County, Ohio. Miller and Brown (1981) incorrectly synonymized *C. pegala borealis* with *C. pegala olympus* (W. H. Edwards, 1880), a putative subspecies which does not occur in Ohio. In addition, Howe (1975) incorrectly states that the type locality of form 'ochracea' (F. & R. Chermock, 1942) is Ohio. The type locality of this form is actually in Rhode Island.

Family DANAIDAE-Milkweed Butterflies

Danaus plexippus plexippus (Linnaeus, 1758). Monarch. Plate 38.

Fig. 8.271 *Danaus plexippus*.

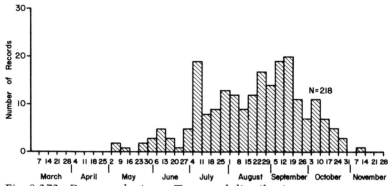

Fig. 8.272 *Danaus plexippus*-Temporal distribution.

STATUS : Regular immigrant; common.

DISTRIBUTION/RANGE: This species occurs throughout North and South America and has established permanent populations on Hawaii and Australia. In North America, *D. plexippus* is a permanent resident only in southern Florida, southern California, and Mexico. Ohio specimens are primarily the result of annual migrations northward from central Mexico. This species has been recorded from all 88 Ohio counties (Figure 8.271).

HABITAT: This species occurs in virtually any open habitat. Typical habitats include old fields, roadsides, prairie remnants, gardens, and urban yards.

HOSTPLANT(S): In Ohio, this species has been found and reared on common milkweed (*Asclepias syriaca* L.). Larvae have also been found on swamp milkweed (*Asclepias incarnata* L) and butterfly-weed (*Asclepias tuberosa* L.). Milkweeds are the primary hosts of this butterfly.

ADULT ENERGY RESOURCES: Red clover (*Trifolium pratense* L.), alfalfa (*Medicago sativa* L.), common milkweed (*Asclepias syriaca* L.), swamp milkweed (*Asclepias incarnata* L.), butterfly-weed (*Asclepias tuberosa* L.), Indian hemp (*Apocynum cannabinum* L.), wild carrot (*Daucus carota* L.), dame's rocket (*Hesperis matronalis* L.), Canada thistle (*Cirsium arvense* [L.] Scop.), thistles (*Cirsium* spp.), horseweed (*Erigeron canadensis* L.), tall ironweed (*Vernonia altissima* Nutt), spotted Joe-Pye weed (*Eupatorium maculatum* L.), common boneset (*Eupatorium perfoliatum* L.), goldenrod (*Solidago* sp.), asters (*Aster* spp.), teasel (*Dipsacus sylvestris* Huds.), lilac (*Syringa vulgaris* L.), and numerous garden flowers. Adults also imbibe moisture from damp soil and damp gravel. This butterfly has also been observed at motor oil stains on pavement.

FLIGHT PERIOD: Two to four overlapping generations, depending on how early in the season this species becomes established (Figure 8.272). Extreme dates range from 5 May to 9 November.

SIMILAR SPECIES: See *Limenitis archippus*. This species can also be confused with *D. gilippus*, but the orange ground color of *D. plexippus* will separate it from the much darker brown *D. gilippus*.

GENERAL COMMENTS: This is probably the most familiar butterfly in the State, and is a common sight in open areas in late summer and early autumn. This is also Ohio's only species which migrates both north and south annually. Each autumn, this species participates in mass migrations, with adults gathering in numbers as they head southward to their overwintering grounds in Mexico. These migrations involve nonreproducing adults from the entire northeastern United States and Canada. Although many adults travel alone, occasionally aggregations are formed. The largest migratory aggregation on record for Ohio occurred in September 1892, when millions of individuals descended into Cleveland from Canada (Webster, 1892; 1912; Anonymous,

1893). This migration coincided with an epidemic of cholera, and many people who witnessed this aggregation believed that the butterflies were disguised cholera germs (Anonymous, 1892). Another large aggregation occurred over Cleveland in 1872 (Saunders et al, 1875).

Today, large gatherings of migrating adults still occur on the Lake Erie Islands, especially Kelleys Island. These individuals apparently gather on the islands to rest and feed after crossing Lake Erie from Canada. The number of individuals arriving on the islands vary considerably from year to year (Teraguchi, 1988). Aggregations apparently move quickly through the State. One aggregation, noted in Seneca County on 3 October 1907 (Henninger, 1910), was observed in Pickaway County the next day (Bales, 1907). Bales noted that this aggregation moved steadily from north to south, and estimated that millions of individuals were involved. Although the majority of Ohio monarchs may eventually reach the overwintering grounds in the mountains of central Mexico, some individuals may pass the winter in southern Florida, or on the Caribbean Islands.

After reaching Mexico, adults gather by the millions in small areas where winter temperatures are slightly warmer than in surrounding habitats. Adults roost on trees and on each other, creating huge forests of orange. Throughout the winter months, the monarchs remain fairly inactive, and only fly about in search of water and, if it can be found, nectar. During this period, adults are in reproductive diapause, primarily existing upon fat reserves that had been accumulated during the larval stage. Many adults die during this period, usually from predation and lethal cold temperatures. As their fat reserves are used up, their reproductive systems begin to develop, and adults become more active. During late winter-early spring, the adults mate and begin to fly northward. It is estimated that less than one percent of the original adults survive to return to northern areas (Opler and Krizek, 1984). As the females fly northward, they search for milkweeds upon which to lay eggs. The overwintering females usually do not survive for long, and it is doubtful that overwintering females ever return as far north as Ohio. It is their offspring that complete the cycle and find their way into Ohio. Because northward flying adults fly as solitary individuals, few people notice this phase of the migration.

Because the monarch depends on its overwintering grounds for survival, any factor which might disturb the suitability of this limited area could have a dramatic impact on this butterfly. Until recently, the overwintering grounds in Mexico had been threatened by lumbering, but with the realization that the area had unique tourism potential, the Mexican government has since protected the sites. However, these sites may still be adversely affected by the pressure of tourism. Further study of the potential impacts of this activity needs to be undertaken. Thus, the status of the monarch in Ohio depends heavily upon the conservation of the overwintering grounds in Mexico.

In 1938, a program of tagging monarchs was initiated by Fred A. Urquhart of Toronto, Canada (Urquhart, 1960). This method of identifying individuals, using identification tags attached to their wings, ultimately led to the discovery in 1975 of the famous overwintering grounds in central Mexico (Urquhart, 1976). This program of tagging is still in progress across North America and includes several sites in Ohio. A number of specimens tagged in Ohio have been recovered and at least two specimens tagged on Kelleys Island in 1983 were later observed in Texas and at Angangueo, Michoacan, Mexico. (Sonja E. Teraguchi, pers comm, 1983; Urquhart, 1960).

The larvae of this species feed on milkweeds, which usually possess poisons known as cardiac glycosides. These chemicals, which are extremely toxic to most vertebrates, are incorporated into the bodies of the larvae and adult monarchs. In addition to the glycosides, monarchs sequester emetic substances which cause vomiting in birds. Thus, birds which eat monarchs do not die, but only become ill. Birds which eat monarchs generally remember the experience as a bad one, and as a result the monarch gains a certain amount of protection from predation. The bright color patterns found on larval and adult monarchs are thought to be aposematic. These easily recognized patterns serve as warnings which are quickly learned by potential predators, because they can associate the striking appearance of this insect with the bad experience of eating one.

The monarch forms a model for the viceroy (*Limenitis archippus*) in probably the most famous example of Batesian mimicry. In this relationship, the adult viceroy (the mimic) has evolved a very similar color pattern to that of the distasteful monarch. By resembling the monarch, the viceroy gains protection from predators who have tasted monarchs and cannot distinguish between the two butterflies. However, an intriguing study (Ritland and Brower, 1991) challenges this theory by concluding that *A. archippus* is also distasteful, suggesting that this species is a Müllerian co-mimic of *D. plexippus*, rather than a Batesian mimic.

The flight of the monarch is very slow and leisurely, and is characterized by long periods of gliding. Only when alarmed does this species exhibit a very rapid flight. Males patrol while searching for females, and will chase after most other large orange butterflies. Adults are avid flower visitors, and feed with the wings together or outstretched. This species is not very wary, and can usually be very closely observed. Roosting adults hang upside down from plants at night.

LITERATURE RECORDS: None.

Danaus gilippus thersippus (Bates, 1863) (= **strigosus** [Bates, 1864]). Queen. Plate 38.

Fig. 8.273 *Danaus gilippus.*

STATUS: Stray; rare. This species has only been recorded once from Ohio.

DISTRIBUTION/RANGE: Within the United States, this butterfly is a permanent resident only in peninsular Florida, southern Georgia, and along the Mexican border (Opler and Krizek, 1984). The single Ohio record was collected in Sharon Township, Franklin County (Gilbert, 1960), and is the farthest northeast that this species has been recorded (Figure 8.273).

HABITAT: Where this butterfly is a resident, it occupies a variety of open habitats such as old fields, pastures, and roadsides.

HOSTPLANT(S): Not known in Ohio. Various species of milkweeds (*Asclepias* spp.) are used as hosts in areas where this butterfly is a resident (Opler and Krizek, 1984).

ADULT ENERGY RESOURCES: Possibly moisture from damp gravel (see below).

FLIGHT PERIOD: The only Ohio record is dated 1 July 1959.

SIMILAR SPECIES: See *D. plexippus* and *Limenitis archippus.*

GENERAL COMMENTS: The only known Ohio record of this species was a specimen captured by Brother Donald Ray Geiger with his fingers as it rested on a gravel road on the grounds of the Pontifical College Josephinum (Gilbert, 1960). A stray from more southern climates, this species cannot survive Ohio's winters. It is doubtful that this species ever reproduces within the State. The lone Ohio specimen is deposited in The Ohio State University Collection of Insects and Spiders.

Two subspecies of this species occur in the United States, and both have the potential of reaching Ohio. Although the southeastern subspecies *D. gilippus berenice* (Cramer, 1780), which is a resident of Florida and southern Georgia, has been observed several times in Kentucky (Charles V. Covell, Jr., pers comm, 1987), the specimen collected in Ohio represents the southwestern subspecies, *D. gilippus thersippus* (Bates, 1863). This subspecies is a resident of southern Texas and Mexico southward to Argentina and is more migratory than *D. gilippus berenice. Danaus gilippus thersippus* has also been recorded from Iowa, North Dakota, Missouri, and Illinois (Opler and Krizek, 1984; Royer, 1988; Heitzman and Heitzman, 1987; Irwin and Downey, 1973). *Danaus gilippus thersippus* can be recognized by the presence of white scaling along the black veins of the dorsal hindwing. This white scaling is usually absent in *D. gilippus berenice.*

LITERATURE RECORDS: None.

9. SPECIES OF POSSIBLE OCCURRENCE IN OHIO

Included here are 18 butterflies not known at present from Ohio that could occur in the State either as breeding residents, or as strays from other regions. Many have been already credited to the State, but sufficient confusion exists concerning their proper identity that we place them here. We hope the following information will lead to the discovery of additional species in Ohio.

Family HESPERIIDAE

***Erynnis zarucco* (Lucas, 1857).** Zarucco Dusky Wing. Plate 39.

This skipper is a resident of the southeast, regularly occurring as far north as New Jersey and Tennessee. It is known to wander and has been recorded in southwestern Pennsylvania (Opler and Krizek, 1984) and in Indiana (Shull and Badger, 1972). *Erynnis zarucco* occurs in a variety of open and forest edge habitats (Opler and Krizek, 1984). It should be watched for during late summer and early autumn. *Erynnis zarucco* is superficially similar to *E. baptisiae* so individuals of *E. baptisiae* found late in the season should be examined closely.

***Erynnis funeralis* (Scudder & Burgess, 1870).** Funeral Dusky Wing. Plate 39.

Although primarily a species of the extreme southwest (Scott, 1986), *E. funeralis* has been recorded rarely in western Kentucky and in northeastern Indiana (Opler and Krizek, 1984). This species should be watched for in open habitats during late summer and early autumn. It has been suggested (Scott, 1986) that *E. funeralis* is a subspecies of *Erynnis zarucco*.

***Lerema accius* (Smith, 1797).** Clouded Skipper. Plate 39.

Lerema accius is a southeastern coastal plain resident which irregularly emigrates northward west of the Appalachian Mountains (Opler and Krizek, 1984). There is an old record of this species from Indiana (Shull and Badger, 1972) and it has also been recorded in west-central Kentucky (Charles V. Covell, Jr., pers comm, 1985). Because this species does wander northward, it should be watched for in open areas during late summer and early autumn.

***Polites vibex vibex* (Geyer, 1832).** Whirlabout. Plate 39.

Wyss (1930b; 1932) and Albrecht (1982) reported this species from Ohio. However, all specimens examined which were originally identified as this species have been *Hylephila phyleus*. *Polites vibex* occurs in a variety of open habitats along the southern Coastal Plain and is known to stray northward along the Atlantic Coast and Mississippi River Valley (Opler and Krizek, 1984). There is a remote chance that this species could stray into Ohio, especially in late summer and early autumn.

***Wallengrenia otho otho* (Smith, 1797).** Broken Dash. Plate 39.

Evans (1955) reported this species from Ohio on the basis of two males in the British Museum of Natural History. However, Burns (1985) found only one specimen, a female, labeled simply "Ohio". John M. Burns (pers comm, 1985) doubts the validity of this specimen, although he believes that the species probably occurs sparingly in Ohio. *Wallengrenia otho* is very similar to *Wallengrenia egeremet* but is more southern in distribution. *Wallengrenia otho* has been recorded as far north as northern Indiana (Burns, 1985). This species could stray into southern Ohio.

***Atrytone arogos iowa* (Scudder, 1869).** Arogos Skipper. Plate 39.

Reported from Auglaize County by Hoying (1975) who remarked "rare, June 18". Specimens identified as this species in the Hoying collection were *Thymelicus lineola*. Also, Price (1970) stated, without reference, that it "has been taken in central Ohio". *Atrytone arogos* is a little-understood prairie and grassland species found in scattered colonies along the Atlantic coast and in the Great Plains (Opler and Krizek, 1984). In Illinois it flies from late June to late July in association with bluestem grasses (*Andropogon scoparius* Michx. and *Andropogon gerardi* Vitman) (Sedman and Hess, 1985). Although this species is not known from the immediate vicinity of Ohio, it could possibly occur on some of the larger and less disturbed prairie remnants in western Ohio where bluestems are common.

***Problema byssus* (Edwards, 1880).** Byssus Skipper. Plate 39.

Problema byssus inhabits marshes along the Southeastern Coastal Plain and prairies and other grassy areas in the Midwest (Opler and Krizek, 1984; Scott, 1986). The Midwestern subspecies, *P. byssus kumskaka* (Scudder, 1887), ranges east to northeastern Indiana (Opler and Krizek, 1984). It has been suggested that this species may be expanding its range in the north (Irwin and Downey, 1973; Sedman and Hess, 1985; Scott, 1986) and may eventually be found in Ohio. In Illinois, adults are found from early June to early August (Sedman and Hess, 1985). In west-central Illinois, *P. byssus* is associated with big bluestem, *Andropogon gerardi* Vitman (Sedman and Hess, 1985). Potential habitats for *P. byssus* exist in northwestern Ohio where *A. gerardi* is abundant. The Oak Openings and adjacent areas in Lucas and Fulton Counties should be monitored for the presence of this species.

***Amblyscirtes aesculapius* (Fabricius, 1793).** Lace-winged Roadside Skipper. Plate 39.

Opler and Krizek (1984) included extreme southwestern Ohio on their distribution map of this species. Paul A. Opler (pers comm, 1985) indicated that this record is in error. *Amblyscirtes aesculapius* is a southeastern species found as far north as northern Kentucky (Opler and Krizek, 1984). A larval host plant, giant cane (*Arundinaria gigantea* [Walt.] Chapm.), is native and occurs locally in southern Ohio (Braun, 1961). However, there are few if any natural stands remaining, and most existing stands probably have spread from ornamental plantings near old homesites (Allison W. Cusick, pers comm, 1984). *Amblyscirtes aesculapius* should be searched for in these areas, especially in Adams and Clermont Counties, where native canebreaks once existed. In Virginia it is bivoltine, flying from late May to late September (Clark and Clark, 1951).

Family PAPILIONIDAE

Papilio joanae Heitzman, 1974. Missouri Woodland Swallowtail. Plate 40.

This recently recognized species (Heitzman, 1973) is known to occur in Missouri, Arkansas, and Kentucky (J. Richard Heitzman, pers comm, 1986). It is restricted to forests and forest clearings which distinguishes it from the very similar and sympatric *Papilio polyxenes*, which occurs in open habitats (Heitzman, 1974). Heitzman feels that as the typical habitat and hostplants are found over a wide range, *P. joanae* probably also occurs over a much wider range than is currently known, and that it is overlooked due to its resemblance to *P. polyxenes*. The hostplants, yellow pimpernel (*Taenidia integerrima* [L.] Drude), and meadow-parsnip (*Thaspium barbinode* [Michx.] Nutt), are both widespread and frequent in the unglaciated counties of Ohio (Cusick and Silberhorn, 1977). Observations of *P. joanae* in Missouri lead us to believe that suitable habitats may exist in southeastern Ohio. Any swallowtails resembling *P. polyxenes* found in forested situations deserve closer examination. *Papilio joanae* is multi-brooded, and flies from early April to early September (J. Richard Heitzman, pers comm, 1989). Although Scott (1986) acknowledges differences in adult appearance and behavior, larval morphology, habitat, and hostplant preference, he treats this species as a synonym of *P. polyxenes*.

Family PIERIDAE

Colias interior Scudder, 1862. Pink-edged Sulfur. Plate 40.

This species was reported from Seneca County by Henninger (1910) who remarked "one specimen taken June 1890". *Colias interior* is primarily a northern and montane Canadian Zone species of acidic habitats (Opler and Krizek, 1984). The nominate subspecies has been recorded in southeastern Michigan (Moore, 1960) and may once have been present in northern Ohio, either as a stray or local breeding resident. The single unverifiable record from Ohio may refer to the very similar *Colias philodice*. The hostplants of *C. interior* are blueberries (*Vaccinium* L. spp.). Three of the five species of blueberries that are listed as hostplants by Scott (1986) are recorded from Ohio (Weishaupt, 1971). It is unlikely that this species is a current breeding resident in the State, but it could stray into our area.

Family LYCAENIDAE

Incisalia polios Cook & Watson, 1907. Hoary Elfin. Plate 39.

Widespread north of Ohio, this species ranges south through the Appalachian mountains to Virginia (Opler and Krizek, 1984). The nominate subspecies has been recorded from southeastern Michigan (Moore, 1960) and western West Virginia (Drees and Butler, 1978). The only confirmed hostplant is bearberry, *Arctostaphylos uva-ursi* (L.) Spreng., but trailing arbutus, *Epigaea repens* L., has been suggested as a host in Pennsylvania (Shapiro, 1966). Although bearberry once occurred locally on beaches and dunes along Lake Erie in Erie and Ashtabula Counties, it is now thought to be extirpated (Braun, 1961). The last significant population of bearberry known from Ohio (Thomas, 1981) was visited in the late 1930's by John S. Thomas (pers comm, 1985) specifically to search for *I. polios*.

Although bearberry is very rare or extirpated in Ohio, trailing arbutus is widespread throughout the Appalachian and Allegheny Plateau Sections westward into the Great Lake Section, especially Erie County (Braun, 1961). In unglaciated Ohio, it is common on dry acidic slopes and in forests (Cusick and Silberhorn, 1977). In southern Michigan, *I. polios* flies from mid-April to late May (Moore, 1960). This species should be watched for in areas where trailing arbutus is common and along Lake Erie if populations of bearberry are discovered.

Leptotes marina (Reakirt, 1868). Marine Blue. Plate 39.

Although this species is not a resident northeast of Texas, strays have been recorded as far east as Kentucky and Indiana (Scott, 1986). This species resembles *Everes comyntas* in flight, and *L. marina* could be overlooked easily in the field. It may occur occasionally in Ohio and should be looked for in late summer and early autumn, particularly in open areas such as clover and alfalfa fields.

Family NYMPHALIDAE

Chlosyne gorgone (Hübner, 1810). Gorgone Checkerspot. Plate 40.

Chlosyne gorgone is endemic to the central United States, with isolated populations occurring as far east as Pennsylvania and New York (Scott, 1986; Shapiro, 1974). The northern subspecies, *C. gorgone carlota* (Reakirt, 1866), has been recorded in all states surrounding Ohio (Opler and Krizek, 1984). In Illinois, it is locally common in a variety of habitats including brushy meadows, wastelands, dry prairies, marshes, and town gardens (Sedman and Hess, 1985), and in Indiana it was reported from a fallow field (Masters and Masters, 1969). Irwin and Downey (1973) suggest that in Illinois *C. gorgone* has recently experienced a dramatic increase in abundance. If it is not present already, *C. gorgone* could spread into Ohio from the west. It should be looked for in association with the reported sunflower hostplants (*Helianthus* spp.), especially in prairie-like sites in gravelly or sandy areas not far from water (David F. Hess, pers comm, 1986). At least 15 species of *Helianthus* are reported from Ohio (Weishaupt, 1971), including several of the species known to be utilized by *C. gorgone*. Other hostplants occur in Ohio, notably greater ragweed, *Ambrosia trifida* L. (Iftner, 1983b) which is abundant throughout the State. In Illinois, *C. gorgone* flies from early May through late September (Irwin and Downey, 1973). In flight, this species can be easily confused with *C. nycteis* and large *P. tharos*.

Phyciodes batesii (Reakirt, 1865). Tawny Crescent. Plate 40.

This species has been reported in Ohio by many authors, the first being Strecker (1878). Bales (1909) considered this species "common along the small water courses" in Pickaway County, but did not list *Phyciodes tharos*. Henninger (1910) called this species "rather rare" in Seneca County. The most recent treatment was by Studebaker and Studebaker (1967), who stated that three specimens from Miami County were "confirmed to be this species" by R. M. Fox of the Carnegie Museum. These specimens were examined by us and found to be two aberrant males and one typical female of *P. tharos*. *Phyciodes batesii* is easily confused with *P. tharos*, and this may explain many of the early reports. *Phyciodes pascoensis*, a recently recognized species, also is confused easily with *P. batesii*. Before it was recognized as a separate entity, many *P. pascoensis* specimens were identified as *P. batesii* (Oliver, 1979).

Phyciodes batesii is primarily a northern species, although it does range south in the Appalachian Mountains to Georgia. This species has been reported in close proximity to Ohio in Michigan, Pennsylvania, and West Virginia. Many of the eastern populations have declined in recent years (Opler and Krizek, 1984). *Phyciodes batesii* is associated with shale barrens and rocky riparian slopes in West Virginia and Pennsylvania (Oliver, 1979), and should be watched for in similar habitats in the eastern and southeastern portions of Ohio. The hostplants include an aster (*Aster umbellatus* Mill.) (Opler and Krizek, 1984), which is common in fields and openings throughout unglaciated Ohio (Cusick and Silberhorn, 1977). In Virginia, this species flies from early June through early July, between the two broods of *P. tharos* (Clark and Clark, 1951).

Polygonia faunus (Edwards, 1862). Green Comma. Plate 40.

This species was reported by Hine (1898a; b) from the vicinity of Cincinnati. *Polygonia faunus* is a northern species closely associated with Canadian Zone forests as far south (in the mountains) as Georgia (Opler and Krizek, 1984). There is a remote chance that the northern nominate subspecies, or the Appalachian subspecies (*P. faunus smythi* Clark, 1937) could stray into Ohio. The single report from Ohio probably refers to *Polygonia comma* or *Polygonia progne*.

Polygonia satyrus (W. H. Edwards, 1869). Satyr Angle Wing. Plate 40.

This is primarily a western species that ranges eastward along the northern United States and Canada to New York and Newfoundland. (Ferris and Brown, 1981). There are several records from northern Indiana from June and July (Shull, 1987) and there is a remote possibility that this species could stray into Ohio. This species is very similar in appearance to *P. comma*, and could be easily overlooked by collectors not actively searching for unusual *Polygonia* species.

Nymphalis californica (Boisduval, 1852). California Tortoise Shell. Plate 40.

Not usually found east of the Rocky Mountains (Scott 1986), this species periodically experiences population explosions that result in emigrations far from its usual range. It has been recorded in at least eight eastern States including Illinois, Michigan, and Pennsylvania (Opler and Krizek, 1984). There is a remote chance that this species could stray into Ohio during a future eastward emigration surge.

Family SATYRIDAE

Enodia creola (Skinner, 1897). Creole Pearly Eye. Plate 40.

This species occurs in canebrakes throughout the southeastern United States as far north as central Kentucky (Opler and Krizek, 1984). Although usually reported from swampy areas, in the Allegheny Plateau Region of Kentucky it occurs in rich forested riparian habitats associated with the hostplant, giant cane, *Arundinaria gigantea* [Walt.] Chapm. (Loran D. Gibson, pers comm, 1984). *Arundinaria gigantea* occurs locally in southern Ohio (Braun, 1961). Although a native species, giant cane may now exist only in stands that have spread from cultivation (Allison W. Cusick, pers comm, 1984). There is a remote chance that *E. creola* occurs with these stands in areas that once supported native canebrakes in Adams and Clermont Counties. In Virginia, this species is multivoltine and flies between mid-June and mid-September (Clark and Clark, 1951). *Enodia creola* is strongly crepuscular, often flying at dusk and sometimes after dark.

10. SPECIES ERRONEOUSLY REPORTED FROM OHIO

Some species which have been attributed to Ohio in error are discussed in the previous section. Included here are those species reported from Ohio in the literature for which no supporting evidence has been found. The large number of skippers included is not surprising, given the difficulty of making accurate determinations prior to the publication of Lindsey's (1921) keys for North American Hesperioidea. We empathize with Klots (1951), who found that sometimes judgment must be based "as much on knowledge about the sources of the records as on the butterflies themselves".

Family HESPERIIDAE

Hesperia uncas Edwards, 1863. Uncas Skipper.

Several authors, including Kirkpatrick (1864) and Hine (1898a; b), listed this species from Ohio. *Hesperia uncas* is a western species and is not known to occur east of Iowa and Minnesota (Opler and Krizek, 1984) and should not be expected in Ohio. The erroneous original type locality of "Philadelphia Pennsylvania" probably contributed to this early confusion. Brown and Miller (1977) have since corrected the type locality to the vicinity of Denver, Colorado. The early Ohio records were probably based upon misidentifications, possibly of female *Atalopedes campestris* which can occasionally possess ventral hindwing patterns very reminiscent of *H. uncas*.

Hesperia comma (L., 1758). Comma Skipper.

This species was reported from Ohio by Henninger (1910) as "rare, taken Oct., 1891". *Hesperia comma* is a northern species and in the eastern United States it is not known to occur regularly south of northern Michigan and Wisconsin (Opler and Krizek, 1984). It should not be expected in Ohio. Henninger's record was probably based upon a misidentified specimen of *H. leonardus*, a species he did not list. The eastern subspecies, *H. comma laurentina* (Lyman, 1892), is similar in appearance to *H. leonardus*. The late date of the record also suggests *H. leonardus*, which flies later into autumn than *H. comma*.

Hesperia attalus (Edwards, 1871). Dotted Skipper.

Lindsey, Bell, and Williams (1931) commented that "the Barnes collection contains specimens labeled Ohio". The Barnes collection currently is deposited in the National Museum of Natural History. John M. Burns and William W. McGuire (pers comm, 1986) examined these specimens and found them to be misidentified. Macy and Shepard (1941) and Klots (1951) reported the species from Ohio but probably followed Lindsey, Bell, and Williams. On the strength of a record in an unpublished student report submitted to John Carroll University, Albrecht (1982) reported this species from Cuyahoga County. The *H. attalus* specimen upon which this record was based is now in the Cleveland Museum of Natural History and is *Polites origenes*. *Hesperia attalus* is primarily a local resident of the southeastern United States and Great Plains (Scott, 1986) and is not expected to occur in Ohio.

Problema bulenta (Boisduval & LeConte, 1834). Rare Skipper.

Kirtland (1854a) and Kirkpatrick (1864) listed this species from Rockport (vicinity of Cleveland), but both listings are probably based on the same record. *Problema bulenta* is found locally only along the Atlantic coast from Maryland south to Georgia (Opler and Krizek, 1984). The occurrence of this species in Ohio is highly unlikely. The reports from Ohio may refer to *Atrytone logan* or a female of some *Euphyes* species.

Poanes taxiles (Edwards, 1881). Taxiles Skipper.

Evans (1955) reported this species from Ohio on the basis of one male and one female in the British Museum of Natural History. Based on his experience with similarly labeled specimens in the British Museum, John M. Burns (pers comm, 1986) suggests that these specimens are probably misidentified or mislabeled, although he has not examined them personally. *Poanes taxiles* is a western species and is not known to occur east of Nebraska and South Dakota (Scott, 1986). Howe (1975), and Tilden and Smith (1986) also question eastern records.

Oligoria maculata (Edwards, 1865). Twin Spot Skipper.

Albrecht (1982) doubted a record included in an unpublished student report submitted to John Carroll University. The doubtful record may be based on a misidentified specimen of *Euphyes vestris* labeled *O. maculata* found in the Cleveland Museum of Natural History. Although strays have been recorded as far north as Pennsylvania (Teitz, 1952) and Massachusetts, this species is resident only along the southeastern coastal plain (Scott, 1986). It is highly unlikely that this species occurs in Ohio.

Family PAPILIONIDAE

Battus polydamas lucayus (Rothschild and Jordan, 1906). Polydamas Swallowtail.

Gerberg and Arnett (1989) noted that this species strays north to Ohio. In the eastern United States, this species is resident only in peninsular Florida (Opler and Krizek, 1984). Although a stray has been recorded from Kentucky (Covell, 1974), *B. polydamas* should not be expected in Ohio.

Family LYCAENIDAE

Fixsenia favonius (Smith, 1797). Southern Hairstreak.

"*Thecla favonius*" was reported from the vicinity of Cleveland and considered "rare" by Kirkpatrick (1864) and "among our most rare species" by Kirtland (1854a) who added that it was "occasionally seen hovering about oak bushes". Kirtland listed red oak (*Quercus rubra* L.) as the hostplant. Kirkpatrick based his report on a single specimen from Kirtland's collection, which apparently was determined by Thaddius William Harris. William Kayser also reported "*Thecla favonius*" from Auglaize County (Williamson, 1905). In the past, there has been much controversy concerning the historical usage of the name "*favonius*" for different species and it is unclear as to what species these authors actually were referring. As a result, Scudder (1876) doubted the accuracy of Kirtland's record. *Fixsenia favonius* is a resident species of southeastern Georgia south through Florida (Opler and Krizek, 1984). Although strays of this species have been reported for New Jersey and West Virginia (Klots, 1951), its occurrence in Ohio is extremely doubtful. The Ohio reports probably refer to a species of *Satyrium, Strymon melinus,* or extreme examples of *Fixsenia ontario*.

Family RIODINIDAE

Calephelis virginiensis (Guérin-Ménéville, 1831). Little Metalmark.

Holland (1931) remarked that this species is "common in parts of Ohio". This statement is probably in error, and intended for his discussion of *C. borealis*, which was discussed immediately after *C. virginiensis* in the text. Klots (1951) also reported this species from Ohio, but probably followed Holland. In addition, there is a specimen of this species bearing Ohio data in the Cincinnati Museum of Natural History. This specimen is undoubtedly mislabeled, as there are several *Calephelis borealis* specimens in the collection with the same date and locality as the above specimen, as well as several specimens of *C. virginiensis* from Florida collected by the same collector in the same year.

    C. virginiensis is a resident of the southeastern Coastal Plain. West of the Appalachian Mountains, it has not been reported north of Alabama (Opler and Krizek, 1984). The hostplant, yellow thistle (*Cirsium horridum* Michx.), does not occur in Ohio (Weishaupt, 1971). Although Drees and Butler (1978) reported this species from West Virginia, it should not be expected to be found in Ohio.

Family SATYRIDAE

Neonympha areolatus (Smith, 1797). Georgia Satyr.

This species was reported from Seneca County by Henninger (1910), who remarked "one specimen taken". Henninger did not collect the specimen personally, and doubted its validity. Except for populations in New Jersey, this species is primarily a resident of the southern coastal plain (Opler and Krizek, 1984), and should not be expected to occur in Ohio. The dubious Ohio record is probably based on a misidentified specimen of *Megisto cymela* or possibly *Neonympha mitchellii*.

GLOSSARY

The terms and definitions that follow relate directly to the preceding text and its context.

aberration. An atypical phenotype, such as an unusual wing pattern, which may be genetically or environmentally induced.

acidic soils. Soils having a pH of less than 7.

alkaline soils. Soils having a pH of greater than 7. These soils are usually derived from materials containing calcium carbonate ($CaCO_3$) such as limestone.

alleles. Two or more genes that occupy the same position on homologous chromosomes and that are responsible for contrasting traits.

anterior. Morphological term referring to areas near or towards the head.

aposomatic coloration. Bright and/or highly contrasting colors and color patterns that serve to warn potential predators of unpalatability and/or danger.

bait. A mixture of ingredients such as beer, molasses, and rotting fruit, used to attract butterflies and moths.

basking. A behavior that maintains or elevates body temperature by positioning the body and wings to absorb energy from sunlight.

Batesian mimicry. Mimicry wherein the mimetic species is palatable and the model species is unpalatable due to chemical or active defense.

bilateral gynandromorph. An aberrant individual that exhibits female traits on one side of the body and male traits on the other side of the body.

bimodal. Double peaked; refers to a temporal distributions in which a single brood has two distinct peaks of emergence.

biodiversity. A concept combining numbers and abundances of species occupying an area. As the numbers of species in an area decrease (or as one species increases in numbers at the expense of other species) biodiversity decreases.

biome. A broad geographical region shared by plants and animals with considerable interdependence (eg prairie, deciduous forest, coniferous forest).

bivoltine. Refers to species which have two generations annually.

calcareous soils. Soils possessing minerals rich in calcium, generally carbonates and bicarbonates, derived from limestone, dolomite, marble, and coral rock.

climax community. Plants and animals that assume final long-term occupation of a habitat if succession is allowed to continue without interruption.

clinal subspecies. Geographically defined subspecies which change gradually from one region to the next, with large areas of intergradation between the subspecies.

crespuscular. Refers to activity during the twilight of dusk, dawn, or both.

cryptic. Refers to an organism which blends into its environment, usually as a result of both color pattern and behavior.

deciduous. Woody plants that shed most or all of their leaves or small twigs at the same season (usually autumn) each year.

diapause. A period of arrested development, during which growth and development proceed at minimal rates if at all. Diapause is usually a developmental response limited to one life stage and allows an individual to survive predictable periods of unfavorable environmental conditions. It may be genetically or environmentally induced (see reproductive diapause).

dimorphism. A special case of polymorphism in which there are two distinct forms, usually variations of wing pattern, size, or shape, that are under direct genetic control.

discal cell. A centralized area of the wing which is nearly or completely enclosed by veins.

disjunct. A distribution in which two or more populations of a species occur at widely separated localities, frequently more than 100 km apart.

diurnal. Refers to activity during daylight hours.

dorsal. Morphological term which refers to the upper wing and body surfaces. (The opposite of ventral).

ecotype. A localized population which differs from other surrounding populations in the frequencies of certain genes.

emetic. An agent that induces vomiting.

endemic. Refers to species that are restricted to a geographic region.

ericaceous. Plants belonging to the heath family (Ericaceae).

extant. Refers to objects that exist at the present time (eg populations and species).

extinct. Refers to populations or species which no longer exist.

extirpated. Refers to species which have been eliminated from a limited geographic or political region.

facultative diapause. Diapause which is induced by environmental conditions such as the interplay between photoperiod and temperature.

falcate. Refers to wings which are hooked or curved at the distal apex.

family. A taxonomic concept used to group genera which are closely related. The concept implies that the genera are evolutionarily related.

foodplant. See hostplant.

form. See phenotype.

genotype. The genetic composition of an individual.

genus (pl, **genera**). A taxonomic concept used to group species which are closely related. The concept implies that the species contained within a genus are evolutionarily related.

geographic barrier. A land form or body of water which has prevented the migration of certain kinds of plants or animals from one side to the other.

glade. An opening within a forest.

gynandromorph. An aberrant individual that exhibits both male and female traits, usually in approximately equal proportions.

herbaceous. Plants having little or no woody tissue.

hill-topping. The congregation of butterflies, primarily males, on hilltops and other elevated areas. This behavior is assumed to be associated with mate location.

holotype. The individual specimen upon which the original description of a species or subspecies is based.

hostplant. A plant species which is suitable for oviposition and subsequent larval development.

immigrant. A species that normally breeds outside of the state, but regularly or irregularly establishes breeding populations within Ohio. These populations usually do not survive the winter.

indicator plants/animals. Species or communities which, by their presence, may denote environmental conditions peculiar to their respective habitats.

melanic. An individual or brood that is characterized by an increase of dark pigments (melanins) relative to typical individuals or broods.

melanin(s). A class of chemical pigments which impart dark gray, brown, or black colors.

mesic. A moist environment characterized by adequate precipitation coupled with slow infiltration of rain and melt-water through the soil.

migration. Directed movement of individuals, usually seasonal.

mimicry. An adaptation through which one species a "mimic" gains protection from predators by its resemblance to an inedible or distasteful species (a "model").

monophagous. Refers to species whose larvae feed on only one species or genus of hostplants.

morph. The physical appearance of an organism.

morphology. The study of the form and structure of organisms.

Müllerian mimicry. Mimicry wherein two or more unpalatable species resemble each other, and thereby gain mutual protection.

multivoltine. Refers to species which have more than two generations per year.

myrmecophily. The association between ants and larvae of certain butterflies, especially larvae of the Lycaenidae.

nectar. A solution found in flowers, generally containing sugar and amino acids.

nomenclature. A system of applying names to objects.

ocellus (pl, ocelli). A wing marking which resembles an eye. (Also, the small single-lens eye of an insect).

oviposition. The act of laying eggs.

palatable. Refers to the acceptability of an object (butterfly) as a food item to a potential predator.

paratype. A specimen included among the series of specimens used to describe a species or subspecies.

patrolling. A strategy used by males for locating potential mates in which the male flies through habitat likely to contain females. Potential mates are investigated as they are encountered.

perching. A strategy used by males for locating potential mates in which the male perches on a characteristic object, and flies out to investigate passing objects. Potential mates are investigated as they fly past the perch.

phenology. The appearance and disappearance of plants and animals throughout the course of the year.

phenotype. The morphological expression of a genotype. Phenotypes, although under genetic control, may also be modified by external factors such as photoperiod, moisture, and temperature.

photoperiod. The amount of daylight during the 24 hour cycle.

polymorphism. Having two or more forms (phenotypes), usually variations of wing pattern, size, or shape, that are under direct genetic control.

polyphagous. Refers to species whose larvae naturally feed on several different hostplants. This implies that the hostplants are spread among unrelated genera or families.

polyphenism. Having two or more forms (phenotypes), usually variations of wing pattern, size, or shape, that are influenced by environmental conditions such as temperature or photoperiod. These forms do not reflect genetic differences between phenotypes.

population. A group of interbreeding organisms, belonging to the same species, subspecies, or variety, which share a limited geographical area.

posterior. Morphological term which refers to regions away from the head and towards the rear.

relict. Species or populations of plants or animals surviving in local situations where surrounding areas are generally unfavorable to their migration or establishment. This implies that they were once part of a community type which once covered a region more extensively, and then disappeared as the result of changes in climate, geology, or human activity.

reproductive diapause. A period of arrested development found in adults, during which growth and development of the reproductive organs proceed at minimal rates. Reproductive diapause allows an individual to survive predictable periods of unfavorable environmental conditions and may be genetically or environmentally induced.

resident. A species that reproduces annually in Ohio and persists as some life stage continuously through the year.

sexual dimorphism. A special case of polymorphism in which males and females differ in morphology due to differences in sex-linked genes. This concept usually refers to differences in wing pattern, color, size, or shape, and is usually not applied to differences related to reproductive systems.

sexual mosaic. An aberrant individual that exhibits both male and female traits, usually with one sex dominating. This concept implies a mixing of sexual characters, rather than symmetry.

sibling species. Two or more species which are presumed to have shared a common ancestor so recently that morphological differences between the species are minimal.

species. A group of individuals or populations that are similar in structure and physiology and are capable of interbreeding and producing fertile offspring, and which are different in behavior, physiology, and/or structure from other such groups and normally do not interbreed with them. Species are usually morphologically recognizable, but need not be.

stigma. A sharply defined patch of scent scales located on the wings of butterflies.

stray. A species that breeds outside of the State, but sporadically wanders into Ohio. These species do not reproduce in Ohio and do not usually survive the winter.

subspecies. An isolated or geographically defined series of populations which differ behaviorally, morphologically, and/or physiologically from other such populations of the same species.

succession. A change in the composition of a biotic community over time, due to a variety of causes, involving changes in the environment and the introduction of competing species.

sympatric. Refers to species which occur in the same area.

synonym. A taxonomic name which is not currently in use because it has been superseded by an earlier or more valid name.

taxonomy. The theory and practice of classifying organisms.

temporal distribution. A species' distribution in time (ie adult flight periods).

territoriality. The active defense of a defined area (territory) containing some resource. In butterflies, it is usually the male which is territorial and the behavior is usually assumed to facilitate mate location.

thermoregulation. The process of regulating body temperature. In butterflies, this is usually accomplished by basking in, or avoiding, sunlight.

tibia (pl, tibiae). The fourth segment of a butterfly's leg.

type. See holotype.

type locality. The locality where the holotype of a species or subspecies was collected.

univoltine. Refers to species which have one generation per year.

unpalatable. Refers to the unacceptability of an object (butterfly) as a food item to a potential predator.

ventral. Morphological term referring to the under surfaces of the wings and body. (The opposite of dorsal).

xeric. An environment characterized by a deficiency of precipitation and therefore frequent drought, coupled usually with rapid run-off or infiltration of rain and melt-water through the soil.

xerothermic period. A warm, dry climatic condition believed to have prevailed in the post-Wisconsinan glacial time, estimated between 3500 and 3000 years ago.

BIBLIOGRAPHY

This bibliography was constructed to serve two purposes. First and foremost, it serves as a guide to the literature referenced throughout this text. Second, we hope that it will be used as a starting point at all levels for future research involving Ohio's butterflies. As such, it serves as a bibliography of the literature dealing with Ohio butterflies and includes all of the papers known to us which specifically treat the Ohio fauna, selected taxonomic revisions and collection inventories which are particularly relevant to Ohio, and faunal lists from adjacent states. Also included are selected general references and books which emphasize various aspects of butterfly biology.

Ackery, Phillip R. and Richard I. Vane-Wright. 1984. Milkweed butterflies. British Museum (Natural History), London. 425p.

Ahearn, Susan G. K. 1978. The potential for managing various insects and their habitats for educational purposes. M.S. Thesis. The Ohio State Univ. Columbus, Ohio. 161p.

Ahearn, Susan K. 1983. An analysis of the butterfly fauna of the Battelle-Darby Metropolitan Park. Unpublished report to the Ohio Dept. of Natural Resources. Columbus, Ohio. 52p.

Albrecht, Carl W. 1973. Lepidoptera of Cedar Bog. Ohio Biol. Surv. Info. Cir. No. 4:43-45.

_____ **1974.** The Lepidoptera of Cedar Bog, Champaign County, Ohio. I. An annotated checklist of the Rhopalocera. Ohio J. Sci. 74(2):126-132.

_____ **1982.** The taxonomy, geography, and seasonal distribution of Rhopalocera in Ohio. Ph.D. Dissert. The Ohio State Univ. Columbus, Ohio. 512p.

Albrecht, Carl W. and Reed A. Watkins. 1983. A cross reference to names of Ohio skippers and butterflies (Insecta: Lepidoptera: Hesperioidea and Papilionoidea). Ohio Biol. Surv. Info. Circ. No. 12. 20p.

Alcock, John and Kevin M. O'Neill. 1987. Territory preferences and intensity of competition in the grey hairstreak *Strymon melinus* (Lepidoptera, Lycaenidae) and the tarantula hawk *Hemipepsis ustulata* (Hymenoptera, Pompilidae). Am. Midl. Nat. 118(1):128-138.

Anderson, Dennis. 1983. The natural divisions of Ohio. Natural Areas J. 3(2):23-33.

Andreas, Barbara K. 1985. The relationship between Ohio peatland distribution and buried river valleys. Ohio J. Sci. 85(3):116-125.

_____ **1989.** The vascular flora of the glaciated Allegheny Plateau Region of Ohio. Ohio Biol. Surv. Bull. N. S. 8 (1). 191p.

Andrews, William V. 1875. [Captures of diurnal Lepidoptera]. Can. Entomol. 7(7):137.

Anonymous. 1883. The cabbage butterfly, or green worm (*Pieris rapae*). First Report of the Ohio Agr. Exp. Station for 1882:82.

_____ **1887.** Elm-leaf caterpillar, *Vanessa antiopa*, Linn. 5th Ann. Report of the Ohio Agr. Exp. Station for 1886:228.

_____ **1892.** [Migration of *Danaus archippus* in Cleveland, Ohio]. Cleveland Plain Dealer, 21 Sept.

_____ **1893.** Swarming of the *Archippus* butterfly. Insect Life 5(3):205-206.

_____ **1905.** Obituary of W. N. Tallant. Entomol. News 16 (3):96.

Arnold, Richard A. 1983. Ecological studies of six endangered butterflies (Lepidoptera, Lycaenidae): island biogeography, patch dynamics, and the design of habitat preserves. Univ. Calif. Publ. Entomol. 99:1-169.

Bales, Blenn R. 1907. [Migrating *Anosia plexippus*]. Entomol. News 18(9):402.

_____ **1909.** A partial list of the Lepidoptera of Pickaway County, Ohio. Entomol. News 20(4):169-177.

Benninghoff, William S. 1964. The prairie peninsula as a filter barrier to postglacial plant migration. Proc. Indiana Acad. Sci. 72:116-124.

Bowers, M. Deane. 1978. Observations on *Erora laeta* (Lycaenidae) in New Hampshire. J. Lepid. Soc. 32(2):140-144.

_____ **1980.** Unpalatability as a defense strategy of *Euphydryas phaeton*. Evolution 34:586-600.

Bracher, Ray W. 1976. Disappearance of Lepidoptera in Indiana and Ohio. Atala 4(1-2):29-30.

Braun, E. Lucy. 1961. The woody plants of Ohio. The Ohio State Univ. Press. Columbus, Ohio. 362p.

_____ **1967.** The Monocotyledoneae [of Ohio]: cat-tails to orchids. With Gramineae by Clara G. Weishaupt. The Ohio State Univ. Press. Columbus, Ohio. 464p.

Britton, Nathaniel L. and Addison Brown. 1913. An illustrated flora of the northeastern United States, Canada and British posses-

sions..., 2nd Edition. Charles Scribner's Sons. New York, New York. Volumes 1-3.

Brower, Lincoln P. 1969. Ecological chemistry. Scientific American 220(2):22-29.

Brown, F. Martin. 1967. Eugene Pilate (1804-1890). Entomol. News 78(3):57-59.

Brown, F. Martin and Lee D. Miller. 1977. Types of the hesperiid butterflies named by William Henry Edwards. Part II. Hesperiinae, Section I. Trans Am. Entomol. Soc. 103 (1):259-302.

Bubna, Mathias. 1897. Entomology at Cleveland, Ohio. Entomol. News 8(5):97-99.

Burns, John M. 1964. Evolution in skipper butterflies of the genus *Erynnis*. Univ. Calif. Publ. Entomol. 37:1-216.

_____ **1966a.** Expanding distribution and evolutionary potential of *Thymelicus lineola* (Lepidoptera: Hesperiidae), an introduced skipper, with special reference to its appearance in British Columbia. Can. Entomol. 98(8):859-866.

_____ **1966b.** Preferential mating versus mimicry: disruptive selection and sex-limited dimorphism in *Papilio glaucus*. Science 153:551-553.

_____ **1984.** Evolutionary differentiation: differentiating gold-banded skippers-*Autochton cellus* and more (Lepidoptera: Hesperiidae: Pyrginae). Smithson. Contr. Zool. 405:1-38.

_____ **1985.** *Wallengrenia otho* and *W. egeremet* in eastern North America (Lepidoptera: Hesperiidae: Hesperiinae). Smithson. Contr. Zool. 423:1-39.

Calhoun, John V. 1985[86]. An annotated list of the butterflies and skippers of Lawrence County, Ohio. J. Lepid. Soc. 39 (4):284-298.

_____ **1987[88].** Aberrant Polyommatinae (Lycaenidae) from Ohio and Florida. J. Res. Lepid. 26(1-4):264-266.

Calhoun, John V., Thomas J. Allen, and David C. Iftner. 1989[90]. Temporary breeding populations of *Phoebis sennae eubule* (L.) (Pieridae) in Ohio and West Virginia. J. Res. Lepid. 28(1-2):123-125.

Calhoun, John V. and David C. Iftner. 1988[89]. An additional natural hostplant of *Pieris virginiensis* (W. H. Edwards) (Pieridae) in Ohio. J. Res. Lepid. 27(2):141-142.

Cappuccino, Naomi and Peter Kareiva. 1985. Coping with a capricious environment: a population study of a rare pierid butterfly. Ecology 66(1):152-161.

Cardé, Ring T., Arthur M. Shapiro, and Harry K. Clench. 1970. Sibling species in the *eurydice* group of *Lethe* (Lepidoptera: Satyridae). Psyche 77(1):70-130.

Chermock, Frank H. 1929. Notes on North American Lepidoptera. Bull. Brooklyn Entomol. Soc. 24(1):20-21.

Chew, Francis S. 1977. The effects of introduced mustards (Cruciferae) on some native North American cabbage butterflies (Lepidoptera: Pieridae). Atala 5(2):13-19.

Clark, Austin H. 1932. The butterflies of the District of Columbia and vicinity. Smithson. Inst. Bull. 157:1-337.

_____ **1936.** The gold-banded skipper (*Rhabdoides cellus*). Smithson. Misc. Coll. 95(7):1-50.

Clark, Austin H. and Leila F. Clark. 1951. The butterflies of Virginia. Smithson. Misc. Coll. 116:1-239.

Claypole, Edward W. 1880. [Insects observed at Yellow Springs, Ohio]. Can. Entomol. 12(6):120.

_____ **1882.** Entomological notes for the summer of 1881. Can. Entomol. 14(1):17-18.

_____ **1897.** Butterflies found in Summit County, Ohio. Ohio State Acad. Sci. 5th Ann. Report 49.

Clench, Harry K. 1972. *Celastrina ebenina*, a new species of Lycaenidae (Lepidoptera) from the eastern United States. Ann. Carnegie Mus. 44:33-44.

_____ **1976.** *Nathalis iole* (Pieridae) in the southeastern United States and the Bahamas. J. Lepid. Soc. 30(2):121-125.

Clench, Harry K. and Paul A. Opler. 1983. Studies on nearctic *Euchloe*. Part 8. Distribution, ecology, and variations of

Euchloe olympia (Pieridae) populations. Ann. Carnegie Mus. 52:41-54.

Comstock, John H. and Anna Botsford Comstock. 1904. How to know the butterflies. D. Appleton and Co. New York, New York. 311p.

Conant, Helen S. 1868. Mid-summer butterflies. The Ohio Farmer 17(31):484-485. (August 1).

Cooperrider, Tom S., ed. 1982. Endangered and threatened plants of Ohio. Ohio Biol. Surv. Biol. Notes No. 11. Columbus, Ohio. 92p.

Courtney, Steven P. 1986. The ecology of pierid butterflies: dynamics and interactions. Advances in Ecological Research 15:51-131.

Covell, Charles V., Jr. 1974. A preliminary checklist of the butterflies of Kentucky. J. Lepid. Soc. 28(3):253-256.

Covell, Charles V., Jr., Loran D. Gibson, Richard A. Henderson, and Michael L. McInnis. 1979. Six new state butterfly records from Kentucky. J. Lepid. Soc. 33(3):189-191.

Cusick, Allison W. 1981. The prairies of Adams County, Ohio: 50 years after the studies of E. Lucy Braun. Pages 56-59 in The Prairie Peninsula-in the "shadow" of Transeau: Proceedings of the Sixth North American Prairie Conference, The Ohio State University, Columbus, Ohio, 12-17 August 1978. Ronald L. Stuckey and Karen J. Reese, eds. Ohio Biol. Surv. Biol. Notes No. 15. 278p.

Cusick Allison W. and Gene M. Silberhorn. 1977. The vascular plants of unglaciated Ohio. Ohio Biol. Surv. Bull. N. S. 5(4). 157p.

Cusick, Allison W. and K. Roger Troutman. 1978. The prairie area survey project. A summary of data to date. Ohio Biol. Surv. Info. Cir. No. 10. 60p.

Denton, Sherman F. 1900. As nature shows them; moths and butterflies of the United States, east of the Rocky Mountains. J. B. Millet Co. Boston, Massachusetts. 361p.

Doubleday, Edward. 1838. Communications on the natural history of North America. Entomol. Magazine 4:487-488; 5:21-34, 199-206, 269-300, 402-407, 409-417.

Doubleday, Edward, William C. Hewitson, and John O. Westwood. 1846-1850. The genera of diurnal Lepidoptera, comprising their generic characters, a notice of their habits and transformations, and a catalogue of the species of each genus; illustrated with 86 plates by W. C. Hewitson. Vol I. Longman, Brown, Green, and Longmans. London, England. 250p.

Douglas, Matthew M. 1986. The lives of butterflies. Univ. Michigan Press. Ann Arbor, Michigan. 241p.

Douglas, Matthew, M. and John W. Grula. 1988. Thermoregulatory adaptations allowing ecological range expansion by the pierid butterfly, *Nathalis iole* Boisduval. Evolution 32(4):776-783.

Drees, Bastiaan M. 1982. Four additional butterflies from Cedar Bog, Champaign County, Ohio. Ohio J. Sci. 82(3):141-142.

Drees, Bastiaan M. and Linda Butler. 1978. Rhopalocera of West Virginia. J. Lepid. Soc. 32(3):198-206.

Dury, Charles. 1878. Catalogue of the Lepidoptera observed in the vicinity of Cincinnati, Ohio. J. Cincinnati Soc. Nat. Hist. 1(1):12-23.

_____ **1898.** Zoological miscellany. J. Cincinnati Soc. Nat. Hist. 19(4):142.

_____ **1900.** Random notes on natural history. J. Cincinnati Soc. Nat. Hist. 19(5):171.

_____ **1910.** Ecological notes on insects. J. Cincinnati Soc. Nat. Hist. 21(2):61-63.

Edwards, William H. 1881. Is *Limenitis arthemis* a double-brooded species? Can. Entomol. 13(12):237-242.

_____ **1882a.** Note on *Limenitis ursula*. Can. Entomol. 14(2):29.

_____ **1882b.** Description of the preparatory stages of *Debis portlandia* Fabr. Can. Entomol. 14(5):84-88.

_____ **1884.** Revised catalogue of the diurnal Lepidoptera of America north of Mexico. Trans. Amer. Entomol. Soc. 11:245-337.

Ehle, George. 1958. *Adopaea lineola* (Hesperiidae) in Pennsylvania, a new state record. Lepid. News. 12(1-2):15-16.

Ehrlich, Paul R. and Ann H. Ehrlich. 1961. How to know the butterflies. W. C. Brown. Dubuque, Iowa. 262p.

Eliot, John N. and A. Kawazoe. 1983. Blue butterflies of the Lycaenopsis group. British Museum (Natural History). London, England. 309p.

Engle, Henry. 1908. A preliminary list of the Lepidoptera of western Pennsylvania collected in the vicinity of Pittsburgh. Ann. Carnegie Mus. 5(1):27-136.

Evans, William H. 1952. A catalogue of the American Hesperiidae indicating the classification and nomenclature adopted in the British Museum (Natural History), Part II, Pyrginae, Section 1. British Museum (Natural History). London, England. 178p.

_____ **1953.** A catalogue of the American Hesperiidae indicating the classification and nomenclature adopted in the British Museum (Natural History), Part III, Pyrginae, Section 2. British Museum (Natural History). London, England. 246p.

_____ **1955.** A catalogue of the American Hesperiidae indicating the classification and nomenclature adopted in the British Museum (Natural History), Part IV, Hesperiinae and Megathyminae. British Museum (Natural History). London, England. 499p.

Ferris, Clifford D. and F. Martin Brown. 1981. Butterflies of the Rocky Mountain States. Univ. of Oklahoma Press. Norman, Oklahoma. 442p.

Ferris, Clifford D., ed. 1989. Supplement to: A catalogue/checklist of the butterflies of America north of Mexico. Lepid. Soc. Memoir No. 3. 103p.

Field, William D. 1938. A manual of the butterflies and skippers of Kansas (Lepidoptera, Rhopalocera). Bull. Univ. Kansas 39(10):1-328.

Field, William D., Cyril F. dos Passos, and John H. Masters. 1974. A bibliography of the catalogs, lists, faunal and other papers on the butterflies of North America north of Mexico arranged by state and province (Lepidoptera: Rhopalocera). Smithson. Contrib. Zool. 157:1-104.

Finke, Mark D. and J. Mark Scriber. 1988. Influence on larval growth of the eastern black swallowtail butterfly *Papilio polyxenes* (Lepidoptera: Papilionidae) of seasonal changes in nutritional parameters of Umbelliferae species. Amer. Midl. Nat. 119(1):45-62.

Forbes, William T. M. 1960. Lepidoptera of New York and neighboring states. Part IV. Agaristidae through Nymphalidae, including butterflies. Cornell Univ. Agr. Exp. Sta., Mem. 371. Ithaca, New York. 188p.

Ford, E. B. 1975. Butterflies. Revised edition. William Collins Sons & Co. Ltd. Glasgow, Scotland. 368p.

Forsythe, Jane L. 1981. Geological setting of Ohio prairies. Pages 54-56 in The Prairie Peninsula-in the "shadow" of Transeau: Proceedings of the Sixth North American Prairie Conference, The Ohio State University, Columbus, Ohio, 12-17 August 1978. Ronald L. Stuckey and Karen J. Reese, eds. Ohio Biol. Surv. Biol. Notes No. 15. 278p.

Freeman, Hugh, A. 1942. Notes on some North American Hesperiidae with the description of a new race of *Polites verna* (Edwards) (Lepidoptera, Rhopalocera). Entomol. News 53(4):103-106.

_____ **1943.** A new form of *Hesperia leonardus* (Harris) from the middle western United States. Bull. Brooklyn Entomol. Soc. 38(5):153-154.

French, George H. 1886. The butterflies of the eastern United States. J. B. Lippincott Co. Philadelphia, Pennsylvania. 402p.

Friedlander, Timothy P. 1986[87]. Taxonomy, phylogeny and biogeography of *Asterocampa* Rober 1916. J. Res. Lepid. 25(4):215-338.

Gall, Lawrence F. 1976. The status of *Satyrium boreale* (Lycaenidae). J. Lepid. Soc. 30(3):214-218.

Gatrelle, Ronald R. and Richard T. Arbogast. 1974. A new subspecies of *Lethe appalachia* (Satyridae). J. Lepid. Soc. 28(4):359-363.

Gerberg, Eugene J. and Ross H. Arnett, Jr. 1989. Florida butterflies. Natural Science Publications, Inc. Baltimore, Maryland. 90p.

Gilbert, William M. 1960. *Danaus gilippus* in Ohio. J. Lepid. Soc. 14(1):36.

Gilbert, Lawrence E. and Michael C. Singer. 1975. Butterfly ecology. Ann. Rev. Ecol. Syst. 6:365-397.

Good, Albert I. 1901. Some observations on the development of *Feniseca tarquinius* Fab. Can. Entomol. 33(8):228.

Goodwin, George H., Jr. 1958. Earlier dates for *Libythea bachmanii* and *Macroglossa balteata*. Lepid. News 12(3-4):123.

Gordon, Robert B. 1966. Natural vegetation map of Ohio at the time of the earliest land surveys. Ohio Biol. Survey. Columbus, Ohio. 1 map.

Gordon, Robert B. 1969. The natural vegetation of Ohio in pioneer days. Ohio Biol. Surv. Bull. N. S. 3(2). 113p.

Gray, John E. and Edward Doubleday. 1844. List of the specimens of Lepidopterous insects in the collection of the British Museum. Part I. British Museum (Natural History). London, England. 150p.

Gunder, Jeane D. 1927. New transition forms or "abs". (Lepid. Rhopalocera). Bull. S. California Acad. Sci. 26(2):53.

Hammond, Paul C. and David V. McCorkle. 1983[84]. The decline and extinction of *Speyeria* populations resulting from human environmental disturbances (Nymphalidae: Argynninae). J. Res. Lepid. 22(4):217-224.

Harvey, Donald J. and Thomas A. Webb. 1980. Ants associated with *Harkenclenus titus*, *Glaucopsyche lygdamus* and *Celastrina argiolus* (Lycaenidae). J. Lepid. Soc. 34(4):371-372.

Heitzman, J. Richard. 1964. The early stages of *Euphyes vestris*. J. Res. Lepid. 3(3):151-153.

_____ 1965a. The life history of *Amblyscirtes belli* in Missouri. J. Res. Lepid. 4(1):75-78.

_____ 1965b. The life history of *Problema byssus* (Hesperiidae). J. Lepid. Soc. 19(2):77-81.

_____ 1973. A new species of *Papilio* from the eastern United States. J. Res. Lepid. 12(1):1-10.

_____ 1974. *Atrytonopsis hianna* biology and life history in the Ozarks. J. Res. Lepid. 13(4):239-245.

Heitzman, J. Richard and Joan E. Heitzman. 1987. Butterflies and moths of Missouri. Missouri Dept. of Conservation. Jefferson City, Missouri. 385p.

Heitzman, J. Richard and Roger L. Heitzman. 1974. *Atrytonopsis hianna* biology and life history in the Ozarks. J. Res. Lepid. 13(4):239-245.

Heitzman, J. Richard and Cyril F. dos Passos. 1974. *Lethe portlandia* (Fabricius) and *L. anthedon* (Clark), sibling species, with descriptions of new subspecies of the former (Lepidoptera: Satyridae). Trans. Amer. Ent. Soc. 100(1):52-99.

Henninger, Walter F. 1910. The Macro-Lepidoptera of Seneca County, Ohio. The Ohio Nat. 11(2):233-242.

Herrick, J. Arthur. 1974. The natural areas project - a summary of data to date. Ohio Biol. Surv. Info. Circ. No. 1. 60p.

Hine, James S. 1898a. List of butterflies known to have been taken in Ohio. Ohio State Acad. Sci. 6th Ann. Report: 22-27.

_____ 1898b. Ohio butterflies. J. Proc. Columbus Hort. Soc. 12(4):77-89.

_____ 1899. Additions to a list of butterflies known to have been taken in Ohio. Ohio State Acad. Sci. 7th Ann. Report 5.

Holland, William J. 1898. The butterfly book. Doubleday, Page, and Co. New York, New York. 382p.

_____ 1931. The butterfly book, new and thoroughly revised edition. Doubleday. Garden City, New York. 424p.

Howe, William H., ed. 1975. The butterflies of North America. Doubleday. Garden City, New York. 633p.

Hoying, Louis A. 1968. A migration of *Vanessa cardui* (Nymphalidae) in Ohio. J. Lepid. Soc. 22(2):118-119.

_____ 1975. A list of west central Ohio butterflies. News Lepid. Soc. No. 2/3:4.

Iftner, David C. 1983a. A new state butterfly record for Ohio. Ohio J. Sci. 83(1):67-68.

_____ 1983b. A new food plant record for *Chlosyne gorgone carlota* (Reakirt) (Nymphalidae). J. Lepid. Soc. 37(1):80-81.

Irwin, Roderick R. and John C. Downey. 1973. Annotated checklist of the butterflies of Illinois. Illinois Nat. Hist. Surv. Biol. Notes No. 81. 60p.

Jewett, Henry S. 1880. Notes on Lepidoptera. Can. Entomol. 12(11):228-231.

Johnson, Kurt. 1982-84[86]. Prairie and plains disclimax and disappearing butterflies in the central United States. Atala 10-12:20-30.

Keil, Ernst. 1915. An aberration of *Vanessa antiopa* (Lep.). Entomol. News 26(9):395.

Kennedy, Clarence H. 1931. Obituary of James Stewart Hine. Ohio J. Sci. 31 (6):510-511.

King, Charles C. 1981. Prairies of the Darby Plains in west-central Ohio. Pages 108-127 *in* The Prairie Peninsula-in the "shadow" of Transeau: Proceedings of the Sixth North American Prairie Conference, The Ohio State University, Columbus, Ohio, 12-17 August 1978. Ronald L. Stuckey and Karen J. Reese, eds. Ohio Biol. Surv. Biol. Notes No. 15. 278p.

Kirkpatrick, John. 1864. List of diurnal Lepidoptera found in the vicinity of Cleveland, Ohio. Proc. Entomol. Soc. Phil. 3 (September):228-230.

Kirtland, Jared P. 1851a. [Comments on Ohio Butterflies]. Trans. Entomol. Soc. London (New Series) 1:101-102.

_____ 1851b. *Libythea bachmanii*. The Family Visitor 2 (24)(Whole No. 76):189.

_____ 1852a. Description of a new species of *Libythea* and of *Macroglossa*. Amer. J. Sci. and Arts (Silliman) Second Series 13(39):336-338.

_____ 1852b. Peculiarities of climate, flora and fauna of the south shore of Lake Erie, in the vicinity of Cleveland, Ohio. Amer. J. Sci. and Arts (Silliman) Second Series 13 (39):215-219.

_____ 1854a. Diurnal Lepidoptera of northern and middle Ohio. Cleveland Acad. Nat. Sci. Ann. Sci. 2(1):5, 45-46; 2(3):73-75.

_____ 1854b. Localities and habits of certain species of insects. Amer. J. Sci. and Arts (Silliman) Second Series 17 (51):444.

_____ 1874a. Description of a new species of *Libythea* and of *Macroglossa*. Proc. Cleveland Acad. Nat. Sci. 1845-1859:171-173.

_____ 1874b. Diurnal Lepidoptera of northern and middle Ohio. Proc. Cleveland Acad. Nat. Sci. 1845-1859:17-25.

_____ 1874c. Peculiarities of climate, flora and fauna of the south shore of Lake Erie, in the vicinity of Cleveland, Ohio. Proc. Cleveland Acad. Nat. Sci. 1845-1859:165-171.

Klots, Alexander B. 1951. A field guide to the butterflies of North America, east of the Great Plains. Houghton Mifflin Co. Boston, Massachusetts. 349p.

Klots, Alexander B. and Cyril F. dos Passos. 1981. Studies of North American *Erora* (Scudder) (Lepidoptera: Lycaenidae). J. New York Entomol. Soc. 89(4):295-331.

Knapp, Ronald O. and Ansel M. Gooding. 1964. A radiocarbon-dated pollen profile from Sunbeam Prairie Bog, Darke County, Ohio. Amer. J. Sci. 262(2):259-266.

Kohler, Steve. 1977. Revision of North American *Boloria selene* (Nymphalidae) with description of a new subspecies. J. Lepid. Soc. 31(4):243-268.

Lafferty, Michael B., ed. 1979. Ohio's natural heritage. Ohio Acad. Sci. Columbus, Ohio. 324p.

Lafontaine, J. Donald. 1970. A redescription of *Strymon borealis* Lafontaine (Lycaenidae). J. Lepid. Soc. 24(2):83-86.

Langlois, Thomas H. 1964. Hackberry butterflies at South Bass Island. The Explorer 6(3):8-11.

Langlois, Thomas H. and Marina H. Langlois. 1964. Notes on the life-history of the hackberry butterfly, *Asterocampa celtis* (Bdvl. & Lec.) on South Bass Island, Lake Erie. Ohio J. Sci. 64(1):1-11.

Lederhouse, Robert. 1982. Territorial defense and lek behavior of the black swallowtail butterfly, *Papilio polyxenes*. Behav. Ecol. and Sociobiol. 10:109-118.

Lepidopterists' Society. 1949a. Annual summary. Lepid. News Vol. 2, supplement: VII.

_____ 1949b. Annual summary. Lepid. News 3(8-9):94.

_____ 1951. Annual summary. Lepid. News 5(8):99.

_____ 1967. Annual summary. News Lepid. Soc. No. 3:10.

_____ 1968. Annual summary. News Lepid. Soc. No. 3:14.

_____ 1969. Annual summary. News Lepid. Soc. No. 3:14.

_____ 1972. Annual Summary. News Lapid. Soc No. 2:17.

_____ 1974. Annual summary. News Lepid. Soc. No. 2:9.

_____ 1975. Annual summary. News Lepid. Soc. No. 2/3:9.

_____ 1976. Annual summary. News Lepid. Soc. No. 2:9.

_____ 1977. Annual summary. News Lepid. Soc. No. 2:11.

_____ 1979. Annual summary. News Lepid. Soc. No. 2:9.

_____ 1980. Annual summary. News Lepid. Soc. No. 2:19.

_____ 1984. Annual summary. News Lepid. Soc. No. 2:19.

Lindsey, Arthur W. 1921. The Hesperioidea of North America. Iowa Stud. Nat. Hist. 9(4):1-114.

Lindsey, Arthur W., Ernest L. Bell, and Roswell C. Williams, Jr. 1931. The Hesperioidea of North America. Denison Univ. Bull. J. Sci. Lab. 26:1-142.

Luebke, Heidi J., J. Mark Scriber, and Brian S. Yandell. 1988. Use of multivariate discriminant analysis of male wing morphometrics to delineate a hybrid zone for *Papilio glaucus glaucus* and *P. g. canadensis* in Wisconsin. Amer. Midl. Nat. 119(2):366-379.

MacNeill, C. Don. 1964. The skippers of the genus *Hesperia* in western North America with special reference to California (Lepidoptera: Hesperiidae). Univ. Calif. Publ. Entomol. 35:1-130.

_____ 1975. Family Hesperiidae. Pages 423-579 *in* W. H. Howe, ed. The butterflies of North America. Doubleday. Garden City, New York. 633p.

Macy, Ralph W. and Harold H. Shepard. 1941. Butterflies,.... Univ. Minn. Press. Minneapolis, Minnesota. 247p.

Mallis, Arnold. 1971. American Entomologists. Rutgers Univ. Press. New Brunswick, New Jersey. 549p.

Martin, Leland L. 1962. A whitish *Lycaena phlaeas* in Ohio. J. Lepid. Soc. 16(1):59.

Martin, Lloyd M. and Fred S. Truxal. 1955. A list of North American Lepidoptera in the Los Angeles County Museum. Part I:

butterflies (suborder Rhopalocera). Los Angeles County Museum. Los Angeles, California. 35p.

Masters, John H. and Wilma L. Masters. 1969. An annotated list of the butterflies of Perry County and a contribution to the knowledge of Lepidoptera in Indiana. Mid-Continent Lepid. Ser. No. 6. St. Paul, Minnesota. 25p.

Mather, Bryant. 1963. *Euphyes dukesi*. A review of knowledge of its distribution in time and space and its habitat. J. Res. Lepid. 2(2):161-169.

Mayfield, Harold F. 1965. Jared Potter Kirtland: Pioneer ornithologist of Ohio. Dept. Natural History, The Ohio Historical Soc. Columbus, Ohio. 8p.

Maynard, Charles J. 1891. A manual of North American butterflies. De Wolfe, Fiske & Co. Boston, Massachusetts. 226p.

McAlpine, Wilbur S. 1937. A case of mistaken identity and the discovery of a new metal mark (*Calephelis*) from Michigan (Lepidoptera, Rhiodinidae). Bull. Brooklyn Entomol. Soc. 32(2):43-49.

McAlpine, Wilbur S., Stephen P. Hubbell, and Thomas E. Pliske. 1960. The distribution, habits, and life history of *Euptychia mitchellii* (Satyridae). J. Lepid. Soc. 14(3):209-226.

McCance, Robert M., Jr., and James F. Burns, eds. 1984. Ohio endangered and threatened vascular plants. Abstracts of state listed species. Division of Natural Areas and Preserves, Ohio Dept. Natural Resources. Columbus, Ohio. 635p.

Metzler, Eric H. 1989. The Lepidoptera of Cedar Bog II. A checklist of the moths (in part) of Cedar Bog. Pages 29-32 in Robert C. Glotzhober, Anne Kochman, and William T. Schultz, eds. Cedar Bog Symposium II. Ohio Historical Society. Columbus, Ohio. 96p.

Metzler, Eric H. and John A. Shuey. 1989. Unusual butterflies and moths of the Oak Openings, Lucas County, Ohio. J. Stranahan Arboretum. Spring, 1989:7-10.

Metzler, Eric H. and Vincent P. Lucas. 1990. An endangered moth in Ohio, with notes on other species of special concern (Lepidoptera: Saturniidae, Sphingiidae, Notodontidae, and Arctiidae). Ohio J. Sci. 90(1):33-40.

Miller, Lee D. and F. Martin Brown. 1981. A catalogue/checklist of the butterflies of America north of Mexico. Lepid. Soc. Mem. No. 2. 280p.

Mitchell, Robert T. and Herbert S. Zim. 1962. Butterflies and moths. A guide to the more common American species. Golden Press. New York, New York. 160p.

_____ 1987. Butterflies and moths. A guide to the more common American species. Revised Edition. Golden Press. New York, New York. 160p.

Moeck, Arthur H. 1957. Geographical variability in *Speyeria*, comments, records, and description of a new subspecies (Nymphalidae). Published by the author. 48p.

Moore, Allen Y. 1875. [*Papilio asterius* larvae]. Can. Entomol. 7 (3):60.

Moore, Sherman. 1960. A revised annotated list of the butterflies of Michigan. Occas. Pap. Mus. Zool. Univ. Michigan. No. 617. 39p.

Morris, John G. 1862. Synopsis of the described Lepidoptera of North America. Part I: Diurnal and crepuscular Lepidoptera. Smithson. Misc. Coll. 358p.

Moseley, Edwin L. 1928. Flora of the Oak Openings. Proc. Ohio Acad. Sci. 8 Special Paper No. 20:80-134.

Myres, M. T. 1985. A southward return migration of painted lady butterflies, *Vanessa cardui*, over southern Alberta in the fall of 1983, and biometeorological aspects of their outbreaks into North America and Europe. Can. Field Naturalist 99(2):147-155.

Nabokov, Vladimir. 1949. The Nearctic forms of *Lycaeides* Hübner (Lycaenidae, Lepidoptera). Psyche 50(1-2):87-99.

Nault, Brian A., Roy W. Rings, and David J. Horn. 1989. Lepidoptera recorded from the islands of western Lake Erie, with a brief account of geology and flora. Great Lakes Entomol. 22(3):111-119.

Nielsen, Mogens C. 1970a. Distribution maps for Michigan butterflies. Part I. Skippers. Mid-Continent Lepid. Ser. No. 16. St. Paul, Minnesota. 10p.

_____ 1970b. New Michigan butterfly records. J. Lepid. Soc. 24(1):42-47.

_____ 1985. Notes on the habitat and foodplant of *Incisalia henrici* (Lycaenidae) and *Pyrgus centaureae* (Hesperiidae) in Michigan. J. Lepid. Soc. 39(1):62-68.

Ogden, J. Gordon, III. 1966. Forest history of Ohio. I. Radiocarbon dates and pollen stratigraphy of Silver Lake, Logan County, Ohio. Ohio J. Sci. 66(4):387-400.

_____ 1967. Radiocarbon and pollen evidence for a sudden change in climate in the Great Lakes region approximately 10,000 years ago. Pages 117-127 in Quaternary paleoecolgy, Edward J. Cushing and Herbert J. Wright, Jr., eds. Yale Univ. Press. New Haven, Conn. 431p.

Oliver, Charles G. 1979. Experimental hybridization between *Phyciodes tharos* and *Phyciodes batesii* (Nymphalidae). J. Lepid. Soc. 33(1):6-20.

_____ 1980. Phenotypic differentiation and hybrid breakdown within *Phyciodes* 'tharos' (Lepidoptera: Nymphalidae) in the northeastern United States. Ann. Entomol. Soc. Amer. 73(6):715-721.

Opler, Paul A. and George O. Krizek. 1984. Butterflies east of the Great Plains. Johns Hopkins Univ. Press. Baltimore, Maryland. 294p.

Osborn, Herbert. 1910. The Tallant collection [donated to Ohio State University]. The Ohio Naturalist 11(3):266.

_____ 1930. Bibliography of Ohio zoology. Ohio Biol. Surv. Bull. 23:353-410.

_____ 1937. Fragments of entomological history, including some personal recollections of men and events. Part I. Spahr and Glenn Co. Columbus, Ohio. 394p.

_____ 1946. Fragments of entomological history, including some personal recollections of men and events. Part II. Spahr and Glenn Co. Columbus, Ohio. 232p.

_____ 1948. Recent insect invasions of Ohio. Ohio Biol. Surv. Bull. 40:357-385.

Pallister, John C. 1927. *Cissia mitchelli* (French) found in Ohio with notes on its habits. Lepidoptera-Satyridae. Ohio J. Sci. 27(4):203-204.

Peattie, Donald C. 1922. The Atlantic Coastal Plain element in the flora of the Great Lakes. Rhodora 24 (280-281):57-70, 80-88.

Pengelly, D. H. 1960. *Thymelicus lineola* (Ochs.) (Lepidoptera: Hesperiidae) a pest of hay and pasture grasses in southern Ontario. Proc. Entomol. Soc. Ont. 91:189-197.

Pilate, George R. 1879. List of butterflies collected in Dayton, Ohio. Can. Entomol. 11(7):139-140.

_____ 1880. Interesting captures [*Thecla m-album* and *Junonia coenia* in Ohio]. Bull. Brooklyn Entomol. Soc. 3 (7):63.

_____ 1882. List of Lepidoptera taken in and around Dayton, Ohio. Papilio 2(5):65-71.

_____ 1906. Rare Ohio Lepidoptera. Entomol. News 17:31.

Pivnick, Kenneth A. and Jeremy N. McNeil. 1985. Mate location and mating behavior of *Thymelicus lineola* (Lepidoptera: Hesperiidae). Ann. Entomol. Soc. Amer. 78(5):651-656.

_____ 1987. Diel patterns of activity of *Thymelicus lineola* adults (Lepidoptera: Hesperiidae) in relation to weather. Ecol. Entomol. 12:197-207.

Platt, Austin P. 1968. Evolution of North American admiral butterflies. Bull. Entomol. Soc. Amer. 29(3):11-22.

Platt, Austin P. and Lincoln P. Brower. 1968. Mimetic versus disruptive coloration in intergrading populations of *Limenitis arthemis* and *astyanax* butterflies. Evolution 22(4):699-718.

Platt, Carolyn V. 1987. The Great Black Swamp. Timeline 4 (1):26-39.

Pliske, Thomas E. 1957[58]. Notes on *Atrytone dukesi*, a rare species new to southern Michigan (Hesperiidae). Lepid. News 11(1-3):42.

Porter, James W. 1965. An annotated list of butterflies for northwestern Ohio. J. Res. Lepid. 4(2):109-112.

Potter, Martha A. and Edward S. Thomas. 1970. Fort Hill. Ohio Historical Society. Columbus, Ohio. 38p.

Prescott, John M. 1984. The butterflies of Presque Isle State Park, Erie County, Pennsylvania. Melsheimer Entomol. Ser. No. 34:19-23.

Price, Homer F. 1961. Lepidoptera as prey of other insects. J. Lepid. Soc 15(2):93-94.

_____ 1970. Butterflies of northwestern Ohio. Mid-Continent Lepid. Ser. No. 14, St. Paul, Minn. 16p.

Price, Homer F. and Ernest M. Shull. 1969. Uncommon butterflies of northeastern Indiana. J. Lepid. Soc. 23(3):186-188.

Price, Peter W. 1984. Insect ecology, 2nd Ed. John Wiley and Sons, Inc. New York, New York. 607p.

Pyle, Robert M. 1981. The Audubon Society field guide to North American butterflies. Alfred A. Knopf, Inc. New York, New York. 916p.

_____ 1984. The Audubon handbook for butterfly watchers. Charles Scribner's Sons. New York, New York. 274p.

Randle, Worth S. 1953. Observations on the life history of *Calephelis borealis*. Lepid. News 7(3-6):119-122, 133-138.

Rawson, George W. 1931. The addition of a new skipper, *Adopaea lineola* (Ochs.), to the list of U.S. Lepidoptera. J. New York Entomol. Soc. 39(4):503-506.

_____ 1948. A new subspecies of *Lycaena epixanthe* Boisduval and LeConte with comments on the identity of typical *epixanthe* (Lepidoptera: Lycaenidae). J. New York Entomol. Soc. 56(1):55-62.

Rawson, George W. and John S. Thomas. 1939. The occurrence of *Hemiargus isola* (Reakirt) in northern Ohio. Ohio J. Sci. 34(1):9-10.

Remington, Charles L. 1942. The distribution of *Hemiargus isola* (Reakirt) east of the Mississippi River. Bull. Brooklyn Entomol. Soc. 37(1):6-8.

Riddlebarger, Joseph E. 1984. *Euchloe olympia*, a butterfly new to Ohio. Ohio. J. Sci. 84(5):267.

Riley, Thomas J. 1980. Effects of long and short day photoperiods on the seasonal dimorphism of *Anaea andria* (Nymphalidae) from central Missouri. J. Lepid. Soc. 34(4):330-337.

Rings, Roy W., Richard M. Ritter, Robert W. Hawes, and Eric H. Metzler. 1987. A nine year study of the Lepidoptera of the Wilderness Center, Stark County, Ohio. Ohio J. Sci. 87(3):55-61.

Rings, Roy W. and Eric H. Metzler. 1988. A preliminary annotated checklist of the Lepidoptera of Atwood Lake Park, Ohio. Ohio J. Sci. 88(4):159-168.

_____ 1989. A preliminary checklist of the Lepidoptera of Mohican State Forest and Mohican State Park, Ashland County, Ohio. Ohio J. Sci. 89(4):78-88.

_____ 1990. The Lepidoptera of Fowler Woods State Nature Preserve, Richland County, Ohio. Great Lakes Entomol. 23(1):43-56.

Ritland, David B. and Lincoln P. Brower, 1991. The viceroy butterfly is not a batesian mimic. Nature 350:497-498.

Robertson-Miller, Ellen. 1912. Butterfly and moth book. Charles Scribner's Sons. New York, New York. 249p.

Rothschild, M. and C. Farrell. 1983. The butterfly gardener. M. Joseph Ltd. London, England. 128p.

Rothschild, Walter, Ernst Hartert, and Karl Jordon. 1906. A revision of the American Papilios. Nov. Zool. 13(3):411-752.

Royer, Ronald A. 1988. Butterflies of North Dakota: an atlas and guide. Sci. Mon. No. 1. Minot State University. Minot, North Dakota. 192p.

Sampson, Homer C. 1930. Succession in the swamp forest formation in northern Ohio. Ohio J. Sci. 30(4):340-357.

Sauer, Jonathan D. 1988. Plant migration. Univ Calif. Press. Berkeley, California. 282p.

Saunders, William E. 1876. Notes of the year. 6th Ann. Rep. Entomol. Soc. Ontario for 1875:29-35.

_____ 1916. European butterfly found at London Ont. Ottawa Nat. 30:116.

Saunders, William E., Charles J. S. Bethune, and Robert V. Rogers. 1875. Meetings of the Entomological Club of the American Association for the Advancement of Science. Can. Entomol. 7(9):177-180.

_____ 1876. Meetings of the Entomological Club of the American Association for the Advancement of Science. 6th Ann. Report of the Entomol. Soc. Ontario for 1875:13-17.

Schultz, William T. 1976. Identifying common insects at Wahkeena Nature Preserve. Ohio Historical Soc. Columbus, Ohio. 7p.

Scott, James A. 1986. The butterflies of North America, a natural history and field guide. Stanford Univ. Press. Stanford, California. 583p.

Scriber, J. Mark and Mark H. Evans. 1986(87). An exceptional case of paternal transmission of the dark form female trait in the tiger swallowtail butterfly, *Papilio glaucus* (Lepidoptera: Papilionidae). J. Res Lepid. 25(2):110-120.

_____ 1987[88]. Bilateral gynandromorphs, sexual and/or color mosaics in the tiger swallowtail butterfly, *Papilio glaucus* (Lepidoptera: Papilionidae). J. Res. Lepid. 26(1-4):39-57.

Scriber, J. Mark and Mark Finke. 1978. New foodplant and oviposition records for the eastern black swallowtail, *Papilio polyxenes* on an introduced and a native umbelifer. J. Lepid. Soc. 32(3):236-238.

Scudder, Samuel H. 1876. Synonymic list of the butterflies of North America, north of Mexico. Part II. Rurales. Bull. Buffalo Soc. Nat. Sci. 3(3):98-129.

_____ 1877. The introduction and spread of *Pieris rapae* in North America, 1860-1885. Mem. Boston Soc. Nat. Hist. 4:53-69.

_____ 1889. The butterflies of the eastern United States and Canada with special reference to New England. 3 Vols. Cambridge, Massachusetts. Published by the author. 1958p.

Sedman, Yale and David F. Hess. 1985. The butterflies of west central Illinois. Western Ill. Univ. Ser. Biol. Sci. No. 11. 120p.

Shane, Linda C.K. 1976. Late-glacial and postglacial palynology and chronology of Darke County, west-central Ohio. Ph.D. Dissert. Kent State Univ. Kent, Ohio. 213p.

Shapiro, Arthur M. 1965. Ecological and behavioral notes on *Hesperia metea* and *Atrytonopsis hianna* (Hesperiidae). J. Lepid. Soc. 19(4):215-221.

_____ 1966. Butterflies of the Delaware Valley. Amer. Entomol. Soc. Special Publ. 79p.

_____ 1970a. Postglacial biogeography and the distribution of *Poanes viator* and other marsh butterflies. J. Res. Lepid. 9(3):125-155.

_____ 1970b. Seasonal polyphenism. Evol. Biol. 9: 259-330.

_____ 1974. Butterflies and skippers of New York State. Search Agriculture 4(3):1-60.

_____ 1979. *Erynnis baptisiae* (Hesperiidae) on crown vetch (Leguminoseae). J. Lepid. Soc. 33(4):258.

Shuey, John A. 1983. An annotated checklist of the butterflies of Athens County, Ohio. Ohio J. Sci. 83(5):262-269.

_____ 1984. A bilateral sexual mosaic of *Mitoura gryneus* (Lycaenidae). J. Lepid. Soc. 38(2):144-146.

_____ 1985. Habitat associations of wetland butterflies near the glacial maxima in Ohio, Indiana, and Michigan. J. Res. Lepid. 24(2):176-186.

_____ 1986. The ecology and evolution of wetland butterflies with emphasis on the genus *Euphyes* (Lepidoptera: Hesperiidae). Ph.D. Dissert. The Ohio State University. Columbus, Ohio. 157p.

_____ 1987. The ethics of introducing species. J. Ohio Native Plant Soc. 5(6):17-18.

_____ 1988(89). The morpho-species concept of *Euphyes dion* with the description of a new species (Hesperiidae). J. Res. Lepid. 27(3-4):160-172.

Shuey, John A., John V. Calhoun, and David C. Iftner. 1987. Butterflies that are endangered, threatened, and of special concern in Ohio. Ohio J. Sci. 87(4):98-106.

Shuey, John A., David C. Iftner, and John V. Calhoun. 1985[86]. The distribution of *Satyrium edwardsii* (Lepidoptera: Lycaenidae) in Ohio. Atala 13(2):1-3.

Shuey, John A., Eric H. Metzler, David C. Iftner, John V. Calhoun, John W. Peacock, Reed A. Watkins, Jeffrey D. Hooper, and William F. Babcock. 1987. Status and habitats of potentially endangered Lepidoptera in Ohio. J. Lepid. Soc. 41(1):1-12.

Shuey, John A. and John W. Peacock. 1985. A bilateral gynandromorph of *Celastrina ebenina* (Lycaenidae) J. Res. Lepid. 24(2):195-196.

_____ 1988(89). A significant new hostplant record for *Pieris virginiensis* (Pieridae). J. Res. Lepid. 27(3-4):259-260.

_____ 1989. Hostplant exploitation in an oligophagous population of *Pieris virginiensis* (Lepidoptera: Pieridae). Am. Midl. Naturalist 122(2):255-261.

Shull, Ernest M. 1977. Colony of *Pieris napi oleracea* (Pieridae) in Indiana. J. Lepid. Soc. 31(1):68-70.

_____ 1987. The butterflies of Indiana. Indiana Acad. Sci. and Indiana Univ. Press. Bloomington and Indianapolis, Indiana. 262p.

Shull, Ernest M. and F. Sidney Badger. 1972. Annotated list of the butterflies of Indiana, 1971. J. Lepid. Soc. 21(1):13-24.

Silberglied, R. E. and O. R. Taylor. 1973. Ultraviolet differences between the sulphur butterflies, *Colias eurytheme* and *C. philodice*, and a possible isolating mechanism. Nature 241:406-408.

Silberhorn, Gene M. 1970. A distinct phytogeographic area in Ohio: the Southeastern Allegheny Plateau. Castanea 35 (4):277-292.

Skinner, Henry. 1907a. The identity of *Thecla calanus* and *edwardsii*. Entomol. News 18(1):47-48.

_____ 1907b. Studies of *Thecla irus* Godart and *I. henrici* Grote and Robinson. Entomol. News 18(4):129-132.

Smalley, Stephen B. 1949. Observations from butterfly rearing. Lepid. News 3(3):25.

Stehr, William C. 1945. Notes and records of Lepidoptera in Ohio. Ohio J. Sci. 45(1):18.

Strecker, Ferdinand H. H. 1878. Butterflies and moths of North America,... a complete synonymical catalogue of Macro-

Lepidoptera, with full bibliography. B. F. Owen. Reading, Pennsylvania. 283p.

Stuckey, Ronald L. and Guy L. Denney. 1981. Prairie fens and bog fens in Ohio: Floristic similarities, difference, and geographical affinities. Pages 1-33 in Geobotany II. R. C. Romans, ed. Plenum Publishing. New York, New York. 271p.

Studebaker, Orville N. and Dennis J. Studebaker. 1967. Butterflies of Miami County, Ohio. Newsletter Assoc. Minnesota Entomol. 1(3):61-65.

Tallant, William N. 1881. [Comments on Terias nicippe in Ohio]. Can. Entomol. 13(1):115.

Teitz, Harrison M. 1952. The Lepidoptera of Pennsylvania, a manual. Penn. State Coll. Ag. Exper. Sta. State College, Pennsylvania. 194p.

Tekulsky, Matthew. 1985. The butterfly garden. Harvard Common Press. Harvard and Boston, Massachusetts. 144p.

Teraguchi, Sonja E. 1988. Migration of the monarch butterfly, Danaus plexippus plexippus (L.) in the island region of western Lake Erie. Pages 179-184 in The biogeography of the island region of western Lake Erie. Jerry F. Downhower, ed. The Ohio State Univ. Press. Columbus, Ohio. 280p.

Thomas, Edward S. 1940. Insect life-stories. Ohio State Archeological and Historical Soc. 15p.

_____ 1952. A European skipper, Adopaea lineola, at Columbus, Ohio. Lepid. News 6(6-8):92-93.

_____,1981. In Ohio woods and fields. Dispatch Printing Co. Columbus, Ohio. 122p.

Thompson, Isabel. 1939. Geographical affinities of the flora of Ohio. Amer. Midl. Nat. 21:730-751.

Tilden, James W. and Arthur C. Smith. 1986. A field guide to western butterflies. Houghton Mifflin Co. Boston, Massachusetts. 370p.

Transeau, H. E. 1935. The prairie peninsula. Ecology 16:423-437.

Trautman, Milton B. 1977. The Ohio country from 1750 to 1977-a naturalist's view. Ohio Biol. Surv. Biol. Notes No. 10. 25p.

_____ 1981. Some vertebrates of the Prairie Peninsula. Pages 40-42 in The Prairie Peninsula-in the "shadow" of Transeau: Proceedings of the Sixth North American Prairie Conference, The Ohio State University, Columbus, Ohio, 12-17 August 1978. Ronald L. Stuckey and Karen J. Reese, eds. Ohio Biol. Surv. Biol. Notes No. 15. 278p.

Tylka, Dave. 1987. Butterfly gardening and conservation. Missouri Dept of Conservation: Urban Wildlife Series Pamphlet No. 2.

United States Department of Agriculture. 1960. Index of plant diseases in the United States. Agriculture Handbook No. 165. 531p.

Urquhart, Fred A. 1960. The monarch butterfly. Univ. Toronto Press. Toronto, Ontario. 361p.

_____ 1976. Found at last: the monarch's winter home. National Geographic 150(2):161-173.

_____ 1987. The monarch butterfly: international traveler. Nelson-Hall. Chicago, Illinois 232p.

Vane-Wright, Richard I. and Phillip R. Ackery. 1984. The biology of butterflies. Academic Press. London, England. 429p.

Voss, Edward G. 1985. Michigan flora. A guide to the identification and occurrence of the native and naturalized seed-plants of the state. Part II. Dicots (Saururaceae-Cornaceae). Cranbrook Inst. Sci. Bull. No. 59 Univ. Mich. Herbarium. 724p.

Wagner, Warren H., Jr. 1978. The northern Great Lakes white, Pieris virginiensis (Lepidoptera: Pieridae) in comparison with its southern Appalachian counterpart. Great Lakes Entomol. 11(1):53-57.

Wagner, Warren H., Jr. and Michael K. Hansen. 1980. Size reduction southward in Michigan's mustard white butterfly, Pieris napi (Lepidoptera: Pieridae). Great Lakes Entomol. 13(2):77-80.

Wagner, Warren H., Jr. and T. Lawrence Mellichamp. 1978. Foodplant, habitat, and range of Celastrina ebenina (Lycaenidae). J. Lepid. Soc. 32(1):20-36.

Wagner, Warren H., Jr. and Amos H. Showalter. 1976. Ecological notes on Celastrina ebenina (Lycaenidae). J. Lepid. Soc. 30(4):310-312.

Warren, E. J. M. 1988. The country diary book of creating a butterfly garden. Henry Holt and Co. New York, New York. 144p.

Webster, Francis M. 1892. A flight of Danais archippus Fabr. Entomol. News 3(9):234-235.

_____ 1893. Some insect immigrants in Ohio. Science 21 (522):57-59.

_____ 1900a. Some notes on the larval habits of the gray hairstreak butterfly. 30th Ann. Report of the Entomol. Soc. Ontario for 1899:56-57.

_____ 1900b. [Larvae of Papilio asterius in Ohio.] Entomol. News 11(6):577.

_____ 1912. The migration of Anosia plexippus Fab. Can. Entomol. 44(12):366-367.

Webster, Reginald P. and Mogens C. Nielsen. 1984. Myrmecophily in the Edwards' hairstreak butterfly Satyrium edwardsii (Lycaenidae). J. Lepid. Soc. 38(2):124-133.

Weed, Clarence M. 1917. Butterflies worth knowing. Doubleday Page & Co. Garden City, New York. 286p.

Weishaupt, Clara G. 1971. Vascular plants of Ohio, a manual for use in field and laboratory. Kendall/Hunt Publ. Co. Dubuque, Iowa. 292p.

_____ 1985. A descriptive key to the grasses of Ohio based on vegetative characters. Ohio Biol. Surv. Bull. N. S. 7 (1). 99p.

Whan, Peter. 1990. The Gulf fritillary, Agraulis vanillae nigrior, recorded from Ohio. The Ohio Lepidopterist 12(4):65.

Whittlesey, Charles. 1874. Biographical notice of John Kirkpatrick, late secretary of the Cleveland Academy of Natural Science... Proc. Clev. Acad. Nat. Sci. 1845-1859:174-178.

Williams, Carrington B. 1930. The migration of butterflies. Oliver and Boyd. Edinburgh, Scotland. 473p.

_____ 1970. The migrations of the painted lady butterfly, Vanessa cardui (Nymphalidae), with special reference to North America. J. Lepid. Soc. 24(3):157-175.

Williams, Nelson N. 1962. Pollen analysis of two central Ohio bogs. Ph.D. Dissert. The Ohio State University. Columbus, Ohio. 68p.

Williamson, Charles W. 1905. History of western Ohio and Auglaize County. W. M. Linn and Sons. Columbus, Ohio. 860p.

Wormington, Alan. 1982. Preliminary annotated list of the butterflies of Point Pelee National Park. Parks Canada. Cornwall, Ontario. Unpublished. 43p.

Wormsbacher, Henry. 1918. Collecting in Ohio during the spring of 1918. Lepidoptera 2(10):75-77.

Wright, David M. 1983. Life history and morphology of the immature stages of the bog copper butterfly Lycaena epixanthe (Boisduval and LeConte) (Lepidoptera: Lycaenidae). J. Res. Lepid. 22(1):47-100.

Wyss, Albert E. 1930a. Papilio asterius, Fabricius, variation. Proc. Junior Soc. Nat. Sci. 1(3):7.

_____ 1930b. A list of Rhopalocera taken in Cincinnati and vicinity. Proc. Junior Soc. Nat. Sci. 1(8-9):4-6.

_____ 1931. Additions to the list of Cincinnati Rhopalocera. Proc. Junior Soc. Nat. Sci. Memorial Number 59.

_____ 1932. Guide to the butterflies of Cincinnati and vicinity. Junior Soc. Nat. Sci. Misc. Publ. 7. 37p.

Wyss, Herbert, E. 1930. Report of the curator of entomology for 1930. Proc. Junior Soc. Nat. Sci. 1(12):7-8.

_____ 1931. Entomological notes of 1930. Proc. Junior Soc. Nat. Sci. 2(1):9-11.

Xerces Society. 1987. Fourth of July butterfly counts for 1986. Supplement to Atala 15:21.

APPENDIX I: REGIONAL LEPIDOPTEROLOGICAL SOCIETIES

ORGANIZATION	FOCUS/FUNCTION
The Idalia Society of Mid-American Lepidopterists c/o J. Richard Heitzman 3112 South Harris Avenue Independence, MO 64052-2732	Focuses on the Lepidoptera of mid-America. Newsletter emphasizes activities of the organization and information pertaining to the Lepidoptera of the region. Sponsors meetings and field trips.
The Kentucky Lepidopterists c/o Dr. Charles V. Covell, Jr. Department of Biology University of Louisville Louisville, KY 40292	Focuses on the Lepidoptera of Kentucky. Publishes quarterly newsletter emphasizing new records, field reports, meeting reports, and membership list. Sponsors annual meeting and field trips.
The Lepidoptera Research Foundation 9620 Heather Road Beverly Hills, CA 90210	Publishes *Journal of Research on the Lepidoptera*, a peer-reviewed journal of international scope. Newsletter emphasizes international news and issues affecting the Foundation.
The Lepidopterists Society c/o Dr. William D. Winter, Jr. 257 Common Street Dedham, MA 02026-4020	Publishes the *Journal of the Lepidopterists Society*, a peer-reviewed journal of international scope. Bi-monthly newsletter emphasizes national/international issues, membership concerns, collecting techniques, collecting records, and membership list. Annual meeting emphasizes Lepidoptera biology and systematics.
Michigan Entomological Society c/o Department of Entomology Michigan State University East Lansing, MI 48824	Publishes *The Great Lakes Entomologist*, a peer-reviewed journal emphasizing insect biology in the Great Lakes region. Sponsors annual meeting and field trips. Quarterly newsletter addresses a wide variety of entomological issues.
The Ohio Lepidopterists c/o Eric H. Metzler 1241 Kildale Square N Columbus, OH 43229-1306	Focuses on the Lepidoptera of Ohio. Quarterly newsletter emphasizes natural history, conservation, collecting, meeting reports, and butterfly gardening. Sponsors the Ohio Survey of Lepidoptera, two annual meetings, numerous field trips, and museum visits.
The Southern Lepidopterists' Society c/o Thomas M. Neal 1705 NW 23rd Street Gainesville, FL 32605	Focuses on the Lepidoptera of the southeastern United States. Quarterly newsletter emphasizes collecting and natural history. Sponsors annual meeting and field trips.
The Xerces Society 10 SE Ash Street Portland, OR 97204	Focuses on global invertebrate conservation issues. Publishes biannual newsletter, *Wings*, which emphasizes ongoing programs. Sponsors 4th of July butterfly counts. Annual meetings emphasize global bioconservation issues.
Young Entomologists' Society 1915 Peggy Place Lansing, MI 48910-2553	Provides publications and programs for younger students of insects. Focuses on natural history, collection, and identification.

APPENDIX II: OHIO COUNTY ABBREVIATIONS CODE

County	Code	County	Code
Adams	ADA	Licking	LIC
Allen	ALL	Logan	LOG
Ashland	ASD	Lorain	LOR
Ashtabula	ATB	Lucas	LUC
Athens	ATH	Madison	MAD
Auglaize	AUG	Mahoning	MAH
Belmont	BEL	Marion	MAR
Brown	BRO	Medina	MED
Butler	BUT	Meigs	MEG
Carroll	CAR	Mercer	MER
Champaign	CHP	Miami	MIA
Clark	CLA	Monroe	MOE
Clermont	CLE	Montgomery	MOT
Clinton	CLI	Morgan	MRG
Columbiana	COL	Morrow	MRW
Coshocton	COS	Muskingum	MUS
Crawford	CRA	Noble	NOB
Cuyahoga	CUY	Ottawa	OTT
Darke	DAR	Paulding	PAU
Defiance	DEF	Perry	PER
Delaware	DEL	Pickaway	PIC
Erie	ERI	Pike	PIK
Fairfield	FAI	Portage	POR
Fayette	FAY	Preble	PRE
Franklin	FRA	Putnam	PUT
Fulton	FUL	Richland	RIC
Gallia	GAL	Ross	ROS
Geauga	GEA	Sandusky	SAN
Greene	GRE	Scioto	SCI
Guernsey	GUE	Seneca	SEN
Hamilton	HAM	Shelby	SHE
Hancock	HAN	Stark	STA
Hardin	HAR	Summit	SUM
Harrison	HAS	Trumbull	TRU
Henry	HEN	Tuscarawas	TUS
Highland	HIG	Union	UNI
Hocking	HOC	Van Wert	VAN
Holmes	HOL	Vinton	VIN
Huron	HUR	Warren	WAR
Jackson	JAC	Washington	WAS
Jefferson	JEF	Wayne	WAY
Knox	KNO	Williams	WIL
Lake	LAK	Wood	WOO
Lawrence	LAW	Wyandot	WYA

INDEX OF REPORTED OHIO HOSTPLANTS

Scientific names are listed *Genus species*. Common names are listed noun, modifier.

166

INDEX TO COMMON NAMES OF BUTTERFLIES AND SKIPPERS

Numerals separated by a hyphen indicate information which continues from one page to the next; numerals separated by a comma indicate disjointed references. A **bold** page number indicates the page upon which the species discussion begins.

INDEX TO TAXA OF BUTTERFLIES AND SKIPPERS

Linnean binomials are listed both *Genus species* and *species, Genus*. Family names also are listed. Numerals separated by a hyphen indicate information which continues from one page to the next; numerals separated by a comma indicate disjoint references. A **bold** page number indicates the page upon which the species discussion begins; a page number in *italics* refers to an illustration within a plate.

PLATES

THE PLATES EXPLAINED

Plates 3-6 illustrate habitats supporting uncommon to rare lepidopterans. As such, they overemphasize the forests and clearings of southern Ohio, the wetlands of glaciated Ohio, and the Oak Openings. Ohio counties named in the captions are abbreviated following a 3-letter code provided by the Ohio Department of Transportation (Appendix II); North = N; South = S; East = E; West = W; Central = C. Butterflies listed also are biased toward the more uncommon species, and are not representative of the entire fauna likely to be encountered.

Plate 7 illustrates butterfly behaviors, emphasizing passive behaviors which facilitate photography. Ohio counties are abbreviated as above.

Plates 8-40 illustrate Ohio's butterflies and skippers. Within the plate heading are spelled out the names of the genera included on that plate; the genus name is spelled out upon first appearance in a caption or row only if more than one genus represented on that plate begins with the same letter. Following the first appearence of a species name within a caption or row is the page number on which the species account begins in the text. Caption rows are arranged vertically from the top to the bottom of each page; specimens making up a row are arranged from left to right. Species are presented in phylogenetic order, approximating the text. Codes used in the captions are: Dorsal = D; Lateral = L; Ventral = V; ♀ = female; ♂ = male; months are abbreviated to their first three letters; Ohio counties are abbreviated as above; only the collector's last name is given.

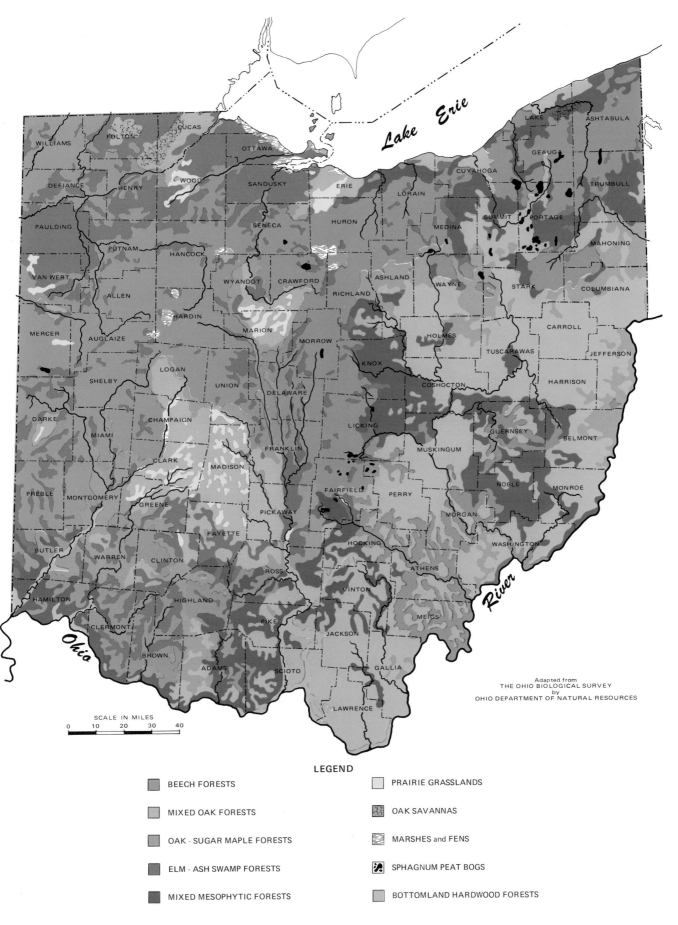

LEGEND

⬛ BEECH FORESTS		⬛ PRAIRIE GRASSLANDS	
⬛ MIXED OAK FORESTS		⬛ OAK SAVANNAS	
⬛ OAK - SUGAR MAPLE FORESTS		⬛ MARSHES and FENS	
⬛ ELM - ASH SWAMP FORESTS		⬛ SPHAGNUM PEAT BOGS	
⬛ MIXED MESOPHYTIC FORESTS		⬛ BOTTOMLAND HARDWOOD FORESTS	

Adapted from
THE OHIO BIOLOGICAL SURVEY
by
OHIO DEPARTMENT OF NATURAL RESOURCES

Plate 1. The natural vegetation of Ohio (Gordon, 1969).

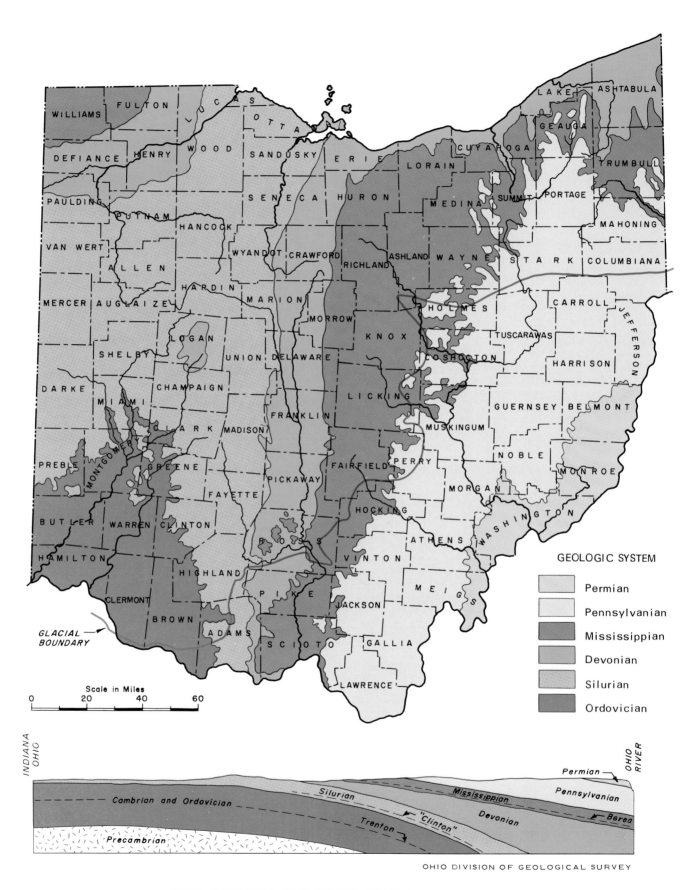

GEOLOGIC SYSTEM

- Permian
- Pennsylvanian
- Mississippian
- Devonian
- Silurian
- Ordovician

Scale in Miles

0   20   40   60

GLACIAL BOUNDARY

INDIANA
OHIO

Cambrian and Ordovician

Precambrian

Trenton

Silurian

"Clinton"

Devonian

Mississippian

Berea

Pennsylvanian

Permian

OHIO RIVER

OHIO DIVISION OF GEOLOGICAL SURVEY

GEOLOGIC MAP AND CROSS SECTION OF OHIO

Plate 2.   Geologic map and cross-section of the bedrock of Ohio. Ohio Department of Natural Resources, Division of Geological Survey.

Plate 3.   **Forested Habitats**

Row 1.   **Oak-pine forest SCI;** rich forest habitat in Shawnee State Forest and associated openings supporting one of the State's most diverse assemblages of butterflies. Less often encounted spp. along this ridgetop include *Hesperia metea, Amblyscirtes vialis, A. hegon, Satyrium edwardsii, Incisalia augustus, I. henrici, I. niphon, Glaucopsyche lygdamus, Cyllopsis gemma, Hemeuptychia sosybius.* **Mixed-oak forest,** SCI; more mesic area of Shawnee State forest, just down-slope from the previous habitat. Uncommon spp. - *Anthocharis midea, Incisalia henrici, Celastrina ebenina.*

Row 2.   **Mixed-oak forest with beech, ATH;** topography provides an ideal setting for "hilltopping" ♂ ♂ , *Eurytides marcellus* and *Anthocharis midea* ♂ ♂ are frequently sighted. Other butterflies - *Erynnis* spp., *Cyllopsis gemma, Cercyonis p. alope.* **Mixed-oak forest, LAW;** near Lake Vesuvius, supports *Euchloe olympia,* remainder of fauna similar to previous photograph.

Row 3.   **Bottomland forest, PIK;** such forests in S Ohio support a rich spring fauna including *Erynnis* spp., *Eurytides marcellus, Papilio glaucus, P. troilus, Anthocharis midea, Celastrina neglecta-major, C. ebenina.* **Bottomland forest, MRW;** such forests in C and NE Ohio support *Pieris virginiensis, Erynnis brizo, E. juvenalis, Papilio cresphontes, Nymphalis antiopa, Polygonia comma, Enodia anthedon.*

Plate 4.   Wetlands and Prairies

Row 1.   **Sedge meadow/fen, ROS;** such habitats in glaciated Ohio support *Polites mystic, Poanes massasoit, P. viator, Euphyes dion, E. conspicua, E. bimacula, Lycaena hyllus, Euphydryas phaeton, Satyrodes eurydice, Cercyonis p. nephele*. **Bog fen, POR;** such fens in NE Ohio support *Polites mystic, Poanes viator, Euphyes dion, E. conspicua, Satyrium acadica, Euphydryas phaeton, Satyrodes eurydice*. Part of the "Streetsboro Swamp", this fen is botanically very similar to habitats supporting *Neonympha mitchellii* and *Lycaena dorcas* in S Michigan.

Row 2.   **Prairie fen, LOG;** typical WC Ohio habitat for *Polites mystic, Poanes massasoit, Euphyes bimacula, Satyrium acadica, Calephelis muticum, Boloria selene, Nymphalis milberti, Satyrodes eurydice*. (Dr. John W. Peacock provides the human scale). **Bog, POR;** Ohio's bogs support many lepidopterans, but support few butterflies-*Ancyloxypha numitor, Euphyes conspicua, Satyrium liparops, Speyeria* spp., *Cercyonis p. nephele. Lycaena epixanthe*, possibly once resident in NE Ohio, is restricted to bogs which support its hostplant, cranberry.

Row 3.   **Swamp, LOG;** C and NW Ohio—typical habitat for *Euphyes dukesi, Satyrodes appalachia;* other uncommon species are *Papilio cresphontes, Satyrium acadica, Fixsenia ontario, Polygonia progne*. **Mesic prairie, MAD;** such moist prairies support *Polites* spp., *Atrytone logan, Papilio polyxenes, Speyeria* spp., *Boloria bellona, Satyrodes eurydice, Cercyonis p. nephele, Danaus plexippus*.

176

Plate 5.   **Prairies and Oak Openings**

Row 1.   **Mesic prairie, ATH;** small prairie with a diverse fauna dominated by species which characterize woodland borders in the Allegheny Plateau — *Thorybes* spp., *Erynnis* spp. (including *martialis*), *Polites* spp., *Atrytone logan, Poanes hobomok, P. zabulon, Amblyscirtes hegon, Anthocharis midea, Incisalia henrici, Celastrina ladon, C. ebenina, Glaucopsyche lygdamus, Speyeria* spp., *Enodia anthedon,* and *Cyllopsis gemma*. **Xeric prairie, ADA;** species — *Erynnis* spp., *Thorybes* spp., *Polites* spp., *Papilio* spp., *Anthocharis midea, Satyrium calanus, S. edwardsii, Calycopis cecrops, Mitoura gryneus, Incisalia henrici, Speyeria cybele, S. aphrodite, Phyciodes tharos, Chlosyne nycteis, Enodia anthedon, Hermeuptychia sosybius, Cercyonis pegala, Danaus plexippus*.

Row 2.   **Xeric opening in deciduous forest (S Ohio).** Species — *Erynnis* spp., *Hesperia metea, H. sassacus, Atrytonopsis hianna, Satyrium calanus, Calycopis cecrops, Polygonia interrogationis, P. comma, Vanessa atalanta*. **Oak Openings old field/prairie, LUC;** disturbed community supporting a rich variety of native plants and several unusual butterflies including *Erynnis baptisiae, E. persius, Hesperia leonardus, Atrytonopsis hianna, Satyrium acadica, S. edwardsii, Incisalia irus, Lycaeides melissa, Boloria selene*. This field supported the last known population of *Lycaeides melissa* in Ohio.

Row 3.   **Dune community, LUC;** endangered community supporting the largest assemblage of rare butterflies in Ohio. Endangered spp.—*Erynnis persius, Incisalia irus,* and (at one time) *Lycaeides melissa samuelis*. Other unusual spp.—*Hesperia leonardus, Atrytonopsis hianna, Satyrium edwardsii*. **Dune community, LUC;** more disturbed than previous community, this photograph shows the spread of lupine (in bloom) into recently disturbed soils. Same spp. as previous habitat.

177

Plate 6.   **Disturbed Habitats**

Row 1.   **Overgrown railroad right-of-way through bottomland forest, ATH;** supports a wide variety of spp.—*Autochton cellus, Amblyscirtes hegon, Anthocharis midea, Parrhasius m-album, Celastrina ebenina, C. neglecta-major, Hermeuptychia sosybius.* **Powerline cut supporting *Andropogon scoparius*, GUE;** typical habitat in S Ohio for *Pyrgus centaureae, Hesperia metea, H. sassacus, Atrytonopsis hianna.*

Row 2.   **Pasture, MAD;** such habitats are notable for supporting immigrants — *Pyrgus communis, Atalopedes campestris, Phoebis sennae, Eurema lisa, E. nicippe, Euptoieta claudia, Junonia coenia.* **Wet clearing, HIG;** such disturbed wetlands are important habitats in S Ohio for *Feniseca tarquinius, Lycaena hyllus, Boloria bellona, Euphydryas phaeton.*

Row 3.   **Alfalfa field, HUR;** such fields support few breeding populations of butterflies but are important sources of nectar and can attract adults of many species from adjacent habitats — most of the common skippers, swallowtails, whites, sulphurs; also *Everes comyntas, Speyeria* spp., *Boloria bellona, Phyciodes tharos, Vanessa* spp., *Danaus plexippus.* **Fallow field, HUR;** such fields are important habitats for butterflies which use hostplants that colonize abandoned agricultural fields rapidly; breeding species include *Staphylus hayhurstii, Pholisora catullus, Pontia protodice, P. rapae, Colias philodice, C. eurytheme, Everes comyntas, Danaus plexippus.*

Plate 7. **Behaviors.**

Row 1. ***Erynnis brizo*, LAW;** dorsal basking behavior with wings held outstretched; a characteristic basking posture of many Pyrginae. ***Hesperia metea*, SCI;** Perching/dorsal basking behavior with wings held at an angle above the body, a basking posture characteristic of Hesperiinae. ***Papilio polyxenes*, FRA;** feeding behavior at flowers.

Row 2. ***Eurytides marcellus*, HIG;** feeding behavior at wet sand, large groups may be encountered, forming "mud puddle clubs". ***Anthocharis midea*, SCI;** early morning roosting posture; this individual presumably spent the night on the protected perch under the leaves of its hostplant, toothwort. ***A. midea*, LAW;** courtship behavior, (♂ hovering over a perched ♀); courtship was unsuccessful and the ♂ flew away.

Row 3. ***Incisalia augustus*, SCI;** feeding behavior at flower. ***I. irus*, LUC;** lateral basking behavior typical of elfins and many hairstreaks; this individual is resting on lupine, its hostplant. ***Satyrium edwardsii*, LUC;** perching behavior; this individual is also rubbing its hindwings together in an alternating up and down fashion, a behavior found in most hairstreaks and elfins, and in some blues.

Row 4. ***Cyllopsis gemma*, SCI;** lateral basking behavior. ***Satyrodes appalachia*, WIL;** dorsal basking behavior. ***S. appalachia*, WIL;** perching behavior with this individual occupying a "strategic" leaf which provides a clear view of all activity occurring in a small swampland clearing.

179

Plate 8. Hesperiidae: *Epargyreus, Urbanus, Autochton, Achalarus, Thorybes.* (Specimens approx. 85% life size).

Row 1. *E. c. clarus*, D♂, 16 Aug 1986, JEF, Iftner, p. 28.
E. c. clarus, D♀, 9 Aug 1986, PUT, Calhoun.
E. c. clarus, V♂, ex-larva, 27 Aug 1988, PIK, Calhoun.

Row 2. *U. p. proteus*, D♂, 9 Jan 1986, Lee Co., FL, Calhoun, p. 28.
U. p. proteus, V♂, 18 Dec 1981, Lee Co., FL, Calhoun.
Autochton cellus, D♂, 16 May 1987, GAL, Iftner, p. 29.

Row 3. *A. cellus*, V♀, 25 Jun 1984, LAW, Calhoun.
Achalarus lyciades, D♂, 17 May 1986, GAL, Iftner, p. 30.
A. lyciades, V♀, 4 Jul 1983, ATH, Calhoun.

Row 4. *T. bathyllus*, D♂, 11 Jun 1988, MOE, Calhoun, p. 30.
T. bathyllus, D♀, 18 Jun 1984, LAW, Iftner.
T. bathyllus, V♂, 1 Jun 1984, LUC, Calhoun.

Row 5. *T. pylades*, D♂, 17 May 1982, VIN, Calhoun, p. 31.
T. pylades, D♀, 4 May 1986, SCI, Iftner.
T. pylades, V♂, 19 Jun 1984, LAW, Calhoun.

Row 6. *T. confusis*, D♂, 11 Jun 1981, Boone Co., KY, Gibson, p. 32.
T. confusis, D♀, 9 Jun 1978, Boone Co., KY, Gibson.
T. confusis, V♂, 29 May 1988, ADA, Parshall.

Plate 9. **Hesperiidae: *Staphylus* and *Erynnis*.** (Specimens approx. life size).

Row 1.
S. hayhurstii, D♂ , 24 Jul 1988, ADA, Calhoun, p. 32.
S. hayhurstii, V♂ , 28 May 1988, ADA, Iftner.
S. hayhurstii, D♀ , 24 Jul 1988, ADA, Calhoun.
S. hayhurstii, V♀ , 28 May 1988, ADA, Iftner.

Row 2.
E. icelus, D♂ , 27 May 1987, TUS, Iftner, p. 33.
E. icelus, V♂ , 12 May 1988, ROS, Calhoun.
E. icelus, D♀ , 14 May 1988, COL, Calhoun.
E. icelus, V♀ , 14 May 1988, COL, Iftner.

Row 3.
E. b. brizo, D♂ , 10 Apr 1988, ADA, Iftner, p. 34.
E. b. brizo, V♂ , 19 Apr 1987, FAI, Calhoun.
E. b. brizo, D♀ , 18 Apr 1987, ADA, Calhoun.
E. b. brizo, V♀ , 12 Apr 1986, SCI, Iftner.

Row 4.
E. j. juvenalis, D♂ , 30 Apr 1988, BRO, Iftner, p. 35.
E. j. juvenalis, V♂ , 16 May 1987, LAW, Iftner.
E. j. juvenalis, D♀ , 7 May 1988, ALL, Iftner.
E. j. juvenalis, V♀ , 15 May 1982, LOG, Calhoun.

Row 5.
E. horatius, D♂ , 25 Apr 1984, LAW, Calhoun, p. 36.
E. horatius, V♂ , 27 Apr 1984, LAW, Calhoun.
E. horatius, D♀ , 3 May 1986, JAC, Iftner.
E. horatius, V♀ , 5 Sep 1987, MIA, Calhoun.

Row 6.
E. martialis, D♂ , 16 May 1987, GAL, Iftner, p. 36.
E. martialis, D♀ , 27 May 1985, LAW, Calhoun.
E. martialis, V♀ , 4 May 1985, LAW, Calhoun.
E. baptisiae, D♂ , spring phenotype, 30 Apr 1987, DEL, Calhoun, p. 38.

Row 7.
E. baptisiae, V♂ , spring phenotype, 30 Apr 1987, DEL, Calhoun.
E. baptisiae, D♂ , summer phenotype, 25 Aug 1986, PER, Calhoun.
E. baptisiae, D♀ , summer phenotype, 16 Aug 1986, HAS, Iftner.
E. baptisiae, V♂ , summer phenotype, 29 Aug 1984, LAW, Calhoun.

Row 8.
E. lucilius, D♂ , 12 May 1962, Middlesex Co., MA, Burns, p. 37.
E. lucilius, V♂ , 14 May 1965, Middlesex Co., MA, Burns.
E. lucilius, D♀ , 14 May 1965, Middlesex Co., MA, Burns.
E. lucilius, V♀ , 30 May 1962, Middlesex Co., MA, Burns.

181

Plate 10. **Hesperiidae: _Erynnis, Pyrgus, Pholisora, Nastra, Ancyloxypha, Copaeodes, Thymelicus, Hylephila, Hesperia._** (Specimens approx. life size).

Row 1.　*E. p. persius*, D♂ , 26 May 1980, LUC, Iftner, p. 39.
　　　　E. p. persius, V♂ , 12 May 1984, LUC, Calhoun.
　　　　E. p. persius, D♀ , 19 May 1984, LUC, Calhoun.
　　　　E . p. persius, V♀ , 19 May 1984, LUC, Calhoun.

Row 2.　*Pyrgus centaureae wyandot*, D♂ , 27 Apr 1986, HOC, Iftner, p. 40.
　　　　P. c. wyandot, V♂ , 27 Apr 1986, HOC, Iftner.
　　　　P. c. wyandot, D♀ , 27 Apr 1986, HOC, Calhoun.
　　　　P. c. wyandot, V♀ , 27 Apr 1986, HOC, Iftner.

Row 3.　*Pyrgus communis*, D♂ , 21 Sep 1986, SCI, Calhoun, p. 40.
　　　　P. communis, V♂ , 8 Sep 1985, GAL, Calhoun.
　　　　P. communis, D♀ , 8 Sep 1985, GAL, Calhoun.
　　　　P. communis, V♀ , 18 Oct 1986, SCI, Calhoun.

Row 4.　*Pholisora catullus*, D♂ , 21 May 1988, WOO, Iftner, p. 41.
　　　　P. catullus, V♂ , 31 Aug 1985, HAN, Calhoun.
　　　　P. catullus, ex-ovum, 7 Aug 1988, ADA, Calhoun.
　　　　P. catullus, V♀ , 9 Jun 1984, PUT, Iftner.

Row 5.　*N. lherminier*, D♂ , 27 May 1985, MEG, Calhoun, p. 42.
　　　　N. lherminier, D♀ , 14 Aug 1983, GAL, Calhoun.

　　　　N . lherminier, V♂ , 16 Aug 1983, GAL, Calhoun.
　　　　A. numitor, D♂ , 16 Aug 1986, JEF, Iftner, p. 43.
　　　　A. numitor, D♀ , 17 Aug 1985, WOO, Calhoun.

Row 6.　*A. numitor*, V♂ , 29 May 1987, LOG, Calhoun.
　　　　C. minima, D♂ , 9 Mar 1987, Lee Co., FL, Calhoun, p. 43.
　　　　C. minima, D♀ , 12 Mar 1987, Dade Co., FL, Calhoun.
　　　　C. minima, V♂ , 10 Dec 1982, Lee Co., FL, Calhoun.
　　　　T. lineola, D♂ , 26 Jun 1983, HOC, Iftner, p. 44.
　　　　T. lineola, D♀ , 26 Jun 1983, HOC, Iftner.

Row 7.　*T. lineola*, V♂ , 20 Jun 1982, POR, Calhoun.
　　　　T. lineola, D♂ , form 'pallida', 26 Jun 1979, FRA, Calhoun.
　　　　Hylephila p. phyleus, D♂ , 30 Aug 1987, MAD, Calhoun, p. 45.
　　　　H. p. phyleus, V♂ , 9 Aug 1987, MAR, Calhoun.
　　　　H. p. phyleus, D♀ , 1 Mar 1987, Lee Co., FL, Calhoun.

Row 8.　*Hylephila p. phyleus*, V♀ , 17 Dec 1981, Lee Co., FL, Calhoun.
　　　　Hesperia l. leonardus, D♂ , 22 Aug 1988, MEG, Iftner, p. 45.
　　　　H. l. leonardus, D♀ , 24 Aug 1986, LUC, Calhoun.
　　　　H. l. leonardus, V♀ , 24 Aug 1986, LUC, Iftner.

182

Plate 11. **Hesperiidae:** *Hesperia, Polites, Wallengrenia, Pompeius.* (Specimens approx. life size).

Row 1.
H. m. metea, D♂ , 29 Apr 1987, ATH, Iftner, p. 46.
H. m. metea, V♂ , 7 May 1988, HOC, Parshall.
H. m. metea, D♀ , 1 May 1987, SCI, Calhoun.
H. m. metea, V♀ , 1 May 1988, PIK, Iftner.

Row 2.
H. s. sassacus, D♂ , 25 May 1987, CAR, Iftner, p. 47.
H. s. sassacus, V♂ , 25 May 1987, CAR, Calhoun.
H . s. sassacus, D♀ , 25 May 1987, STA, Calhoun.
H. s. sassacus, V♀ , 19 Jun 1984, POR, Iftner.

Row 3.
Polites coras, D♂ , 9 Jun 1984, FUL, Iftner, p. 48.
P. coras, V♂ , 26 Jul 1986, ALL, Calhoun.
P. coras, D♀ , 23 Aug 1986, KNO, Iftner.
P. coras, V♀ , 16 Aug 1987, FAY, Iftner.

Row 4.
Polites themistocles, D♂ , 17 May 1986, JAC, Calhoun, p. 48.
P. themistocles, V♂ , 17 May 1986, GAL, Iftner.
P. themistocles, D♀ , 31 Jul 1986, KNO, Iftner.
P. themistocles, V♀ , 5 Sep 1986, FAI, Calhoun.

Row 5.
Polites o. origenes, D♂ , 18 Jun 1984, LAW, Iftner, p. 49.
P . o. origenes, V♂ , 29 Aug 1983, LAW, Calhoun.
P . o. origenes, D♀ , 17 Aug 1986, BEL, Iftner.
P. o. origenes, V♀ , 1 Jun 1986, FAI, Calhoun.

Row 6.
Polites m. mystic, D♂ , 9 Jun 1984, LUC, Calhoun, p. 50.
P. m. mystic, V♂ , 6 Jun 1982, POR, Calhoun.
P. m. mystic, D♀ , 9 Jun 1984, FUL, Iftner.
P. m. mystic, V♀ , 6 Jun 1982, POR, Calhoun.

Row 7.
W. egeremet, D♂ , 28 Jun 1985, FRA, Calhoun, p. 51.
W. egeremet, V♂ , 16 Jun 1986, HOL, Calhoun.
W. egeremet, D♀ , 2 Jul 1987, FRA, Calhoun.
W. egeremet, V♀ , 6 Jun 1983, VIN, Calhoun.

Row 8.
Pompeius verna, D♂ , 14 Jun 1987, GAL, Calhoun, p. 52.
P. verna, V♂ , 26 Jun 1983, HOC, Iftner.
P. verna, D♀ , 16 Jun 1985, DEL, Calhoun.
P. verna, V♀ , 28 Jun 1986, VIN, Peacock.

Plate 12. **Hesperiidae:** *Atalopedes, Atrytone, Poanes, Euphyes.* (Specimens approx. life size).

Row 1.
Atalopedes campestris huron, D♂ , 19 Sep 1987, HAM, Iftner, p. 52.
A. c. huron, V♂ , 19 Sep 1987, HAM, Iftner.
A. c. huron, D♀ , 8 Sep 1985, GAL, Calhoun.
A. c. huron, V♀ , 14 Sep 1984, LAW, Calhoun.

Row 2.
Atrytone l. logan, D♂ , 6 Jul 1986, MAR, Iftner, p. 53.
A. l. logan, D♀ , 5 Jul 1987, MAR, Iftner.
A. l. logan, V♂ , 19 Jun 1987, LOG, Calhoun.
P. m. massasoit, D♂ , 28 Jun 1984, CHP, Iftner, p. 54.
P. m. massasoit, D♀ , 6 Jul 1986, LOG, Calhoun.

Row 3.
P. m. massasoit, V♂ , 9 Jul 1982, WIL, Calhoun.
P. h. hobomok, D♂ , 21 May 1988, SAN, Iftner, p. 55.
P. h. hobomok, V♂ , 5 May 1987, CAR, Iftner.
P. h. hobomok, D♀ , 28 May 1988, ADA, Calhoun.

Row 4.
P. h. hobomok, V♀ , 1 Jun 1987, CLA, Iftner.
P. h. hobomok, D♀ , form 'pocahantas', 1 Jun 1988, PIK, Calhoun.

P. h. hobomok, V♀ , form 'pocahantas', 13 Jun 1980, FRA, Calhoun.
P. zabulon, D♂ , 21 May 1988, SAN, Iftner, p. 56.

Row 5.
P. zabulon, V♂ , 21 May 1988, SAN, Iftner.
P. zabulon, D♀ , 10 Aug 1987, MOR, Calhoun.
P. zabulon, V♀ , 22 May 1988, MEI, Calhoun.
P. v. viator, D♂ , 17 Jul 1983, POR, Iftner, p. 57.

Row 6.
P. v. viator, D♀ , 13 Jul 1986, HUR, Calhoun.
P. v. viator, V♂ , 17 Jul 1983, POR, Iftner.
E. dion, D♂ , 10 Jul 1986, CHP, Calhoun, p. 57.
E. dion, D♀ , 11 Jul 1987, PUT, Calhoun.

Row 7.
E. dion, V♀ , 10 Jul 1986, CHP, Calhoun.
E. dukesi, D♂ , 11 Jul 1987, PUT, Calhoun, p. 58.
E. dukesi, D♀ , 5 Jul 1987, WYA, Iftner.
E. dukesi, V♂ , 10 Jul 1986, UNI, Calhoun.

Plate 13. **Hesperiidae: *Euphyes, Atrytonopsis, Amblyscirtes, Lerodea, Panoquina, Calpodes.*** (Specimens approx. life size).

Row 1.   *E. c. conspicua*, D♂ , 7 Jul 1984, HEN, Calhoun, p. 59.
            E. c. conspicua, V♂ , 5 Jul 1987, MAR, Iftner.
            E. c. conspicua, D♀ , 13 Jul 1986, MAR, Iftner.
            E. c. conspicua, V♀ , 8 Jul 1987, DEL, Calhoun.

Row 2.   *E. b. bimacula*, D♂ , 27 Jun 1986, Clinton Co., PA, Calhoun, p. 60.
            E. b. bimacula, V♂ , 10 Jun 1985, LOG, Iftner.
            E. b. bimacula, D♀ , 25 Jun 1939, STA, Baker.
            E. b. bimacula, V♀ , 26 Jun 1939, STA, Baker.

Row 3.   *E. vestris metacomet*, D♂ , 17 May 1986, GAL, Iftner, p. 61.
            E. v. metacomet, V♂ , 24 Jul 1987, MAD, Calhoun.
            E. v. metacomet, D♀ , 11 Jun 1988, MOE, Calhoun.
            E. v. metacomet, V♀ , 12 Jul 1987, DAR, Iftner.

Row 4.   *Atrytonopsis h. hianna*, D♂ , 16 May 1987, LAW, Calhoun, p. 61.
            A. h. hianna, V♂ , 23 May 1981, LUC, Iftner.
            A. h. hianna, D♀ , 5 Jun 1984, LUC, Calhoun.
            A. h. hianna, V♀ , 23 May 1986, LUC, Iftner.

Row 5.   *Amblyscirtes hegon*, D♂ , 4 May 1986, SCI, Calhoun, p. 62.
            A. hegon, D♀ , 22 May 1988, MEG, Iftner.
            A. hegon, V♀ , 22 May 1988, MEG, Calhoun.
            A. vialis, D♂ , 1 May 1987, JAC, Iftner, p. 63.
            A. vialis, D♀ , 12 May 1988, ROS, Calhoun.

Row 6.   *A. vialis*, V♀ , 18 May 1987, GAL, Iftner.
            A. belli, D♂ , 16 May 1987, Christian Co., KY., Gibson, p. 64.
            A. belli, D♀ , 30 Jul 1982, Davidson Co., TN, Ashby.
            A. belli, V♂ , 16 May 1987, Christian Co., KY, Gibson.
            L. eufala, D♂ , 3 Mar 1987, Highlands Co., FL, Calhoun, p. 64.

Row 7.   *L. eufala*, D♀ , 18 Sep 1983, Monroe Co., FL, Calhoun.
            L. eufala, V♂ , 9 Mar 1987, Lee Co., FL, Calhoun.
            P. ocola, D♂ , 30 Aug 1987, MAD, Calhoun, p. 65.
            P. ocola, V♂ , 18 Mar 1984, Collier Co., FL, Calhoun.
            C. ethlius, D♂ , 13 Dec 1982, Lee Co., FL, Calhoun, p. 65.
            C. ethlius, V♂ , 9 Mar 1987, Lee Co., FL, Calhoun.

Plate 14. **Papilionidae: *Battus*, *Eurytides*, *Papilio*.** (Specimens approx. 50% life size).

Row 1.   *B. p. philenor*, D♂ , 1 May 1987, JAC, Iftner, p. 66.
           B. p. philenor, D♀ , 21 May 1980, FRA, Calhoun.
           B. p. philenor, V♀ , 4 May 1986, SCI, Iftner.

Row 2.   *E. m. marcellus*, D♂ , form 'marcellus', 10 Apr 1988, ADA, Iftner, p. 67.
           E. m. marcellus, D♂ , form 'telamonides', 4 Jun 1979, FRA, Calhoun.
           E. m. marcellus, D♂ , form 'lecontei', ex-ovum, 3 Jun 1988, ROS, Calhoun.

Row 3.   *E. m. marcellus*, V♂ , form 'marcellus', 14 Apr 1986, NOB, Iftner.
           P. polyxenes asterius, D♂ , 15 May 1980, DEL, Calhoun, p. 68.

Row 4.   *P. p. asterius*, D♀ , ex-ovum, 11 Oct 1988, KNO, Calhoun.
           P. p. asterius, V♀ , 31 Aug 1986, CRA, Iftner.

Plate 15. **Papilionidae:** *Papilio.* (Specimens approx. 50% life size).

Row 1. *P. cresphontes*, D♂ , ex-larva, 23 Jul 1988, FRA, Calhoun, p. 69.
P. cresphontes, D♀ , 14 Jul 1987, SAN, Calhoun.

Row 2. *P. cresphontes*, V♂ , 4 Aug 1984, LAW, Calhoun.
P. g. glaucus, D♂ , 25 May 1982, HIG, Calhoun, p. 70.

Row 3. *P. g. glaucus*, D♀ , 12 Sep 1984, LAW, Calhoun.
P. g. glaucus, V♂ , 28 May 1980, VIN, Calhoun.

187

Plate 16. **Papilionidae:** *Papilio.* (Specimens approx. 50% life size).

Row 1. *P. g. glaucus*, D♀ , form 'glaucus', 17 Aug 1986, TUS, Iftner, p. 70.
         P. g. glaucus, V♀ , form 'glaucus', 2 Aug 1980, DEL, Calhoun.

Row 2. *P. t. troilus*, D♂ , 3 Aug 1983, VIN, Calhoun, p. 71.
         P. t. troilus, D♂ , blue hindwing form, 12 May 1979, FAI, Iftner.

Row 3. *P. t. troilus*, D♀ , 26 May 1980, LUC, Iftner.
         P. t. troilus, V♂ , 14 Jul 1987, WOO, Calhoun.

Plate 17. **Pieridae: *Pontia, Pieris.*** (Specimens approx. 85% life size).

Row 1. *Pontia protodice*, D♂, form 'vernalis', 19 Apr 1931, STA, Baker, p. 72.
P. protodice, V♂, form 'vernalis', 19 Apr 1931, STA, Baker.
P. protodice, D♀, form 'vernalis', 13 Mar 1946, STA, Baker.

Row 2. *Pontia protodice*, V♀, form 'vernalis', 7 Apr 1929, STA, Baker.
P. protodice, D♂, summer phenotype, 17 Jul 1984, LAW, Calhoun.
P. protodice, V♂, summer phenotype, 29 Jul 1984, LAW, Calhoun.

Row 3. *Pontia protodice*, D♀, summer phenotype, 17 Jul 1984, LAW, Calhoun.
P. protodice, V♀, summer phenotype, 8 Aug 1987, ADA, Calhoun.
P. protodice, V♀, autumn phenotype, 21 Sep 1986, ADA, Calhoun.

Row 4. *Pieris napi oleracea*, D♂, summer phenotype, 26 Jun 1987, Oakland Co., MI, Iftner, p. 73.
P. n. oleracea, D♀, summer phenotype, 27 Jun 1987, Oakland Co., MI, Calhoun.
P. n. oleracea, V♂, summer phenotype, 21 Jun 1986, Oakland Co., MI, Calhoun.

Row 5. *Pieris n. oleracea*, V♂, spring phenotype, 12 May 1984, Lagrange Co., IN, Calhoun.
Pieris virginiensis, D♂, 25 Apr 1988, DEL, Iftner, p. 74.
P. virginiensis, D♀, 25 Apr 1988, MRW, Iftner.

Row 6. *Pieris virginiensis*, V♂, 10 May 1984, POR, Calhoun.
Pieris rapae, D♂, summer phenotype, 17 Aug 1986, TUS, Iftner, p. 75.
P. rapae, D♀, summer phenotype, 1 Jun 1986, FAI, Calhoun.

Row 7. *Pieris rapae*, V♀, summer phenotype, 27 Aug 1979, WAY, Iftner.
P. rapae, D♂, spring phenotype, 12 Apr 1988, DEL, Calhoun.
P. rapae, V♂, spring phenotype, 12 Apr 1980, VIN, Calhoun.

Plate 18.   Pieridae: *Euchloe, Anthocharis, Colias*. (Specimens approx. life size).

Row 1.   *E. olympia*, D♂ , 5 May 1984, LAW, Calhoun, p. 76.
 E. olympia, D♀ , 26 May 1984, Allegan Co., MI, Calhoun.
 E. olympia, V♂ , 26 May 1984, Allegan Co., MI, Calhoun.

Row 2.   *A. midea annickae*, D♂ , 12 Apr 1986, SCI, Iftner, p. 77.
 A. m. annickae, D♀ , 30 Apr 1988, BRO, Iftner.
 A. m. annickae, V♀ , 30 Apr 1988, BRO, Iftner.

Row 3.   *C. p. philodice*, D♂ , 23 Aug 1986, KNO, Iftner, p. 78.
 C. p. philodice, D♀ , 1 Oct 1979, FRA, Calhoun.
 C. p. philodice, V♂ , 5 May 1979, VIN, Iftner.

Row 4.   *C. p. philodice*, D♀ , white form, ex-ovum, 9 Sep 1988, MOT, Calhoun.
 C. p. philodice, V♀ , white form, 7 Aug 1988, MED, Iftner.
 C. eurytheme, D♂ , 18 Oct 1987, PER, Iftner, p. 79.

Row 5.   *C. eurytheme*, D♀ , 5 Sep 1978, WAY, Iftner.
 C. eurytheme, V♂ , 16 Aug 1986, JEF, Iftner.
 C. eurytheme, D♀ , white form, 18 Oct 1987, MRG, Iftner.

Row 6.   *C. eurytheme*, V♀ , white form, 10 Sep 1979, FRA, Calhoun.
 C. eurytheme, D♂ , spring phenotype, 5 May 1984, LAW, Calhoun.
 C. eurytheme, D♀ , spring phenotype, 26 Apr 1987, CLA, Iftner.

190

Plate 19. **Pieridae:** *Colias, Phoebis.* (Specimens approx. life size).

Row 1. *C. c. cesonia*, D♂ , 19 Sep 1987, Dearborn Co., IN, Calhoun, p. 80.
      C. c. cesonia, D♀ , 4 Mar 1987, Marion Co., FL, Calhoun.

Row 2. *C. c. cesonia*, V♂ , 19 Sep 1987, Dearborn Co., IN, Iftner.
      C. c. cesonia, V♀ , form 'rosa', 21 Sep 1981, Boone Co., KY, Calhoun.

Row 3. *P. sennae eubule*, D♂ , 5 Aug 1987, MAD, Calhoun, p. 80.
      P. s. eubule, V♂ , 3 Sep 1987, MAD, Calhoun.

Row 4. *P. s. eubule*, D♀ , 8 Aug 1987, ADA, Calhoun.
      P. s. eubule, V♀ , 25 Jul 1987, LAW, Calhoun.

Plate 20. **Pieridae: *Phoebis, Eurema, Nathalis*.** (Specimens approx. life size).

Row 1.   *P. p. philea*, D♂ , 11 Dec 1982, Lee Co., FL, Calhoun, p. 81.
        P. p. philea, D♀ , 4 Sep 1982, Lee Co., FL, Calhoun.

Row 2.   *E. l. lisa*, D♂ , 17 Aug 1986, TUS, Iftner, p. 82.
        E. l. lisa, V♂ , 20 Jul 1986, PIC, Calhoun.
        E. l. lisa, D♀ , 24 Aug 1986, LUC, Iftner.

Row 3.   *E. l. lisa*, V♀ , 21 Sep 1986, ADA, Calhoun.
        E . l. lisa, D♀ , white form, 1 Sep 1980, ATH, Calhoun.
        E. nicippe, D♂ , 14 Sep 1984, LAW, Iftner, p. 83.

Row 4.   *E. nicippe*, V♂ , 17 Jul 1987, MAD, Calhoun.
        E. nicippe, D♀ , 18 Aug 1987, MAD, Calhoun.
        E. nicippe, V♀ , 14 Jul 1981, FAI, Calhoun.

Row 5.   *E. mexicana*, D♂ , 7 Aug 1984, Mexico, Unknown, p. 83.
        E. mexicana, D♀ , 30 Jul 1986, Cochise Co., AZ, Peacock.
        E. mexicana, V♀ , 30 Jul 1986, Cochise Co., AZ, Peacock.

Row 6.   *N. iole*, D♂ , 11 Jul 1985, LOG, Parshall, p. 84.
        N. iole, V♂ , 22 Mar 1981, Lee Co., FL, Calhoun.
        N. iole, D♀ , 10 Sep 1983, Union Co., KY, Calhoun.
        N. iole, V♀ , 21 Apr 1985, Dade Co., FL, Iftner.

Plate 21. Lycaenidae: *Feniseca, Lycaena, Atlides.* (Specimens approx. life size).

Row 1.
F. t. tarquinius, D♂ , 16 Jun 1986, KNO, Calhoun, p. 85.
F. t. tarquinius, D♀ , 9 May 1982, ADA, Calhoun.
F. t. tarquinius, V♀ , 4 May 1985, GAL, Calhoun.

Row 2.
L. phlaeas americana, D♂ , 17 Jul 1988, STA Iftner, p. 86.
L. p. americana, D♀ , 25 May 1987, CAR, Iftner.
L. p. americana, V♂ , 10 Sep 1978, FRA, Calhoun.
L. p. americana, D♀ , aberration 'fasciata', 19 Jul 1951, STA, Baker.

Row 3.
L. hyllus, D♂ , 10 Jun 1984, POR, Iftner, p. 87.
L. hyllus, D♀ , 13 Jul 1986, MAR, Calhoun.
L. hyllus, V♂ , 27 Jul 1983, ATH, Calhoun.

Row 4.
L. e. epixanthe, D♂ , 28 Jun 1987, Preston Co., WV, Iftner, p. 88.
L. e. epixanthe, V♂ , 21 Jun 1986, Oakland Co., MI, Calhoun.
L. e. epixanthe, D♀ , 28 Jun 1987, Preston Co., WV, Iftner.
L. e. epixanthe, V♀ , 26 Jun 1987, Oakland Co., MI, Calhoun.

Row 5.
L. d. dorcas, D♂ , 13 Jul 1984, Jackson Co., MI, Iftner, p. 89.
L. d. dorcas, V♂ , 12 Jul 1982, Jackson Co., MI, Calhoun.
L. d. dorcas, D♀ , 21 Jul 1983, Jackson Co., MI, Iftner.
L. d. dorcas, V♀ , 12 Jul 1982, Jackson Co., MI, Calhoun.

Row 6.
L. helloides, D♂ , 5 Jun 1984, FUL, Iftner, p. 89.
L. helloides, V♂ , 5 Jun 1984, FUL, Calhoun.
L. helloides, D♀ , 9 Jun 1984, LUC, Calhoun.
L. helloides, V♀ , 19 Jul 1987, McHenry Co., IL, Iftner.

Row 7.
A. halesus ssp., D♂ , 20 Oct 1980, Bexar Co., TX, Iftner, p. 90.
A. h. halesus, D♀ , 16 Sep 1972, Cumberland Co., NC, Parshall.
A. h. halesus, V♂ , 15 Jun 1985. Dorchester Co., MD, Grooms.

193

Plate 22. **Lycaenidae: *Harkenclenus, Satyrium, Calycopis*.** (Specimens approx. life size).

Row 1.   *H. titus* ssp., D♂ , 21 Jun 1986, MAD, Iftner, p. 91.
        H. t. mopsus, V♂ , 14 Jun 1987, GAL, Calhoun.
        H. titus ssp., D♀ , 3 Jul 1988, DEL, Calhoun.
        H. titus ssp., V♀ , 27 Jun 1980, DEL, Calhoun.

Row 2.   *S. a. acadica*, D♂ , 13 Jul 1984, LUC, Iftner, p. 92.
        S. a. acadica, V♂ , 7 Jul 1984, HEN, Calhoun.
        S. a. acadica, D♀ , 19 Jun 1987, LOG, Parshall.
        S. a. acadica, V♀ , 13 Jul 1983, POR, Iftner.

Row 3.   *S. edwardsii*, D♂ , 27 Jun 1987, Allegan Co., MI, Calhoun, p. 93.
        S. edwardsii, V♂ , 24 Jun 1988, ADA, Parshall.
        S. edwardsii, D♀ , 13 Jul 1984, LUC, Iftner.
        S. edwardsii, V♀ , 7 Jul 1984, LUC, Calhoun.

Row 4.   *S. calanus falacer*, D♂ , 19 Jun 1984, LAW, Calhoun, p. 94.
        S. c. falacer, V♂ , 20 Jun 1980, VIN, Calhoun.
        S. c. falacer, D♀ , 18 Jun 1984, LAW, Iftner.
        S. c. falacer, V♀ , 20 Jun 1988, UNI, Iftner.

Row 5.   *S. caryaevorum*, D♂ , 11 Jun 1986, LOG, Parshall, p. 95.
        S. caryaevorum, V♂ , 20 Jun 1988, UNI, Iftner.
        S. caryaevorum, D♀ , 10 Jul 1987, UNI, Parshall.
        S. caryaevorum, V♀ , 27 Jul 1981, POR, Shuey.

Row 6.   *S. liparops strigosum*, D♂ , 25 Jun 1984, UNI, Parshall, p. 96.
        S. l. strigosum, V♂ , ex-larva, 15 Jun 1980, WAY, Iftner.
        S. l. strigosum, D♀ , 28 Jun 1984, LOG, Parshall.
        S. l. strigosum, V♀ , 19 Jun 1984, LAW, Calhoun.

Row 7.   *C. cecrops*, D♂ , 29 Jul 1984, LAW, Calhoun, p. 97.
        C. cecrops, V♂ , 27 Aug 1988, ADA, Parshall.
        C. cecrops, D♀ , 22 May 1987, VIN, Peacock.
        C. cecrops, V♀ , 4 May 1986, SCI, Iftner.

Plate 23. Lycaenidae: *Mitoura, Incisalia, Fixsenia, Parrhasius.* (Specimens approx. life size).

Row 1.
M. g. gryneus, D♂ , spring phenotype, 30 Apr 1988, ADA, Iftner, p. 97.
M. g. gryneus, D♀ , spring phenotype, 30 Apr 1988, BRO, Iftner.
M. g. gryneus, D♂ , summer phenotype, 3 Jul 1987, GAL, Parshall.
M. g. gryneus, D♀ , summer phenotype, 3 Jul 1987, GAL, Parshall.
M. g. gryneus, V♀ , spring phenotype, 8 May 1987, GAL, Calhoun.

Row 2.
I. augustus croesioides, D♂ , 5 Apr 1986, SCI, Calhoun, p. 98.
I. a. croesioides, V♂ , 13 Apr 1986, SCI, Calhoun.
I. a. croesioides, D♀ , 12 Apr 1986, SCI, Iftner.
I. a. croesioides, V♀ , 13 Apr 1986, SCI, Calhoun.

Row 3.
I. i. irus, D♂ , 19 May 1984, LUC, Calhoun, p. 99.
I. i. irus, V♂ , 26 May 1984, Allegan Co., MI, Calhoun.
I. i. irus, D♀ , 12 May 1984, LUC, Calhoun.
I. i. irus, V♀ , 19 May 1984, LUC, Calhoun.

Row 4.
I. h. henrici, D♂ , 5 Apr 1986, SCI, Iftner, p. 100.
I. h. henrici, V♂ , 13 Apr 1985, LAW, Calhoun.

I. h. henrici, D♀ , 9 Apr 1988, ADA, Calhoun.
I. h. henrici, V♀ , 30 Apr 1988, BRO, Iftner.

Row 5.
I. n. niphon, D♂ , 13 Apr 1985, LAW, Calhoun, p. 101.
I. n. niphon, V♂ , 29 Apr 1984, LAW, Iftner.
I. n. niphon, D♀ , 19 Apr 1986, MEG, Calhoun.
I. n. niphon, V♀ , 16 May 1987, GAL, Iftner.

Row 6.
F. o. ontario, D♂ , 5 May 1986, Mobile Co., AL, Ashby, p. 102.
F. o. ontario, V♂ , 10 Jun 1988, UNI, Parshall.
F. o. ontario, D♀ , 11 Jun 1988, UNI, Parshall.
F. o. ontario, V♀ , 6 Jun 1985, UNI, Parshall.

Row 7.
P. m. m-album, D♂ , 24 Apr 1986, PER, Calhoun, p. 103.
P. m. m-album, V♂ , 26 Apr 1975, VIN, Parshall.
P. m. m-album, D♀ , 18 Apr 1987, ADA, Calhoun.
P. m. m-album, V♀ , 26 Apr 1975, VIN, Parshall.

Plate 24. **Lycaenidae: *Strymon, Erora, Hemiargus, Everes, Celastrina.*** (Specimens approx. life size).

Row 1. *S. melinus humuli,* D♂ , 2 Apr 1986, LAW, Calhoun, p. 103.
S. m. humuli, V♂ , 4 May 1982, VIN, Calhoun.
S. m. humuli, D♀ , ex-larva, 20 Aug 1987, DEL, Calhoun.
S. m. humuli, V♀ , 17 Aug 1986, TUS, Iftner.

Row 2. *Erora laeta,* D♂ , 10 Jul 1976, Harlan Co., KY, Gibson, p. 104.
E. laeta, V♂ , 10 Jul 1976, Harlan Co., KY, Gibson.
E. laeta, D♀ , 29 May 1980, near Manchester, VT, Wright.
E. laeta, V♀ , 7 Jul 1977, Harlan Co., KY, Gibson.

Row 3. *H. isola alce,* D♂ , 30 Apr 1988, Santa Cruz Co., AZ, Gibson, p. 105.
H. i. alce, V♂ , 15 Jul 1973, Manitoba, Canada, Parshall.
H. i. alce, D♀ , 15 Oct 1986, Travis Co., TX, Iftner.
H. i. alce, V♀ , 2 May 1988, Cochise Co., AZ, Gibson.

Row 4. *Everes c. comyntas,* D♂ , summer phenotype, 24 Jul 1988, PIK, Calhoun,
p. 106.
E. c. comyntas, V♂ , summer phenotype, 7 Aug 1988, MED, Iftner.
E. c. comyntas, D♀ , spring phenotype, 25 May 1987, STA, Iftner.
E. c. comyntas, D♀ , summer phenotype, 20 Jul 1986, PIC, Calhoun.
E . c. comyntas, V♀ , summer phenotype, 3 Jul 1980, FRA, Calhoun.

Row 5. *C. l. ladon,* D♂ , spring phenotype, form 'violacea', 25 Apr 1988, MOR, Iftner,
p. 107.

C. l. ladon, D♀ , spring phenotype, form 'violacea', 4 Apr 1986, JAC, Iftner.
C. l. ladon, V♂ , spring phenotype, form 'violacea', 17 Apr 1988, MOR,
Calhoun.
C. l. lucia, V♂ , 17 May 19??, Sussex Co., NJ, Unknown.
C. l. lucia, V♀ , form 'marginata', 27 May 19??, Sussex Co., NJ, Unknown.

Row 6. *Celastrina* sp., spring phenotype, D♂ , 14 May 1988, COL, Calhoun.
Celastrina sp., spring phenotype, D♀ , 14 May 1988, COL, Calhoun.
Celastrina sp., spring phenotype, V♂ , 14 May 1988, COL, Calhoun.

Row 7. *C. l. ladon,* D♂ , summer phenotype, form 'neglecta', 30 Aug 1987, MAD,
Calhoun.
C. l. ladon, D♀ , summer phenotype, form 'neglecta', 11 Jun 1988, NOB,
Calhoun.
C. l. ladon, V♂ , summer phenotype, form 'neglecta', 14 Jun 1986, CHP,
Calhoun.

Row 8. *C. neglecta-major,* D♂ , 4 May 1985, LAW, Calhoun, p. 108.
C. neglecta-major, D♀ , 16 May 1987, LAW, Calhoun.
C. neglecta-major, V♂ , 7 May 1982, VIN, Calhoun.

Row 9. *C. ebenina,* D♂ , 10 Apr 1988, ADA, Iftner, p. 109.
C. ebenina, D♀ , ex-larva, 17 Jun 1988, JAC, Calhoun.
C. ebenina, V♂ , 9 Apr 1988, ADA, Calhoun.

Plate 25. **Lycaenidae, Riodinidae, Libytheidae, and Heliconiidae:** *Glaucopsyche, Lycaeides, Calephelis, Libytheana, Agraulis.* (Specimens approx. life size).

Row 1.
- *G. l. lygdamus*, D♂, 5 May 1984, LAW, Calhoun, p. 110.
- *G. l. lygdamus*, V♂, 25 Apr 1984, LAW, Calhoun.
- *G. l. lygdamus*, D♀, 1 May 1987, JAC, Iftner.
- *G. l. lygdamus*, V♀, 29 Apr 1987, HOC, Iftner.

Row 2.
- *Lycaeides melissa samuelis*, D♂, 13 Jul 1984, LUC, Iftner, p. 111.
- *L. m. samuelis*, V♂, 1 Jun 1984, LUC, Calhoun.
- *L. m. samuelis*, D♀, 30 May 1974, LUC, Parshall.
- *L. m. samuelis*, V♀, 2 Aug 1956, LUC, Price.

Row 3.
- *C. borealis*, D♂, 25 Jun 1984, LAW, Calhoun, p. 112.
- *C. borealis*, V♂, 25 Jun 1984, LAW, Calhoun.
- *C. borealis*, D♀, 2 Jul 1984, LAW, Calhoun.
- *C. borealis*, V♀, 11 Jul 1984, DEL, Iftner.

Row 4.
- *C. muticum*, D♂, 4 Jul 1985, LOG, Calhoun, p. 113.
- *C. muticum*, V♂, 4 Jul 1985, LOG, Calhoun.
- *C. muticum*, D♀, 7 Jul 1985, LOG, Calhoun.
- *C. muticum*, V♀, 10 Jul 1968, CHP, Amrine.

Row 5.
- *Libytheana b. bachmanii*, D♂, 12 Jul 1987, DAR, Iftner, p. 114.
- *L. b. bachmanii*, V♀, form 'kirtlandi', 26 Sep 1980, HAM, Calhoun.
- *L. b. bachmanii*, V♂, 22 Jul 1979, FRA, Calhoun.

Row 6.
- *A. vanillae nigrior*, D♂, 5 Mar 1987, Volusia Co., FL, Calhoun, p. 115.
- *A. v. nigrior*, V♂, 19 Apr 1985, Monroe Co., FL, Iftner.

Row 7.
- *A. v. nigrior*, D♀, 29 Dec 1974, Monroe Co., FL, Iftner.
- *A. v. nigrior*, V♀, 22 Mar 1981, Lee Co., FL, Calhoun.

Plate 26. **Nymphalidae: *Euptoieta, Speyeria.*** (Specimens approx. 50% life size).

Row 1.   *E. claudia,* D♂ , 16 Sep 1982, UNI, Calhoun, p. 116.
               E. claudia, D♀ , 19 Sep 1987, HAM, Iftner.
               E. claudia, V♀ , 8 Sep 1986, MEG, Calhoun.

Row 2.   *S. diana,* D♂ , 14 Jul 1984, Wise Co., VA, Calhoun, p. 117.
               S. diana, V♂ , 14 Jul 1984, Wise Co., VA, Calhoun.

Row 3.   *S. diana,* D♀ , 9 Jul 1988, Letcher Co., KY, Iftner.
               S. diana, V♀ , 21 Jul 1981, Letcher Co., KY, Iftner.

Row 4.   *S. c. cybele,* D♂ , 1 Jun 1985, LOG, Calhoun, p. 118.
               S. c. cybele, V♂ , 19 Jun 1988, SAN, Iftner.

Row 5.   *S. c. cybele,* D♀ , 23 Jul 1988, TUS, Iftner.
               S. c. cybele, V♀ , 17 Jul 1979, WAY, Iftner.

Plate 27. **Nymphalidae:** *Speyeria.* (Specimens approx. 50% life size).

Row 1.   *S. a. aphrodite*, D♂ , 11 Jun 1982, KNO, Calhoun, p. 119.
           S. a. aphrodite, V♂ , 22 Jun 1980, HOC, Calhoun.
           S. aphrodite alcestis, V♂ , 21 Jul 1983, Allegan Co., MI, Iftner.

Row 2.   *S. a. aphrodite*, D♀ , 4 Jul 1986, MRG, Iftner.
           S. a. aphrodite, V♀ , 17 Jul 1988, COL, Calhoun.
           S. aphrodite alcestis, V♀ , 27 Jun 1987, Allegan Co., MI, Iftner.

Row 3.   *S. idalia*, D♂ , 7 Jul 1946, STA, Baker, p. 120.
           S. idalia, V♂ , 27 Jun 1980, DEL, Calhoun.

Row 4.   *S. idalia*, D♀ , 3 Jul 1980, DEL, Calhoun.
           S. idalia, V♀ , 27 Jul 1957, STA, Baker.

Row 5.   *S. a. atlantis*, D♂ , 28 Jun 1982, Warren Co., PA, Calhoun, p. 121.
           S. a. atlantis, V♂ , 29 Jul 1984, Mackinac Co., MI, Iftner.

Row 6.   *S. a. atlantis*, D♀ , 16 Aug 1986, ATB, Godwin.
           S. a. atlantis, V♀ , 29 Jun 1982, Warren Co., PA, Calhoun.

Plate 28. **Nymphalidae:** *Boloria, Chlosyne, Phyciodes.* (Specimens approx. life size).

Row 1.
B. selene ssp., D♂, 1 Jun 1984, FUL, Calhoun, p. 121.
B. selene ssp., D♀, 2 Jun 1985, LUC, Calhoun.
B. selene ssp., V♂, 1 Jun 1984, FUL, Calhoun.

Row 2.
B. b. bellona, D♂, 14 Apr 1986, MOE, Iftner, p. 122.
B. b. bellona, D♀, 30 Aug 1978, WAY, Iftner.
B. b. bellona, V♂, 14 Apr 1986, MOE, Iftner.

Row 3.
C. n. nycteis, D♂, 19 May 1985, LAW, Calhoun, p. 123.
C. n. nycteis, D♀, 20 Jun 1980, ATH, Calhoun.
C. n. nycteis, V♂, 16 Aug 1986, JEF, Iftner.

Row 4.
C. harrisii liggetti, D♂, 6 Jun 1982, POR, Calhoun, p. 124.
C. h. liggetti, D♀, 19 Jun 1984, POR, Iftner.
C. h. liggetti, V♂, 14 Jun 1980, POR, Calhoun.

Row 5.
C. h. harrisii, D♂, 21 Jun 1986, Oakland Co., MI, Calhoun.
P. t. tharos, D♂, form 'marcia', 21 May 1988, SAN, Iftner, p. 125.
P. t. tharos, V♂, form 'marcia', 13 May 1980, FRA, Calhoun.

Row 6.
P. t. tharos, D♀, form 'marcia', 22 May 1988, MEG, Calhoun.
P. t. tharos, V♀, form 'marcia', 8 Sep 1986, MEG, Calhoun.
P. t. tharos, D♂, form 'morpheus', 23 Jul 1985, DEL, Calhoun.

Row 7.
P. t. tharos, V♂, form 'morpheus', 30 Jun 1981, FRA, Calhoun.
P. t. tharos, D♀, form 'morpheus', 11 Jul 1983, MAR, Iftner.
P. t. tharos, V♀, form 'morpheus', 17 Jul 1979, WAY, Iftner.

Plate 29. **Nymphalidae:** ***Phyciodes, Euphydryas, Polygonia.*** (Specimens approx. life size).

Row 1. *Phyciodes pascoensis*, D♂ , 27 Jun 1986, Elk Co., PA, Calhoun, p. 126.
P. pascoensis, V♂ , 27 Jun 1986, Elk Co., PA, Calhoun.
P. pascoensis, D♀ , 27 Jun 1986, Elk Co., PA, Calhoun.
P. pascoensis, V♀ , 27 Jun 1986, Elk Co., PA, Calhoun.

Row 2. *E. p. phaeton*, D♂ , 9 Jun 1984, POR, Iftner, p. 126.
E. p. phaeton, D♀ , 19 Jun 1984, POR, Iftner.
E. p. phaeton, V♂ , 14 Jun 1980, POR, Calhoun.

Row 3. *Polygonia interrogationis*, D♂ , ex-larva, 19 Sep 1988, DEL, Calhoun, p. 127.
P. interrogationis, V♂ , 21 Sep 1986, SCI, Calhoun.

Row 4. *P. interrogationis*, D♀ , 8 Aug 1988, Otsego Co., MI, Peacock.
P. interrogationis, V♀ , 3 Aug 1983, LAW, Calhoun.

201

Plate 30. **Nymphalidae:** *Polygonia.* (Specimens approx. 90% life size).

Row 1.   *P. interrogationis*, D♂ , form 'umbrosa', 11 Sep 1983, FUL, Calhoun, p. 127.
              P. interrogationis, V♂ , form 'umbrosa', 5 Jul 1987, CLA, Overracker & Stafford.

Row 2.   *P. interrogationis*, D♀ , form 'umbrosa', 18 Jun 1988, UNI, Iftner.
              P. interrogationis, V♀ , form 'umbrosa', 26 May 1981, UNI, Calhoun.

Row 3.   *P. comma*, D♂ , 14 Sep 1988, FAY, Iftner, p. 128.
              P. comma, V♂ , 21 Sep 1982, Boone Co., KY, Calhoun.

Row 4.   *P. comma*, D♀ , 19 Oct 1982, VIN, Calhoun.
              P. comma, V♀ , 19 Apr 1980, VIN, Calhoun.

Plate 31. **Nymphalidae: *Polygonia, Nymphalis*.** (Specimens approx. 85% life size).

Row 1.   *P. comma*, D♂ , form 'dryas', 19 Jun 1988, WYA, Iftner, p. 128.
             P. comma, V♂ , form 'dryas', 14 Jul 1987, WOO, Calhoun.

Row 2.   *P. comma*, D♀ , form 'dryas', 24 Jun 1984, MAR, Peacock.
             P. comma, V♀ , form 'dryas', 17 Aug 1987, VIN, Parshall.

Row 3.   *P. p. progne*, D♂ , 3 Sep 1987, MAD, Parshall, p. 129.
             P. p. progne, D♀ , 8 Apr 1978, Boone Co., MO, Iftner.
             P. p. progne, V♂ , 30 Sep 1976, Texas Co., MO, Iftner.

Row 4.   *P. p. progne*, D♂ , form 'l-argenteum', 7 Aug 1987, MAD, Parshall.
             P. p. progne, D♀ , form 'l-argenteum', 9 Aug 1986, PUT, Calhoun.
             P. p. progne, V♂ , form 'l-argenteum', 10 Jul 1985, Mason Co., IL, Calhoun.

Row 5.   *N. vau-album j-album*, D♂ , 1 Aug 1981, Otsego Co., MI, Gibson, p. 130.
             N. v. j-album, V♂ , 8 Aug 1982, Otsego Co., MI, Gibson.

Plate 32. **Nymphalidae:** *Nymphalis, Vanessa.* (Specimens approx. 90% life size).

Row 1.   *N. a. antiopa*, D♂ , 27 Jun 1979, WAY, Iftner, p. 131.
                N. a. antiopa, V♀ , 3 Jun 1986, GAL, Iftner.

Row 2.   *N. m. milberti*, D♂ , 6 Sep 1978, WAY, Iftner, p. 132.
                N. m. milberti, D♀ , 29 May 1987, LOG, Calhoun.
                N. m. milberti, V♂ , 5 Aug 1987, MAD, Calhoun.

Row 3.   *V. virginiensis*, D♂ , 22 May 1988, MEG, Iftner, p. 133.
                V. virginiensis, V♀ , 23 Jul 1988, TUS, Iftner.

Row 4.   *V. cardui*, D♂ , 27 Aug 1988, SHE, Iftner, p. 134.
                V. cardui, V♀ , 14 Sep 1988, FAY, Iftner.

Plate 33. **Nymphalidae: *Vanessa, Junonia, Limenitis.*** (Specimens approx. life size).

Row 1. *V. atalanta rubria*, D♂ , 7 Aug 1988, ERI, Iftner, p. 135.
         V. a. rubria, V♀ , 3 Jul 1987, CLA, Overracker & Stafford.

Row 2. *J. coenia*, D♂ , 14 Sep 1984, ADA, Iftner, p. 135.
         J. coenia, D♀ , 14 Sep 1984, ADA, Iftner.

Row 3. *J. coenia*, V♂ , 23 Aug 1986, LUC, Calhoun.
         J. coenia, V♀ , form 'rosa', 21 Sep 1986, ADA, Calhoun.

Row 4. *L. a. archippus*, D♂ , 3 Jul 1987, FAY, Calhoun, p. 137.
         L. a. archippus, V♂ , 19 Jun 1988, WOO, Iftner.

Plate 34. **Nymphalidae: *Limenitis*.** (Specimens approx. 50% life size).

Row 1. *L. arthemis astyanax*, D♂ , 24 Aug 1986, LUC, Iftner, p. 136.
L. a. astyanax, D♀, 4 Sep 1983, LAW, Calhoun.
L. a. astyanax, V♂ , 19 Jun 1988, WOO, Iftner.

Row 2. *L. a. astyanax*, D♂ , form 'viridis', 1 Jun 1988, JAC, Calhoun.
L. arthemis, D♂ , form 'proserpina', 28 Jun 1982, Warren Co., PA, Calhoun.
L. arthemis, V♂ , form 'proserpina', 23 Aug 1983, GAL, Calhoun.

Row 3. *L. arthemis*, D♂ , form 'albofasciata', 23 Jun 1940, STA, Unknown.
L. arthemis, D♂ , form 'arthemis', 25 Aug 1985, ATB, Godwin.
L. arthemis, D♀ , form 'arthemis', 20 Aug 1984, ATB, Godwin.

Row 4. *L. a. arthemis*, D♂ , 3 Jul 1983, Luce Co., MI, Shuey.
L. a. arthemis, D♀, 3 Jul 1983, Luce Co., MI, Shuey.
L. a. arthemis, V♂ , 30 Jul 1984, Ontario, Canada, Iftner.

Plate 35. **Apaturidae: *Anaea, Asterocampa.*** (Specimens approx. 85% life size).

Row 1. *Anaea andria*, D♂ , 17 Oct 1987, Bexar Co., TX, Iftner, p. 138.
A. andria, V♂ , 22 Oct 1980, Bexar Co., TX, Iftner.

Row 2. *A. andria*, D♀ , 22 Oct 1980, Bexar Co., TX, Iftner.
A. andria, V♀ , 22 Oct 1980, Bexar Co., TX, Iftner.

Row 3. *Asterocampa celtis celtis*, D♂ , 31 Jul 1987, MAD, Iftner, p. 139.
A. c. celtis, V♂ , 8 Aug 1984, Pike Co., IL, Iftner.
A. c. celtis, D♀ , 11 Aug 1986, PIC, Calhoun.

Row 4. *A. c. celtis*, V♀ , 18 Jun 1988, UNI, Iftner.
A. clyton clyton, D♂ , 3 Jul 1987, FAY, Calhoun, p. 140.
A. c. clyton, D♂ , form 'proserpina', 12 Jul 1987, DAR, Iftner.

Row 5. *A. c. clyton*, V♂ , 21 Jul 1988, MAD, Calhoun.
A. c. clyton, D♀ , 7 Sep 1984, Switzerland Co., IN, Calhoun.
A. c. clyton, V♀ , 19 Sep 1987, HAM, Calhoun.

Plate 36. **Satyridae: *Enodia, Satyrodes, Cyllopsis, Hermeuptychia, Neonympha, Megisto.*** (Specimens approx. 85% life size).

Row 1.
    E. anthedon, D♂ , 28 May 1988, HIG, Iftner, p. 141.
    E. anthedon, D♀ , 23 Aug 1986, COS, Iftner.
    E. anthedon, V♂ , 28 Jul 1985, GAL, Calhoun.

Row 2.
    S. e. eurydice, D♂ , 20 Jul 1983, WIL, Iftner, p. 142.
    S. e. eurydice, D♀ , 10 Jun 1985, LOG, Iftner.
    S. e. eurydice, V♂ , 28 Jun 1984, CLA, Calhoun.

Row 3.
    S. appalachia leeuwi, D♂ , 3 Jul 1988, DEL, Calhoun, p. 143.
    S. a. leeuwi, D♀ , 13 Jul 1982, UNI, Calhoun.
    S. a. leeuwi, V♂ , 30 Jun 1982, UNI, Calhoun.

Row 4.
    C. g. gemma, D♂ , 12 Apr 1986, SCI, Iftner, p. 144.
    C. g. gemma, D♀ , 1 May 1987, SCI, Iftner.
    C. g. gemma, V♂ , 14 Aug 1984, LAW, Calhoun.

Row 5.
    H. sosybius, D♂ , 29 Jul 1984, LAW, Calhoun, p. 144.
    H. sosybius, D♀ , 14 Aug 1983, LAW, Calhoun.
    H. sosybius, V♂ , 28 May 1988, ADA, Calhoun.

Row 6.
    N. m. mitchellii, D♂ , 13 Jul 1984, Jackson Co., MI, Iftner, p. 145.
    N. m. mitchellii, D♀ , 13 Jul 1984, Jackson Co., MI, Iftner.
    N. m. mitchellii, V♂ , 13 Jul 1984, Jackson Co., MI, Iftner.

Row 7.
    M. c. cymela, D♂ , 22 May 1988, MEG, Calhoun, p. 146.
    M. c. cymela, D♀ , 11 Jun 1988, MOE, Calhoun.
    M. c. cymela, V♂ , 28 May 1988, ADA, Iftner.

Plate 37. **Satyridae:** *Cercyonis.* (Specimens approx. 85% life size).

Row 1.   *C. pegala 'alope'*, D♂ , 25 Jul 1981, FRA, Iftner, p. 147.
             C. pegala 'alope', D♀ , 12 Jul 1987, PIC, Calhoun.

Row 2.   *C. pegala 'alope'*, V♂ , 11 Jul 1979, FRA, Calhoun.
             C. pegala, D♂ , intermediate phenotype, 30 Jun 1982, UNI, Calhoun.

Row 3.   *C. pegala*, D♂ , intermediate phenotype, 10 Jul 1983, MAD, Iftner.
             C. pegala 'nephele', D♂ , 29 Jun 1986, FRA, Calhoun.

Row 4.   *C. pegala 'nephele'*, D♀ , 31 Jul 1986, PUT, Iftner.
             C. pegala 'nephele', V♂ , 7 Jul 1981, POR, Calhoun.

Plate 38. **Danaidae: *Danaus*.** (Specimens approx. 85% life size).

Row 1. *D. p. plexippus*, D♂ , 23 Sep 1987, LIC, Iftner, p. 148.

Row 2. *D. p. plexippus*, V♀ , 14 Sep 1979, FRA, Calhoun.

Row 3. *D. gilippus thersippus*, D♂ , 17 Oct 1980, Bexar Co., TX, Iftner, p. 150.

D. g. thersippus, V♀ , 20 Oct 1980, Hidalgo Co., TX, Iftner.

210

Plate 39. **Species of Possible Occurrence: Hesperiidae and Lycaenidae.** (Specimens approx. 85% life size).

Row 1. *Erynnis zarucco,* D♂ , 7 Sep 1982, Monroe Co., FL, Calhoun, p. 151.
 E. zarucco, D♀ , 10 Sep 1982, Lee Co., FL, Calhoun.
 E. zarucco, V♂ , 8 Aug 1984, Lee Co., FL, Calhoun.
 E. funeralis, D♂ , 14 Jul 1924, Pima Co., AZ, Poling, p. 151.

Row 2. *E. funeralis,* D♀ , 14 Jul 1924, Pima Co., AZ, Poling.
 E. funeralis, V♂ , 14 Jul 1924, Pima Co., AZ, Poling.
 Lerema accius, D♂ , 18 Oct 1980, Bexar Co., TX, Iftner, p. 151.
 L. accius, D♀ , 13 Dec 1984, Lee Co., FL, Calhoun.

Row 3. *L. accius,* V♂ , 1 Mar 1987, Lee Co., FL, Calhoun.
 Polites v. vibex, D♂ , 3 Mar 1987, Highlands Co., FL, Calhoun, p. 151.
 P. v. vibex, V♂ , 18 Mar 1984, Collier Co., FL, Iftner.
 P. v. vibex, D♀ , 9 Mar 1987, Lee Co., FL, Calhoun.

Row 4. *P. v. vibex,* V♀ , 9 Mar 1987, Lee Co., FL, Calhoun.
 Wallengrenia o. otho, D♂ , 9 Mar 1987, Lee Co., FL, Calhoun, p. 151.
 W. o. otho, D♀ , 11 Mar 1987, Monroe Co., FL, Calhoun.
 W. o. otho, V♂ , 21 Mar 1984, Monroe Co., FL, Calhoun.

Row 5. *Atrytone arogos iowa,* D♂ , 26 Jun 1923, Omaha, NB, Leussler, p. 151.
 A. a. iowa, V♂ , 7 Jul 1924, Omaha, NB, Leussler.
 A. a. iowa, D♀ , 26 Jun 1923, Omaha, NB, Leussler.
 A. a. iowa, V♀ , 21 Jun 1923, Omaha, NB, Leussler.

Row 6. *Problema byssus kumskaka,* D♂ , 13 Jun 1986, Green Co., IL, Iftner, p. 151
 P. b. kumskaka, V♂ , 3 Jul 1988, Green Co., IL, Iftner.
 P. b. byssus, D♀ , 5 Sep 1981, Jasper Co., SC, Finkelstein.
 P. b. kumskaka, V♀ , 11 Jul 1971, Mercer Co., IL, Conway.

Row 7. *Amblyscirtes aesculapias,* D♂ , 31 May 1987, Powell Co., KY, Iftner, p. 151.
 A. aesculapias, V♂ , 31 May 1983, Menifee Co., KY, Calhoun.
 A. aesculapias, D♀ , 31 May 1987, Powell Co., KY, Iftner.
 A. aesculapias, V♀ , 30 May 1983, Menifee Co., KY, Calhoun.

Row 8. *Incisalia p. polios,* D♂ , 1 May 1971, Ocean Co., NJ, Wright, p. 152.
 I. p. polios, V♂ , 11 May 1971, Ocean Co., NJ, Wright.
 I. p. polios, D♀ , 20 May 1978, Lake Co., IL, Iftner.
 I. p. polios, V♀ , 20 May 1978, Lake Co., IL, Iftner.

Row 9. *Leptotes marina,* D♂ , 27 Jul 1986, Pima Co., AZ, Peacock, p. 152.
 L. marina, V♂ , 27 Jul 1986, Pima Co., AZ, Peacock.
 L. marina, D♀ , 11 Aug 1986, Pike Co., IL, Iftner.
 L. marina, V♀ , 11 Aug 1986, Pike Co., IL, Iftner.

Plate 40. **Species of Possible Occurrence: Papilionidae, Pieridae, Nymphalidae, and Satyridae.** (Specimens approx. 50% life size).

Row 1. *Papilio joanae*, D♂ , 18 Jul 1978, Benton Co., MO, Iftner, p. 152.
P. joanae, D♀ , 18 Jul 1978, Benton Co., MO, Iftner.

Row 2. *Colias i. interior*, D♂ , 30 Jul 1984, Ontario, Canada, Iftner, p. 152.
C. i. interior, D♀ , 11 Jul 1983, Tucker Co., WV, Calhoun.
C. i. interior, V♀ , 11 Jul 1983, Tucker Co., WV, Calhoun.

Row 3. *Chlosyne gorgone carlota*, D♂ , 15 Jun 1979, Manitoba, Canada, Parshall, p. 152.
C. g. carlota, V♂ , 15 Jun 1979, Manitoba, Canada, Parshall.
C. g. carlota, D♀ , 15 Jun 1979, Manitoba, Canada, Parshall.
C. g. carlota, V♀ , 31 Aug 1986, Jackson Co., MO, Heitzman.

Row 4. *Phyciodes batesii*, D♂ , 6 Jun 1985, Crawford Co., MI, Peacock, p. 153.
P. batesii, V♂ , 16 Jun 1984, Ontario, Canada, Sutton.
P. batesii, D♀ , 20 Jun 1983, Ontario, Canada, Sutton.

P. batesii, V♀ , 6 Jun 1985, Crawford Co., MI, Peacock.

Row 5. *Polygonia f. faunus*, D♂ , 30 Jul 1984, Ontario, Canada, Iftner, p. 153.
P. f. faunus, D♀ , 30 Aug 1987, New Brunswick, Canada, Hensel.
P. f. faunus, V♂ , 15 Aug 1987, New Brunswick, Canada, Hensel.
P. satyrus, D♂ , 10 Aug 1982, New Brunswick, Canada, Hensel, p. 153.

Row 6. *P. satyrus*, D♀ , 10 Aug 1982, New Brunswick, Canada, Hensel.
P. satyrus, V♀ , 30 Aug 1987, New Brunswick, Canada, Hensel.
Nymphalis c. californica, D♂ , 25 Jul 1987, Linn Co., OR, Iftner, p. 153.
N. c. californica, V♂ , 28 Jul 1987, Linn Co., OR, Iftner.

Row 7. *Enodia creola*, D♂ , 31 May 1987, Powell Co., KY, Iftner, p. 153.
E. creola, D♀ , 6 Jun 1985, Cumberland Co., NC, Parshall.
E. creola, V♀ , 31 May 1987, Powell Co., KY, Calhoun.

EDITOR'S NOTE

Butterflies and Skippers of Ohio, Ohio Biological Survey Bulletin New Series Volume 9 Number 1, is set in Trump Roman type. The type was set, the black-and-white artwork was made camera-ready, and the publication was printed by The Ohio State University Printing Services. The color separates for the Plates were produced by the Mid-Ohio Graphics Company. The Bulletin is printed on 60 lb. white offset paper and bound in 80 lb. Vintage Glossy coverstock. It was sewn and bound by H.&H. Bookbinders, Indianapolis, Indiana.

PUBLISHER'S NOTE

Butterflies and Skippers of Ohio, Ohio Biological Survey Bulletin New Series Volume 9 Number 1, is the first Bulletin to be presented in the new 8½" X 11" size.

It is not easy to break with nearly eight decades of tradition, especially when the content of the old 6¾" X 10" size Bulletins was of such consistent high quality. We conducted research into print-shop trends and users' preferences, and came to the conclusion that the 8½" X 11" size would only became more desirable in the future.

The Executive Committee of the Ohio Biological Survey, on 29 April 1988, authorized increasing the size of the Bulletins New Series to 8½" X 11", effective with Volume 9, Number 1.

PUBLICATIONS OF THE
OHIO BIOLOGICAL SURVEY

For a current price list and ordering information, please write to:

Ohio Biological Survey
Museum of Biological Diversity
1315 Kinnear Road
Columbus, Ohio 43212-1192
Phone: 614-292-9645